Atlas of Classical History

Featuring over 130 colour maps of ancient physical and human landscapes spanning Britain to India and deep into the Sahara, this atlas is a compact kaleidoscope of peoples, migrations, empires, strife, cultures, cities and travels from Greece's Bronze Age to Rome's fall in the West.

This revised edition of the *Atlas of Classical History* equips readers with a clear visual grasp of the spatial dimension, a vital aspect for understanding history. Users gain insight into the formative roles of physical landscape – seas, rivers, mountains, deserts – in Mediterranean peoples' development. The maps in all their variety of scope, scale and colour offer an absorbing means to track the growth of states on the ground, especially their relationships, conflicts, urbanization, communications and cultures. Each map is enriched by readily identifiable symbols and concise accompanying texts, as well as recommendations for further reading. With its vast geographical sweep in a compact format, this book is a comprehensive reference work primarily aimed at non-specialists.

With updated text and thoroughly revised maps now presented in colour, the *Atlas of Classical History* remains an essential reference volume for all those interested in the civilizations of ancient Europe, North Africa and Western Asia, as well as for students and scholars of ancient Greek and Roman history.

Richard Talbert is Research Professor of History at the University of North Carolina, Chapel Hill, US. His publications include the *Barrington Atlas of the Greek and Roman World*, *Rome's World: The Peutinger Map Reconsidered*, *Challenges of Mapping the Classical World* and *The Romans from Village to Empire*.

Lindsay Holman is Visiting Assistant Professor of History at Mercyhurst University (Erie, Pennsylvania, US). Her research explores the materiality of inscriptions naming slaves from the Roman Empire. She is the author of "Two Unpublished *Tesserae Nummulariae* from the Lewis Collection, Cambridge," *ZPE* 210 (2019).

Benet Salway is Senior Lecturer in Ancient History at University College London, UK; a director of the British Academy 'Projet Volterra' on Roman Law; and a contributor to *L'Année épigraphique*. He has published widely on aspects of Greco-Roman geography, including "Putting the world in order" (Chicago, 2012).

Atlas of Classical History

Revised Edition

Edited by Richard Talbert, Lindsay Holman and Benet Salway

LONDON AND NEW YORK

Cover image: Roman Thamugadi (Timgad, Algeria) and beyond to the north-west; Triple Imperial Arch in left foreground. See plan, p. 139. Photograph courtesy of J.D. Falconer.

First published 2023
by Routledge
4 Park Square, Milton Park, Abingdon, Oxon OX14 4RN

and by Routledge
605 Third Avenue, New York, NY 10158

Routledge is an imprint of the Taylor & Francis Group, an informa business

© 2023 selection and editorial matter, Richard Talbert, Lindsay Holman and Benet Salway; individual chapters, the contributors

The right of Richard Talbert, Lindsay Holman and Benet Salway to be identified as the authors of the editorial material, and of the authors for their individual chapters, has been asserted in accordance with sections 77 and 78 of the Copyright, Designs and Patents Act 1988.

All rights reserved. No part of this book may be reprinted or reproduced or utilised in any form or by any electronic, mechanical, or other means, now known or hereafter invented, including photocopying and recording, or in any information storage or retrieval system, without permission in writing from the publishers.

Trademark notice: Product or corporate names may be trademarks or registered trademarks, and are used only for identification and explanation without intent to infringe.

First edition published by Croom Helm Ltd in 1985 and by Routledge in 2013.

British Library Cataloguing-in-Publication Data
A catalogue record for this book is available from the British Library

Library of Congress Cataloging-in-Publication Data
Names: Talbert, Richard J. A., 1947– editor. | Holman, Lindsay, editor. | Salway, Benet, editor.
Title: Atlas of classical history / Richard Talbert, Lindsay Holman, Benet Salway.
Description: 2. revised edition | New York City: Routledge, 2022. |
Includes bibliographical references and index.
Identifiers: LCCN 2022025669 (print) | LCCN 2022585129 (ebook) |
ISBN 9781138785823 (hardback) | ISBN 9781138785830 (paperback) |
ISBN 9781003125228 (ebook) | ISBN 9781003125228q(ebook) |
ISBN 9781138785823q(hardback) | ISBN 9781138785830q(paperback)
Subjects: LCSH: Geography, Ancient--Maps. | LCGFT: World atlases.
Classification: LCC G1033 .A8 1994 (ebook) |
LCC G1033 (print) | DDC 911 23/eng/20220—dc12
LC record available at https://lccn.loc.gov/2022025669

ISBN: 978-1-138-78582-3 (hbk)
ISBN: 978-1-138-78583-0 (pbk)
ISBN: 978-1-003-12522-8 (ebk)

DOI: 10.4324/9781003125228

Typeset in Times New Roman
by codeMantra

To Mary Smallwood, senior contributor,
in her 103rd year, and to her fellow contributors
who did not live to see this revision completed:

Alan Astin
Michael Ballance
Robert Jordan
Simon Keay
Michael McGann
Timothy Potter
Peter Rhodes
John Salmon
Brian Warmington

Contents

Preface to the Revised Edition	ix
Preface to the Original Edition	xii
Key	xiii
Contributors (with their current institutional affiliations)	xiv

Maps

Battles, Cities, Regions, Shrines to around 300 BCE: **Locator**	1
Egypt and the Near East, 1200–500 BCE	2, 201
Troy: Citadel	4, 201
Troy: Lower Town	5, 201
Neolithic and Bronze Age Greece and the Aegean	6, 201
Neolithic and Bronze Age Crete	9, 201
Neolithic and Bronze Age Cyprus	9, 201
Knossos	10, 202
Mycenae: Citadel	11, 202
Mycenae Outside the Citadel	11, 202
Homer's World	13, 202
Mainland Greece in Homer's Epics	14, 202
Iron Age Greece	16, 202
Greek Colonization, 800–500 BCE	18, 202
Archaic Greece	21, 202
Persian Empire, 550–330 BCE	22, 202
Persepolis	25, 202
Marathon, 490 BCE	25, 202
Persian Wars	27, 202
Thermopylae, 480 BCE: Ephialtes' Route	28, 202
Artemision, 480 BCE	28, 202
Salamis, 480 BCE	29, 202
Plataea, 479 BCE	29, 203
Greece and the Aegean (Hellespont inset)	30, 203
Classical Greece	32, 203
Cimmerian Bosphorus	34, 203
Olympia	35, 203
Attica	36, 203
Athens	37, 203
Classical Athens (Fifth and Fourth Centuries BCE)	38, 203
Roman Athens	38, 203
Delphi	39, 203
Sparta	40, 203
Miletus	40, 203
Priene	41, 203
Halicarnassus	41, 203
Akragas	42, 203
Greek and Punic Sicily	43, 203
Athenian Empire	45, 203
Greek Dialects around 450 BCE	47, 203
Peloponnesian War, 431–404 BCE (Sicily inset)	48, 203
Pylos/Sphacteria, 425 BCE	51, 204
Syracuse (and Athenian Siege, 415–413 BCE)	51, 204
Explorers	53, 204
Anabasis (Spring 400 to Winter 400/399 BCE)	54, 204
Leuctra, 371 BCE	55, 204
Second Athenian League	56, 204
Chaeronea, 338 BCE	57, 204
Growth of Macedonian Power, 359–336 BCE	58, 204
Alexander's Campaigns, 334–323 BCE	60, 204
Granicus River, 334 BCE	63, 204
Issus, 333 BCE	63, 204
Tyre, 332 BCE	64, 204
Gaugamela, 331 BCE	64, 204
Hydaspes River, 326 BCE	65, 204
Alexandria Oxiana (Ai Khanoum)	65, 204
Alexandria	66, 205
Hellenistic World: Kingdoms	68, 205
Hellenistic World: Aegean	70, 205
Hellenistic World: Asia Minor	72, 205
Hellenistic World: Syria–Egypt	74, 205
Pergamum	77, 205
Delos City	78, 205
Delos Centre	79, 205
Delos Island	79, 205

Etruria and Etruscan Expansion	81, 205	Lepcis Magna	143, 208
Early Italy and its Neighbours	83, 205	Africa Proconsularis and Numidia	144, 208
Peoples of Italy, and their Languages to the First Century CE	85, 205	Cyrene	145, 208
		Lutetia Parisiorum (Paris)	145, 208
Latium, 600–300 BCE	86, 205	Gaul	147, 208
Campania	87, 205	Germany	149, 208
Roman Expansion in Italy to 241 BCE	89, 205	Rhine-Danube *Limes*, 40–260 CE	151, 208
Cosa	90, 205	Danube–Black Sea	152, 208
Rome by 300 BCE	91, 205	Crete	154, 208
Roman Colonization in Italy to the Time of Augustus (Campania inset)	92, 205	Greece	155, 208
		Cyprus	156, 208
Second Punic War (First Punic War inset)	94, 206	Aphrodisias	157, 208
		Asia Minor	159, 209
Cannae, 216 BCE	97, 206	Paul's Journeys	160, 209
Zama, 202 BCE	97, 206	Syria–Persian Gulf	162, 209
Roman Campaigns in the Iberian Peninsula, 218–133 BCE	99, 206	Antioch (Syria)	165, 209
		Dura	166, 209
Numantia: Roman Siege, 133 BCE	100, 206	Jerusalem/Aelia Capitolina, Second–Third Centuries CE	167, 209
Numantia: Region	100, 206		
Rome in the Late Republic	101, 205	Jerusalem on Madaba Map	167, 209
Rome's Empire around 60 BCE	103, 206	Judaea	168, 209
Roman Campaigns, 58–30 BCE	104, 206	Masada (and Roman Siege, 73 CE)	169, 209
Actium, 31 BCE	107, 206	Egypt	171, 209
Augusta Praetoria (Aosta)	107, 206	Arabia	172, 209
Italy from Alps to Campania (including Corsica)	108, 206	India	174, 209
		Rome's Empire around 211 CE	178, 209
Italy from Apulia to Bruttium	111, 206	Circuit of the Roman Empire by Aurelius Gaius, 285–299 CE	180, 209
Sicily and Sardinia	113, 206		
Rome's Empire and Beyond: **Locator**	114	Etesian Winds and Sea Currents	182, 210
Rome at the Death of Augustus, 14 CE	116, 205	Sea Routes in Diocletian's Edict on Prices	182, 210
Environs of Imperial Rome	117, 206	Rome at the Death of Constantine, 337 CE	184, 205
Ostia	119, 207		
Portus	120, 207	Split	186, 210
Second Battle of Cremona, 69 CE	121, 207	Constantinople	187, 210
Pompeii	123, 207	Rome's Empire around 314 CE	188, 210
Herculaneum	124, 207	Christianity by the Early Fourth Century	192, 210
Italian Towns with Alimentary Schemes	127, 207		
		Roman World on Two Portable Sundials	195, 210
Rome at the Death of Trajan, 117 CE	128, 205		
Rome's Empire around 60 CE	130, 207	Barbarian Invasions of the Roman Empire, 370–500 CE	196, 210
Britain	132, 207		
Hadrian's Wall	135, 207	Roman Empire and Successor Kingdoms around 530 CE	199, 210
Antonine Wall	136, 207		
Iberian Peninsula	138, 207		
Vipasca	139, 207	Further Reading	201
Thamugadi (Timgad)	139, 207	Gazetteer	211
Africa	140, 207		

Croom Helm Ltd Publishers

are pleased to announce
the publication of the
ATLAS OF CLASSICAL HISTORY
Edited by R.J.A. Talbert
the twenty-fifth title in Croom Helm's
classical studies list
*and invite you to attend a celebration
to mark the event*
on Wednesday 17th April 1985
at Chez Solange
35 Cranbourn Street, London WC2H 7AH
at 5.30-7.30 pm

RSVP: Judy Simpson
Croom Helm Ltd
Provident House, Burrell Row
Beckenham, Kent BR3 1AT
Tel: 658 7813

Croom Helm Limited Publishers
&
The University of Belfast Bookshop

*Request the pleasure of your company at a
publication launch of three books by local authors.*

The Atlas of Classical History
by R.J.A. Talbert

The First Labour Party
by K.D. Brown

Studies in Linguistic Geography
by John Kirk

*on 9th May from 5.30 – 7.30
at
The University Bookshop
91 University Road, Belfast BT7 1NL.*

R.S.V.P. Elizabeth McWatters The University Bookshop 91 University Road,
Belfast BT7 1NL.

Preface to the Revised Edition

First, Richard Talbert looks back forty years. Before continuing, however, you are urged to read his 1984 Preface (reprinted below), because the present revision retains formative features of the original edition of the *Atlas*, which Croom Helm published in April 1985.

The publishers had good reason to feel pleased, so also their editor Richard Stoneman, who conceived the initiative and nurtured it unfailingly throughout. The *Atlas* was the twenty-fifth title in Croom Helm's expanding classical studies list, and with energetic promotion – including celebratory events in both London and Belfast – it sold well from the start, offered initially in both hardback and paperback. The paperback has remained in print ever since (in due course along with an e-book), and a handsome hardback Japanese translation appeared in 1996.

At the outset back in 1981, Richard Stoneman told me that he foresaw the *Atlas* long continuing to provide students with a lucid, useful and affordable reference tool – a vision that has been amply fulfilled, much to his credit. Scholars, too, have valued the *Atlas*, many of them finding it an ideal source of maps for illustrating their books and articles, a step taken indeed in some egregious instances without permission or even acknowledgement. It is still fair to claim, I think, that for a work of its size and type the *Atlas* has no serious rival. The superb cultural and historical atlases published in colour by Phaidon come closest perhaps, but in them text and images upstage the maps, and the large format far outclasses that of a handy textbook.

Naturally, I also was pleased with the distinct strengths of the *Atlas*, as well as thankful that this perilous collaborative enterprise with twenty-four fellow contributors (all in the British Isles) had been brought to a fruitful conclusion with minimal delay. At the same time, I was very conscious that for various reasons the cartography had patent limitations, several acknowledged in the Preface, others noted subsequently by reviewers. Privately, it was always my hope that at some future date a much-improved revision could be produced, remote though the prospects seemed for actually accomplishing this. What I by no means anticipated was that quite soon (early 1988), as a consequence of having both edited Croom Helm's *Atlas* and moved to Canada by then, I would be asked by the American Philological Association to undertake a far more ambitious project: the creation from scratch of a major, definitive classical atlas on a scale not achieved for well over a century. William Harris, as chair of APA's Cartography Committee formed in 1980, had contacted me three years later enquiring about just what was in preparation for Croom Helm, but he did not elaborate on APA's plans, and I never learned of them, let alone of their eventual collapse in 1987.

The outcome of my acceptance of APA's invitation in 1988 to rethink and relaunch its project was the publication of the *Barrington Atlas of the Greek and Roman World* and its *Map-by-Map Directory* by Princeton University Press in 2000 (since 2013, the *Atlas* has also been available as an app for iPad). The goals determined for this project, as well as its stressful progress, are treated in my book *Challenges of Mapping the Classical World* (Routledge, 2019). Fortunately, *Barrington's* maps and the now indispensable resource *Pleiades.stoa.org* (which expands and updates its *Directory*), together with the shift to digital mapmaking and the growing productivity of the Ancient World Mapping Center (www.unc.awmc), have all served to render revision of the wholly pre-digital Croom Helm *Atlas* a more realistic prospect. I established the Mapping Center in 2000 to build on *Barrington's* foundation, and Tom Elliott initiated *Pleiades* there.

Even so, for revision of the *Atlas* numerous dilemmas – fundamental, inescapable, intertwined – awaited resolution. What involvement was I prepared to accept myself, for instance, if any? For long, my inclination was to decline a leading role (because of other preoccupations), although I welcomed the possibility that whoever else undertook the revision might commission the Mapping Center to produce the maps according to their specifications – as was done there principally by Gabriel Moss and Ray Belanger for Trevor Bryce's *Atlas of the Ancient Near East: From Prehistoric Times to the Roman Imperial Period* (Routledge, 2016), a work in fact modelled on the Croom Helm *Atlas*. Then who was to be the publisher? A transfer from Routledge (to whom the title eventually came in 1992 after Croom Helm ceased to be independent in 1986) looked awkward to arrange and not necessarily acceptable there, despite Routledge's evident lack of enthusiasm for sponsoring the revision itself. Equally daunting was the issue of how the actual mapmaking would be funded – once, needless to say, the extent of the revision had been settled, likewise the use it would make of colour (unaffordable in the 1980s!), and so forth.

The colleague who formulated plans most successfully was Benet Salway at University College London, an old friend and collaborator in other projects. Eventually, I agreed to join him as co-editor, not least so that the unique support and expertise of the Mapping Center could be harnessed most effectively. Next, lengthy negotiations with Routledge fortunately led to an agreement that it would publish the revision we envisaged, with all maps to appear in colour and costs shared with the Mapping Center. Work started there in earnest in 2017 just after Lindsay Holman became its director. Not only did her role in map design and production soon become invaluable, but she has also proved willing to remain the Center's director and in consequence has stayed closely involved with the revision throughout. In due course, Benet and I were eager for her to gain recognition as co-editor, and so we were delighted when she agreed to join us in this capacity. In March 2020, during the last hour before physical access to the Mapping Center was cut off at less than a day's notice because of COVID, Lindsay miraculously reconfigured three of its machines for remote working. By this most timely and deft of interventions, progress could be maintained throughout the next seventeen months, until the Mapping Center again became accessible.

****

Second, from here on all three co-editors write jointly about the scope and character determined for the revised *Atlas*. On balance, there has seemed no strong reason to alter the original trim-size and format; nor, with an eye to handiness and list price, have we been keen to extend the length by much. We certainly wish to engage the same primary audience: students at the high school and college levels, who are not specialists in ancient history and cannot realistically be expected to read academic works in languages other than English. The scope remains largely unchanged too, because most of the original content is retained, with its mix of regional and thematic maps along with city- and battle-plans, each accompanied by a concise explanatory text and a few recommendations for further reading aimed at non-specialists. To be sure, in the course of digital redrafting at the Mapping Center, each original map and plan has been revised in accordance with its contributor's instructions, and each is now presented using a full-colour palette; accompanying texts and recommended readings have similarly been revised and updated.

As might be expected, the amount of revision varies, with contributors having our assurance that they need not strain to make a change when really none is called for. Users familiar with the original edition will notice that some content is now transferred to a different map for better comprehension and use of space (Italy's peoples and languages, for example, on p. 85). In other instances – plans especially – frames have been enlarged to show a core in a wider context (Mycenae, Delos and

Pergamum, for example). By the same token, coverage of Rome's world now reaches deep into the Sahara, as well as much further east to Arabia and India. To accommodate such extensions while also not increasing the original overall length by much has inevitably required dropping some maps and plans. These were tough choices made with reluctance, but in consequence we have also been able to lengthen the timeframe (now to around 500 CE), and to add several themes and cities in which intense interest has developed during the past forty years – among the latter, for example, Portus, Aphrodisias and Syrian Antioch. The Gazetteer now appends (where possible) the modern equivalent name and country to each ancient placename listed.

For regional maps, use of the *Map Tiles* developed at the Mapping Center by Ryan Horne has been hugely beneficial. The *Tiles* show changes in elevation, return the landscape so far as practicable to its ancient aspect and present it consistently throughout – thereby overcoming some of the original edition's most visible limitations. *Barrington's* maps (laid out on a different physical base, and at larger scales than those of the *Atlas*) have in turn proved invaluable for selecting settlements, features and peoples. We have made it our principle to spell their names as in *Barrington* – thus eliminating inconsistencies which it was impossible to resolve in the 1980s.

We offered every contributor to the original edition who was still living, and whose map(s) or plan(s) were to be included in the revision, the opportunity to update them along with any accompanying text and recommended readings. As was only reasonable after so long an interval, several declined in whole or in part. In such instances, as well as for everything that deceased contributors had been responsible, we then took over, often soliciting the generous help of appropriate experts. We sought them too for many of the new maps and plans, and now from a wider orbit than the British Isles alone. In several instances, work that the Mapping Center had itself undertaken – the *Wall Maps* series (Routledge, 2011), for example, and plans in *The Romans from Village to Empire* (Oxford University Press, ed. 2, 2012) – has been adapted and updated. Far from expected, and most gratifying, has been the high total of original contributors glad to revise their work – eleven, including Richard Stoneman – an inspiration in the struggle to ensure the project's completion! Four had already contributed to *Barrington*. One other, Peter Rhodes, sadly passed away after his revisions had been delivered; so too did a new contributor, Simon Keay, at the same stage. Although John Falconer opted not to revise what he had contributed to the original edition, he generously provided the new cover image, a memorable vista captured on a Queen's University, Belfast, Easter 1984 Study Tour to eastern Algeria.

The warmest thanks are due therefore to the thirty colleagues who joined us in producing this edition, as well as to the fourteen students at the Mapping Center whose assistance in its preparation was likewise invaluable: the names of all forty-four are listed below. At Routledge, we heartily thank Marcia Adams, editor Amy Davis-Poynter, and Elizabeth Risch. Completion of the revision has been a lengthy and often stressful struggle; inevitably, limitations and shortcomings remain. Even so, our hope is that the result offers an instructive demonstration of how rewardingly the scholarship, resources and technology for mapping the classical world and its history have advanced over the past forty years. This collaborative, interdisciplinary progress is exciting, and we are eager to see its remarkable potential tapped still further.

Richard Talbert
Benet Salway
Lindsay Holman
Chapel Hill, NC, and London
April 2022

Preface to the Original Edition

In all likelihood, this book has its origin in a chance encounter between Richard Stoneman, the humanities editor of Croom Helm Ltd, and myself at the classical societies' Oxford Triennial Conference in summer 1981. The subject of our conversation on that occasion eludes me. At any rate, it was an unexpected pleasure to be approached by Richard in the autumn with a tentative proposal for the compilation of an atlas of classical history. We soon found that we were in close agreement on what was needed: a volume in which lucid maps offered the high school student and the undergraduate a reasonably comprehensive, up-to-date and scholarly coverage of classical history down to the time of Constantine, accompanied by modest elucidation of the material and by some suggestions for further reading. Explanation and discussion were felt to be especially important, so long as they did not outweigh the maps.

A concern to keep production costs under control has restrained us from including everything that we might have wished. The same concern has affected the size and number of pages in the atlas, while colour printing has proved out of the question. Use of some standard bases has helped to limit expenditure on cartography. Equally, without the help of expert colleagues the desired coverage of classical history would have been impossible to achieve. The warmest gratitude is therefore due to those throughout the British Isles who agreed with alacrity to contribute to the atlas and have done such excellent work. It has been deliberate editorial policy to be ready with guidance when required, but otherwise—in view of the contributors' specialist knowledge—to leave them a fairly free hand in the presentation of their material. Inevitably, however, restraint did have to be exercised when texts submitted overran their allotted space.

In particular, no standard convention for the spelling of names has been imposed. Since a convention which meets with general satisfaction has yet to be devised, in a work of this character an editor who sought to impose one of his own making would only face exceptions, pleas, arguments, delay, as well as increasing the possibility of mistakes and diverting attention from more important issues. Whatever an editor does, he has no hope of pleasing everybody where this perennial controversy is concerned. As it is, notably outlandish or unusual spelling of names has been discouraged, Latin forms have been recommended where serious doubt has arisen, and an effort has been made to keep each individual contributor's usage consistent (since sometimes it was not!). Nonetheless, throughout the atlas as a whole inconsistency does still remain. While any distress caused to purists who read through from cover to cover is regretted, arguably the degree of inconsistency present should hardly cause undue difficulties of comprehension anywhere, and should prove of little account to those who refer just to two or three maps at a time.

Richard Talbert
Queen's University, Belfast
1984

KEY

Except where a North arrow indicates otherwise, all maps and plans are oriented North.

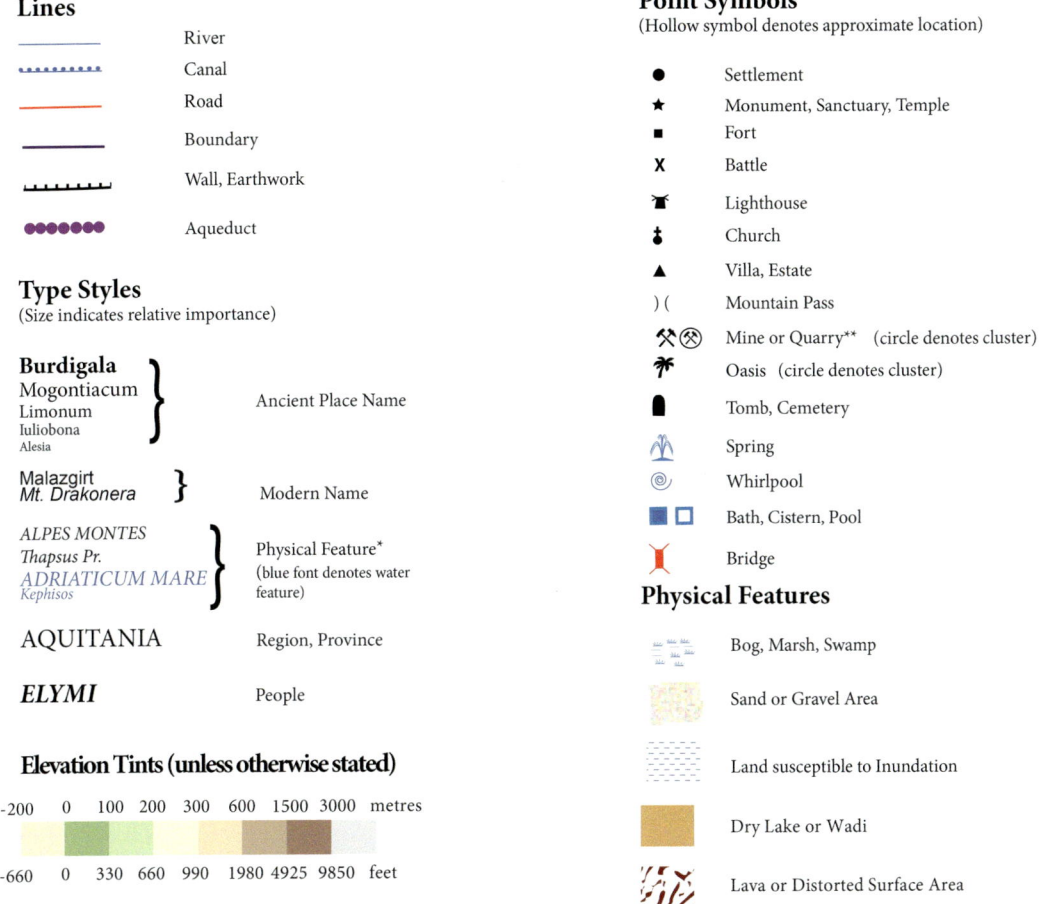

Lines

- River
- Canal
- Road
- Boundary
- Wall, Earthwork
- Aqueduct

Type Styles
(Size indicates relative importance)

- **Burdigala** / Mogontiacum / Limonum / Iuliobona / Alesia — Ancient Place Name
- Malazgirt / Mt. Drakonera — Modern Name
- ALPES MONTES / Thapsus Pr. / ADRIATICUM MARE / Kephisos — Physical Feature* (blue font denotes water feature)
- AQUITANIA — Region, Province
- ELYMI — People

Elevation Tints (unless otherwise stated)

-200 0 100 200 300 600 1500 3000 metres

-660 0 330 660 990 1980 4925 9850 feet

Point Symbols
(Hollow symbol denotes approximate location)

- Settlement
- Monument, Sanctuary, Temple
- Fort
- Battle
- Lighthouse
- Church
- Villa, Estate
- Mountain Pass
- Mine or Quarry** (circle denotes cluster)
- Oasis (circle denotes cluster)
- Tomb, Cemetery
- Spring
- Whirlpool
- Bath, Cistern, Pool
- Bridge

Physical Features

- Bog, Marsh, Swamp
- Sand or Gravel Area
- Land susceptible to Inundation
- Dry Lake or Wadi
- Lava or Distorted Surface Area

Map bases are derived from the Ancient World Mapping Center's *Map Tiles*, which use the WGS 84 coordinate system and web Mercator projection (EPSG: 3857). So far as is practicable, the *Tiles* restore landscape, rivers and shorelines to their ancient aspect.

***Latin** is normally used as follows to identify features, but some Greek terms are also called for:

Latin			
Aestuarium *estuary*	Mons/Montes *mountain(s)*		
Ager (pl. Agri) *territory*	Oceanus *ocean*		
Aqua *aqueduct*	Palus (pl. Paludes) *marsh*		
Campus *plain*	Pons *bridge*		
Chersonesus *peninsula*	Portae *gates*		
Fossa(tum) *canal, earthwork*	Portus *harbour*		
Fretum *strait*	Promunturium *cape*		
Insula (pl. Inss) *island*	Salinae *salt marsh*		
Lacus *lake*	Saltus *forest*		
Litus *coast*	Silva *forest*		
Mare *sea*	Sinus *bay, gulf*		
Metallum *mine*	Via *road*		

Greek terms for features:

- Akra, Akron *cape*
- Antron *cave*
- Aulon *gulf*
- Chora *district*
- Limen (pl. Limenes) *harbour*
- Limnai *marshes*
- Nesos (pl. Nesoi) *island*
- Oros *mountain*
- Pedion *plain*
- Pelagos *sea*
- Porthmos *strait*
- Stoma *mouth*

**Materials Mined or Quarried:

Ag	Silver		
Au	Gold		
Bs	Basalt		
Cu	Copper		
Fe	Iron		
Gr	Granite		
Hg	Mercury		
Ls	Limestone		
M	Marble		
Pb	Lead		
S	Sulphur		
Sn	Tin		

Contributors (with their current institutional affiliations)

Those asterisked also contributed to the first edition.
The editors are responsible for maps on which no contributor's name appears, together with their accompanying texts and further readings.
For maps credited to more than one contributor, the first named is responsible for the accompanying texts and further readings.

*Maureen Alden, Queen's University, Belfast
Rebecca Benefiel, Washington and Lee University, Lexington, VA
Mary Boatwright, Duke University, Durham, NC
Alan Bowman, Brasenose College, Oxford
Lisa Cooper, University of British Columbia, Vancouver
*Raymond Davis, Queen's University, Belfast
Andrea De Giorgi, Florida State University, Tallahassee
*John Drinkwater, University of Sheffield
Jonathan Edmondson, York University, Toronto
Charles Gates, Bilkent University, Ankara
Lindsay Holman, University of North Carolina, Chapel Hill, editor
Simon James, University of Leicester
Alicia Jiménez, Duke University, Durham, NC
Simon Keay, University of Southampton
Noel Lenski, Yale University, New Haven, CT
David Mattingly, University of Leicester
Katherine McDonald, University of Durham
Brian McGing, Trinity College Dublin
Dimitri Nakassis, University of Colorado, Boulder
*Edwin Owens, Swansea University, Wales
*Andrew Poulter, University of Nottingham
*Nicholas Purcell, Brasenose College, Oxford
William Race, University of North Carolina, Chapel Hill
*Peter Rhodes, University of Durham
Elizabeth Robinson, University of Dallas Rome Program
Benet Salway, University College London, editor
Thomas Schneider, University of British Columbia, Vancouver
*Clemence Schultze, University of Durham
*Richard Stoneman, University of Exeter
*Richard Talbert, University of North Carolina, Chapel Hill, editor
Ross Twele, Catholic University of America, Washington, DC
*Christopher Tuplin, University of Liverpool
*Roger Wilson, University of British Columbia, Vancouver

STUDENTS WHO ADVANCED THE REVISION OF THE ATLAS DURING THEIR ASSISTANTSHIPS AT THE ANCIENT WORLD MAPPING CENTER:

Safiatou Bamba, Tyler Brown, Coleman Cheeley, Daniel Hawke, Leah Hinshaw, Bryanna Ledbetter, Kimberly Oliver, Laura Roberson, Rachel Sarvey, Hannah Shealy, Peter Streilein, Lauren Taylor, Faith Virago, Hania Zanib.

Egypt and the Near East, 1200–500 BCE

The 1200s BCE saw disruptions here (p. 2) from political strife, climate crises, internal rebellions and population movements. The shattered palatial systems of the Bronze Age were replaced by new political orders, often with vastly different socio-cultural configurations. In Anatolia, the once-powerful state of Hatti disintegrated, with smaller Neo-Hittite and Aramaean city-states emerging in southern Anatolia and north-west Syria. Along Anatolia's west coast, Greek-speaking migrants founded thriving cities, while further inland the wealthy kingdom of Lydia emerged, as did Phrygia. In far east Anatolia and into Armenia, the formidable kingdom of Urartu established cities on mountain peaks.

Phoenician cities along the Levant coast thrived as bases for maritime trade stretching across the Mediterranean. Further south, the newly arrived Philistines occupied the coastal plain. Inland, unified Israel was ruled by the biblically attested kings David and Solomon, before subsequently separating into two kingdoms, Israel and Judah.

In Egypt, the remaining pharaohs of the once-powerful New Kingdom failed to arrest its decline caused by low Nile inundations, civil unrest, and invasions by both Libyans and Sea Peoples from Mediterranean islands and coastal regions. The subsequent Third Intermediate Period brought renewed political instability, marked repeatedly by fragmentation of the state and control by non-native Egyptian rulers, some of Libyan ancestry (Dynasty 22), others from Nubia (Dynasty 25). After short-lived Neo-Assyrian rule, the 26th Dynasty of Saite kings enjoyed a period of unification and cultural renaissance, which the Persians ended in 526. They ruled Egypt until ousted by Alexander in 332 (p. 60).

In northern Mesopotamia, the early first millennium saw the steady growth of Assyria, an imperial kingdom centred on cities such as Nimrud and Nineveh on the Tigris river. Under successive militarily ambitious rulers, Assyrian expansion led – in the 800s and 700s especially – to the conquest of vast swathes of the Near East, including much of Anatolia, the Levant and even Egypt. But there were still other powers with imperial ambitions, including the Babylonians of southern Mesopotamia (who inherited Assyria's territories after Nineveh fell in 612), and finally the Persians from south-west Iran, who toppled the Medes and Babylonians. By 500, the Persians had established the largest empire to date in this part of the globe (p. 22).

DOI: 10.4324/9781003125228-1

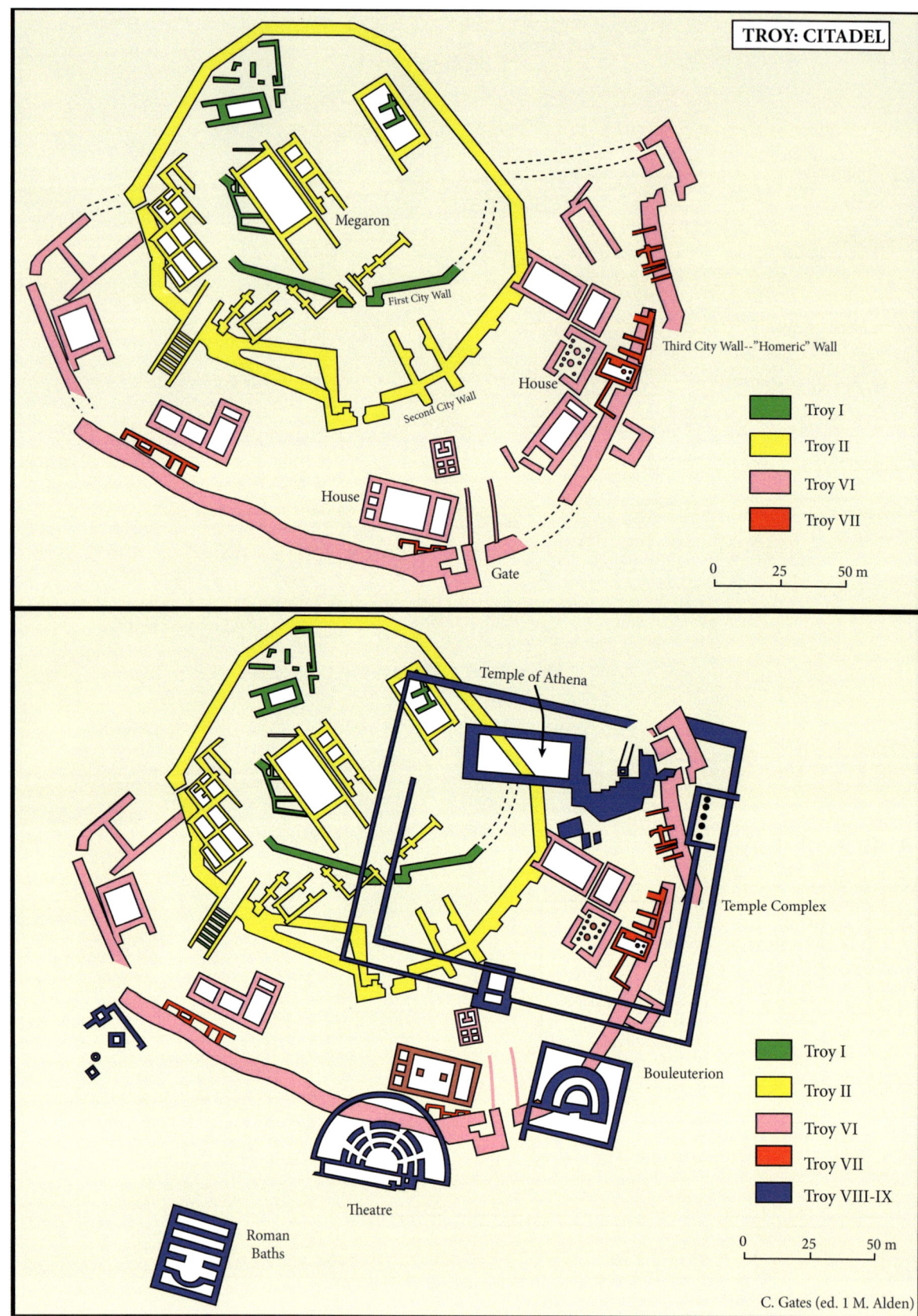

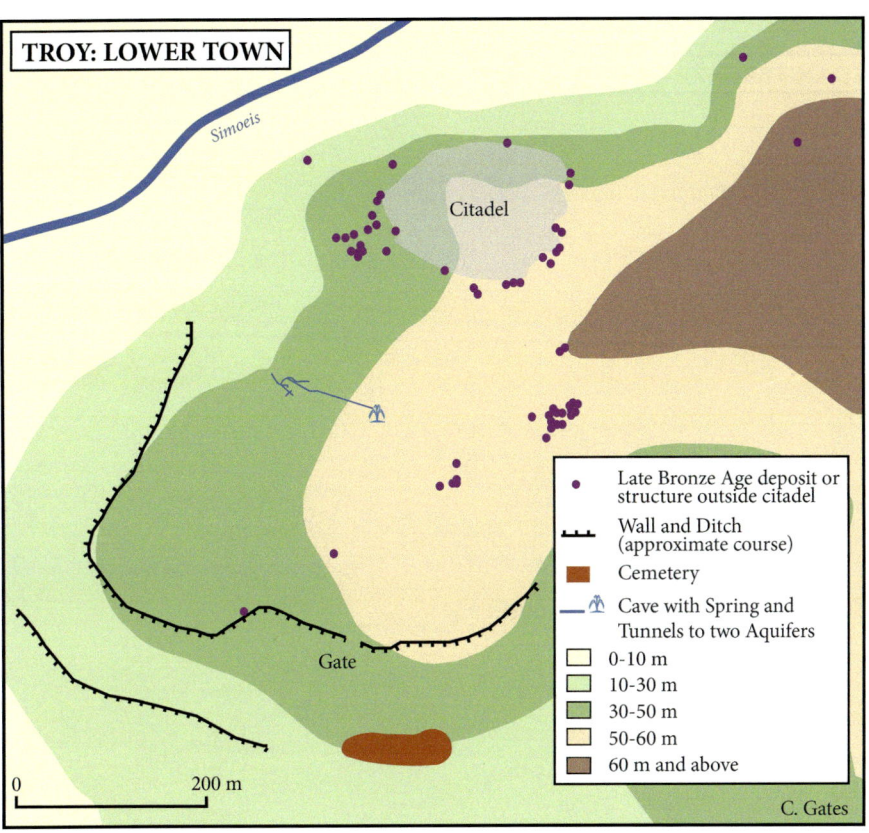

Troy: Citadel and Lower Town

The archaeological site of Hisarlık in northwest Turkey has been intensively investigated since the mid-nineteenth century. Heinrich Schliemann identified it with ancient Troy, the city whose siege and capture by Achaeans (Mycenaeans) figured prominently in ancient Greek views of their past. Although it is impossible to determine whether the Trojan War truly happened, the site itself has given important evidence for settlement from the Early Bronze Age through the Byzantine period. The superimposed remains of settlements have been divided into nine major levels (I–IX), with numerous subdivisions. Levels I–VII represent the Bronze Age; Troy VIII the Iron Age and Classical Greek city, and Troy IX the Roman city. Post-Roman medieval remains are not encompassed by this traditional system.

From the start, excavations focused on the fortified citadel. Recent campaigns, however, have brought to light traces of the Bronze Age walls of a lower town. The earliest settlement, Troy I (around 3000–2550 BCE), lay on the coast. Yet over the centuries silt deposited by local rivers filled in the bay here, leaving the citadel some distance from the sea. The larger and wealthier Troy II (around 2550–2300) featured *megarons* (rectangular halls with a porch) as its prominent architecture. Troy VI (around 1750–1300), larger still, is best known for the imposing stone foundations of its fortification wall. This wall's superstructure, made of sun-dried mud bricks, is long gone. Also gone is the centre of Troy VI, destroyed when the Athena Sanctuary was constructed during the third century. Troy VI may have been wrecked by an earthquake. The successor settlement, Troy VIIa (around 1300–1180), used the same walls; its houses have yielded unusual quantities of *pithoi* (large storage jars), sometimes interpreted as preparation for a siege. After a final Bronze Age phase and a gap in occupation, the town returned to life, now named Ilium.

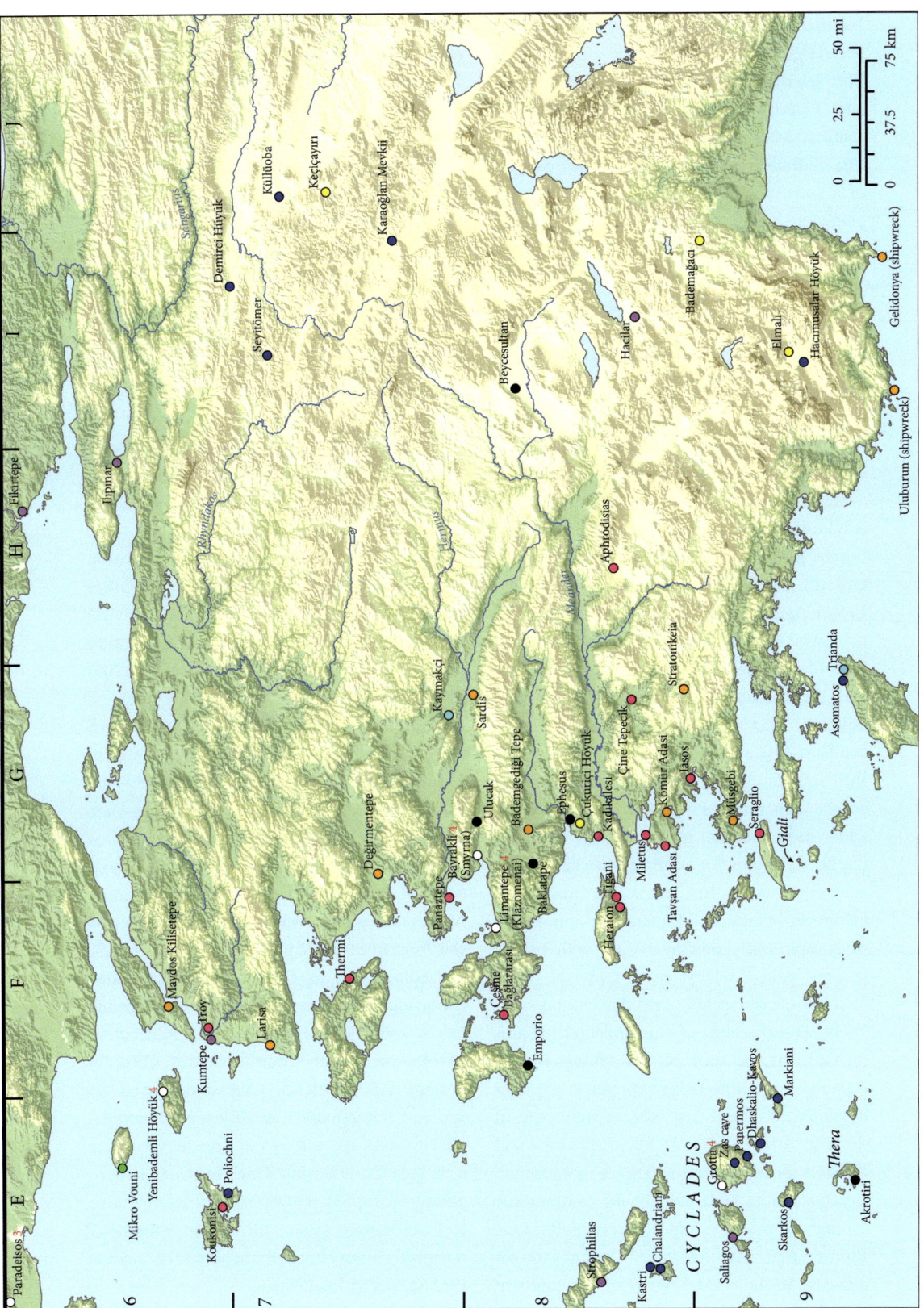

Neolithic and Bronze Age Greece and the Aegean, Crete, Cyprus

The Neolithic period across Greece, the Aegean and Cyprus (around 6800–3100 BCE) is characterized by farming village communities. The diversified agricultural economy made use of a wide range of domesticated animals and plants, including the olive and vine. Obsidian (volcanic glass), quarried from the islands of Melos and Giali and knapped into blades by specialists, was a valuable resource with a wide distribution. Thus, although the Neolithic period is sometimes characterized as simple and egalitarian, its communities were in fact complex, in contact with the wider Aegean as well as the Balkan world to the north, and engaged in sophisticated craft production.

The Early Bronze Age (around 3100–2100) is traditionally defined by the increasing use of bronze, an alloy of copper and another metal, typically tin. As in the Neolithic period, Early Bronze Age communities lived in villages with a diversified economy based on agriculture; these were highly interconnected across the Aegean and the eastern Mediterranean. Some sites, especially larger coastal centres, were fortified. In southern Attica and the Cycladic islands – with their sources of obsidian, copper and marble – coastal communities were in regular contact with neighbouring areas. Hence Cycladic marble sculptures, for example, have been found across the Aegean. In Crete, whose Bronze Age culture is known as Minoan, the appearance of conspicuously wealthy burials with bronze daggers, gold jewellery, beads and seal stones indicates the emergence of an elite culture.

The construction of monumental palaces on Crete at the start of the Middle Bronze Age (around 2100–1650) represents a major development. These first palaces were built at the large urban centres of Malia, Phaistos and Knossos (p. 10). Palaces and other monumental structures were built and rebuilt continuously throughout this Age and the start of the Late Bronze Age. At this time Cretan cultural influence in the coastal towns of the southern Aegean is pronounced. The phenomenon is sometimes explained as political power – a Minoan maritime empire – but recent work has argued that the evidence is more consistent with local communities selectively and strategically emulating Cretan practices. Whatever the explanation, the massive eruption of the volcano on Thera around 1560 buried the important port town of Akrotiri there in metres of ash, removing an important node of maritime trade and diminishing Cretan influence. The eruption may have destabilized Crete, since about a century later (around 1450), a broad surge of destruction left few settlements across the island unaffected. Knossos, however, survived the worst of the chaos and maintained its dominance over much of Crete for a further century, if not longer.

On the Greek mainland, wealthy Shaft Graves at Mycenae (p. 11) beginning around 1750 demonstrate growing prosperity, competition and influence from Crete and the islands. Other novel tomb forms, especially the monumental tholos, also proliferate. This mainland culture in the Late Bronze Age (around 1650–1100) is called Mycenaean. It gradually replaces Minoan influence in the Cyclades and eastern Aegean, where it encountered the powerful Hittite empire and its vassal cities, such as Troy (p. 4). Between 1400 and 1200, palaces were built in many parts of the mainland, from Pylos in the southwest to Volos in the northeast, some of them located within fortified citadels. Mycenaean pottery was widely exported across the Aegean and Mediterranean. Cyprus took a leading role in this international trade, exporting copper in addition to other goods (see p. 156). For reasons that are still debated, Mycenaean palatial culture ended abruptly around 1180, with its palaces destroyed by fire and not rebuilt. The following century – which marks the end of the Bronze Age – was a turbulent one during which settlements were greatly disrupted. However, this century also features a lively urban culture that introduced numerous innovations; these paved the way for the succeeding Iron Age.

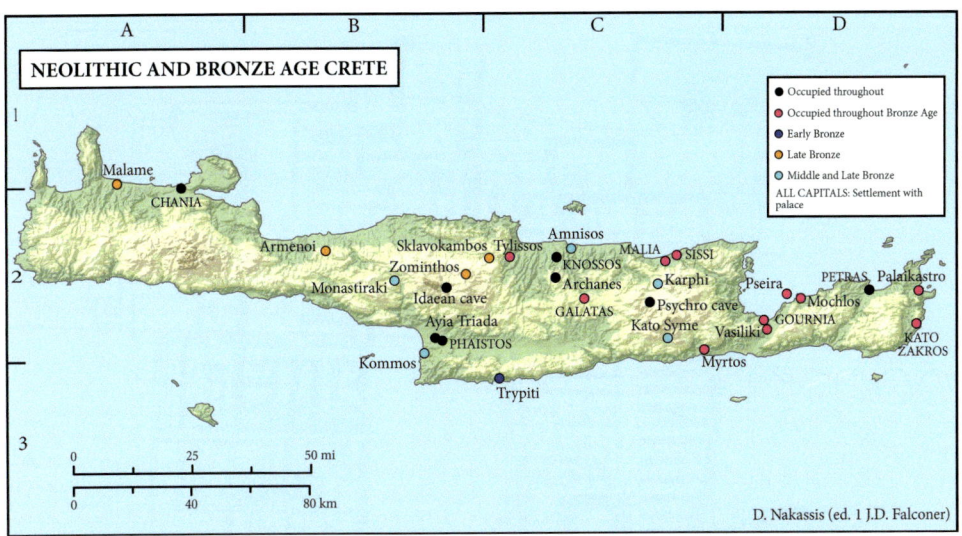

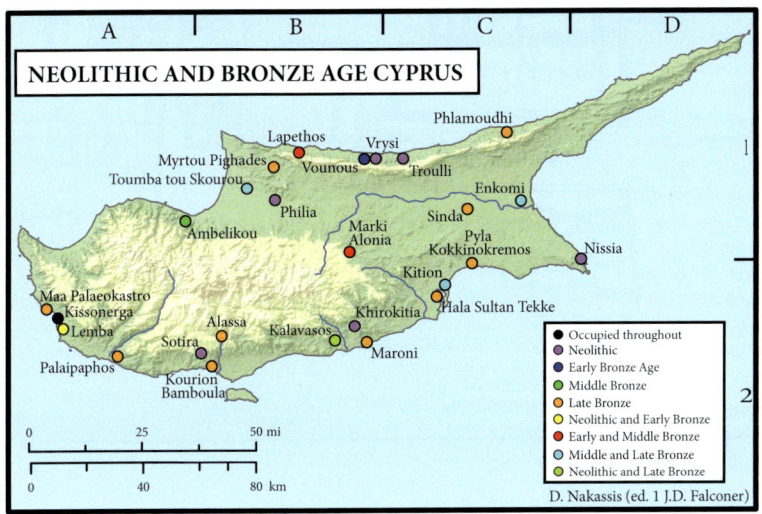

Knossos

Successive palatial structures known as 'The Palace of Minos' at Knossos in Crete were uncovered by the British archaeologist Arthur Evans from 1900 onwards. They were built on the Neolithic tell site of Kephala, south of modern Heraklion. The site was first occupied by about 6000 BCE. Around 2000, a monumental building was erected in the northwest area. The Old Palace – on the same alignment – was built during the following century: its remains include the West Court with stone-lined circular pits ('koulouras'), the West Façade and the Central Court. The Old Palace continued to develop and grow until it was destroyed by a major earthquake around 1700: by that time it included the North Entrance Passage and the Throne Room, Royal Pottery Stores, West Magazines, and the Magazines of the Giant Pithoi. Domestic quarters (with drainage system) were on the east side of the Central Court.

A New Palace, an ambitious multi-level structure with four wings around a central court, was constructed after 1700. Earthquake damage about a century later was remedied by modifications made during the 1500s: they included restoration of the West Façade and

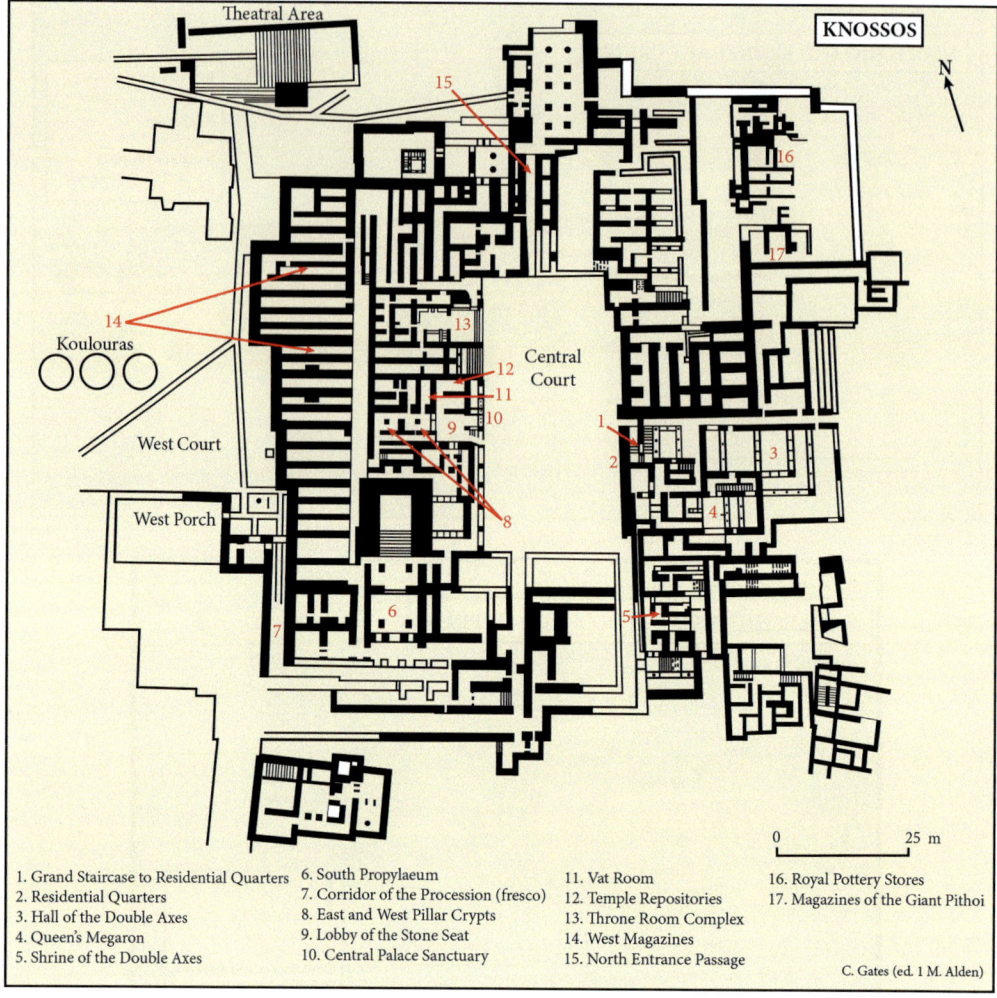

1. Grand Staircase to Residential Quarters
2. Residential Quarters
3. Hall of the Double Axes
4. Queen's Megaron
5. Shrine of the Double Axes
6. South Propylaeum
7. Corridor of the Procession (fresco)
8. East and West Pillar Crypts
9. Lobby of the Stone Seat
10. Central Palace Sanctuary
11. Vat Room
12. Temple Repositories
13. Throne Room Complex
14. West Magazines
15. North Entrance Passage
16. Royal Pottery Stores
17. Magazines of the Giant Pithoi

C. Gates (ed. 1 M. Alden)

South Propylaeum, bastions to support the North Entrance Passage, and new walls to give additional support to upper floors. The West Porch was rebuilt. Decorative frescoes now appear. Also part of this phase are the Central Palace Sanctuary (with its East and West Pillar Crypts), Vat Room (with cult paraphernalia cleared and placed in a pit after destruction), Temple Repositories (where faience 'snake goddess' figures were found), and the Lobby of the Stone Seat.

Despite again suffering earthquake damage (in Colin Macdonald's view), this New Palace remained in limited use, and reconstruction was undertaken between 1500 and 1450 approximately when it was violently destroyed. During the next century, it was succeeded by the Last Palace: the Throne Room as it now appears belongs to this phase. This Last Palace was badly damaged by fire sometime during the later 1300s, but it probably remained an administrative centre, albeit on a much-reduced scale. The date of the Linear B tablets found here remains unclear.

A larger settlement with lavish villas built between 1700 and 1450, as well as extensive cemeteries, surrounds the Bronze Age site. The population of Knossos during this period has been estimated at between 13,400 and 16,750.

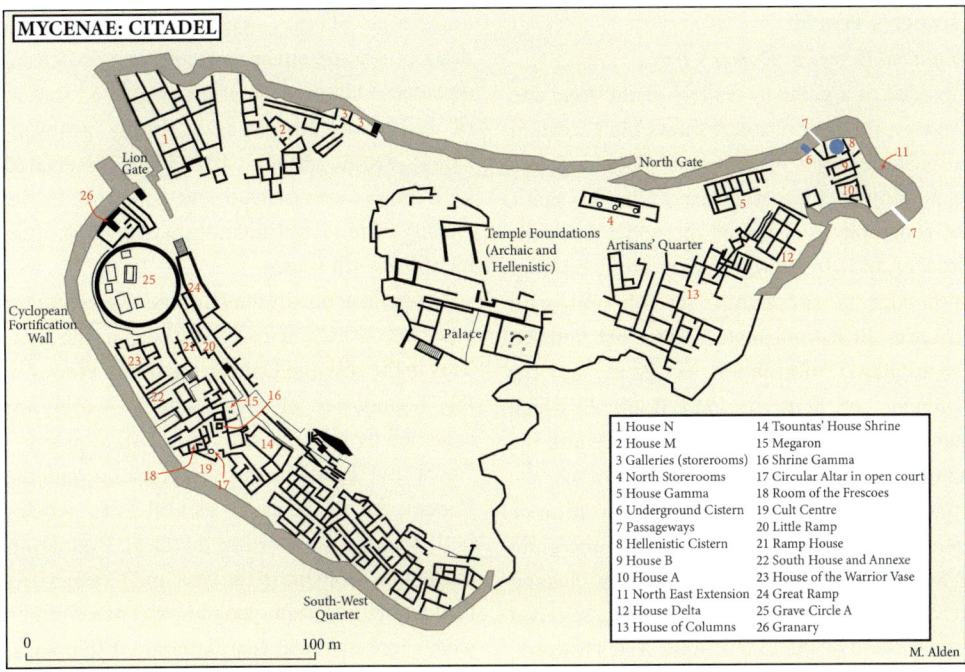

Mycenae: Citadel and Outside

Mycenae's citadel stands on a low hill between a pair of mountains (not shown) to the north and south, separated from them by deep ravines. To the west is an extensive cemetery, its earliest graves dug between 2000 and 1500 BCE. Grave Circles A (found by Heinrich Schliemann in 1876) and B, with their wealthy Shaft Graves, were established here during the late 1600s and the 1500s. Three of the site's nine 'tholos' (domed, beehive) tombs – dating to between 1500 and 1200 – are located here; six more, along with numerous chamber tombs, are cut into the soft rock of the surrounding hills. The citadel's buildings include the palace of the 1300s, a cult centre (with idols and frescoes), artisans' workshops, and storerooms; clay tablets in Linear B script are among the finds. The earliest fortifications (enclosing the top of the hill) were built in massive 'Cyclopean' style around 1350; the Lion and North Gates were part of a second phase (mid-1200s) enclosing Grave Circle A. A north-east extension made around 1200 ensured a water supply: it enclosed an underground fountain fed by the Perseia spring. Major rebuilding had followed an earthquake around 1230; further destruction around 1200 ended written record-keeping. Again some rebuilding occurred, but the site was burned between 1130 and 1100.

Survey and excavation outside the citadel have revealed a sizeable town with associated cemeteries. Some of the houses excavated – like the Petsas House and Ivory Houses – were impressive structures, presumably built for important individuals; more Linear B tablets were found here.

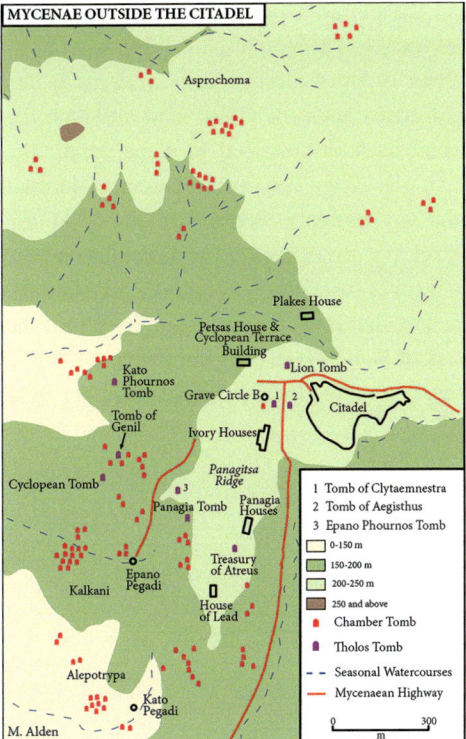

Homer's World
Mainland Greece in Homer's Epics

Intended as a guide to readers of the *Iliad* and *Odyssey*, this pair of maps shows the known or probable location of the main places referred to by Homer. Like other aspects of his epics, the geography is a mix of memories from the Bronze and Iron Age past, contemporary knowledge of the eighth, seventh and sixth centuries BCE, and myth. The most detailed geographical information is given by the *Catalogue of Ships* in *Iliad* Book 2, which names 152 towns or districts in Greece and the islands, together with nineteen in Thrace, the Troad and Asia Minor. Because the position of many of these places was unknown or uncertain to later Greeks, scholars were initially inclined to suggest that the *Catalogue* was a survival from the end of the Late Bronze Age. However, as archaeological knowledge of the Bronze Age grew, they began to argue that the *Catalogue* more plausibly reflected Homer's contemporary world, albeit with an archaizing patina. Even so, many features of the *Catalogue* cannot be easily explained in historical terms, so it seems best to understand it as a poetic composition that is largely shaped by mythical traditions and the narrative of the *Iliad*, in addition to historical and geographical realities.

The Trojan section of the *Catalogue* is less informative than the Greek, and although the Troad itself is described in some detail, the territories of the Trojan allies cannot be located with any certainty. For the geography of the Troad, the rest of the *Iliad* adds details that are sometimes surprisingly accurate – for example, the fact that Poseidon could see Troy from the peak of Samothrace. This feature has led to the suggestion that Homer may have had personal knowledge of the area. Other geographical descriptions are either vague or, in a few cases, invented. Odysseus' description of the location of his home, Ithaca, is a thorny problem. Consequently, Ithaca has been associated with almost every island and peninsula in the vicinity of modern Ithaki, the island most often identified with Ithaca.

The main action of the *Iliad* and *Odyssey* takes place in a world enclosed by Ithaca in the west, Troy in the east and Crete in the south. However, the boundaries of the Homeric world are extended by references to more distant places – Egypt and Libya in the south, Sidon and the Phoenicians in the east – as well as to peoples both real and more or less mythical: Pygmies in the south, Taphians in the west and Cimmerians in the north. Certain geographical descriptions seem more mythical than accurate. Ethiopians, for example, are described as living split in two, some at the dawn and others at the sunset; but historical Ethiopians lived to the south of the Aegean, not at the extreme east or west. Again, the wanderings of Odysseus from the time when he was blown off course rounding Cape Malea seem to occur in mythical surroundings. These stories perhaps stem from traditional ones that lacked any specific geographical location. Nonetheless, attempts were made from quite an early date by the Greeks themselves to fit the wanderings into the geography of the Mediterranean: thus, the Phaeacians were placed on Corcyra, Circe at the location of Circeii south of Rome, Scylla and Charybdis in the Straits of Messina and the Cyclopes on Mount Etna in Sicily. These localizations of Odysseus' wanderings in the West must reflect increasing Greek knowledge of the Mediterranean from the eighth century onwards.

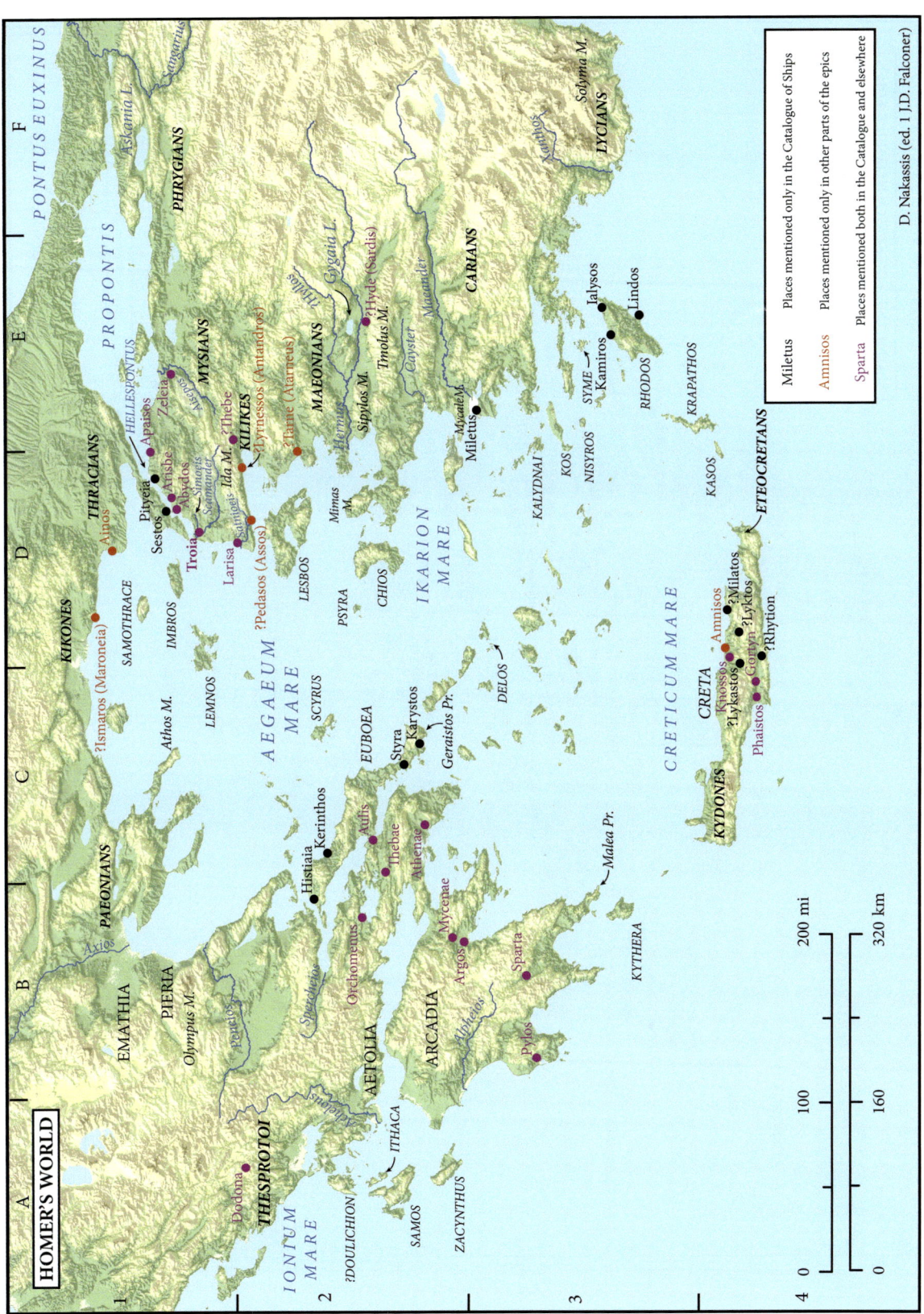

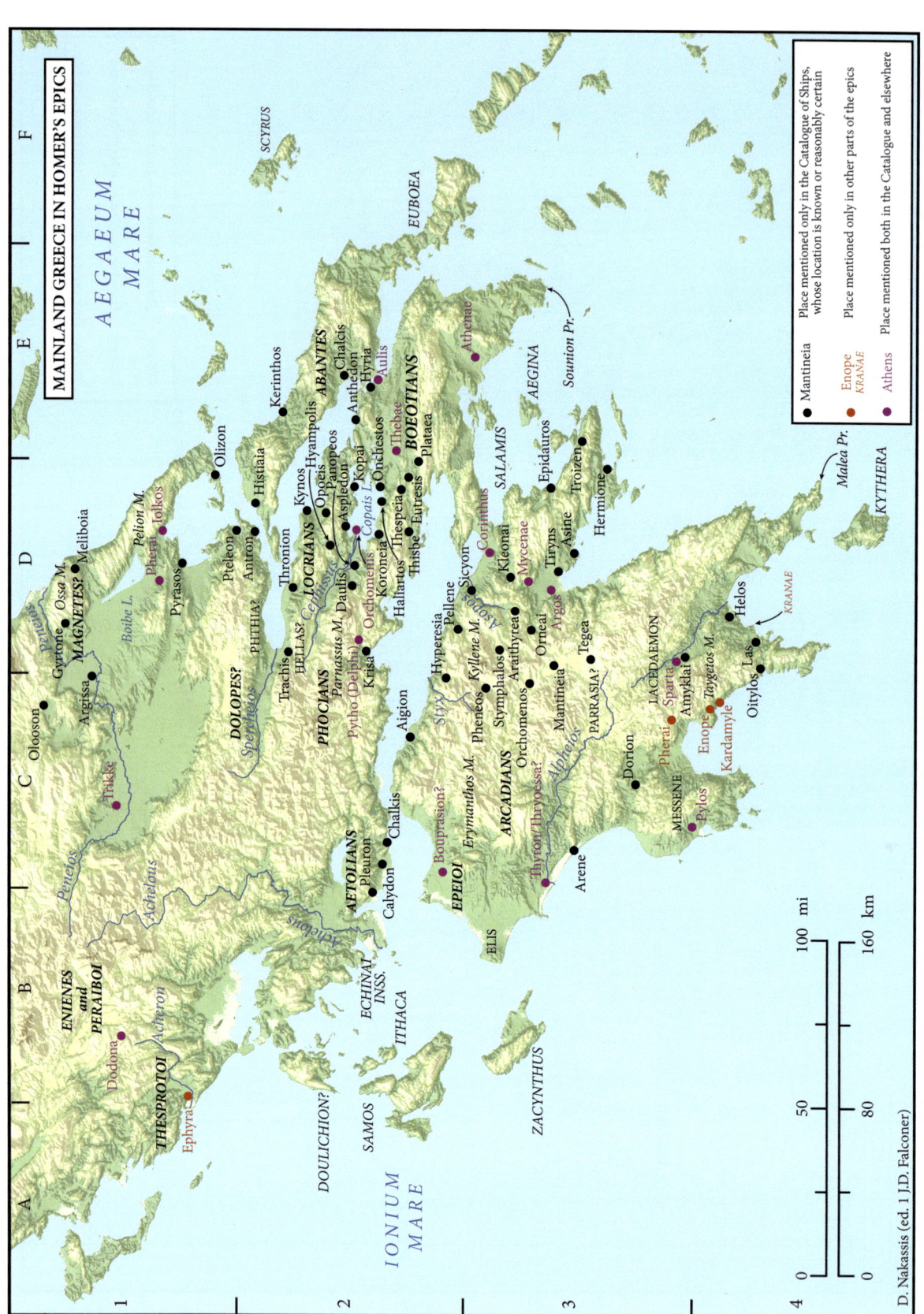

Iron Age Greece

Traditionally, the period of Greek history from the collapse of Mycenaean civilization around 1200 BCE to the early eighth century is viewed as a 'Dark Age,' one during which material culture was much reduced and generally poorer in quality by comparison with the preceding and following periods; documentary evidence is lacking too. However, archaeological research has now modified extreme views of abandonment, social and economic disintegration and cultural poverty associated with the period. Some sites do show continued habitation, albeit at a diminished level, and evidence of occupation is coming to light in areas – such as Messenia and Macedonia – once thought to have been totally depopulated. Nichoria in Messenia documents a fairly continuous sequence of occupation. Clearly, not all regions of Greece suffered to the same extent. Crete, Attica, the Argolid, Euboea and parts of Thessaly survived the worst difficulties; it was here that the recovery of Greece was stimulated.

New technological skills and cultural practices were developed, while old skills were rediscovered. Iron-working technology spread widely. Cupellation of silver was undertaken at Argos and Thorikos by 900, and bronze working has come to light at Lefkandi on Euboea. New regional burial practices and pottery styles emerge. Athens led the rest of Greece with the development of the proto-Geometric style of pottery, from which the full Geometric style evolved around 900 onwards. By 1000, the first Greek settlements were made in the Aegean islands and along the west coast of Asia Minor. The appearance of open-air sanctuaries is the first indication of a change in places of worship.

Excavation of several sites has offered new interpretations of the transition from Bronze Age to Iron Age. Lefkandi on Euboea has proven especially revealing. It was continuously occupied to the end of the eighth century, and seems to have flourished in the century or so after the collapse of Mycenae. Evidence of its prosperity includes monumental architecture in the form of a large stone and mudbrick building with interior plastering, traces of a defensive wall, and bronze working. Two associated burials here stand out, their rich grave-offerings and four sacrificed horses indicating a wealthy elite who possibly practiced a burial ritual later described in Homer. Grave goods from Cyprus and the Near East confirm continued trade beyond Greece.

To date, Lefkandi remains exceptional. However, by the early eighth century, widespread recovery was underway. Many more sites were occupied, and the increased size of numerous settlements indicates substantial population growth. Contacts with the Near East (p. 2) were expanded, with consequent stimulus in multiple ways. By the century's end, the earliest colonies had been established in Chalcidice and the western Mediterranean (see p. 18).

While graves and cemeteries remain the principal source of evidence for the eighth century, there is important insight into architecture to be gained from such sites as Emporio on Chios, Old Smyrna, and Zagora on Andros, as well as from sanctuaries such as the Heraion on Samos. Their substantial remains confirm a more settled and prosperous existence. Even so, the defensive nature of many sites, often in inaccessible or hidden locations, and the construction of fortification walls at places like Old Smyrna and Zagora, all suggest that life was by no means secure.

New sanctuaries appear during this period, and it is clear that some were gaining a reputation beyond their immediate area. About half contain remains of temples and exotic dedications from places in the Levant, Italy and Egypt, demonstrating the extent of Greek contacts across the Mediterranean. The dedication of votive offerings at former Bronze Age sites indicates an interest in the heroic past. With the introduction of the Phoenician alphabet and its adaptation to the Greek language, Greece can be said to have finally put aside its Dark Age.

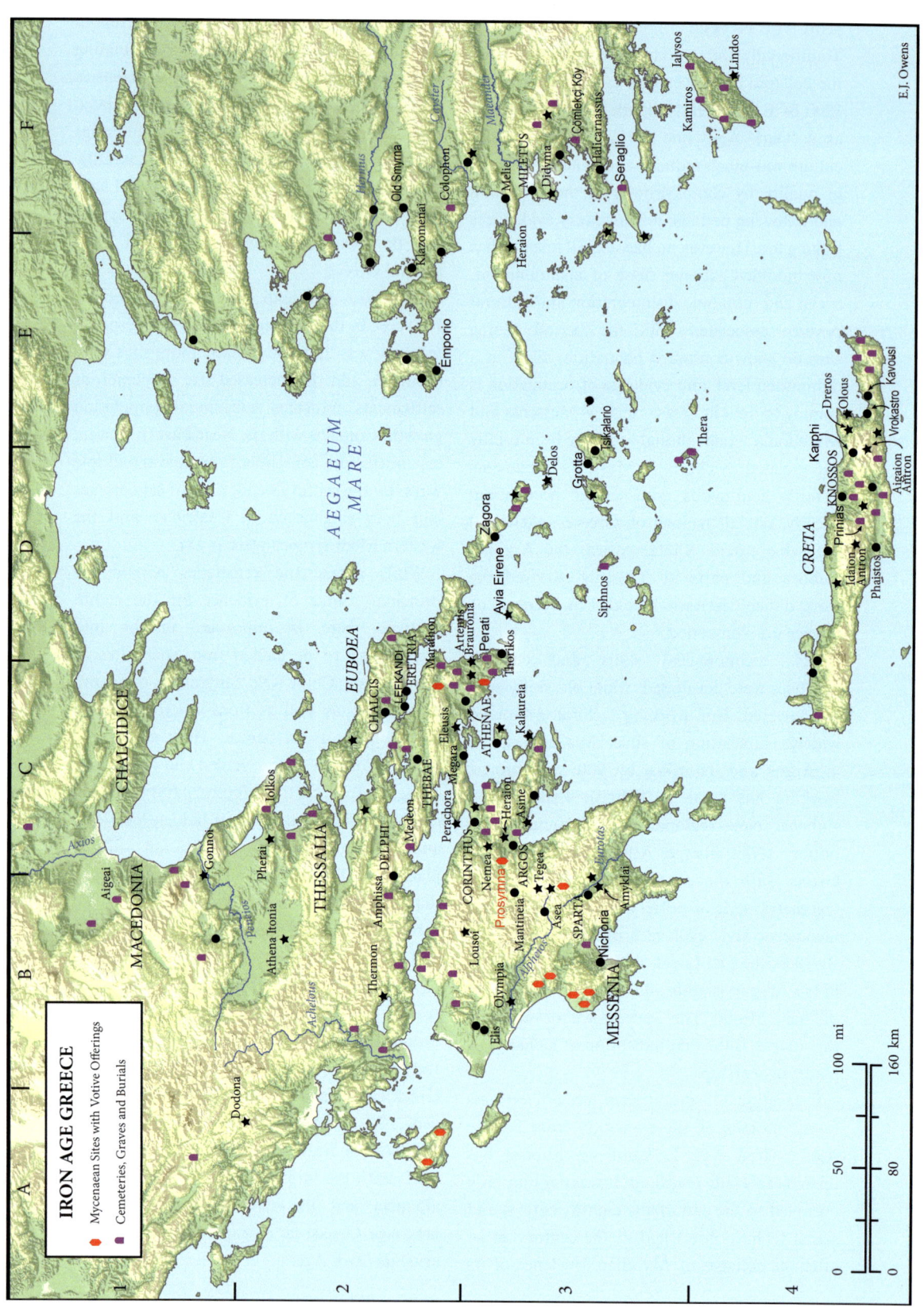

Greek Colonization, 800–500 BCE

By around 800 BCE Greek traders had begun to venture beyond the Aegean with such confidence and regularity that Euboeans from Chalcis and Eretria had set up a 'trading station' (*emporion*) at Al Mina (the place called Posideion by Herodotus) on the Orontes river delta, excavated in the 1930s. Arguably, these traders sought iron and copper above all. A comparable 'trading station' which Euboeans sailing west founded before 750 at Pithekoussai was succeeded during the late 700s by their establishment of 'ports of call' at Zancle and Rhegion, and of settlements in fertile areas at Cumae, Leontini and Katane. Though Greeks were not blind to trading opportunities and valuable resources, it was principally the prospect of fertile land free for occupation which prompted others to follow the Euboean example, in an effort to gain relief from the generally acute problems of increased population and unequal division of landholdings throughout Greece. Further sites in eastern Sicily were quickly settled, and in the 600s these acted as the springboard for foundations on the north and south coasts of the island (for Akragas and Syracuse, see pp. 42, 51). In south Italy development of the same type occurred simultaneously, with settlers from Achaea taking the lead.

To the north, it was again Euboeans who led the way by establishing settlements in Chalcidice during the late 700s. In the 600s other Greeks settled further along the northern shore of the Aegean, either side of the Hellespont, and around the Propontis. Despite its harsher climate, the Pontus was even penetrated by a few settlers at this date, but the main wave of foundations here did not come until the 500s, mainly at the instigation of Miletus.

Elsewhere, Greeks principally from Asia Minor were permitted to establish a 'trading station' and settlement at Naucratis, 50 miles up the Canopic branch of the Nile Delta, in the late 600s. Cyrene near the North African coast was founded from Thera around 630 (see p. 145). Later, in the early 500s, Phocaea planted settlements as far distant as southern France, Spain and Corsica. These areas, together with western Sicily, were also being settled by Phoenicians and Carthaginians (see p. 43). Though their motives seem to have been broadly similar to those of Greeks, hostile relations were the exception, usually the result of provocation.

The modern translation 'colony' for the Greek *apoikia* misleads if it is taken to imply any degree of long-term dependence upon, or control by, the founders from mainland Greece. Rather, from the outset the settlements were in principle independent, with links to their founders in normal circumstances never more than those of culture, religion and sentiment. To be sure, each foundation would enjoy the formal sponsorship of a community, which was thus recognized as the 'mother city' (*metropolis*). Although the extent of its role was prone to vary, typically the *metropolis* would appoint a leader (*oikistes*), furnish ships or other help, and gather colonists, who did not necessarily have to be its own citizens. However, its positive role would often lapse at this point, although less so in the case of Corinth. In special circumstances, where the *metropolis* was suffering particularly bad social or agrarian problems, the colonists might not even be volunteers – as, for example, when Sparta founded Taras and Thera Cyrene.

Cyrene is among the best documented colonial ventures, thanks to the survival of not only Herodotus' narrative, but also an inscription embodying at least the gist of an archaic record; it even grants the colonists leave to return if after five years their settlement still cannot thrive. Herodotus and Thucydides are the authors who furnish the most useful information about colonization; later writers, like Strabo, contribute much less. Excavation and the analysis of material remains (especially pottery) have been essential to exposing the character and development of colonization, even if there is only so much that they can reveal. Frustratingly little survives to deepen our insight into relations between colonists and the local peoples of the areas settled.

Archaic Greece

For Greece, the seventh and sixth centuries BCE are a formative period of the utmost importance, the first to be illuminated significantly by written records as well as by archaeology. Though its origins lie obscurely in the preceding Dark Age, the emergence of the *polis* as the predominant political and social unit was without question a crucial step forward. Autonomous communities of this type – centred on a defensible town in control of its surrounding territory – became a distinctive feature of Greek civilization throughout the Mediterranean and beyond.

Even so, the speed and character of change varied considerably. In many areas, especially the north and west, there was at best only a slow shift away from tribal organization. Elsewhere, Crete (p. 154) and Sparta (p. 40) are distinguished by their idiosyncratic development. The latter, having at last achieved success in a struggle to conquer fertile Messenia shortly before 700, was then faced with bitter hostility not only from Messenians permanently subjected as helots, but also from jealous neighbouring states, Argos especially. A great battle at Hysiai in 669 resulted in a narrow Argive victory. During the late seventh century, the strain which Sparta faced in containing a prolonged Messenian rebellion led to a permanent transformation in the character of the state: most strikingly the Spartiates, or citizen males, became an exclusive military caste. Only during the sixth century was Sparta able to extend its influence further in the Peloponnese. Checked initially by failure to annex Tegea, Sparta proceeded instead to forge alliances, a policy which led to its formation of the Peloponnesian League. By the late sixth century, Sparta was the strongest of the mainland states.

As seen above (p. 18), the Archaic period was one of widespread expansion and of increasing prosperity through trade and settlement. Communities either side of the Aegean – like Chalcis, Eretria, Miletus and Samos – were especially well placed to benefit, as was Crete. On the mainland, this growth caused constant rivalry between ambitious neighbours such as Athens, Megara and Corinth. Corinth built up a formidable fleet and consolidated its influence in north-west Greece. It was also one of the first states where the impact of new wealth weakened the exclusive hold of a traditional landed aristocracy upon government. As a consequence of such strife *(stasis)*, Corinth was seized around 655 by a single ruler or 'tyrant' – not necessarily a pejorative term. Elsewhere too (as at Argos, Sicyon and Samos in particular), powerful tyrants established themselves for one or two generations before giving way to oligarchy or democracy. At Athens – not yet among the leading states – a political and economic crisis was alleviated in 594 by a mediator, Solon. But faction fighting persisted here, so that eventually from 545, at his third attempt, Peisistratus set himself up as a tyrant. He proved a wise ruler who, followed by his sons, did much to unify and stabilize Attica over thirty-five years, as well as to strengthen its economy. Athenian interest in Sigeion and the Thracian Chersonese – on the trade route to the Black Sea – dates from the sixth century.

On the eastern seaboard of the Aegean, the Greek cities first withstood Cimmerian incursions, and then from the 670s more persistent onslaughts by the Mermnad rulers of Lydia, a power which came to stimulate its Greek neighbours as well as to antagonize and dominate them. Coinage, for example, was a Lydian invention imitated by Greeks from about 600. The most successful resistance was that of Miletus, arguably the greatest Greek city of the time, celebrated for its encouragement of culture and scientific inquiry as well as of colonial ventures northwards. Yet Lydia, and with it the Greek cities beyond, fell to Persia in the mid-sixth century. Thereafter Persian encroachment westwards was to make a lasting impact upon the Greeks.

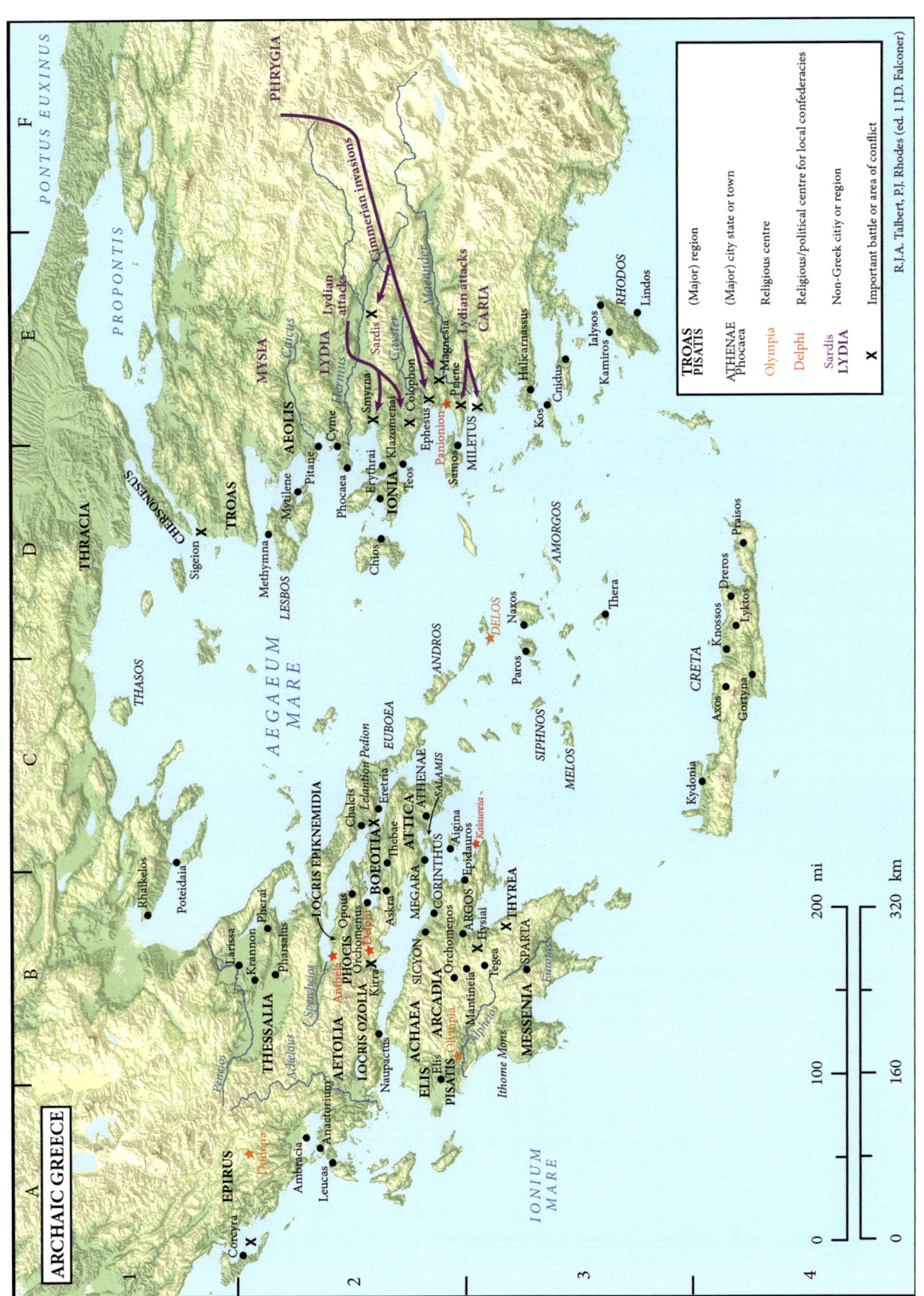

Persian Empire, 550–330 BCE

The empire was largely created by the violent absorption in turn of four existing territorial powers. First, around 550 BCE, a Median area of influence stretching from the Halys river to an uncertain eastern frontier; by 522/521, Persian rule had reached Sogdiana and even further east, but some territory in this direction may have been acquired separately by Cyrus, who died (530) campaigning beyond the Iaxartes river. Second, around 540, the Lydian kingdom, extending west of the Halys to the Aegean. Third, from 539, the Neo-Babylonian empire, comprising Mesopotamia, Elam and Abarnahara ('Beyond the River,' Syria/Palestine). Fourth, from 526, Egypt, up the Nile to Elephantine.

In addition, Cyprus was gained at much the same time as Egypt. Cambyses had Arabians' help in 526, and Darius claimed 'Arabia' in 522/521. Cilicia voluntarily submitted to Cyrus, retaining a native dynasty until the fourth century. Herodotus and the Persian 'Lists of Peoples' show significant additions by Darius: around 518, India (West Indus valley); some east Aegean islands – Samos, Lesbos, Chios among them – and around 513 Greek cities on the north Aegean coast; also around 513, Thracians south, and possibly north, of Mount Rhodope; around 512 or 492, Macedonia; around 513, Libya. The Persian lists add Ethiopia, Caria and, untruthfully, 'Scythians beyond the Sea.' Two new names appear in Xerxes' reign, Akaufaciya (unlocated) and Daha. However, his failure in Greece ended expansion and lost European subjects permanently except at Doriskos.

At best, the empire now stretched from west Anatolia, the Levant and Egypt to Bactria-Sogdiana and India. Chorasmia was certainly lost by the 330s, though some Indians did fight at Gaugamela in 331 (p. 64), coming perhaps from areas where Alexander later encountered native rulers still calling themselves hyparchs or satraps. Even so, the empire never truly included *all* areas lying within the geographical limits outlined. Mysia, Pisidia and the Cardouchoi, for example, appear autonomous around 400, and may always have been. Rebellion was a chronic problem – both nationalist secession, and satraps' attempts to seize the throne or establish independent principalities. In 522, Darius' usurpation occasioned rapidly suppressed disturbances in Elam, Babylonia, Assyria, Armenia, Egypt, Media, Parthia-Hyrcania, Sattagydia, Scythia as well as in Persia itself. Lydia had revolted immediately after Cyrus' conquest, the Asiatic Greeks and Caria in 499–494, Cyprus in 498–497 and possibly 478, Egypt in 486–485 and Babylon in 484–483. Certain unsatisfactory satraps had to be forcibly removed.

After 480/479, the Asiatic Greeks rebelled again, and were only regained securely by the King's Peace of 387/386. Egypt was persistently troublesome: a major rebellion in the 460s was not suppressed until 455 and even later in the Nile Delta; further rebellion around 404 brought independence until 343; a third rebellion erupted in 338–336. Various parts of Phoenicia, Cilicia and Cyprus saw disturbances in the 380s, 360s and 340s. Dissident satraps emerged in Abarnahara (440s, 416), Lydia (416, 401, 360s), Hellespontine Phrygia (360s, 350s), Caria (360s), Cappadocia (370s–360s), and Armenia (360s). Further east the evidence is scantier, but shows a Median rebellion around 408, Cadusian secession from 405 to the 350s, and rebel satraps in Bactria (late 460s), Hyrcania (425/424), and possibly eastern Iran.

The political geography of the empire is a contentious topic. This map seeks at least to take account of four types of enumeration of its constituent parts, although locations are often conjectural and some have not been attempted:

(a) the subject peoples in various royal texts, mostly from Darius' reign;
(b) the 20 *nomoi* or satrapies in Herodotus 3.89–97;
(c) the nations found in Persian armies, especially those of Xerxes in 480 and of Darius in 331; in the former cases, the account of Herodotus 7.61–99 is nearly identical with (b) above;
(d) the nations represented, either singly or in conjunction with others, in attested satrapal titles; this is a fluid list, especially in better-documented areas, compiled almost entirely from *Greek* sources.

Persepolis

This ceremonial capital of the Persian Empire lies in south-west Iran, on the north side of the Marvdasht plain. Though the site may have been used by his predecessor Cambyses, it was Darius the Great (reigned 522–485 BCE) who founded the present complex. Most of the construction was undertaken during the reign of his successor Xerxes between 485 and 472. Buildings of this period include the Gateway of All Lands, the Hall of a Hundred Columns and the Northern Staircase. Persepolis was the gathering place for the annual presentation of tribute to the Great King, a scene represented in the magnificent reliefs of the Northern Staircase. The palace was destroyed by fire by Alexander the Great – by accident or design – in 330. Many of the stone slabs exhibit the marks of cracking by fire. Further columns have collapsed with the passing centuries. Not far west are the tombs of the Achaemenid kings at Naqsh-i-Rustam, and further north Pasargadae and the tomb of Cyrus.

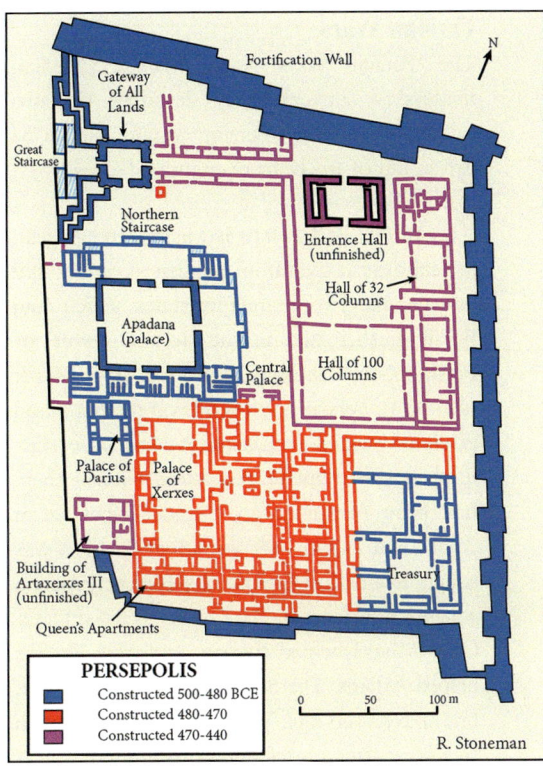

Marathon, 490 BCE

The presumable position of the Athenian camp by the western foothills (at a Herakleion, not securely identified), and the certain position of the *Soros* (Athenian mass-grave), guarantee the main battle's location west of the Charadra river. Also, if the remains of the later trophy were not significantly moved when reused in the Middle Ages, they may confirm the slaughter of fleeing Persians by the Great Marsh, shown in the Stoa Poecile painting. (The supposed 'Plataean Grave' near Vrana, and all dependent suppositions about the battle, should be rejected.) Much about the campaign is disputed. Did the Athenians move their camp during the days before the battle? What eventually precipitated the engagement? Likewise with regard to the battle itself, were the lines parallel with, or at right angles to, the shore? In this connection Herodotus' reference to the Persian centre pushing towards the interior (*mesogaia*) is unhelpful. Why did the Persian cavalry make no significant contribution?

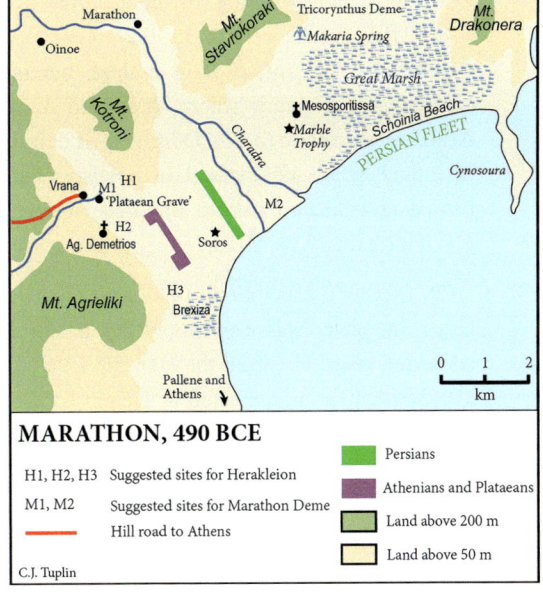

Persian Wars

The 'Persian Wars' – *ta Mēdika*, 'Median matters' – conventionally describes the two occasions on which Persian armies had to be driven out of the heart of mainland Greece:

(1) In 490 BCE, Datis led across the Aegean a seaborne expedition against Eretria and Athens, the two mainland states which had briefly participated in the 'Ionian revolt' of Persia's Greek subjects in western Asia Minor (499–494). Persian aspirations on the mainland extended beyond Eretria and Athens. An earlier, unsuccessful punitive expedition against them had been instructed to conquer whatever it could, and in 491–490 formal submission was sought from other Greek cities. But there was no general movement by the Greeks to resist Datis. Only Athens helped Eretria, and only Plataea helped Athens. The Spartans did march north, but arrived too late. When Eretria fell through treachery after a brief siege, the population was deported to Cissia (Elam). However, a different fate was presumably intended for Athens, since the exiled tyrant Hippias, who accompanied Datis, was hardly going to be restored to a deserted, smoking ruin. In the event, the Athenians chose not to await a siege, but to confront the Persians where they landed in Attica, at Marathon (p. 25). Despite their defeat here, the Persians did then sail on to Athens, but proved unwilling to risk an opposed landing, and returned to Asia Minor.

(2) Xerxes' expedition (480–479), much larger in scale, was confronted by a more concerted resistance from the Hellenic League. The Serpent Column erected at Delphi (p. 39, #22) as a thank-offering after the battle of Plataea listed thirty-one participants in the war, though it omits states that medized after initial resistance and some others. Xerxes planned a steady advance into the Greek peninsula from the north, with his army and fleet acting in conjunction. The overriding concern of the League's Spartan leaders – protection of the Peloponnese – was not shared by Athens, whose fleet was vital to the Greek cause. There were therefore persistent and deep-rooted differences over strategy among the Greeks. But they did agree upon successive attempts to halt Xerxes at Tempe (abandoned as unsuitable before his arrival there), Thermopylae/Artemision (p. 28) and Salamis/Corinthian Isthmus (p. 29). Both the latter were co-ordinated land/sea positions designed to keep the enemy army and fleet out of mutual contact. In the event the Persian army never reached the Isthmus, but it did ravage Athens. After suffering defeat at Salamis in September 480, Xerxes returned to Asia Minor with his fleet and part of the army. The remainder, under Mardonius, wintered in Thessaly and Macedonia.

Neither side hurried into action the following year. In particular, the Hellenic League, dominated by Sparta, showed little enthusiasm for searching out the Persians in northern Greece. Mardonius, after failing to detach Athens by diplomacy, re-invaded Attica. But when the Peloponnesian states eventually mobilized, he chose southern Boeotia as more favourable ground for a decisive confrontation. After their defeat at Plataea (p. 29), the Persians evacuated European Greece, except for garrisons in Thrace and the Black Sea approaches. Meanwhile, after some hesitation, a League fleet crossed the Aegean and defeated the Persians at Mycale, provoking a second Ionian revolt. The subsequent capture of Sestos (479) and Byzantium (478) completed the Hellenic League's operations, and ended the Persian Wars.

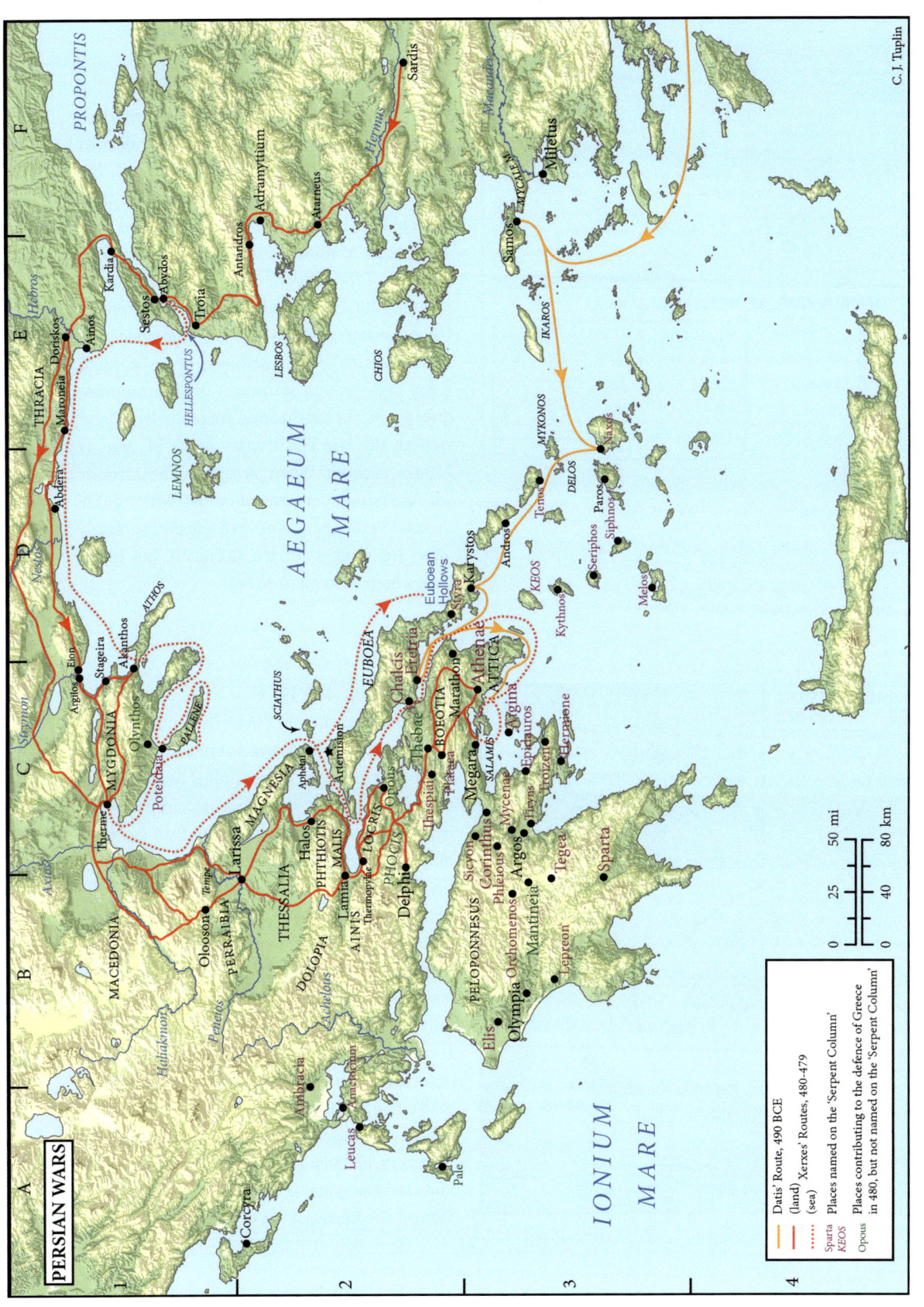

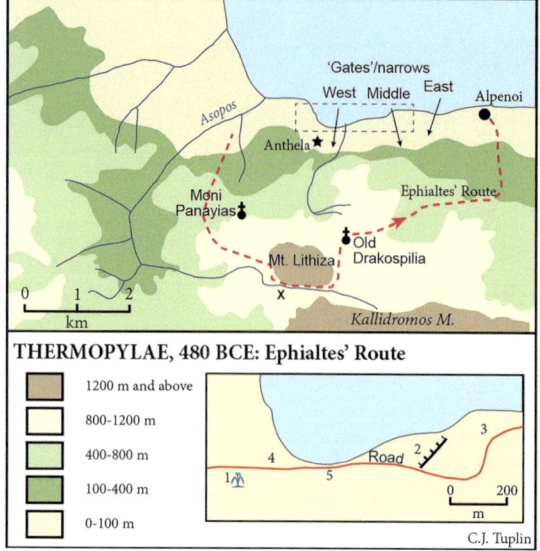

Thermopylae, 480 BCE: Ephialtes' Route

The fighting around the 'Middle Gate' near the Hot Springs [1] is straightforward. For two days the Greeks repelled the Persians' uphill assaults at a point [5] in front of the Phocian wall [2]; on the third day, they pushed west [4], but then retreated to a hillock [3] east of the wall, and were annihilated by attacks from front and rear. The location of the 'Middle Gate' is clear, thanks to identification of the wall [2]. Ephialtes' route is the major topographical problem. Disagreement centres around four questions: Did the route reach high ground southwest of Thermopylae directly, or via the Asopos gorge, or by a long western detour? Did it pass north of Mount Lithiza, or south? Where along it did the skirmish with a Phocian detachment occur? Where did it descend to the coast? The map reflects Pritchett's views (marking x for the skirmish), but many others have been put forward.

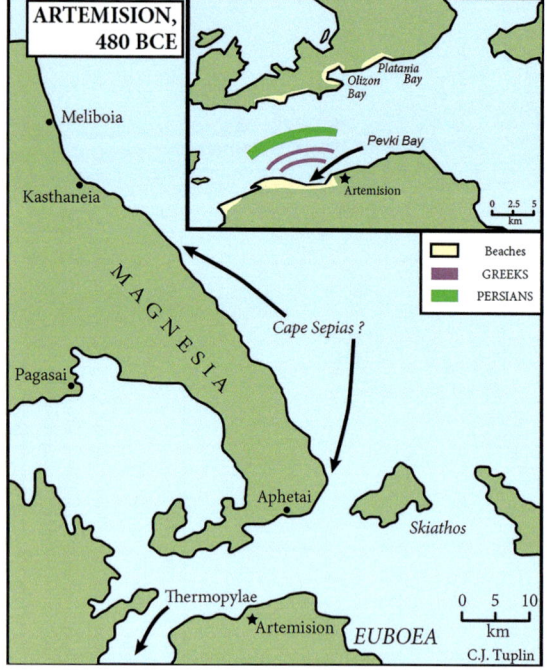

Artemision, 480 BCE

The Greek position at Pevki Bay is guaranteed by discovery of the Artemis shrine. Aphetai, the Persians' headquarters, was probably at Platania, though their fleet doubtless occupied several beaches (suitable areas are marked on the inset map). The fighting involved two afternoon raids on Persian positions (not shown), and a full-scale Persian attack on Artemision. Herodotus' account of the first engagement – the ships fighting in concentric circles, with the Greeks *inside* – is incredible, while of the last he says only that the Persians attacked in a crescent. It is crucially unclear how far north this encounter occurred. The map assumes a position near Pevki and, consequently, two Greek lines. Other related problems include the location of earlier Persian moorings 'between Kasthaneia and Cape Sepias,' and the timing and credibility of the attempted Persian circumnavigation of Euboea.

Salamis, 480 BCE

All discussions revolve around crucial obscurities: (1) Was the Greek fleet largely in Ambelaki or Paloukia Bay? (2) Was the Persian fleet's dawn position (a) along the Attic shore facing Ambelaki and/or Paloukia [I], (b) across the strait from Kynosoura to the Attic shore [II] or (c) from Kynosoura towards Peiraieus facing north [III]? (3) If (c), was the battle precipitated by the Persians sailing into the channel (and if so, was the eventual engagement of type I or II?), or by the Greeks coming out to a position across the channel entrance opposite the Persians [III]? The ancient battle monument on Kynosoura favours a southerly position, but does not decide other issues; and Xerxes' reported expectation that Psyttaleia (surely Lipsokoutali) would be near the battle could have been falsified in the event.

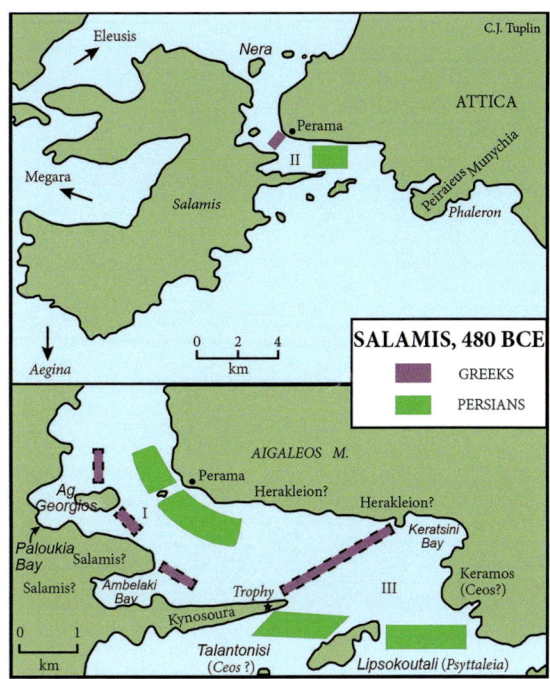

Plataea, 479 BCE

Cavalry attacks and lack of water caused the Greeks to move from their initial position (inset) to the Ag. Demetrios-Pyrgos line (this location depends on the usual equation of Gargaphia with the modern Rhetsi springs). The Persians did likewise north of the Asopos river. After twelve days – during which the Persian cavalry harassed Greek watercarriers by the Asopos, cut supply lines over Dryoskephalai (day 8), and fouled Gargaphia (day 12) – the Greeks moved south in some confusion. The positions of P indicated here, in front of Plataea, and of S, by a Demetrion (site fixed by the find-spot of inscriptions relating to Demeter), are fairly certain; that of A much less so. In their ensuing attack, the two Persian wings were defeated and fled to the fort (M) or to Thebes (G), while the centre withdrew without engaging. The left wing of P, moving to support A, was severely mauled by Theban cavalry.

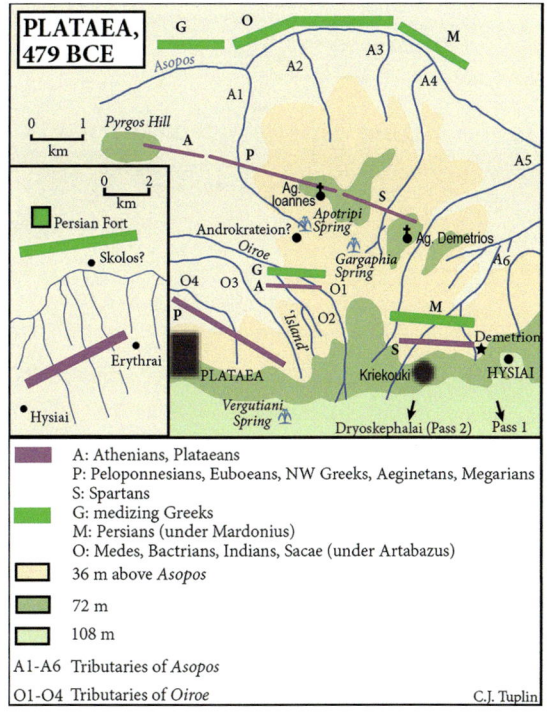

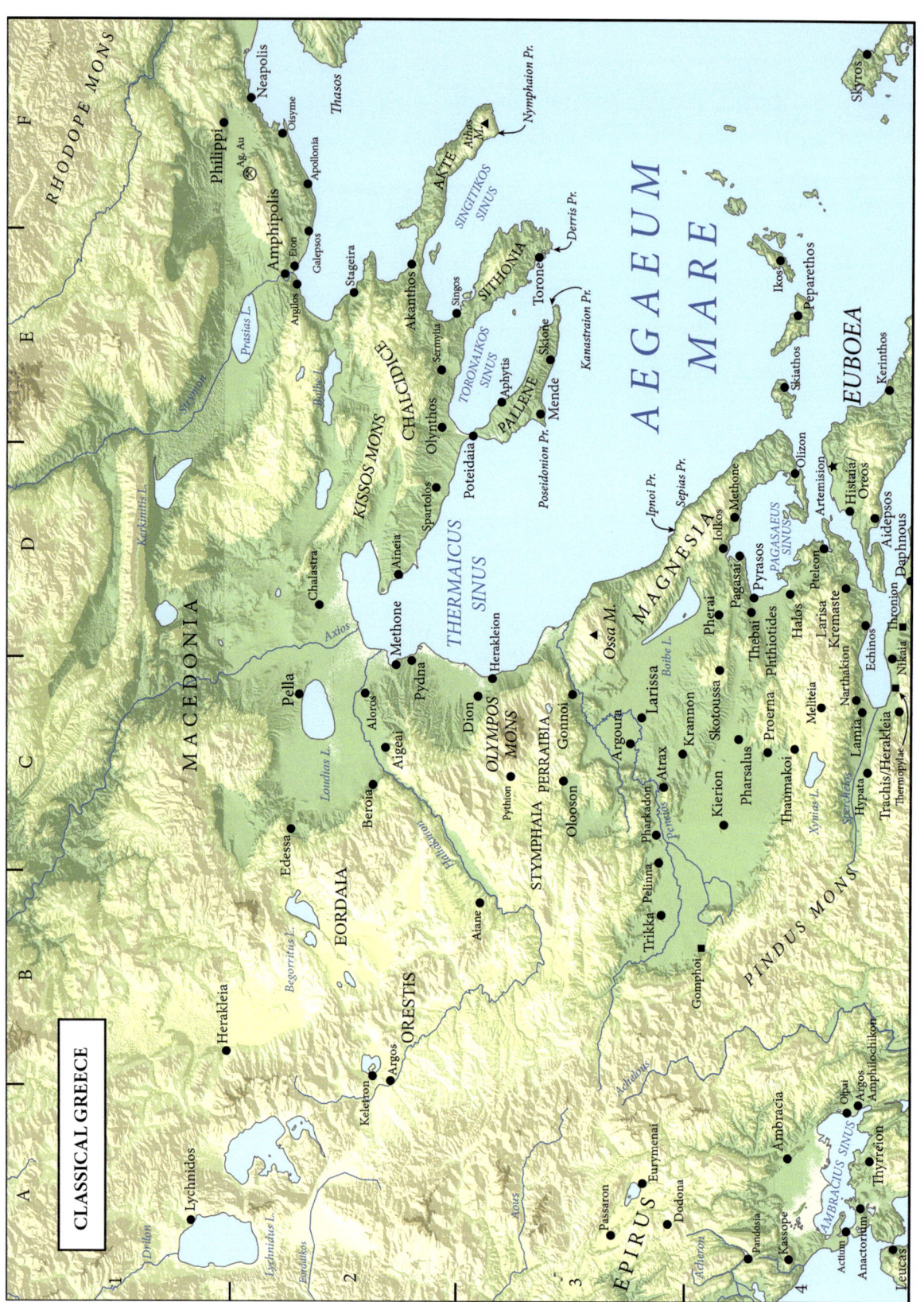

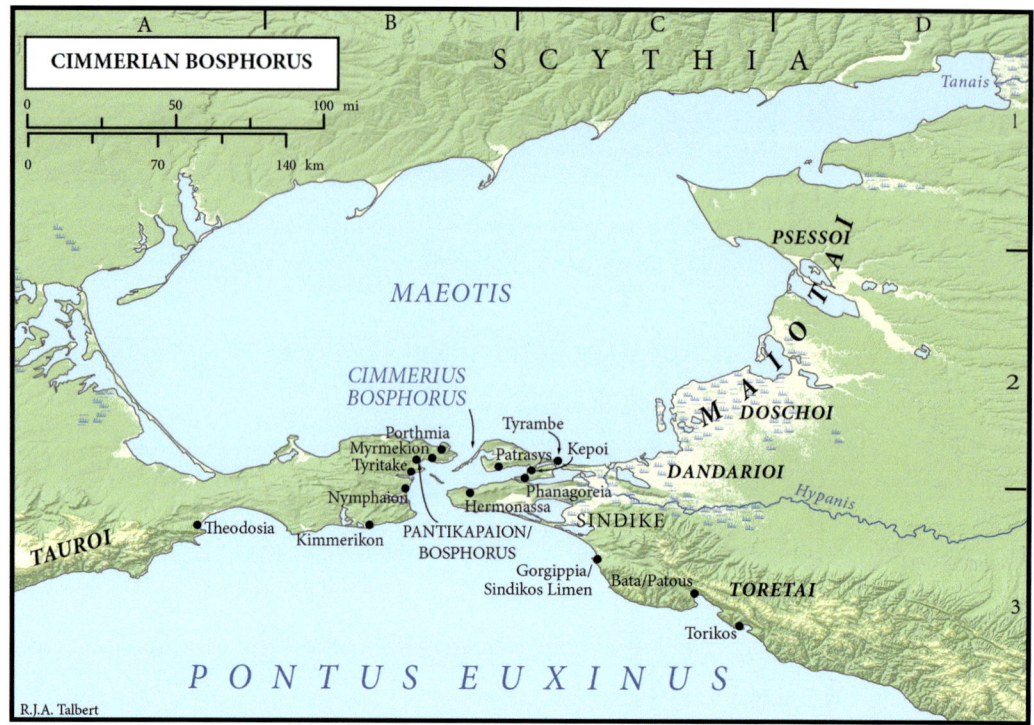

Cimmerian Bosphorus

By the fifth century BCE, Pantikapaion had emerged as the leading Greek settlement on the Cimmerian Bosphorus. Power was seized here around 480 by Archaeanax. His descendants (of whom nothing is known) were displaced in 438 by Spartocus, whose family was to maintain its rule till 109. To the west, the Spartocids eventually secured control of Theodosia, a large port, even though from across the Pontus Heraclea's fleet (p. 68) assisted its resistance. Eastwards the Spartocids sought control first of the Taman peninsula (with its cities Hermonassa and Phanagoreia), and then gradually of the peoples along the eastern shore of the Maeotis – objectives brought to completion during the rule of Paerisades (349–311), when the realm reached its zenith.

Various circumstances enabled the Spartocids to maintain their rule for an exceptionally long span. Not only did they continue to produce suitably capable, long-lived successors over generations. But also, despite being autocrats, they exercised moderation, causing little friction at home, and abroad shunning any reckless expansion such as came to harm many Greek tyrannies; in addition, they successfully incorporated local peoples. Above all, however, the state was unusually wealthy. Since both rulers and ruled benefited, the poverty and consequent tensions common elsewhere were absent, and there was unanimous recognition that continued prosperity rested upon the maintenance of peace and stability.

Bosphoran wealth derived principally from fish (herring, sturgeon, tuna), vines and, above all, grain. This was both grown locally, and brought from the plains beyond the Maeotis for export all over the Greek world. Far into the third century at least, Bosphorus was the largest single supplier of grain to mainland Greece, especially to Athens, whose merchants enjoyed preferential treatment during the late fifth and fourth centuries. Wine was also made, and fish salted, on a substantial scale, as shown by the excavation of winemaking establishments and pickling vats, notably at Tyritake and Myrmekion.

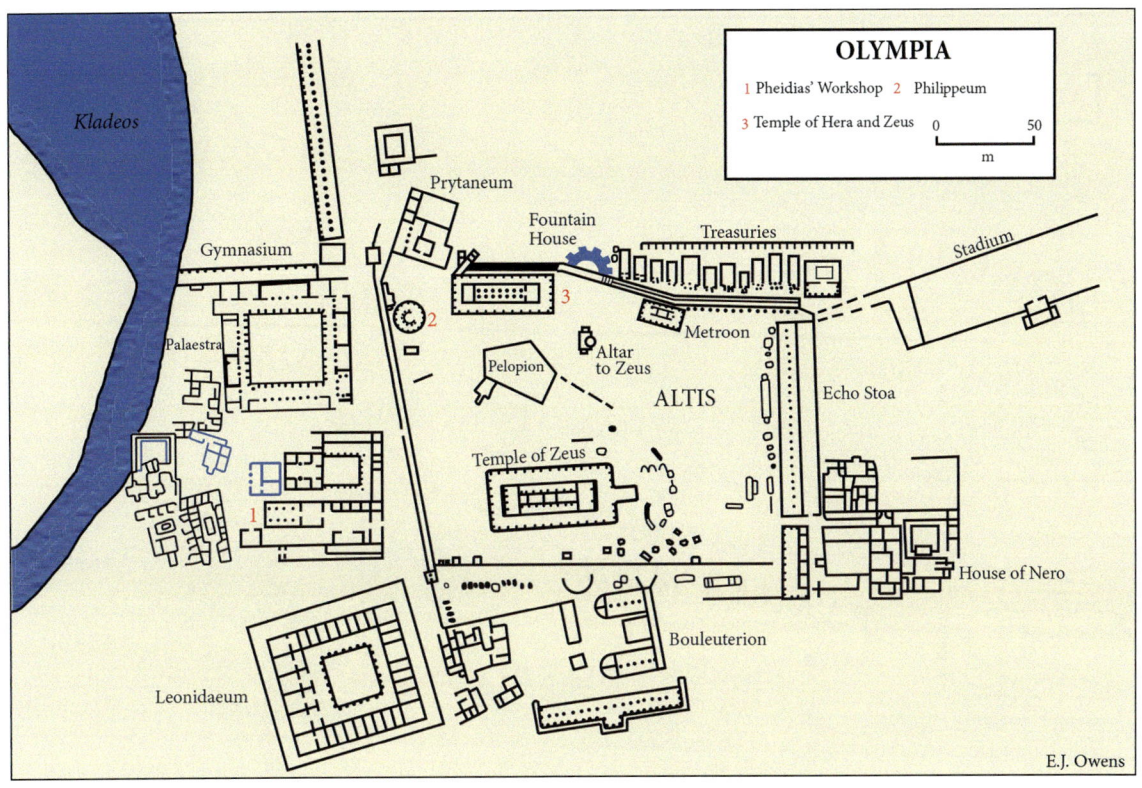

Olympia

The sanctuary of Zeus at Olympia, situated in a pleasant, wooded valley close to where the Kladeos and Alpheios rivers meet, was among the most famous shrines in Greece. Because of the four-yearly games celebrated here, the sanctuary was embellished by dedications of buildings, sculptures and other monuments.

The precinct itself, the Altis, stood at the foot of a hill (not shown) and contained the major religious buildings. On its northern side lay a temple of Hera and Zeus as well as a small Metroon. This temple was originally constructed of mud brick with wooden entablature and columns, although parts were later replaced in stone. The Metroon ('mother-shrine'), built in the fourth century, honoured Rhea, Zeus' mother. An immense temple to Zeus stood on the southern side; built around 460 BCE, it housed Pheidias' great chryselephantine statue of the god. Other religious monuments within the precinct included the Philippeum, a circular structure begun by Philip II of Macedon (west of the temple of Hera); the mound covering the supposed tomb of Pelops; and an open-air altar in honour of Zeus.

Because the Altis was the gods' preserve, monuments associated with the administration of the site and the celebration of the games were located outside it. To the west were the gymnasium and palaestra, the workshop of the sculptor Pheidias (identified by tools and a cup bearing his name), priests' lodgings, baths, and the Leonidaeum which provided accommodation for distinguished visitors. To the east, the precinct was flanked by the stadium (which originally encroached upon it), the late fourth-century Echo Stoa (replacing a classical one), and the house constructed centuries later for Nero's visit (66 CE). A row of treasuries lay along the northern boundary, mostly dedicated by Greek cities in southern Italy and Sicily. Just west of them, Herodes Atticus erected a fountain house in the 150s CE, the first at Olympia. The appeal of the sanctuary remained strong until its closure by Theodosius I in 393.

Attica

By the seventh century BCE, the whole of Attica (about 2,500 km²) belonged to the city state of Athens. Eleusis was the last area to be fully incorporated in the state. The island of Salamis, acquired from Megara in the sixth century, was ruled as subject territory, as was Oropia, an area disputed between Athens and Boeotia. By Cleisthenes' reforms of 508–507 Attica was organized into 139 demes. These were grouped to form ten tribes in such a way that each tribe comprised one *trittys* ('third') based on, but probably not wholly located in, each of the three regions, namely, City, Coast and Inland. The demes forming a *trittys* were sometimes, but not always, adjacent to one another. The ten tribes and their subdivisions formed the basis of the army and of every aspect of Athenian public life. The Long Walls linking Athens to its harbour town of Peiraieus were built in the mid-fifth century.

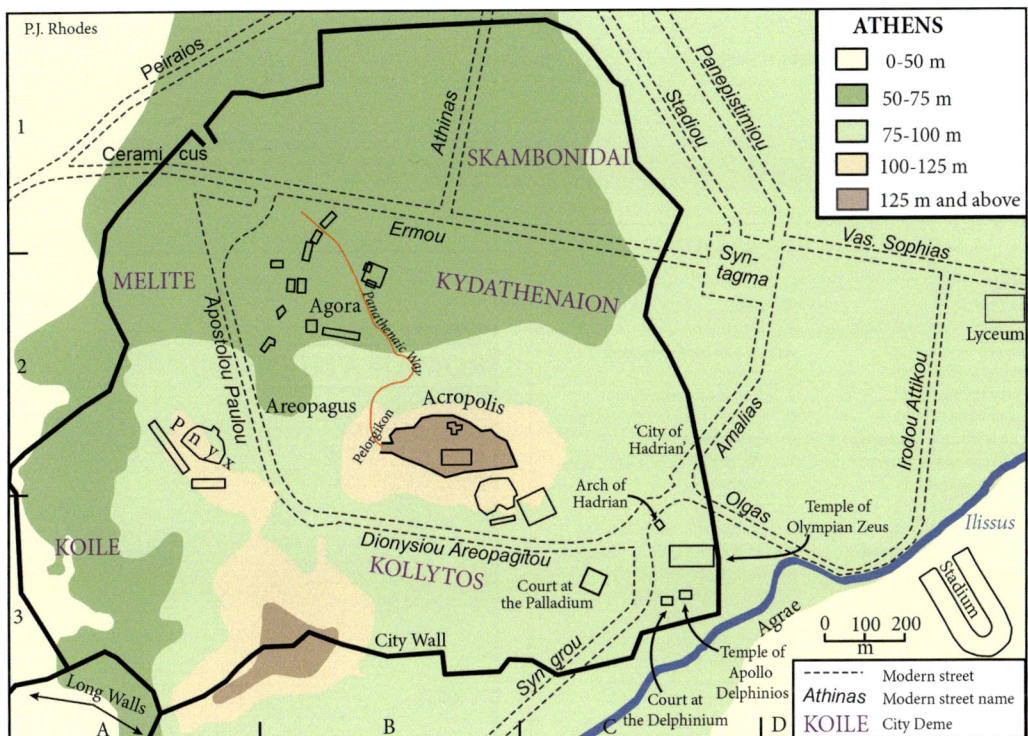

Athens

Athens, 8 km from the sea, was occupied from the Neolithic period; a wall was built round the Acropolis in the Late Mycenaean period (thirteenth century BCE). In classical Athens, the Acropolis was the religious centre, where the principal temple of Athena stood (from around 440 onwards, the Parthenon). The oldest civic buildings seem to have been to the east and south of the Acropolis, but the Areopagus, the meeting-place of the oldest council of state, was to the west. During the sixth century, the area to the north of the Areopagus – after being cleared of private houses and graves – became the Agora, the main square of the city; major civic buildings were erected on its west side in the fifth century. This may have been the original meeting-place of the assembly: the Pnyx was laid out for the assembly in the fifth century.

In the Roman period, a new Agora and the Library of Hadrian were built to the east of the Agora, and there was expansion beyond the Arch of Hadrian in the 'City of Hadrian,' an area occupied in classical times, but outside the city wall at that period. Athens was sacked by the Persians in 480–479, by Sulla in 86, by the Herulians in 267 CE, and on various occasions thereafter. Although in prosperous times a greater area was occupied, a new wall built after 267 CE enclosed merely the Acropolis and the area due north as far as the Roman Agora. The Parthenon, Erechtheum and Hephaesteum were all converted into Christian churches, and later the Parthenon became a mosque: that so much of them survives is due to this re-use.

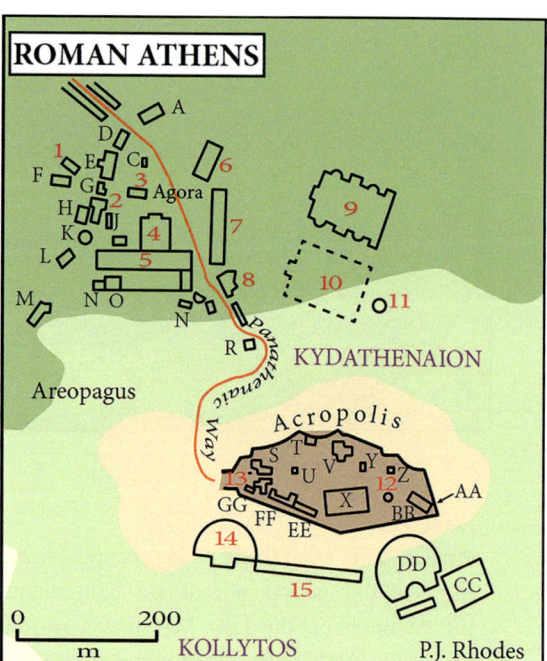

Classical (and Roman) Athens

Agora
- A Stoa Poecile
- B Lawcourts (two small buildings replaced by one large)
- C Altar of Twelve Gods
- D Stoa of the Basileus
- E Stoa of Zeus
- F Hephaesteum ('Theseum')
- G Temple of Apollo Patrous
- H New Bouleuterium
- I Old Bouleuterium
- J Statues of Tribal Heroes (fourth-century location)
- K Tholos
- L Strategeum (?)
- M Gaol
- N Fountain Houses
- O Aeaceum
- P South Stoa
- Q Mint
- R Eleusinium

Acropolis and Beyond
- S Propylaea
- T House of Arrhephori
- U Statue of Athena Promachus
- V Erechtheum
- W Site of old Temple of Athena
- X Parthenon
- Y Altar of Athena
- Z Shrine of Zeus Polieus (?)
- AA Shrine of Aglaurus (on slope)
- BB Shrine of Pandion (?)
- CC Odeum of Pericles
- DD Theatre of Dionysus
- EE Chalcothece
- FF Sanctuary of Artemis Brauronia
- GG Temple of Athena Nike

Roman Athens

Agora
1. Arsenal?
2. Metroum
3. Temple of Ares
4. Odeum of Agrippa
5. Middle Stoa
6. Basilica
7. Stoa of Attalus
8. Library of Pantaenus
9. Library of Hadrian
10. Roman Agora
11. Tower of the Winds

Acropolis and Beyond
12. Temple of Rome and Augustus
13. Monument of Agrippa
14. Odeum of Herodes Atticus
15. Stoa of Eumenes

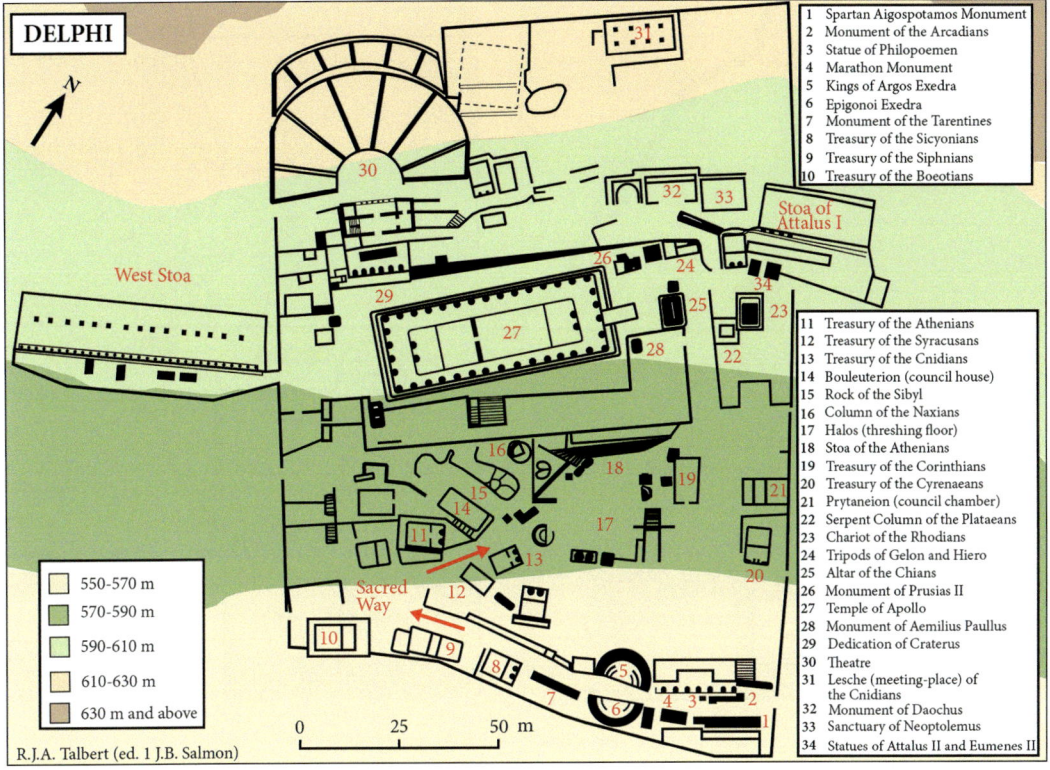

Delphi

Delphi was a *polis* where an oracular cult of Apollo – its origins obscure – was situated. Because of its association with the foundation of colonies in the West from the 700s BCE (see p. 18), the oracle gained extraordinary prestige, which only began to tarnish when it took a defeatist attitude to Xerxes' invasion of Greece in 480. Even so, struggles between leading states to control the sanctuary (demarcated by a wall) persisted. The present temple of Apollo (27) was built during the mid-300s, funded by contributions from Greeks everywhere. The previous one was destroyed by an earthquake (373) and its predecessor by fire (548). The earliest temple has not yet been traced, but the first known treasury (19) was built by Cypselus, tyrant of Corinth, before 600. There followed numerous similar buildings – some half-dozen by 500 – to house moveable dedications.

Other monuments commemorated notable events. Like the treasuries, they were placed along the Sacred Way, which worshippers climbed to reach the temple. Near it, the combined Greek states placed the Serpent Column (22) dedicated after their victory at Plataea in 479 (p. 29). Lower down, the inter-city rivalries which prompted numerous dedications are reflected in their locations: just beyond the sanctuary's main entrance are Sparta's monument for victory at Aigospotamos in 405 (1), an Arcadian one from the fourth century (2), Athens' after Marathon in 490 (4), and two Argive structures (5, 6). The Syracusan Treasury (12), built after the defeat of the Sicilian Expedition in 413 (p. 51), faces the Athenian Treasury (11) erected nearly a century before. The changed conditions of the late 300s are reflected in Craterus' dedication (29), which depicted his rescue of Alexander the Great during a hunt. Later, Hellenistic kings and Romans left conspicuous marks. Nearly a kilometre to the south-east was a sanctuary of Athena (not shown).

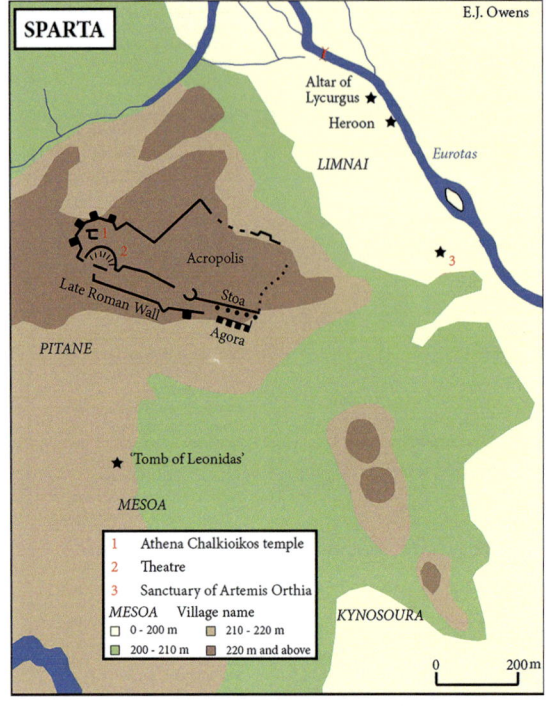
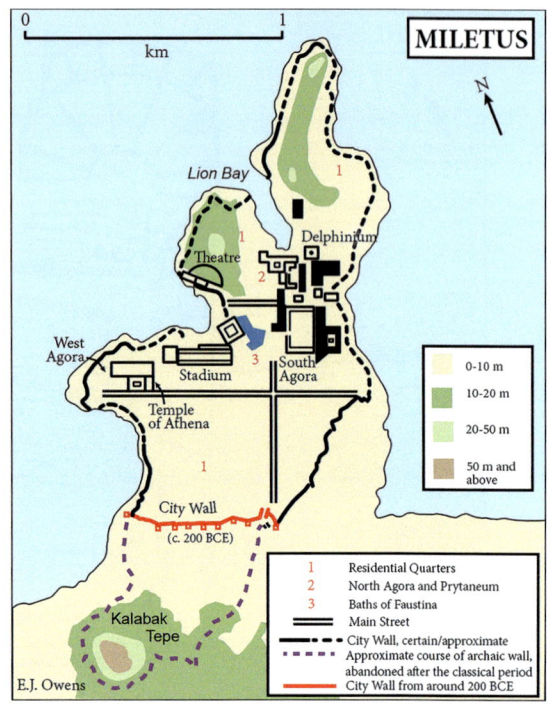

Sparta

Sparta's abnormal development (see p. 20) affected it in two striking respects. First, Spartans claimed that their soldiers were their walls, so only during the fourth century BCE was the settlement partially walled, and not until the second was it completely fortified. Second, Sparta for long remained no more than a group of loosely-knit villages along the Eurotas river. Thucydides' observation (1.10.2) that there were few public buildings seems correct.

Archaeologists have concentrated on the acropolis, where the site of the archaic temple of Athena Chalkioikos has been identified. The theatre here, however, is Hellenistic, as is the small temple to the south, wrongly identified as the Tomb of Leonidas. The stoa above the agora is of Roman date. East of the acropolis, close to the river, some monuments have been found: most important is the sanctuary of Artemis Orthia, where an early altar and temple have been identified. A theatre for spectators was added during the second century CE (not shown).

Miletus

Situated on a peninsula opposite the mouth of the Maeander river, Miletus became an outstanding cultural and commercial centre during the seventh and sixth centuries BCE. Traces of the extensive archaic city have emerged around Lion Bay and the Delphinium (temple of Apollo), on the Theatre hill, around the Temple of Athena, and as far south as the acropolis of Kalabak Tepe.

After suffering destruction by the Persians in 494, Miletus was rebuilt on a grid (only partially known). A large central area was reserved for future public use. In typical fashion, the defences were not integrated with the street system. Although the surviving structures are Hellenistic or Roman (the theatre dates to around 100 CE), several buildings can be traced to the classical period – especially the North Agora, the Delphinium and the Temple of Athena – and the Prytaneum to even earlier. Silting of the Maeander river eventually led to Miletus' decline.

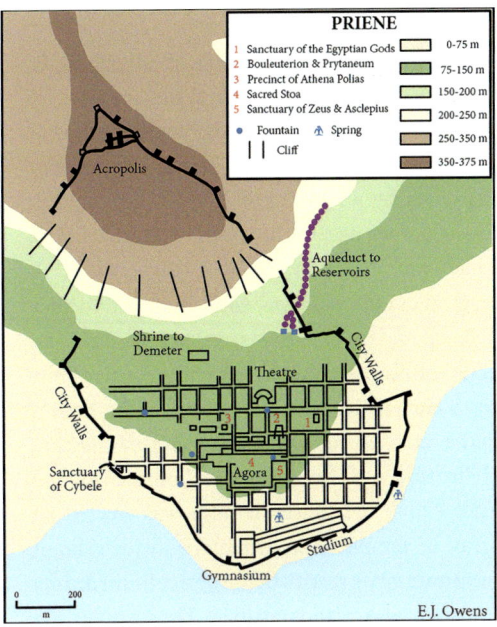
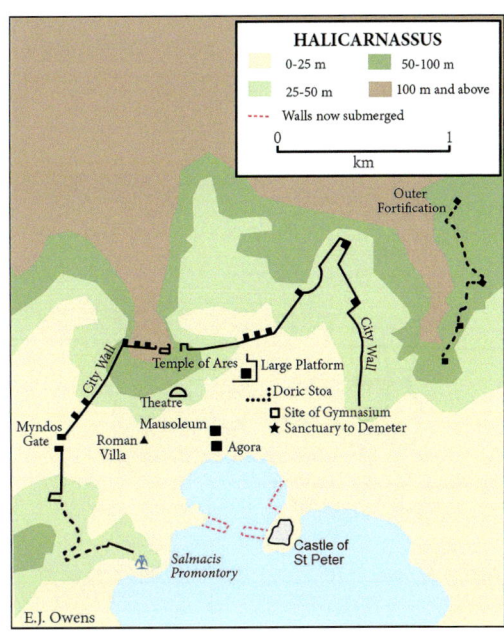

Priene

Priene was always overshadowed by nearby Miletus and suffered even more than it did from the silting of the Maeander river. By the mid-fourth century BCE, the coast had receded so far that the city was refounded on a spur of Mount Mycale further downstream from its original site. A remarkable feature is the application of a grid plan to a difficult, steeply sloping location, where the major arterial streets run east-west, while others – sometimes narrower, and in places reduced to flights of steps – cross these at regular intervals to form rectangular blocks. Most public buildings cluster round the centrally sited agora and conform to the grid plan. Exceptionally, the stadium – located at the lowest point in the city – is misaligned to take advantage of the level ground of the coast. The well-preserved theatre is above the civic centre. On his visit here in 334, Alexander dedicated the temple to Athena Polias. The terrain allowed water, conveyed by an aqueduct, to be piped throughout the city.

Halicarnassus

Occupying a naturally fortified position and having a good, sheltered harbour, the site was originally colonized by Dorians at the eastern promontory of the harbour (Zephyrion), where the ruined castle of St. Peter now stands. Although by the classical period the town had expanded to include the western promontory (Salmacis), and the population had been increased by Ionian and native elements, Halicarnassus remained small until the accession of Mausolus to the satrapy of Caria in 377/376 BCE. Realizing the advantages of the site, he chose it as his new capital, and transformed Halicarnassus into an exceptionally splendid city. According to Vitruvius (2.8.11), the buildings, rising on terraces, resembled the tiers of a theatre with the agora close to the shore, the Mausoleum on a broad avenue running across the middle of the city, and the temple to Ares 'on the uppermost tier.' A considerable part of the ancient city lies underneath the modern Turkish town of Bodrum. However, the line of much of the ancient walls (including the imposing Myndos gate) remains visible, as does the theatre, as well as the location of the Mausoleum and other public buildings. Modern archaeological research has clarified the rectangular street grid, located the Ares temple on the large platform north-east of the theatre, and uncovered some Hellenistic houses and the famous Salmacis fountain.

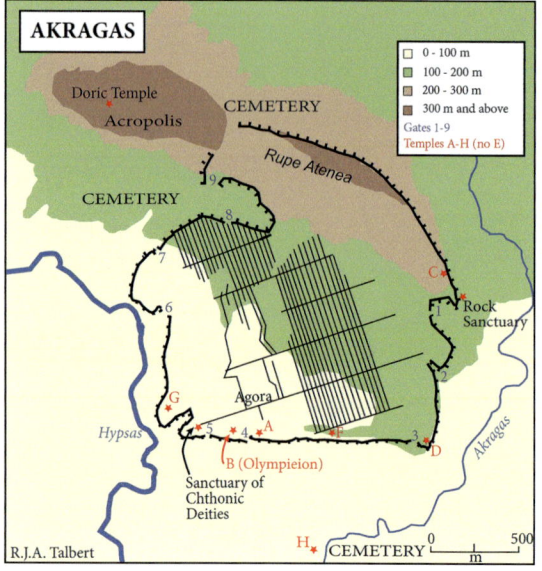

Akragas

Supposedly founded from Gela about 580 BCE, Akragas occupied a vast hilltop site – praised by Polybius (9.27) – which slopes southwards and overlooks the coastal plain. It was protected to the north by a long acropolis hill (the modern town-centre), and to the south by a ridge below which ran the Hypsas and Akragas rivers. A lengthy circuit wall was soon built for further defence, and the extensive street grid (revealed by aerial photography) laid out. As a result of the city's later violent history, nearly all the houses in the relatively limited area so far excavated are Hellenistic and Roman, yet still on the original grid. Along the southern ridge was erected an array of temples and sanctuaries which flaunt the proud city's wealth (from agriculture) during the sixth and fifth centuries. The temples are lettered because the deity of only one is certain. Temple F owes its exceptional preservation to being made a church.

Greek and Punic Sicily

All names on this map are in their Greek forms. Sicily was one of the first areas colonized by Greeks from the latter part of the eighth century BCE onwards, in particular along its eastern and southern seaboards. The settlers' search for fertile agricultural land was amply rewarded. A flourishing export trade to the Italian peninsula, North Africa and mainland Greece brought the leading communities an enviable level of prosperity, reflected especially in ambitious temple-building programmes: these have left impressive remains at Syrakousai (p. 51), Akragas and Selinous especially. The character of relations between Greek settlers and native peoples varied, but the archaeological record shows how everywhere the natives' territory was gradually infiltrated, so that after the fourth century the significance of their ethnic divisions fades from the historical record. By the second century, if not earlier, many of the indigenous hilltop settlements of the interior had gained the trappings of Hellenic culture, with theatres, stoas and small Greek-style shrines.

Quite independently, Phoenicians were attracted to the far west of the island around the same time as Greeks reached the east. The first Phoenician settlement, on the tiny island of Motya, was perhaps intended initially as no more than a port of call on long-distance trading voyages. Thereafter, however (though the time-scale is obscure), cultivation of good land was the principal purpose of settlements at Panormos (Phoenician Ziz) and Soloeis (on the bay below the later Hellenistic hill-town), both perhaps dating from the seventh century. Motya became more accessible once a causeway was built from the mainland. These communities were independent of Carthage, and they generally remained on excellent terms with their Greeks neighbours until around the end of the fifth century. Even later, when a Punic *epikrateia* came to be recognized in treaties, this term is best taken to signify a loose 'zone of influence,' in no way presupposing some rigid barrier between the two groups of peoples. Any notion that Carthage desired to pursue imperialistic ambitions in Sicily is misplaced, despite Agathocles of Syracuse's aggression towards the Carthaginians in the late fourth century.

Athenian Empire

In 478 BCE certain east Aegean members of the Hellenic League invited Athens to assume effective leadership of military action against Persia. The result was the alliance system commonly known as the Delian League. The name is modern, derived from the location of the treasury on Delos and the consultative meetings there (p. 78); contemporaries spoke simply of 'the Athenians and their allies.' Membership involved support of the League's military enterprises by provision of ships, or of money (tribute), in quantities determined by the Athenians. After 454 there were regular reassessments of tribute, theoretically every fourth year, but occasionally out of sequence (443 instead of 442, 428 and 425 instead of 426). The original membership and relative frequency of one or other type of contribution are obscure (Thucydides' valuation of the 'first tribute' at 460 talents being questionable). However, it is certain that choice or compulsion gradually made tribute payment the norm, so that by 431 only Chios and the cities of Lesbos were still furnishing ships (although Samos, which lost its fleet in 440/439, was paying war indemnity rather than tribute). By this time, too, Athenian official parlance was referring to 'the cities which the Athenians rule,' and it had long been appropriate to speak of an Athenian Empire. Tribute is thus a central characteristic of the empire until its temporary replacement in 413–410 by a 5% import/export levy at the empire's harbours.

In 454 the treasury was moved to Athens, and a $1^2/_3$% quota taken from tribute receipts for dedication to Athena began to be recorded on stone. The remains of these annual 'tribute lists' and of assessment lists from 425, 422 and (?)410 are the fundamental sources for knowledge of the extent of the empire. Some 278 places are recorded as paying tribute at one time or other after 454/453 (thirty-two for the first time in 429 or later); a further sixty-nine places can be named which were first assessed in 425 or later, but are not *known* to have paid (the total number of such new assessments was certainly much larger).

The map largely confines itself to states whose payments show an assessment of one talent or more at some date between 454/453 and 429/428 – thus before pressures of war caused assessments to rise much higher. A few places with lower assessments are marked for other reasons. Also shown are the five tribute areas in which quotas were arranged in 442–438 (Ionia and Caria were later amalgamated), together with indicative figures (in brackets) for the total number of actual paying states in each area. The wartime assessments introduced two new areas, *Actaean Cities* (between Ionia and Hellespont), and *Euxine* (cities in the Crimea, and on the west and south coasts of the Black Sea, not shown).

Two other features of the empire are illustrated: (1) Overseas settlement. Here we may distinguish Thurii (in Italy, p. 83) and Amphipolis – both indisputably colonies with minority Athenian participation – from the rest, which present problems of categorization between 'colony' and 'cleruchy.' (2) Revolt. The map distinguishes places where revolt on one or more occasions is attested either in literary sources or by documents relating to organization after revolt with evidence of non-payment in the quota lists. Not recognized, however, are cases where suspicion of revolt depends solely on the quota lists. Such are Miletus (447, 445–443); Aegina (447); Cos (446–443); various islands which never appear in 453–450; twenty-one apparently regular payers in Ionia, Hellespont and Thraceward absent on various occasions in 442–441, 439, 434 and 432; some twenty places in Thraceward whose absence in 431 and later may be connected with the revolts of Poteidaia, Spartolos and Olynthos; and over twenty-five Carian places absent in 441–439 and not recorded as paying after 443 at the latest.

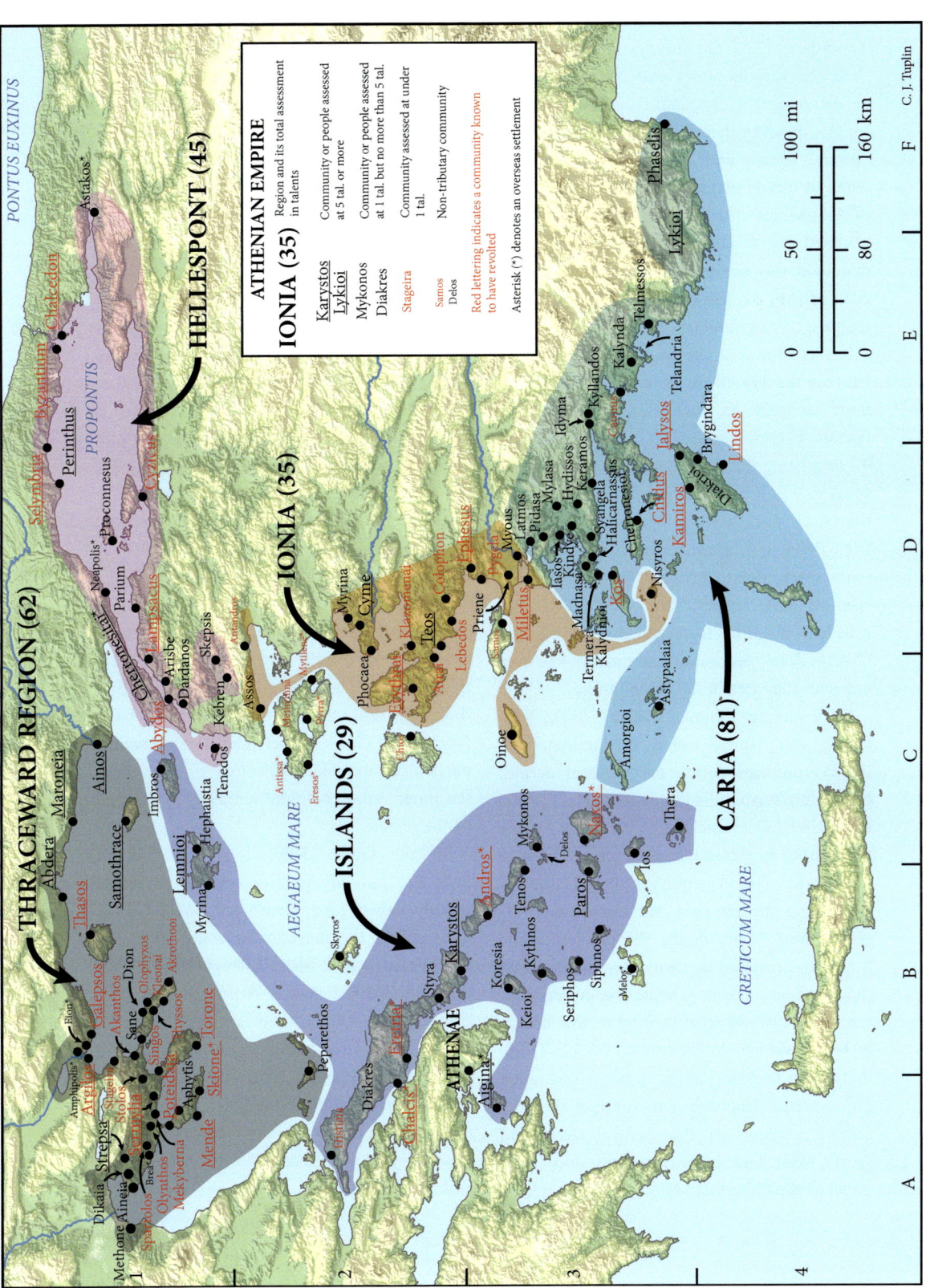

Greek Dialects around 450 BCE

Thucydides (7.57–58) surveys the contingents from the various states and islands involved in the Athenian expedition against Syracuse (p. 51), dividing them into three main groups: Dorian, Ionian and Aeolic. The three were living in clearly divided bands along the coast of Asia Minor in the classical period. So it was assumed that this triple division applied to the mainland also, since according to tradition the cities of the Asia Minor coast and islands were founded by mainland communities.

In fact, however, the linguistic relationships between the dialects on the mainland are much more complex. In particular, the dialect of Arcadia is closely related to that of Cyprus (p. 9), suggesting that the island was colonized by speakers of an earlier form of Arcadian. Also, the Greek discovered on the Linear B tablets from Pylos and elsewhere on the mainland is more closely akin to Arcadian than to any other classical dialect: hence the supposition that a dialect of Greek from which Arcadian and Cypriot developed was at one time spoken over a much wider area in the Peloponnese.

Yet it was two different dialects, North West Greek and Doric, which predominated in the Peloponnese during the classical period, completely surrounding Arcadian. The two are closely related to each other, and the former was spoken in classical times over a very wide area north of the Corinthian Gulf. Traditions concerning the Dorians and the speakers of North West Greek in the Peloponnese relate how they travelled to their later homes from the north in various groups; the evidence of the dialects would seem to support this notion in broad outline. A few traces of a pre-Doric dialect can be found in inscriptions from some Doric areas. Thus we may suppose that the remote ancestors of the classical Doric and North West Greek speakers had once lived north of the Corinthian Gulf, perhaps not even along its north shore, but across the high, wild land dominated by the Pindus mountains.

The second of Thucydides' groups, the Ionian speakers, could be found in his lifetime in many coastal cities and islands (except the southernmost) around the Aegean. He states clearly an accepted historical fact of the time, that the Athenians were Ionians: for it was believed that the first Ionian colonists of Asia Minor had set out from Athens. The evidence of inscriptions certainly confirms the very close linguistic bond between the Attic speakers of Athens and the Ionians. Just how widespread the speakers of Ionic were on the mainland in the period before the arrival of the Dorians is much debated. Equally, the precise relationship between Ionic and Arcado-Cypriot in this early period can in all likelihood never be known.

Aeolic, the third of Thucydides' groups, is in many ways the most mysterious. In Asia Minor, it formed the most northerly of the three dialect bands, and it is there that inscriptions show it in its least contaminated form. Linguistic evidence from the two Aeolic areas on the mainland, Boeotia and Thessaly, strongly suggests that there the dialects had been infiltrated by a North West Greek dialect. This development is particularly marked in Boeotian; in Thessalian, the purer Aeolic is found naturally in the east of the region.

All the Greek dialects can be split on linguistic grounds into two broad divisions, usually called East Greek and West Greek. They reflect the most fundamental split, one that seems to have historical significance, with the East Greek dialects – Attic-Ionic, Arcado-Cypriot and Aeolic – representing the Greek spoken in the areas of Greece prominent during the Mycenaean period. By contrast, the dialects of West Greek – Doric and North West Greek – represent the Greek speakers who came to their classical period homes after the Mycenaean collapse.

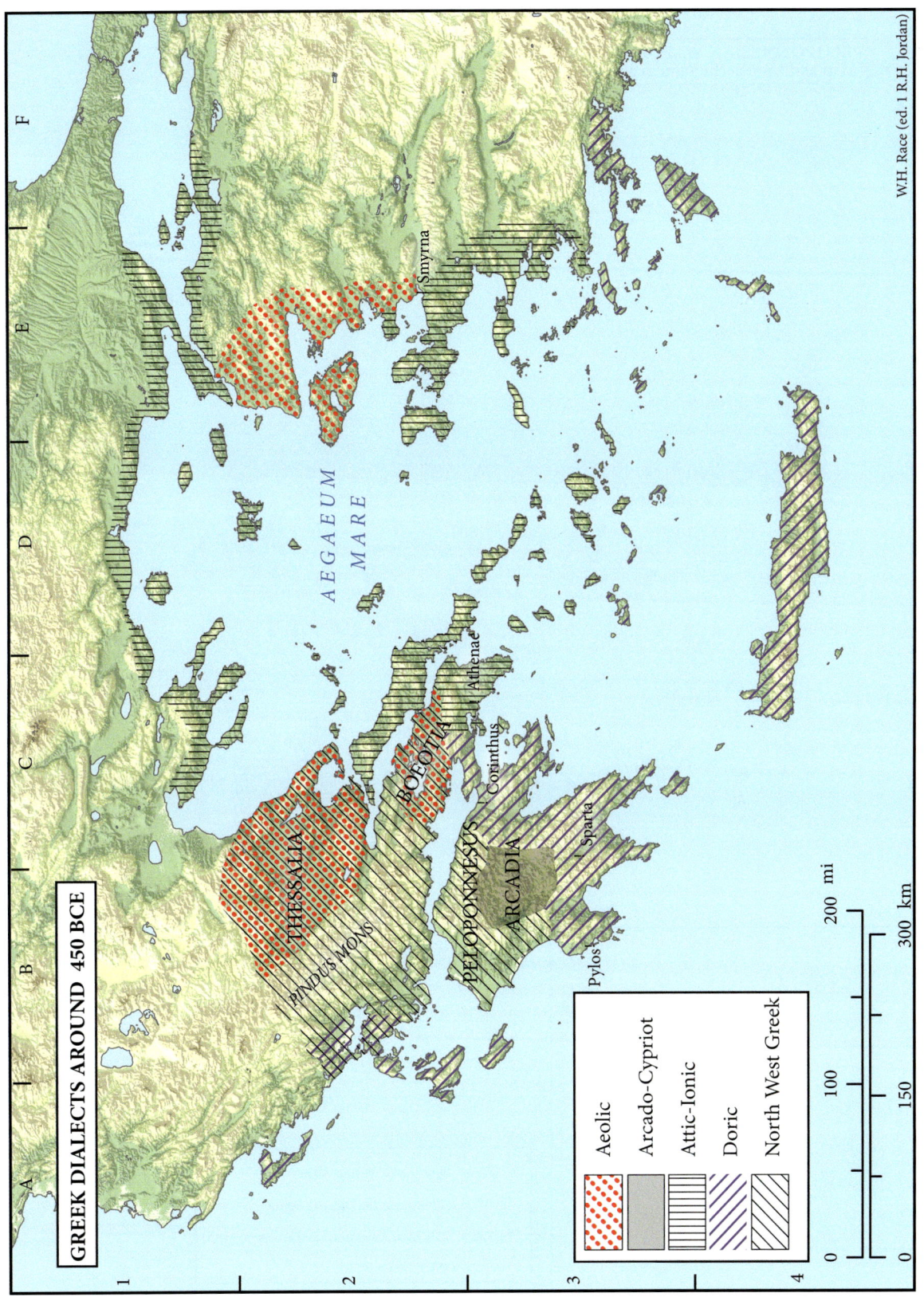

Peloponnesian War, 431–404 BCE

'Peloponnesian War' (term not attested until the first century BCE) signifies the whole period from Sparta's declaration of war in 431 – as supposed champion of the autonomy of the Greeks – until Athens' surrender and reduction to the status of a Spartan subject ally in 404. A single map can only 'illustrate' the fighting of this twenty-seven-year period by indicating the whereabouts of as many places mentioned in the sources as the scale permits. Three phases can be discerned:

(1) 431–421, the 'Ten Years' or 'Archidamian' War (an early term, though inappropriate), with fighting in various theatres: Attica (regular Spartan invasions until 425); Peloponnese (Athenian maritime raids in 431, 430, 426; introduction of garrisons in Pylos, Methone, Kythera in 425–424); central Greece (Spartan siege of Plataea, 429–427; Athenian attempts to capture Megara and various parts of Boeotia, 424); north-west Greece (429–426) and Corcyra (427–425); 'Thraceward' region (431–429; 424–421); Lesbos (428–427); Sicily (427–424).

A major turning point was the Pylos campaign (425, p. 51). After it, Sparta was not only under greater pressure at home, but also had to abandon invasions of Attica to protect the lives of 120 Spartiates taken prisoner. Sparta was ready to negotiate a year's truce in 423–422, and a fifty-year peace in 421, when Brasidas' successful encouragement of rebellion among Athens' Thraceward allies strengthened Sparta's position. The resultant 'Peace of Nicias,' accompanied as it was by a defensive alliance, required each side to surrender certain territorial gains (chiefly in the Peloponnese and Thrace) and all prisoners taken. But the territorial requirements were never properly implemented, and the peace was very tense from the outset.

(2) 421–413, an interlude – lasting until Sparta's occupation of Dekeleia in northern Attica – which Thucydides insisted was mostly no better than a 'suspicious truce' and therefore really part of the war. There was sporadic fighting in Thrace. Active hostility between Athens and Sparta appears in two main areas: Sicily, where resistance to Athens' major onslaught against Syracuse came to be directed by the Spartan Gylippus (415–413, p. 51); and Peloponnese, where Athens' defensive alliance with three anti-Spartan states, Argos, Mantineia and Elis (420), led to military operations, including some direct action against Sparta or its unequivocal allies – incursions from Pylos (419 onwards), capture of Orchomenos (418) and Orneae (416/415), siege of Epidauros (418–417), battle of Mantinea (418), maritime attacks on eastern Laconia (414).

(3) 413–404, the 'Decelean' (cf. Dekeleia above), or 'Ionian' War, because it was mostly fought along the coasts from Byzantium to Rhodes. Both names underline crucial differences from the first period, when Sparta had not attempted either to *occupy* Attica or, normally, to encourage or exploit disorder in the eastern Aegean or Black Sea approaches. The latter development was now prompted by over-optimistic expectations after Athens' Sicilian disaster. Another vital new element was Persian co-operation with Sparta. For five years this did not prevent Athenian recovery, in 410–408 especially. Only after the arrival of the Great King's son, Cyrus, in 407 was Persian wealth used effectively, at least whenever Lysander was in office as navarch (407 and 405–404). The change is well illustrated by the contrast between Sparta's hesitant reaction to loss of a fleet at Cyzicus (410), and the immediate replacement of the losses at the Arginoussai islands (406) with the ships which destroyed Athenian naval power at Aigospotamos (405).

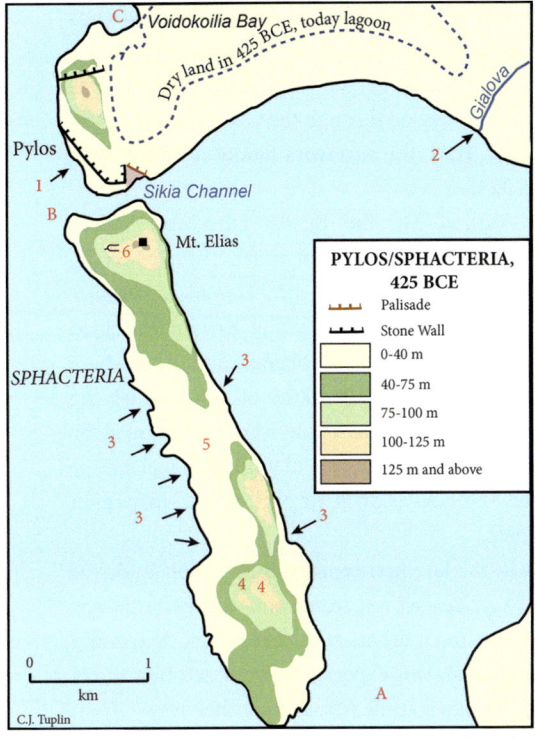
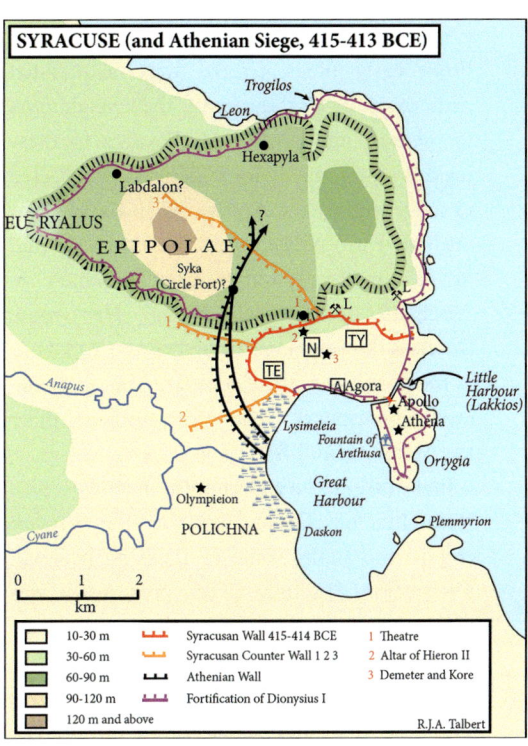

Pylos/Sphacteria, 425 BCE

Five stages can be discerned in the events of 425 BCE described by Thucydides (4.2–6, 8–23, 26–41): (1) Fortification of Pylos (one or two stone walls and a palisade), and its occupation by a small Athenian force. (2) Encampment of Spartan land and naval forces around Gialova river, and installation of 420 hoplites on Sphacteria. Allegedly, the Spartans intended to block the harbour entrances, i.e., either A and B, or B and C. In context Thucydides' words must refer to A/B, but unless the text is emended the reported dimensions of the entrances will only fit B/C. The tactical value of the plan, which was not carried out, is in any case dubious. (3) Two days of unsuccessful seaborne attacks on Pylos [1]. (4) Spartan naval defeat in the harbour [2]. (5) Athenian landings on Sphacteria [3]: a first wave disposed of southern outposts [4]; a second forced the main body [5] to retreat to the fort on Mount Elias [6], where it surrendered after some Messenians scaled the western cliffs.

Syracuse (and Athenian Siege, 415–413 BCE)

Initially, in 734 BCE, Corinthians settled on Ortygia island with its freshwater Fountain of Arethusa. Sanctuaries of Apollo and Athena were erected there early (later enlarged), and by the sixth century a causeway was built to the mainland, where nearby Achradina (A) was settled, with agora and fortification wall. Expansion into the districts Temenites (TE), Neapolis (N) and Tyche (TY) followed later. Thucydides narrates the siege by Athenian forces: their bases were in the marshy area Lysimeleia, on the waterless Plemmyrion headland, and on Epipolae, a steep, uninhabited plateau which dominates the city. However, Athens' plan to confine Syracuse within a wall running north from Lysimeleia, then further north or east across Epipolae, was never achieved; Syracuse built three counter-walls. Around 400 Dionysius I protected both the city and Epipolae with a circuit wall, and built a fortress at Euryalus. Remains of fine public buildings erected in Neapolis from the third century survive. Elsewhere modern occupation has limited investigation.

Explorers

From early times Greeks were acquainted with, or at the least aware of, their neighbours to the east and north-east. Voyages to these regions – presumably for trading – are reflected in the legend of the Argonauts, in the exploits attributed to Aristeas of Proconnesus, and in Io's mythical wanderings recounted in Aeschylus, *Prometheus Bound*. Her route traverses the Scythians, Chalybes and Amazons to the north; then the Caucasus, Asia, and one-eyed Arimaspians. Finally, she turns south to the Aethiopes and Nile river.

In the fifth century, Herodotus made extensive researches on Egypt, Scythia, the Persian empire and India, some of them by personal observation. His only Greek predecessor was Scylax of Karyanda who – in a voyage of coastal exploration undertaken around 510 BCE for the Great King Darius – set off down the Indus river and sailed all the way up the Red Sea. Earlier, two Carthaginians – Himilco around 525, and Hanno around 500 – are credited with having sailed to north and south respectively out of the Pillars of Hercules. Himilco reached Brittany, but probably did not go as far as Britain. From the surviving record, it would seem that Hanno reached Sierra Leone, or possibly even Cameroon. This is further than any other known traveller before the Middle Ages, unless we accept Herodotus' report of a circumnavigation of Africa by a Persian named Sataspes during Xerxes' reign (486–465).

Notable elsewhere is the March of the Ten Thousand led by Cyrus the Younger (401–399), the subject of Xenophon's *Anabasis* (p. 54). It seemingly inspired Alexander the Great, who in 334 began his remarkable campaign of conquering the Persian empire (p. 60). So that a scientific record might be made, he was accompanied by a geographer and other experts. In 329, after passing through the 'Caspian Gates,' he entered hitherto unexplored territory. He remained in central Asia and northern India until 326. His admiral Nearchus was despatched down the Indus to seek a sea route back to Persia, while Alexander and his army struggled through the Gedrosian desert of south Iran, the survivors finally reaching Susa in 324.

Around 310 the British Isles were visited by Pytheas, who sailed north from Massalia through the Pillars of Hercules. Besides apparently circumnavigating Britain he sailed into the North Sea, reporting a condition where sea and air merge in a kind of jelly (a thick fog plus floating ice?). Thule island mentioned by him has been variously identified as Iceland, or the Shetland Islands, or part of the Norwegian coast.

In the late first century BCE, when Eudoxus of Cyzicus set out from India to Egypt, he was blown down the coast of east Africa. According to Strabo, this experience prompted him to try circumnavigating Africa the other way – from Gades. However, he was driven aground by the north-east trade wind, and so headed back. After returning via the Canary Islands, he made a second attempt, but then disappeared from causes unknown.

Several explorers penetrated the Sahara desert. Herodotus records one journey through it by five men of the Nasamones, a Berber people. But this lead was hardly followed until Roman times. Then, in 19 BCE, Cornelius Balbus, proconsul of Africa, explored south into the desert. In the late first century CE another proconsul, Septimius Flaccus, made a three-month march inland, while Julius Maternus later extended the route to Sudan. In 42 CE, Suetonius Paulinus crossed the Atlas range, and some trading contacts evidently did develop (see p. 140). But in general, Romans were not prompted by such scientific curiosity as Greeks. Much ancient geographical knowledge is diluted and distorted in medieval travellers' tales; it was the taste for pilgrimage that again opened up distant lands as objects of interest.

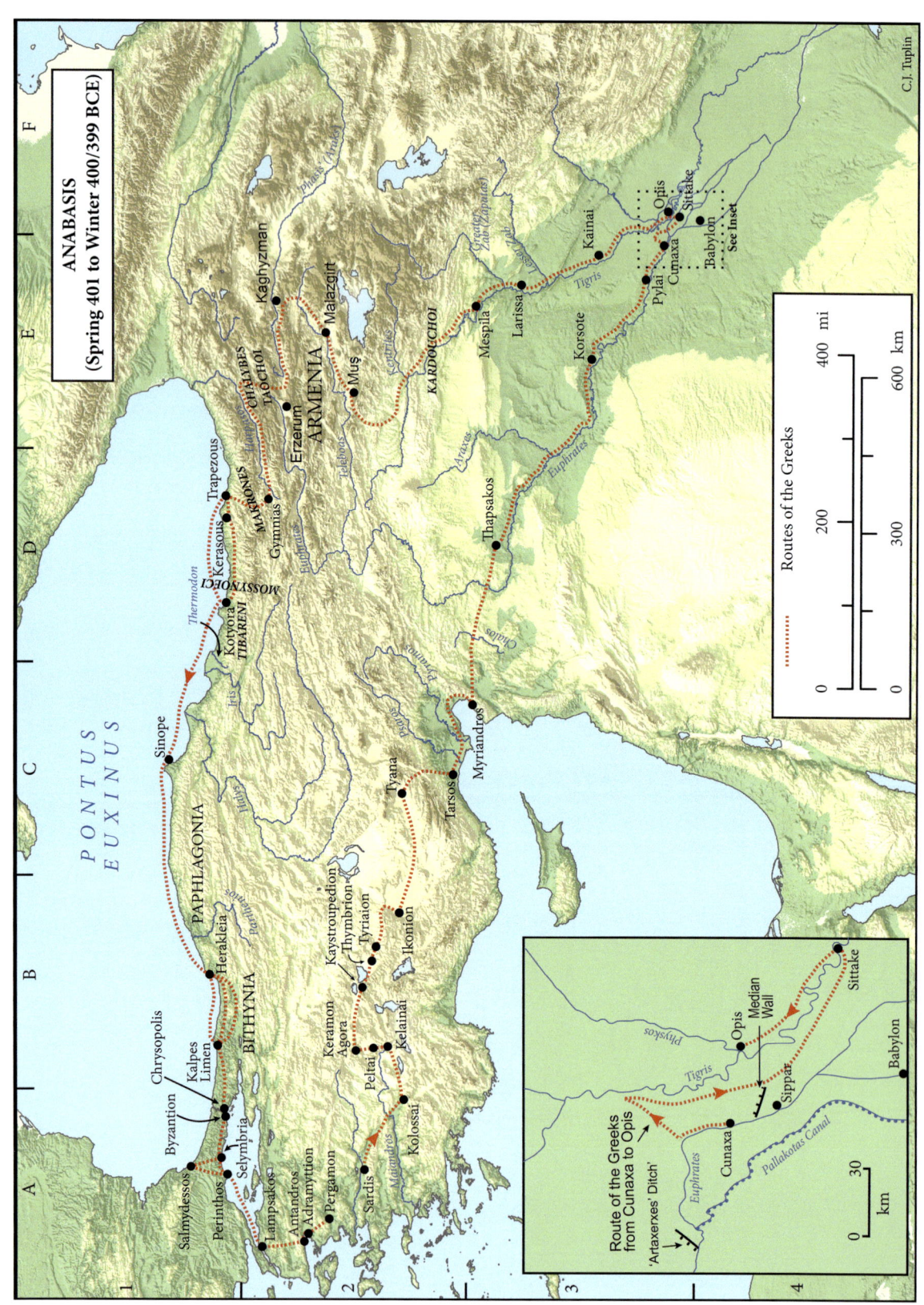

Anabasis (Spring 401 to Winter 400/399 BCE)

The map shows the routes taken successively by: Cyrus' rebel army from Sardis to Cunaxa, where it was defeated by Artaxerxes; the Greek and non-Greek remnants, marching separately, from Cunaxa to the Zapatas river, where the Greek generals were treacherously murdered by Tissaphernes; and the Greeks from the Zab river to Byzantium, eastern Thrace and Pergamum. There are two problematic sections:

(1) *Cunaxa to Opis*. The Greeks marched north/north-east for three days, then stopped for almost a month negotiating with the Persians and waiting in vain for Tissaphernes to escort them back to the Aegean. They then marched to the Median Wall in three days, to the Tigris river at Sittake in another two, and up its east bank to the Physkos river and Opis in a further four. The location of all the named points is controversial: it has even been suggested that Xenophon carelessly interchanged Opis and Sittake. The inset illustrates Barnett's solution: Cunaxa = Nuseffiat, Median Wall = Nebuchadnezzar's Opis-Sippar fortifications (partly preserved between Sippar and Nuseffiat), Sittake = Humaniye (near Azizye), Physkos river and Opis = Diyala river and a site at its confluence with the Tigris.

(2) *Mespila (Nineveh)-Trapezus*, a three-and-a-half month march, the course of which depends on deciding where the Greeks crossed, or marched along, the Kentrites, Teleboas, Euphrates, 'Phasis' (i.e. Araks) and Harpasos rivers. The sources provide no help beyond a record of distances (in days and *parasangs*, rather inexact measurements), general descriptions of terrain, and a scatter of tribal names, valueless in themselves. The solution shown is that of Lehmann-Haupt. Most others are generally similar: they tend to reduce or eliminate the detour to Malazgirt and Kaghyzman, but the final section from the upper Harpasos is common to all. Distinct alternatives either keep to a more westerly line after Muş, or go even further east than Kaghyzman before circling back to the Harpasos.

Leuctra, 371 BCE

The approximate location is established by the Theban battle monument. Combination of the individually incomplete ancient accounts of the battle reveals three key points:

(a) The Spartan cavalry [3] was placed opposite the enemy's initial position and therefore (contrary to normal practice) in front of the infantry. When easily defeated by the Boeotian cavalry [4], it put some of the infantry behind out of action (Phase I).

(b) Sparta's King Cleombrotus attempted to counter a diagonal Boeotian advance by swinging his right wing forward, but he could not complete the move before the arrival of the Thebans [5], spearheaded by the Sacred Band.

(c) The fifty-deep Theban hoplite contingent [5] crushed the isolated Spartans [1] (especially Cleombrotus' Spartiate entourage), while the other Boeotians [6] and the Peloponnesians [2] remained unengaged (Phase II, actually almost simultaneous with Phase I).

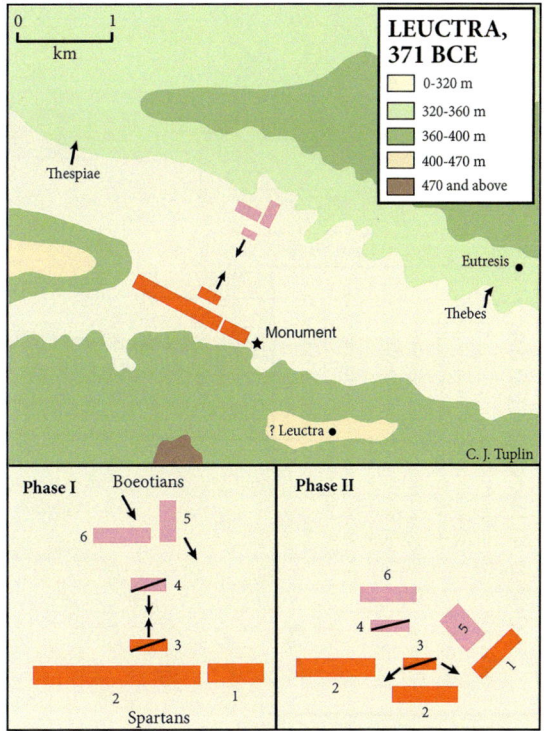

C. J. Tuplin

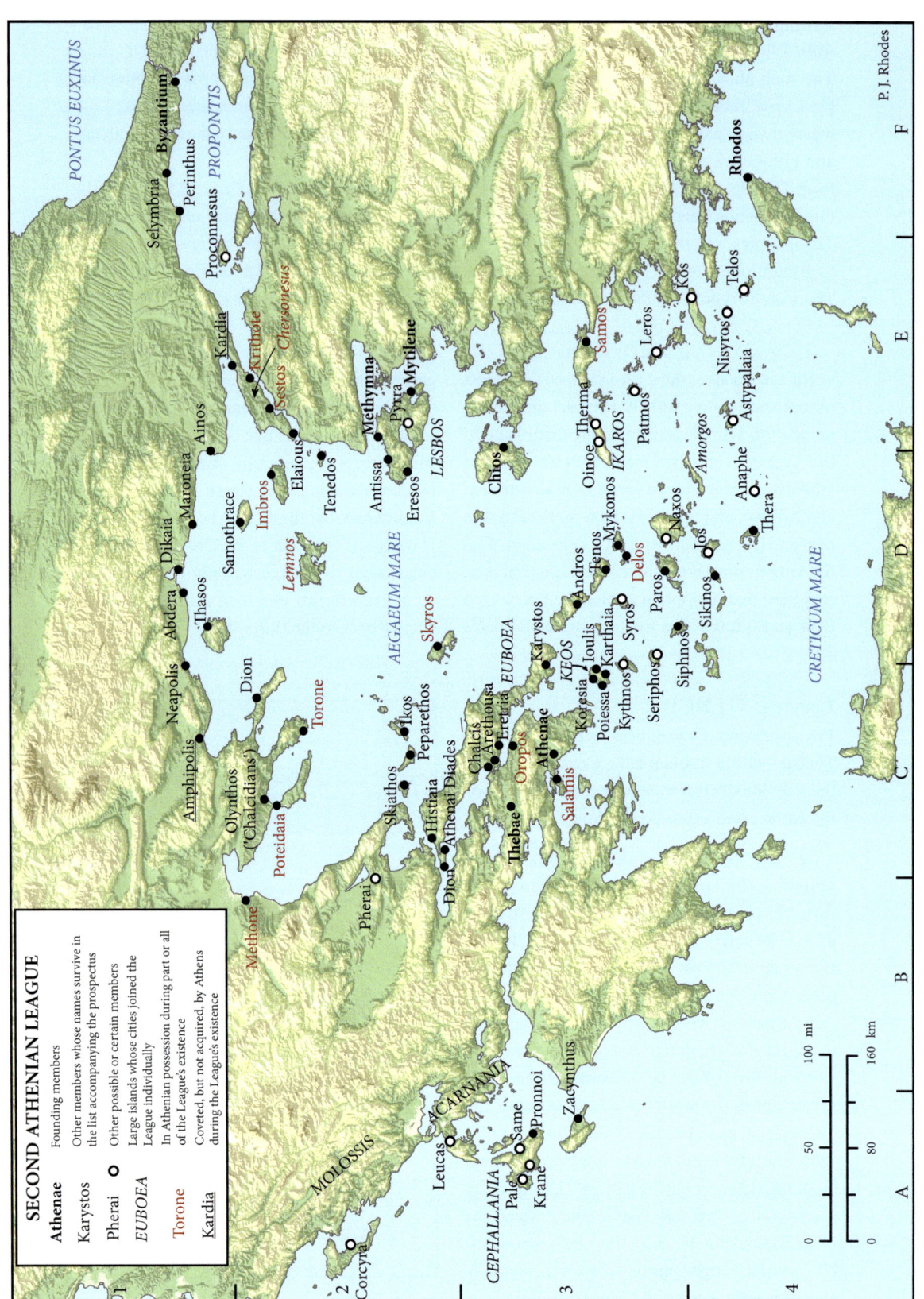

Second Athenian League

In 378–377 BCE, exactly a century after the founding of the Delian League (see p. 45), the Second Athenian League was founded. We possess its prospectus, a decree of the Athenian assembly which declares defence of the freedom of Greek and barbarian states against Spartan imperialism as the League's purpose; all states outside Persia's domains are invited to join on specified terms, designed to protect members against the encroachments on their freedom implemented by Athens in the Delian League. Appended to the decree is a list of members, to which additions were made on various occasions between 377 and around 375, but not thereafter.

The League was never as large or as prosperous as the Delian League, but fear of Sparta, and Athens' promises of good behaviour, won it widespread support during the 370s, mostly among former members of the Delian League. However, at the battle of Leuctra in 371 (p. 55) Sparta was decisively beaten by Thebes, and the threat of Spartan imperialism was destroyed. During the 360s, Athens turned to supporting Sparta against Thebes; it and the cities of Euboea left the League. In the Aegean, Athens not only began making conquests and planting settlements, but also broke several promises made at the League's foundation. Some members, especially in the south-east Aegean, left the League as a result of the Social War (356–355), but certain former members rejoined when they felt threatened by the growing power of Philip of Macedon (see p. 59). After his victory over Athens and Thebes at Chaeronea in 338, Philip organized the mainland Greeks in the League of Corinth, and the Second Athenian League ceased to exist.

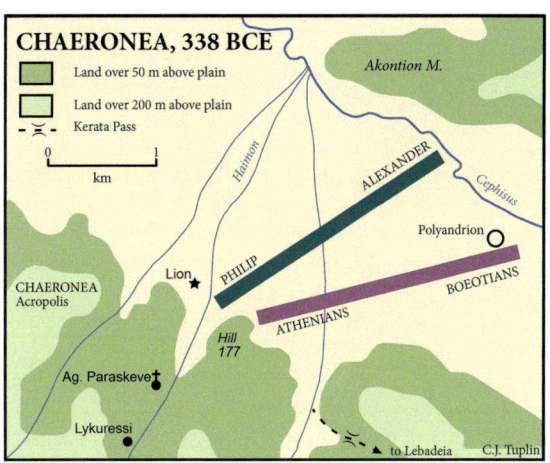

Chaeronea, 338 BCE

The relative positions of Athenian and Boeotian hoplites, Philip and Alexander are clear; an eastern limit for the battlefield is provided by the Macedonian *polyandrion* (containing cremated remains of the dead) and by the Greeks' withdrawal to Lebadeia. The identity of the 254 skeletons under the Lion monument is too uncertain to assist a grasp of the topography; but the Haimon river, near which some of the Greeks camped, must be west of Hill 177, which favours the placement of the Greek left near it rather than at the end of the Lebadeia road. Both Macedonian wings routed the enemy, with Alexander achieving the first breakthrough. However, a more precise picture depends on whether he was leading the Companion Cavalry, and on whether Polyaenus is reliable in his report of a deliberate retreat by the Macedonian right, which tempted the Athenians into disastrous pursuit. These problems are linked, for if Alexander led a cavalry charge (the usual view), Polyaenus must be used to explain why there was a gap in the Greek line for him to attack.

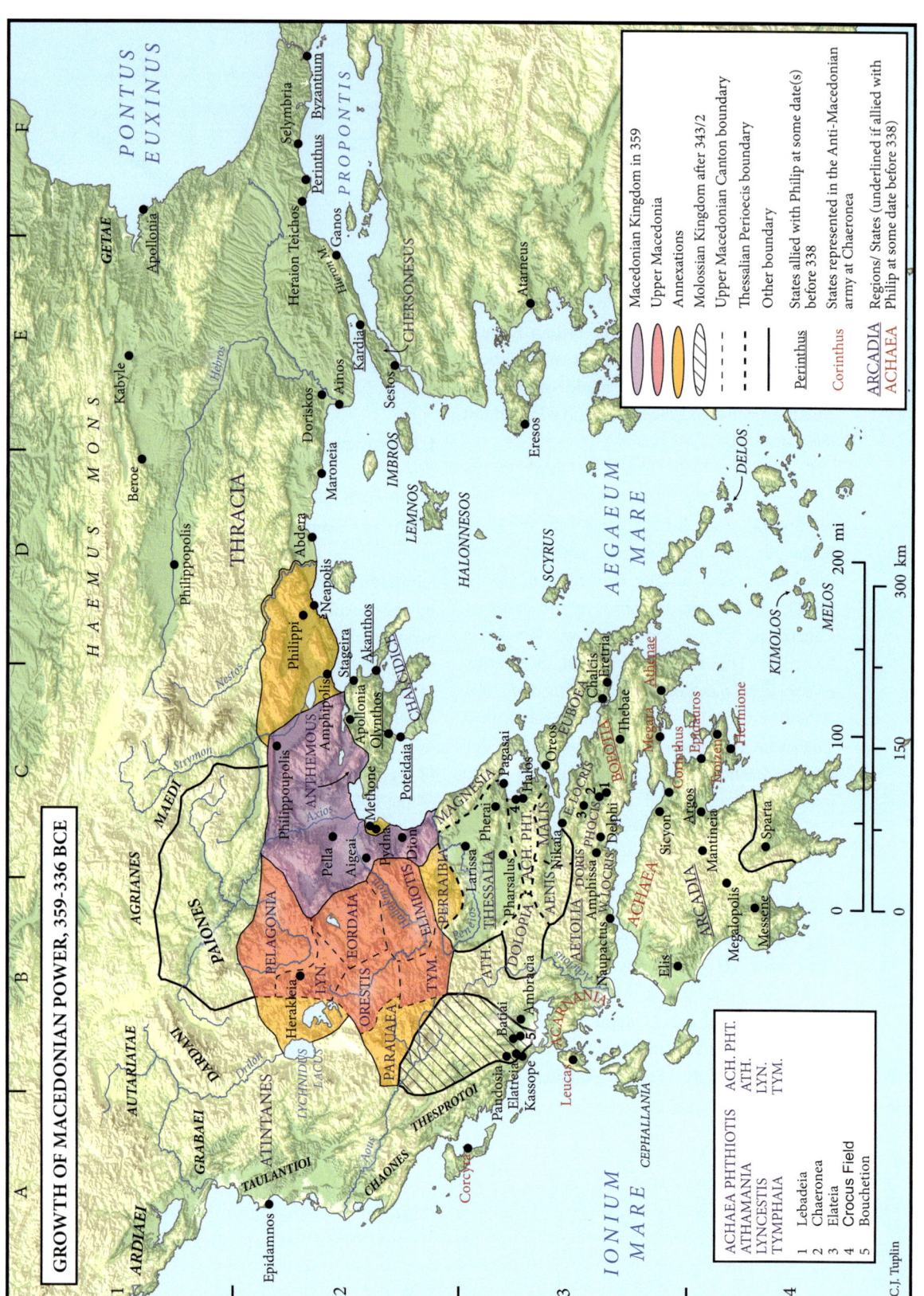

Growth of Macedonian Power, 359–336 BCE

Two distinct developments occur:

(1) *The extension of the Macedonian Kingdom proper.* This was achieved partly by the imposition of unprecedentedly firm control on the Upper Macedonian cantons, and partly by actual annexation of adjacent non-Macedonian territory. The scale of such annexations is debatable. The map registers the acquisition of the region up to lake Lychnidus (358), Pydna (357), the Strymon-Nestos area (356), Methone (354), Perraibia (352) and Parauaea (351?). Some would add Paionia (356) and all of Chalcidice (348). The alternative view is that Paionia simply became a vassal principality and that, although the land of Poteidaia and Olynthos (cities destroyed in 356 and 348) was occupied by Macedonians, the surviving cities of Chalcidice became Philip's allies. At least one Macedonian cavalry squadron was named after a Chalcidian town, Apollonia.

(2) *The acquisition of effective control in areas outside the Kingdom.* Here three phenomena may be distinguished:

(i) The imposition of vassal status on tribal areas: Paionians (356, see above); Dardanians (345); Odrysian Thracians under Cetriporis (towards Nestos river, 356), Amadocus (between Nestos and Hebros, 352) and Cersobleptes (beyond Hebros, 352); also on the Molossian kingdom (around 351–343/342). It is not clear what implications vassaldom had for this kingdom's allies among the Chaones and Thesprotioi, let alone for the Getae (?) under Cothelas (around 341), or for Scythians further north under Atheas (340). It is unlikely that the Agrianes were vassals, and the evidence that some or all of the Grabaei, Autariatae and Ardiaei were in that category is weaker than sometimes suggested. The Taulauntioi certainly were not vassals. The situation in Thrace after 342/341 is uncertain: some believe that a tribute-paying province stretching north to the Haemus mountains was established under a Macedonian *strategos* (first attested under Alexander).

(ii) Thessaly: Philip's suppression of Pherai in 352 was followed by his acclamation as *archon* of the Thessalian League, an extraordinary position for a Macedonian king, entitling him to receive taxes, command military support, and generally control the cities as he saw fit; after 344 the ancient office of tetrarch was revived to assist the process. The status of the *perioecis* (areas theoretically dependent on individual cities) is debatable: Perraibia and Magnesia were annexed in 352, but it is unclear whether the non-annexed areas (including Magnesia after 346) were subject to Philip as *archon* directly, or through the cities.

(iii) Other Greek states: Philip's alliances with several states between 359 and 338 may in varying degrees be construed as expressions of his growing power, and the same goes for his more or less open interference in the politics of Euboea, Megara and the Peloponnese after 346; so too for his addition of certain small Greek towns to the Molossian kingdom in 343/342. But the chief expression and instrument of hegemony was the Corinthian League of 338, established after the battle of Chaeronea (p. 57). It involved assertions of Greek autonomy (but also the outlawing of socio-economic revolution); freedom from tribute and garrisons (except in Ambracia, Corinth and Thebes); the right of deliberation in League synods (albeit occasional and carefully orchestrated); and the obligation to provide military support for the projected Persian expedition. Precise evidence is lacking, but the League must be presumed to have included all mainland and Aegean Greek states which were neither part of Macedonia nor in Persian hands; the only known exception is Sparta.

It should be stressed that, notwithstanding the erection of a far-flung Macedonian *Reich*, the fundamental fact of Macedonian power remained the military potential of Macedonia itself. The chief development here was the creation of a well-disciplined infantry force. In this context the use of population transfers to alter settlement patterns and to create the appropriate human raw material was vital, but the references in the sources are too general to provide insight into the process.

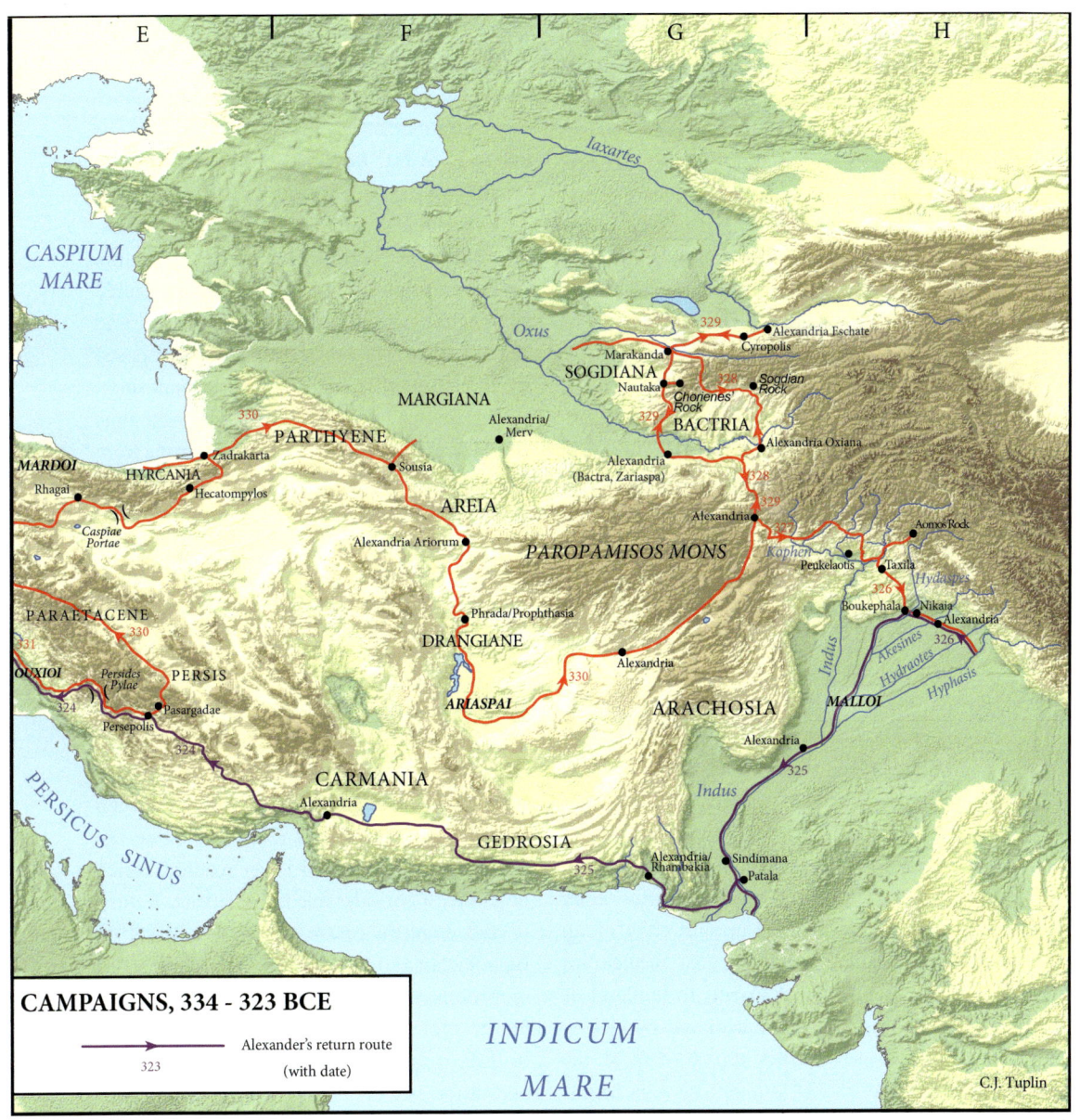

Alexander's Campaigns, 334–323 BCE

The map illustrates Alexander's movements between his departure from Pella in 334 and death at Babylon in 323. The general picture of his progress is not in doubt: 334–331 Asia Minor, Levant; 331–330 Mesopotamia, Iran, Afghanistan; 329–327 Afghanistan, Central Asia; 327–325 Pakistan, India; 325–323 Iran, Mesopotamia. But lack of precise ancient evidence, conflict between sources and differences of opinion about logistical probabilities all render the exact identification of his routes controversial. Sections where even an outline map must reflect a disputed interpretation include: Ancyra-Tarsus; Tyre-Thapsacus (site of the latter is a notorious problem); Ecbatana-Rhagai; Zadrakarta-Alexandria Ariorum (= Herat); Herat-Alexandria in Arachosia (= Kandahar); movements either side of the Oxus river in 328 (in particular, did Alexander actually visit Alexandria in Margiana (= Merv)?); Patala-Alexandria in Carmania.

The campaigns fall into four periods:

(1) The war against Darius, ending in 330 with the burning of Persepolis (p. 25) and his murder as he fled east from Rhagai. Though Alexander had claimed the Persian throne in 332, and had been hailed as 'King of Asia' by his army after Gaugamela, with Darius' opportune death such claims became a reality; further fighting would be against usurpers – like Darius' killer Bessus, who adopted the upright tiara of an Achaemenid king – and against recalcitrant 'subjects.' Reduction of Darius to the level of a fugitive was principally achieved by victory in three set-piece battles (pp. 63–64): at the Granicus river in 334 (attempt by Asia Minor forces to contain the invader); Issus in 333 (Darius' first personal appearance, and a defeat even though he first outmanoeuvred Alexander strategically); and Gaugamela in 331 (defeat which exposed the empire's Mesopotamian and Iranian heartland). The delay between Issus and Gaugamela, which gave Darius another chance, was due to the time Alexander expended on the sieges of Tyre (p. 64) and Gaza, and the occupation of Egypt – diversions that his strategy of neutralizing the Persian navy by control of its bases made essential.

(2) In 330–327 Alexander slowly asserted control in the eastern satrapies against resistance from: Satibarzanes, his own appointee as satrap of Areia; Bessus, satrap of Bactria and would-be Great King; and Spitamenes, leader of a rebellion in initially submissive Sogdiana. These struggles occupied Alexander's attention for eighteen months of hard and ill-documented campaigning in alternately mountainous and desert terrain. The successful outcome disposed of all concerted Iranian nationalist opposition to the foreign King of Kings. The next time trouble arose – in Bactria, in 325 – it came from discontented Greek mercenaries who disliked being settled in such an un-Greek environment.

(3) In 327 Alexander crossed into India (mostly staying within Pakistan in modern terms), capturing the supposedly impregnable Aornos rock (Pir-Sar) early on, and then eliminating resistance by King Poros at the Hydaspes river (p. 65). Further advance eastward stopped at the Hyphasis river, when the army refused to endorse a decision to make for the Ganges. Instead, Alexander then set off down the Indus river to subdue the tribes of its middle and lower reaches, which he did with considerable bloodletting. Return to the empire's centre along the coasts of Baluchistan and Iran became impossible when monsoons delayed the fleet, so Alexander had to cross the Gedrosian desert, losing up to three-quarters of his army there to hunger and thirst.

(4) 324–323 saw Alexander back in Babylonia and Media. Military activity was limited to a winter campaign against the Cossaei, and preparations for an expedition to Arabia which his death forestalled.

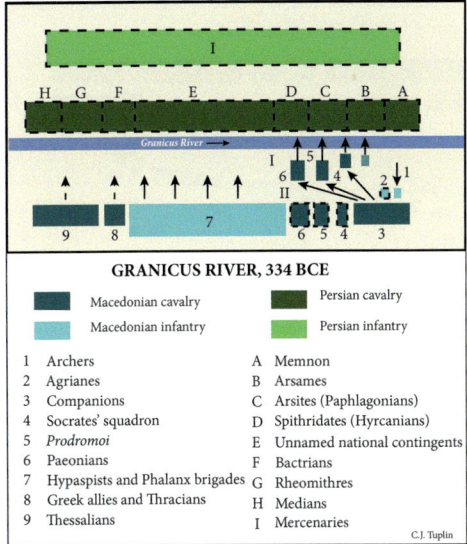
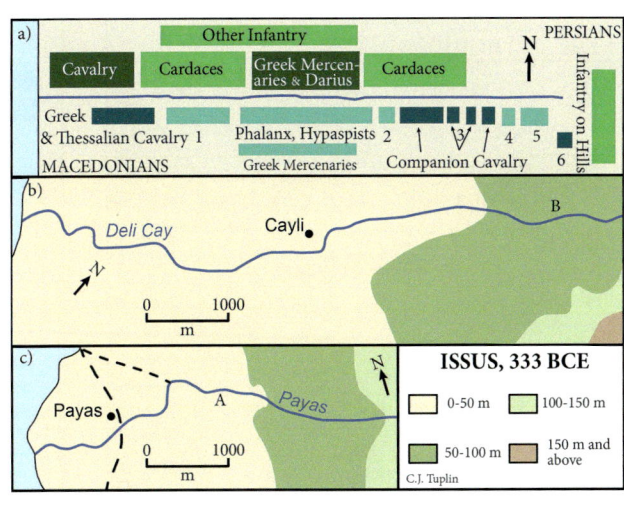

Granicus River, 334 BCE

There is fundamental conflict between the main accounts. In Arrian, Alexander fights his way across the river against Persian cavalry ranged on the east bank, while in Diodorus he makes an unopposed dawn crossing and fights a normal engagement in the plain east of the river. Arrian's somewhat more circumstantial account is perhaps the lesser of two evils, though Diodorus supplies the Persian dispositions. There are two phases: first, the crossing, with two cavalry attacks on the Macedonian right, the second of these co-ordinated with infantry advance; second, the annihilation of the Persians' Greek mercenaries in the plain (not shown). The limited extent of the areas where crossing was unimpeded by either high banks or trees, or both, may explain Alexander's oblique line of attack and his ultimate success (the very localized fighting neutralizing Persian numerical advantage). But the process can only be represented schematically, since precise topographical information is lacking; possibly it is no longer even obtainable, as the river may have shifted course.

Issus, 333 BCE

(a) represents schematically one interpretation of the final pre-battle dispositions recorded in Arrian: 1 Thracian javelineers, Cretan archers; 2 archers; 3 *prodromoi*, Paeonians; 4 archers, Agrianians; 5 Greek mercenaries; 6 small cavalry unit. The Macedonian centre/right routed the enemy – the first breakthrough being led by Alexander against the Cardaces – while the left checked the Persian cavalry. Detailed reconstruction is difficult, not least of the initial Macedonian attack. A crucial problem here is the identification of the Pinarus river. It seems most likely to have been either (b) the Deli Cay (30 km north of modern Iskenderun, Turkey), or (c) the Payas (20 km north), where coastline and riverbed may have changed: see the dashed lines in (c). The Payas fits various reported distances less badly, but steep banks above A preclude the initial Macedonian cavalry charge implied by the sources – and indeed *any* orderly cavalry advance. So, either the battle occurred on the Deli (between B and the sea), or infantry brigades opened the attack.

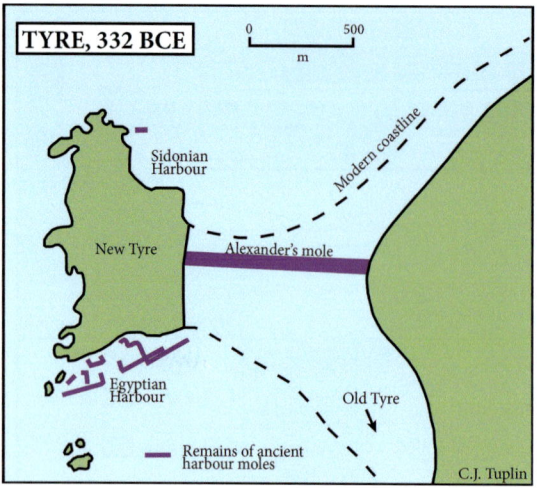

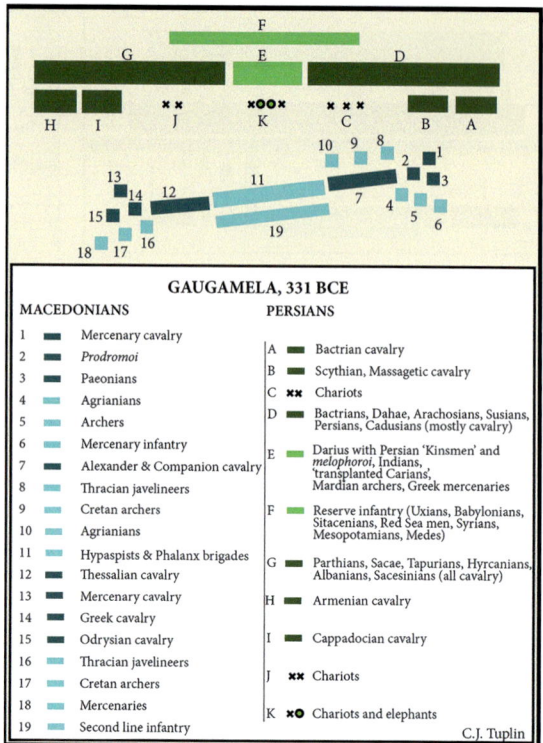

Tyre, 332 BCE

The sources are only in broad agreement, and none offers enough incident for a siege of seven months. Initial Macedonian attempts to provide a platform for siege engines by constructing a mole encountered the insuperable difficulty of protecting the workmen against Tyrian attacks from the walls and from ships. Alexander's acquisition of 224 ships from Cyprus, Phoenicia, Rhodes, Cilicia and Lycia was crucial. The Tyrian fleet then dared not venture out; a small sortie from the Sidonian harbour failed. The mole was completed – though in the event its role was largely diversionary – and a successful assault was mounted. Two ship-borne engines inflicted sufficient damage for an assault party under Alexander to seize a stretch of wall (adjacent to the Egyptian harbour?), while his fleet broke into the harbours. However, no source explains satisfactorily why this attack succeeded when earlier ones had failed.

Gaugamela, 331 BCE

To quote Brunt: "The diversity of modern accounts…shows that agreement…has not been attained and suggests that it is unattainable." This entirely schematic plan shows the position just before the first contact. The dispositions are from Arrian. The oblique Macedonian line, position of the wings, and extent of the Persian overlap, are all arguable. Thereafter three stages may be identified:

(1) The Macedonian right [1–6] stalls attack by Darius' left wing [A, B, parts of D], while light-armed troops [8–10] neutralize a chariot attack [C].

(2) The Companions and infantry phalanx [7, 11] rout the now exposed Persian left/centre [rest of D, E]; Darius flees; the extreme left panics.

(3) The Macedonian left and left-centre phalanx comes under severe pressure: some Persian cavalry may have advanced through it, or around it, to the baggage camp. But apparently, the phalanx holds its own unaided, since the Companions and other cavalry [7, 1] moving behind the lines encounter retreating Parthian cavalry. Controversy attaches particularly to this entire last stage of the battle.

Hydaspes River, 326 BCE

The map illustrates: (a) Alexander's surprise river crossing (scholars vacillate between Stein's view and locations around Jhelum); and (b) the subsequent decisive battle in two stages. Poros' dispositions derive from Arrian; Alexander's are nowhere properly described. The extent of Indian overlap is debatable.

Alexander's initial cavalry victory drove the Indian horse onto the infantry line, and the elephants/infantry attempted a leftward counter-movement; the Indian left's coordination was thus broken, exposing it to the Macedonian infantry, which pelted the elephants with missiles and mounted a crushing mass charge. The chief problem is unit 3, which made for the Indian right but still participated in the cavalry battle. Probably it doubled back as shown, but some believe that Poros transferred his right-wing cavalry to the left – likely in any case – and that unit 3 followed them behind the Indian lines and attacked as they reached their goal.

Alexandria Oxiana (Ai Khanoum)

Discovered by accident and now wrecked by looting, this site – possibly Alexandria Oxiana – on Afghanistan's border with Tajikistan was excavated by French archaeologists (1964–1978). They uncovered here the first evidence (beyond coins) of the Greco-Bactrian civilization. Alexander or Seleucus may have been the founder, but the city hardly developed till the reign of Antiochus I (280–261 BCE). It then flourished, even becoming a royal capital, until severe damage by nomads around 145 caused the Greeks to leave. Thereafter it was only a village occupied by local peoples (a period not represented here). The site at the confluence of the Oxus and Kokcha rivers was well chosen, with an acropolis rising to 60 m reinforced by an escarpment and ramparts, especially to the exposed northeast. Below, the city's best residential area (to the south) and its extensive public buildings lay in the flat area between the Oxus and a straight main street.

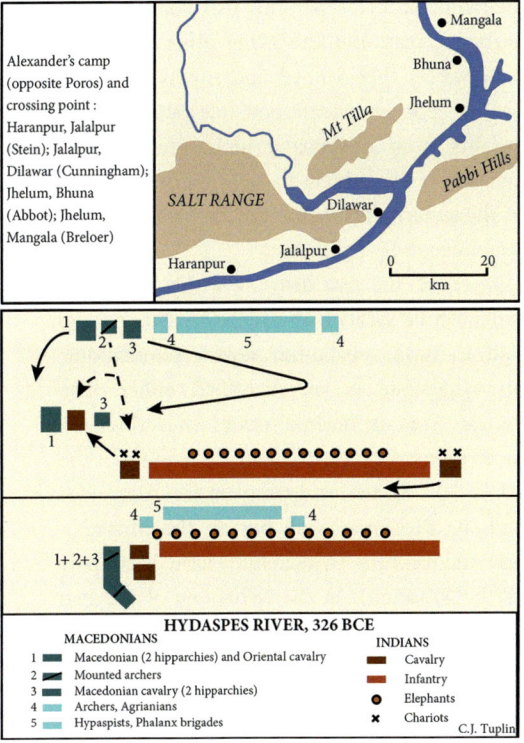

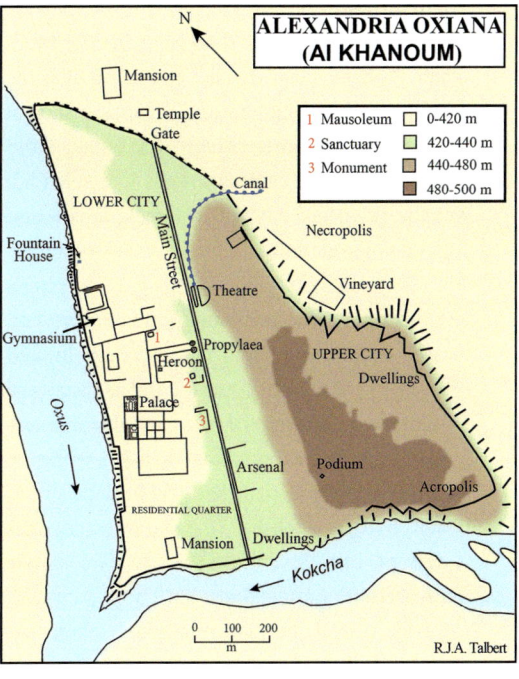

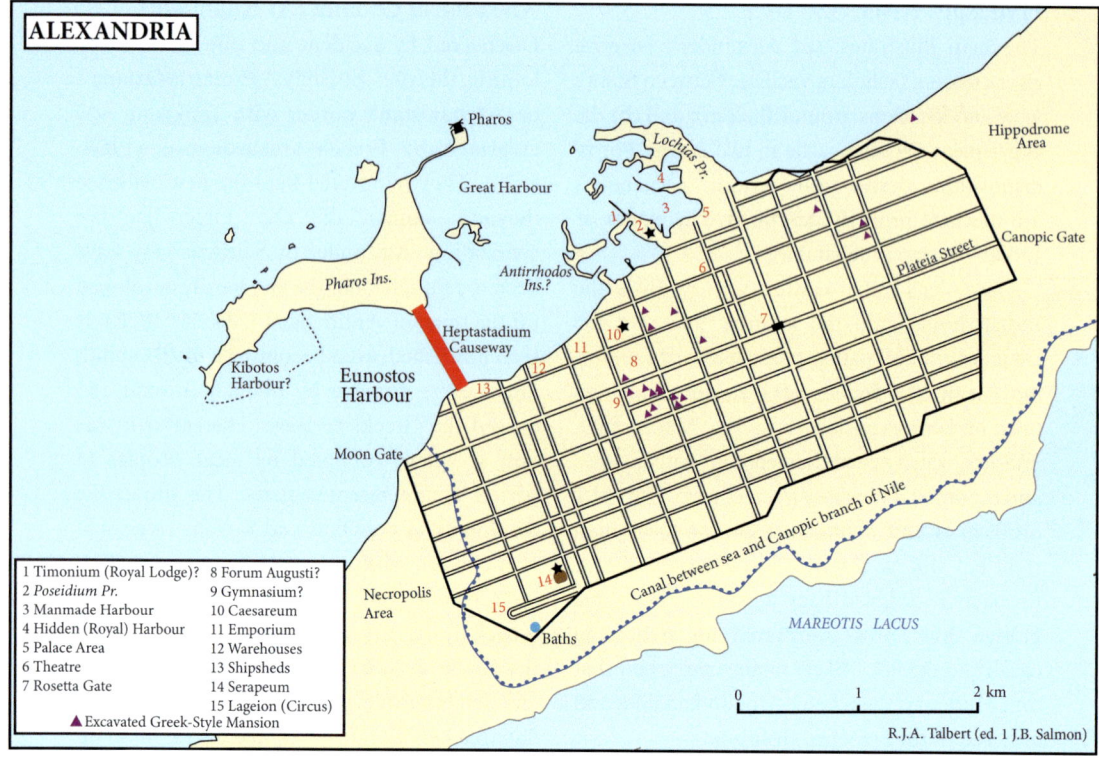

Alexandria

Founded by Alexander the Great in 331 BCE, under Ptolemy I and II Alexandria became the capital of their kingdom and Egypt's principal Mediterranean port. Later Ptolemies, and thereafter Roman emperors, kept it a splendid, wealthy, privileged city with a Greek, Jewish and Egyptian population, often referenced in literary sources (notably Strabo, Philo and Josephus). Even so, uninterrupted occupation to the present, as well as environmental change, have limited recovery of the ancient cityscape and its successive developments. During the past two millennia sea-level here has risen approximately 1.5 m, while the land has sunk up to 6 m. The grid of wide streets is well enough established (the two principal ones widest of all). Several impressive Greek-style mansions with mosaic floors have been excavated from the period the plan represents – first two centuries CE. Also known is the causeway (Heptastadium) connecting Pharos island to the mainland and separating two extensive deep harbour areas. But the many other manmade breakwaters that defined and subdivided these remain poorly understood, despite growing insights from underwater archaeology. Rocks and reefs were a threat to navigation in and out of the eastern area; hence the importance of the celebrated, lofty lighthouse.

None of the five districts within the city's walls can be located, let alone the two of them said to have substantial Jewish populations; no synagogue is yet identified either. The Palace Area is beyond doubt, but three of its famous structures have disappeared: the Soma (or Sema) enclosure where Alexander and the Ptolemies were buried, the Museum, and the Library (which may have been part of the Museum). In the 1870s one of the two tall obelisks ('Cleopatra's Needles') erected in front of the Caesareum temple was shipped to London, the other to New York.

Hellenistic World

In varying degrees, Alexander the Great's career of conquest (p. 60) spread Greek power and culture from his base in Macedonia to Afghanistan and Pakistan in the east, to Egypt in the south, and to most regions in between. No single one of his generals proved powerful enough to hold this entire vast area, although they fought fiercely with each other to carve out their own territories. The generation after Alexander's death in 323 BCE is marked by a series of complicated struggles that by the early third century saw the emergence of three major kingdoms – Antigonids in Greece, Seleucids in the central part of Alexander's domains, Ptolemies in Egypt – and several minor kingdoms and independent states. Geographical boundaries, however, were fluid, as kings, states and subject peoples continued to jockey for political and territorial advantage. Eventually, the clouds that the second century Greek historian Polybius saw gathering in the West – that is, the growing power of Rome – spread, as he feared, over the Greek world. Octavian's defeat of Mark Antony and his Egyptian queen Cleopatra at the battle of Actium in 31 (p. 107), which led to Rome's annexation of Egypt as a province, is usually taken to mark the close of the Hellenistic period after three centuries. By then too, Pompey the Great had brought the ailing Seleucid kingdom to an end, after the Parthians had won control of the central part of its lands and had established themselves as the main threat to Rome's eastern frontier. The Antigonid kingdom had already been abolished by Rome in 167. Even so, despite the end of the independent kingdoms, the date 31 should not be stressed unduly. In fact, numerous cultural, social and economic continuities saw the Hellenistic world live on far into the period of the Roman empire, and they were given a further lease of life when Constantine moved his capital to Byzantium in 324 CE.

The most geographically discrete of the major Hellenistic monarchies was Egypt, although during the third century BCE the Ptolemies also controlled Coele Syria and some parts of Asia Minor, as well as exerting considerable influence on the Greek mainland; moreover, they kept hold of Cyprus and Cyrene well into the first century. They lost most of their possessions in the Aegean and Asia Minor during the reign of Ptolemy V Epiphanes (210–182), and in 200 the Seleucid king Antiochus III also deprived them of Coele Syria. This loss brought the Jewish people under Seleucid rule. As Seleucid power weakened, the Jews were able to enjoy a brief period as an almost independent state, before Rome arrived in the 60s and absorbed them into its empire. In Egypt itself, the Ptolemies inherited the millennia-old land of the Pharaohs with its long-established population centres and economic and religious infrastructure. There was little scope for new city foundations in the centre of the kingdom along the Nile, where Ptolemais Hermiou (p. 75 B7) was their only major new settlement. Alexander had already founded Alexandria (p. 66). The Ptolemies made it their capital and developed it to become one of the Mediterranean's greatest cities. Substantial numbers of military settlers were planted on reclaimed land in the Fayum district of Lower Egypt, where new settlements grew up. Trade with the East saw several towns and harbours established on the Red Sea coast, most prominent among them the ports of Myos Hormos and Berenice.

In contrast to the Ptolemies, the Seleucids created an entirely new cityscape throughout their empire, especially on the Tigris river and in northern Syria, with an extraordinary number of new settlements: recent counts show some eighty-seven west of the Euphrates, thirty-five to the east. Seleucus I (305–281) initiated the policy by founding the four great cities of the Tetrapolis in northern Syria: Seleukeia Pieria and Laodicea on the sea, Antiochia (p. 165) and Apamea on the Orontes river. This was clearly an

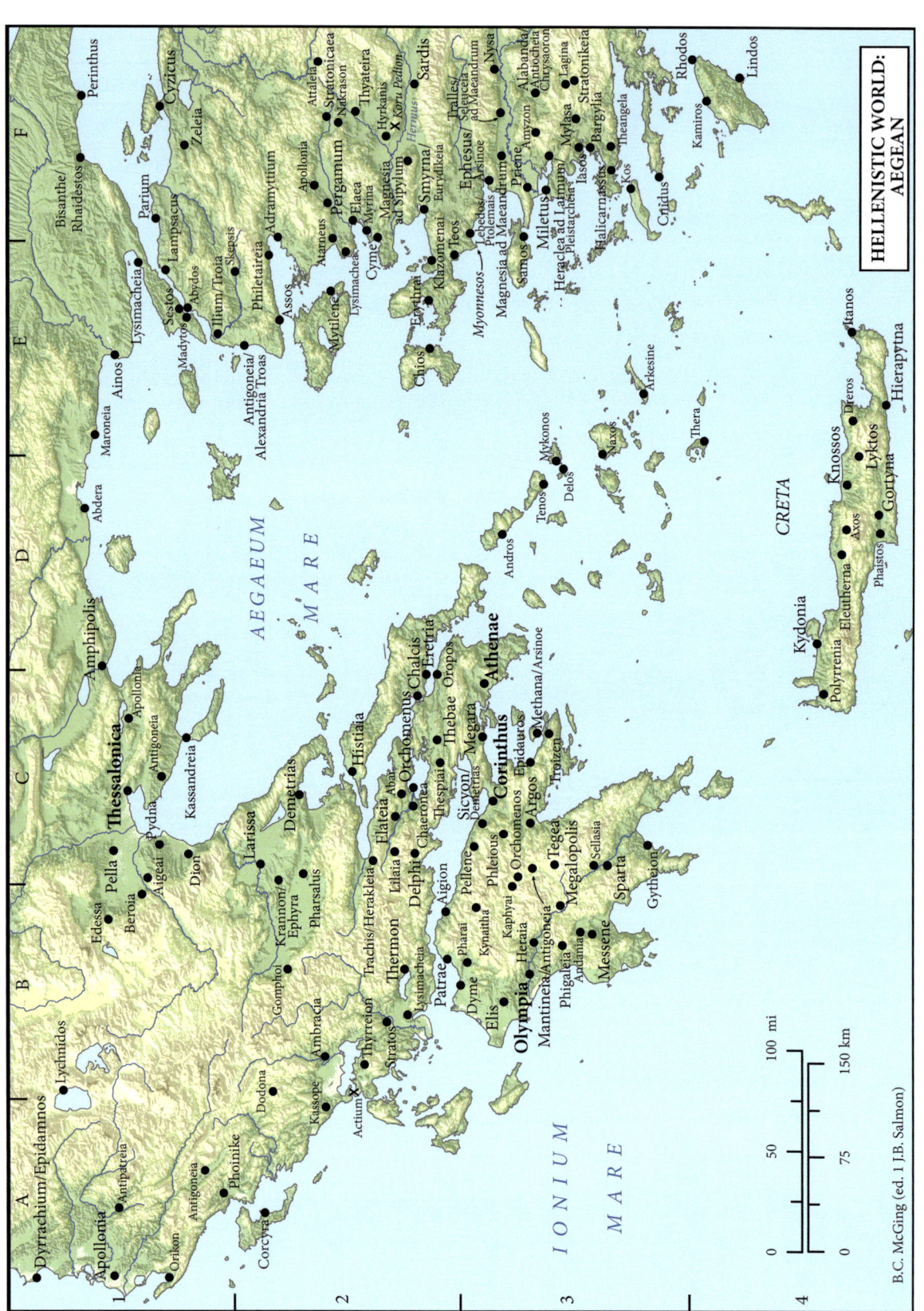

attempt to create a new Macedonian heartland for the Seleucids' vast and heterogeneous territories, the extremities of which were never stable. That the Seleucids would be able to retain control of their distant eastern subjects inherited from Alexander was always unlikely; even Seleucus I had to cede extensive territory to the Indian king Chandragupta Maurya. In the West, the Seleucids started out with interests in Asia Minor, but never extended their control far there. When Antiochus III attempted to establish Seleucid rule in the Aegean and Asia Minor, he met with dramatic defeat by Rome in 190. The Antigonids were also too busy in the Aegean to make inroads in Asia Minor. Without a Macedonian presence there, from the early third century, this became a fruitful zone for local dynasts to establish their own fiefdoms and to declare themselves kings. Thus arose the kingdoms of Pergamum on the Aegean coast, Bithynia and Pontus on the south shore of the Black Sea, and Cappadocia in the centre. Although not a Greek-style kingdom, Galatia, which had been settled by Gauls migrating across the Bosphorus in the first half of the third century, became a separate entity. All these independent units of Asia Minor succumbed to Roman power in the course of the second and first centuries.

The efforts of the Antigonid kings of Macedon were largely limited to maintaining their power on the Greek mainland, although in the early years they too had wider ambitions. While remaining the dominant force in Greece, they were constantly challenged, in particular by the old cities of Greece (most prominently Athens) and two new federal organizations, the Aetolian League in central Greece and the Achaean League in the Peloponnese. Moreover, even during the third century the Romans were beginning to cast their eyes across the Adriatic; once they assumed the role of protector of Greece, it was almost inevitable that Macedonian and Roman interests would prove incompatible. Philip V of Macedon unwisely sided with Hannibal against Rome (see p. 94). Immediately after defeating Carthage in 201, Rome therefore started a new war against Macedon and heavily defeated Philip in 197. Even so, his son Perseus soon provoked Rome, and was defeated at Pydna (167). Having now lost patience with Macedon, Rome then abolished the monarchy and divided the land into four separate republics.

Although kings ruled in most of what we call the Hellenistic world, the Greek *polis* as an institution continued to be the main form of urban organization. While cities often had to tailor their activities to coincide with the wishes of particular kings, they went about their business in traditional ways, sometimes independently. The island state of Rhodes, for instance, after famously withstanding a siege by the Antigonid king Demetrius I in 305-304, enjoyed nearly a century and a half without subjection to any of the major monarchies. Its powerful fleet brought great commercial success and wealth, before Rome put an end to Rhodes' independent existence in the 160s. Numerous Greek settlements around the circuit of the Black Sea likewise retained a considerable degree of freedom, even if they did come under pressure from nearby native peoples and kings, and had to make compromises with them.

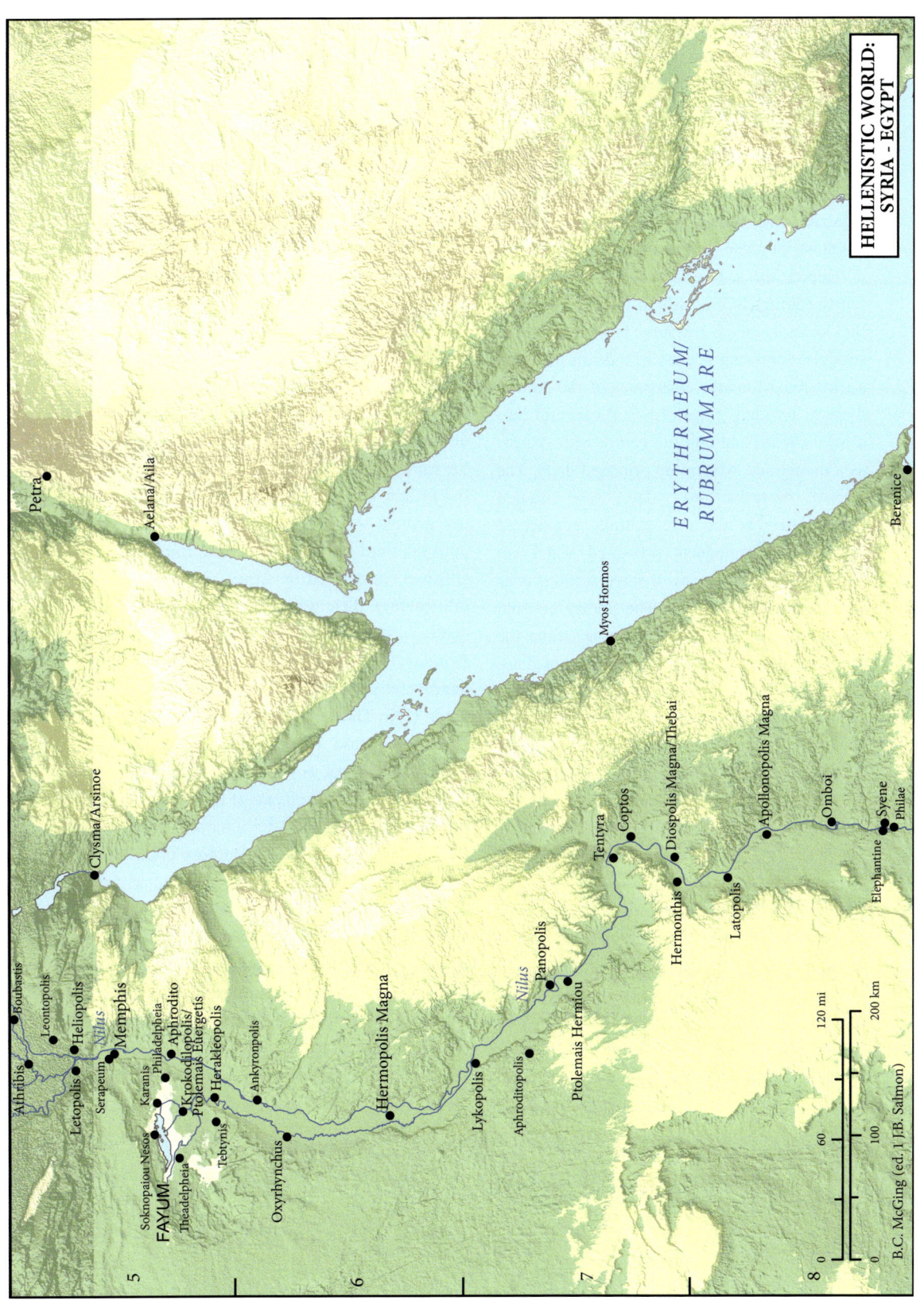

Pergamum

The city's core lies on a mountain ridge rising to around 300 m, with steep drops in all directions except south, where three natural terraces in succession provide an approach. The site – about 30 km inland – is strategic, commanding the rivers Selinos (west) and Keteios (east). Local Mysians settled here at some early date, but little is known of their community's growth until it developed into a Greek-style polis during the fourth century BCE. Early in the third century, the location of a treasury here during the struggles following Alexander's death provided a springboard for the emergence of the Attalid dynasty. Its kings transformed Pergamum into a royal capital and cultural centre with Athens as a model and Athena its principal deity. The arsenal, barracks and palace were situated appropriately at the top; skilfully engineered underground aqueducts pressured water up here. The gymnasium, with three sections, was the Greek world's largest. The library boosted the Attalids as patrons of learning, while the sculptural decoration of the Great Altar of Zeus, depicting the battle between Gods and Giants, symbolized Attalus I's victories over Galatian marauders around 230. Once Rome accepted Attalus III's bequest of his kingdom a century later, Pergamum lost its independence, but not its cultural prominence. After setbacks, during the Principate it gained from being made the meeting-place of the provincial council (*koinon*) responsible for the celebration of Rome's ruler cult in Asia. A lower city, Roman in character, developed, with a colonnaded street leading to the prestigious healing sanctuary of Asclepius. It was enlarged early in the second century CE, when the immense Temple of the Egyptian Gods – bridging the Selinos – was also built. Pergamum suffered from earthquake and attacks by Goths in the third century, but even so, continued to attract intellectuals in the fourth. Thereafter, however, it gradually declined.

Delos

Rocky, barren and parched, this tiny island at the centre of the Cyclades was sacred to the cult of Apollo from an early date. Its western, more sheltered side was settled. A terrace (23) overlooking the original approach to the sanctuary (later it was from the south) was embellished with a line of marble lions around 600 BCE. Then too, a huge marble statue of Apollo was erected against the north wall of the House of the Naxians (7), who took the leading role here until ousted by Athenians during the sixth century. This is also the date of the earliest known temple of Apollo (11). When the Delian League was founded in the 470s, a new temple was begun (9), but not completed until the third century. Although a third temple (10) was constructed by Athens during the late fifth century, there was never a large one. Other deities with temples included Apollo's twin sister Artemis (15) and their mother Leto (21); a sacred dance was performed in front of the Keraton Altar (14). The largest structures date to the Hellenistic period. Two stoas (3, 17) were built by Macedonian kings, as was the Monument of the Bulls (16, so-called from part of its decoration) to house a ship dedicated after a naval victory; the pillared Hypostyle Hall (19, purpose uncertain) was erected around 200. With commercial development (especially slave-trading), and a more cosmopolitan population, came the construction of additional agoras (1, 18, 22), also new residential quarters and public buildings to the north, as well as warehouses to the south, a theatre, and a sanctuary of the Syrian Gods. Delos – lacking defences – was sacked twice in the early first century BCE, and never recovered. French teams have excavated here since the 1870s.

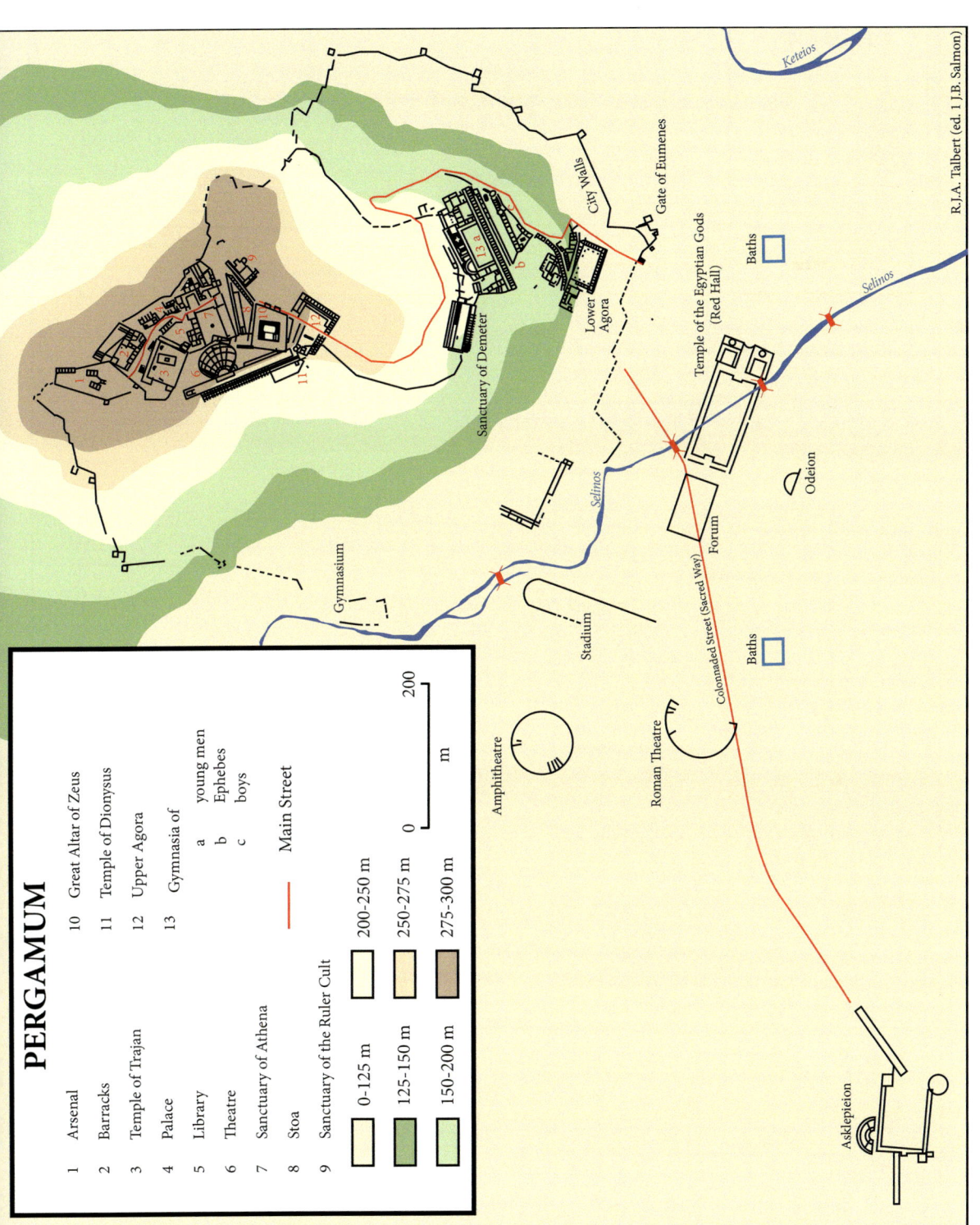

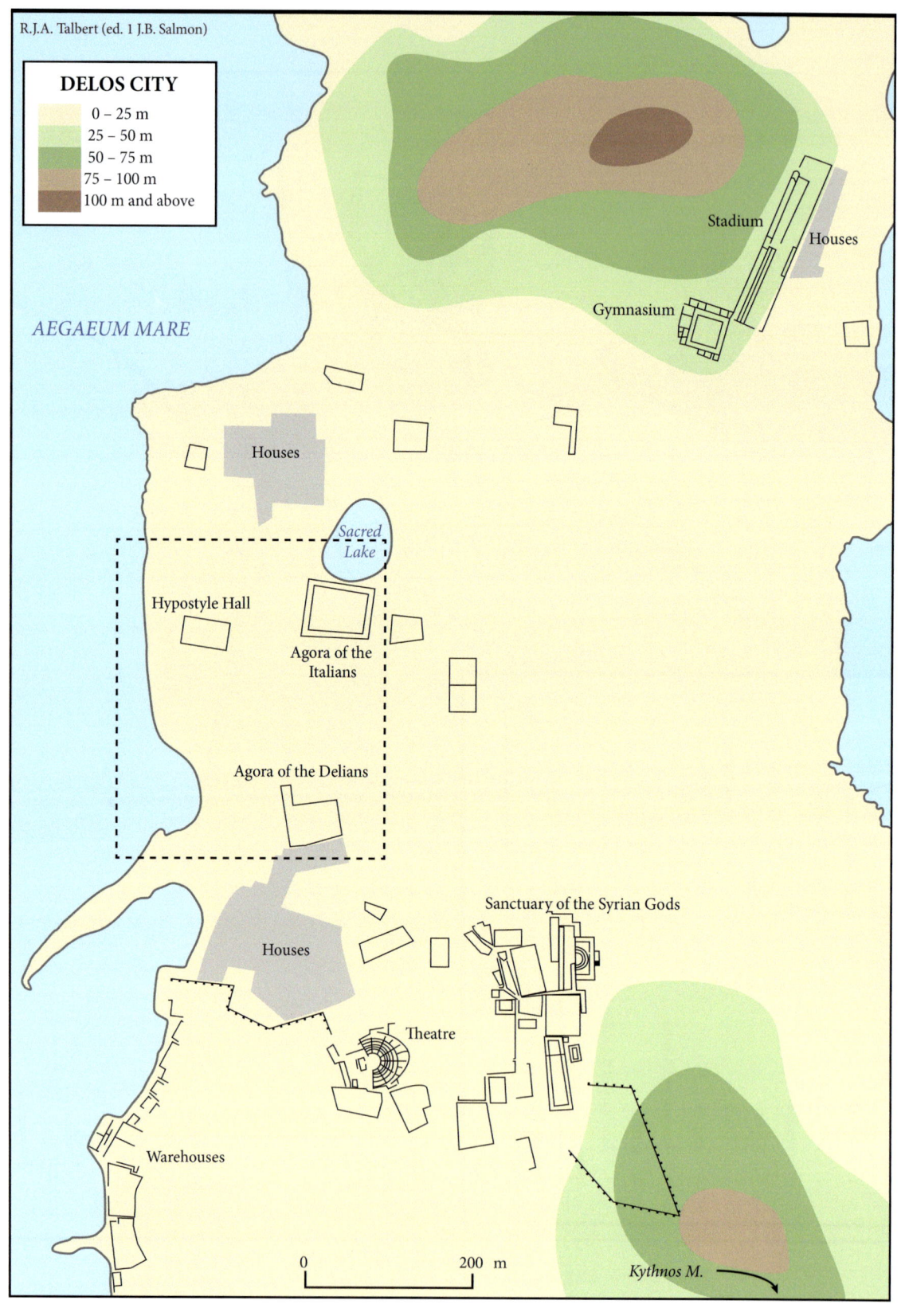

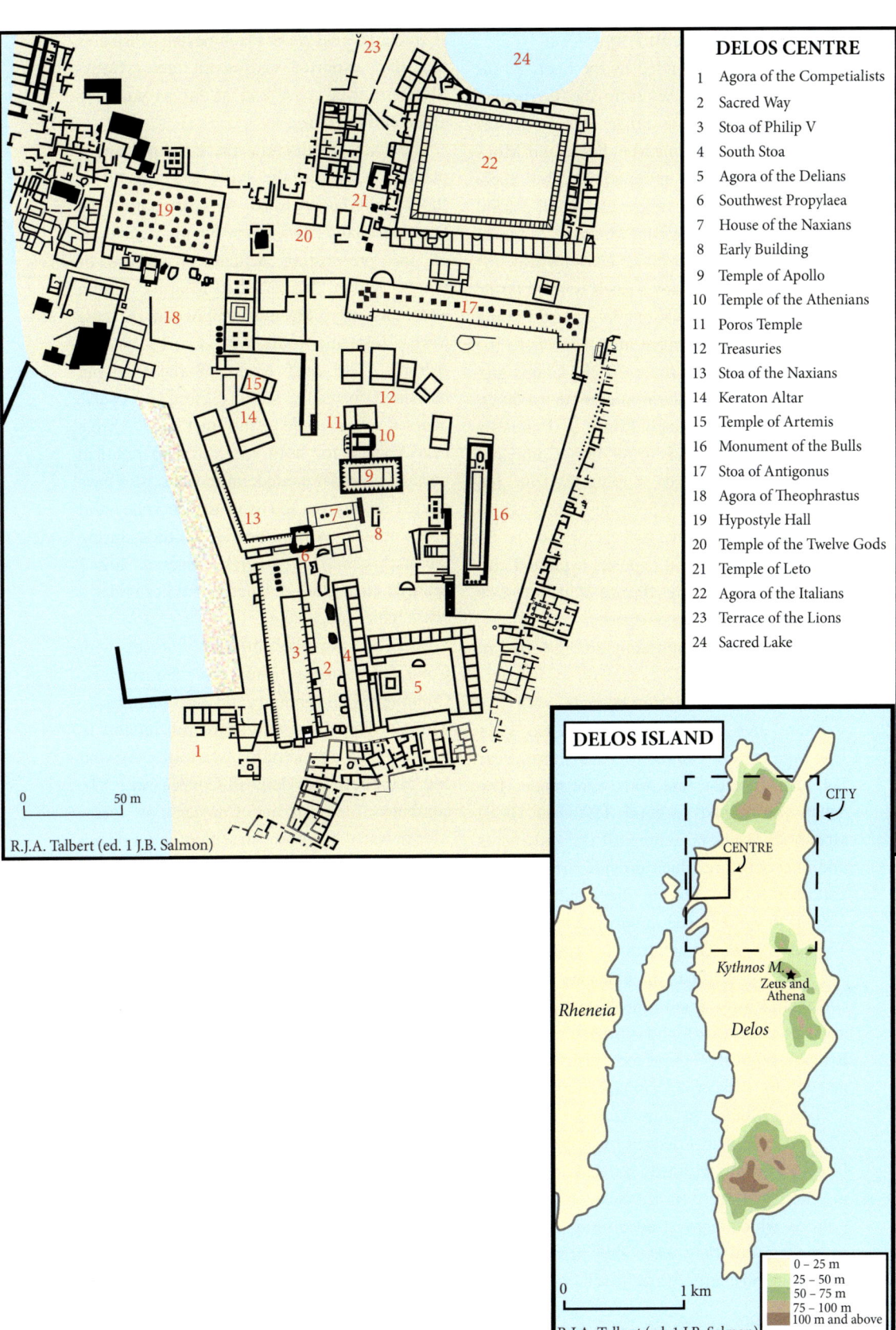

Etruria and Etruscan Expansion

Etruria proper is bounded by the rivers Arnus and Tiber, and stretches from the Tyrrhenian Sea to the Apennine range. Much of the terrain – like the Colline Metallifere and Mons Amiata – is hilly or mountainous, but there are also alluvial river valleys and small coastal plains. The volcanic activity which created Lake Volsiniensis and other crater lakes formed soft tufa rock that breaks down easily to form fertile soil. Good communications by sea and along the navigable rivers linked inland towns to the coast. An important route via the Clanis and Tiber joined the northern and southern cities, and gave access through Rome or Praeneste to the Liris-Volturnus route into Campania (see p. 86). Northwards, a route led from the mid-Arnus over the Apennine watershed to the Rhenus, and thence to Felsina and the Po (Padus) valley. Mineral deposits exploited and traded from the Late Bronze Age onwards explain early Etruscan prosperity: iron, copper, tin, lead, silver and antimony are all found in the region.

Etruria's heartland corresponds with the southern area of Villanovan influence – an Iron Age culture named after Villanova, near Felsina, where the first finds were made. The Villanovan period (around 1000–800 BCE) already shows the beginnings of the settlements and infrastructure which provide the basis for Etruscan culture. During the eighth century urbanization developed rapidly in Etruria itself. The subsequent 'Orientalizing' period (around 730–580) is marked by extensive overseas contacts: luxury goods, both imported and home produced, are found in aristocratic tombs. Etruscans greatly impacted their southern neighbours – Falerii, Campania and Latium, including Rome. In this period, too, they adopted an alphabet derived from that used by Euboean Greeks with whom they had contacts in Campania (p. 87). Etruscans were noted both as wide-ranging traders and (reputedly) as pirates, but they were also producers of various goods: metalware, jewellery, and the characteristic *bucchero* black pottery. Probably too, they exported textiles all along Gaul's Mediterranean coast and as far as southern Spain and Carthage.

The sixth century saw the development of planned towns in the Po valley area. This should not be regarded as 'colonization' by Etruria's inland cities, but rather as an outcome of the pre-existing Villanovan culture of the Po region. Marzabotto, Mantua, Hatria and Spina were the most important of these towns, fostering trade with Greece via the Adriatic. The chief towns of the Etruscan heartland formed a shifting group of twelve peoples (*dodekapolis*) who met at a shrine near Volsinii for both religious and political purposes; similar confederations may also have existed among the towns in the Po valley and in Campania. Within individual cities, during the sixth century aristocratic regimes shifted towards oligarchies or quasi-republics under a *zilath* (chief magistrate).

Etruscan seapower brought contact with Corsica, Sardinia and the Phoenicians. Commercial and military alliances were made with Carthaginians, who shared an interest in resisting Greek penetration westwards. Around 540, at the battle of Aleria off Corsica (see p. 83), combined Etruscan and Carthaginian forces were defeated by Phocaean settlers, but retained control of Corsica and Sardinia because the Greeks' losses were so heavy. Etruscan naval domination of the Tyrrhenian Sea ended in 474 after a defeat inflicted by Syracusans off Cumae. Etruscan land power also declined with the fall (traditionally in 509) of the Etruscan dynasty that had ruled Rome for most of the sixth century, and with the victory (around 504) of Cumaeans and Latins over Etruscans at Aricia. In the north, Celts kept pressing on the Po region and reached northern Etruria in the fourth century. The fall of Veii to Rome (396) and attacks by Dionysius of Syracuse upon Pyrgi (384) initiated a long period of conflict which ended with Rome's conquest of Falerii (241) and all Etruria.

Early Italy and its Neighbours

Peoples of Italy

Italy in the early historical period presented a diversity of peoples, with different languages (see the following text), cultures and forms of organization. Overland population movements, invasions and resettlement all created considerable flux. Seaborne trade and settlements on coastal plains contributed to the spread of cultural influences, and the Apennine range probably blocked interaction less than is sometimes supposed.

Archaeological investigations are transforming our understanding of Iron Age Italy (from around 1000 BCE onwards). Its regional cultures are hard to map from the information about language and ethnicity to be gained from later written accounts. For certain, despite variations in extent and numbers, larger proto-urban settlements did develop, ones with increasingly centralized populations who undertook communal activities. By contrast, in the Apennines especially – where habitation was mostly in small upland valleys – tribal peoples developed forms of association reliant not on urban centres, but on sanctuaries serving as gathering places.

Impact from overseas is clear, through both trade and settlement. There were contacts with Phoenicians and Carthaginians based in Corsica, Sardinia and Sicily. From the eighth century onwards, Greeks (Italiotes) settled permanently on the coast from Cumae to Tarentum, as well as in Sicily (p. 43); meantime, the heel of Italy shows marked Illyrian influences from across the Adriatic. From at least the eighth century, greater socio-economic differentiation is apparent, with varying forms of elite display that often demonstrate wide-ranging exchange networks and high levels of cultural interaction. The seventh and early sixth centuries saw a widespread 'Orientalizing' phase of wealthy, cosmopolitan aristocracies. More generally, the sixth century was marked by urban growth and monumental building that indicate well-organized political communities recognizable as 'city-states.'

By contrast, the fifth century shows widespread disruption, evidenced by changes in settlement and trade practices that suggest some decline in prosperity (though not everywhere), and by social developments perhaps symptomatic of power struggles among elite groups. Concurrently, population movements occurred both in the north (from the Alps to the Po valley) and in central Italy. These are characterized in the ancient sources – with considerable exaggeration – as abrupt, violent incursions by semi-civilized peoples, but they are better understood as longer term processes.

Undeniably important was the westward and southward movement of Oscan-speaking Sabellic peoples from the central Apennines into Campania as Etruscan influence there declined from the early fifth century. The Samnites are identifiable from around this time, beginning to be differentiated into a number of tribes or peoples not highly urbanized but living in upland settlements. The pattern is one of hillforts and of cult centres functioning also as hubs for political and legal activity. Samnites migrated into many Campanian towns, notably Capua, Cumae and Paestum: these migrants became Oscanized and adopted elements of the towns' existing political organization and culture.

In Lucania and Bruttium similar movements of Oscan-speaking peoples occurred, creating a new cultural character there from the fourth century onwards. Similarly, Aequi, Hernici and Volsci migrated into Latium – as best seen at Satricum, which became Volscian in character. Roman sources represent the migrants as invaders, and describe some two centuries of intermittent warfare against them in the Alban hills and over the coastal plain as far as Tarracina. In Italy's far north, the arrival of 'Gauls' or 'Celts' in the early fourth century was represented by Greek and Roman authors as a sudden major incursion by a new invading people from the Alps, but this view over-dramatizes the reality. Some disruption and shift in settlement patterns did result, but in several areas of northern Italy and Picenum a syncretic culture emerged or former practices persisted. Most famously, in (traditionally) 390, a Gallic band reached Rome and supposedly sacked it, though causing less damage than later sources suggest.

Languages of Italy to the First Century CE

It is impossible to represent accurately with clear-cut boundaries the languages spoken in ancient Italy at a specific time. With the exception of Latin, our knowledge of them derives mainly from inscriptions – very few in the case of some languages, and for the most part impossible to date with precision. To a much lesser degree, we may learn from proper names and from a few individual words (glosses) preserved by classical writers. However, not only is this latter evidence chronologically ill-defined, but it also does not necessarily provide reliable information about *speech* communities. The map therefore must confine itself to illustrating the linguistic diversity of Italy and Sicily before Rome's dominance made Latin their common language.

Several of ancient Italy's languages – including Latin – belong to the linguistic group called Indo-European, which during antiquity was spoken in areas as far apart as Ireland and India. The group's languages share certain features usually held to point to a common origin in one not directly attested (termed proto-Indo-European). From it, through a process of differentiation, the historically attested Indo-European languages derive.

Even so, one language widespread in ancient Italy was almost certainly not Indo-European, namely that of Etruria, *Etruscan*, attested also in the north-east of the peninsula and in Campania. Over 10,000 texts in Etruscan survive, most of them short, comprising proper names and recurring formulae. These can be understood; by contrast, the few longer texts (legal and religious) are harder to interpret. Moreover, *Raetic* (in the Adige area to the north) shows considerable resemblances to Etruscan (and also to Lemnian, attested from the Aegean island of Lemnos), and may well also be non-Indo-European. The sparse evidence for *Ligurian* makes it impossible to establish whether or not it is Indo-European.

The other languages known from Italy all belong to the Indo-European group. *Celtic* was introduced there by settlers who established themselves in the north Italian plain and were called Galli by the Romans. From an area further north come inscriptions in what may also be a Celtic language, called *Lepontic*. Some inscriptions from eastern Sicily are in a language called *Sicel*.

In the northern Adriatic region, *Venetic* is found: this may perhaps belong to the Italic branch of Indo-European, as *Latin* and *Sabellic* certainly do. Latin was originally the language of the city of Rome and, with some dialectal differences, of the Latium region. Very similar to Latin is the language of some inscriptions from Falerii, north of Rome: known as *Faliscan*, it shows in addition some influence from Etruscan, its neighbour.

Sabellic (or Sabellian) languages are attested from Umbria to Bruttium, and may conveniently be classified into three broad divisions: (1) *Umbrian*, *Sabine*, *Marsian* and *Volscian* in the north; (2) *Oscan*, *Paelignian*, *Vestinian*, *Marrucinian* and *Hernician* in central and southern Italy; (3) *South Picene*, attested in Picenum and elsewhere, mainly around 600–400 BCE. Inscriptions in *Oscan* abound; these mostly postdate 400. Oscan came to be the dominant language of southern Italy before the Roman conquest, used by Bruttii, Campani, Lucani, Samnites and Sidicini. An important corpus of religious inscriptions from the city of Iguvium constitutes the chief evidence for *Umbrian*.

A language attested in the heel of Italy, *Messapic*, may have Illyrian connections across the Adriatic. In addition to these languages, *Greek* was spoken and written widely in Sicily and southern Italy. This latter region saw a period of stable bilingualism between Greek and Oscan for some three centuries until around 100 BCE. Thereafter Oscan was pushed out by Latin, a process completed by around 100 CE. By then, various contributory factors – contiguity, practicality and Latin's perceived prestige – ensured that Latin was the dominant language throughout peninsular Italy.

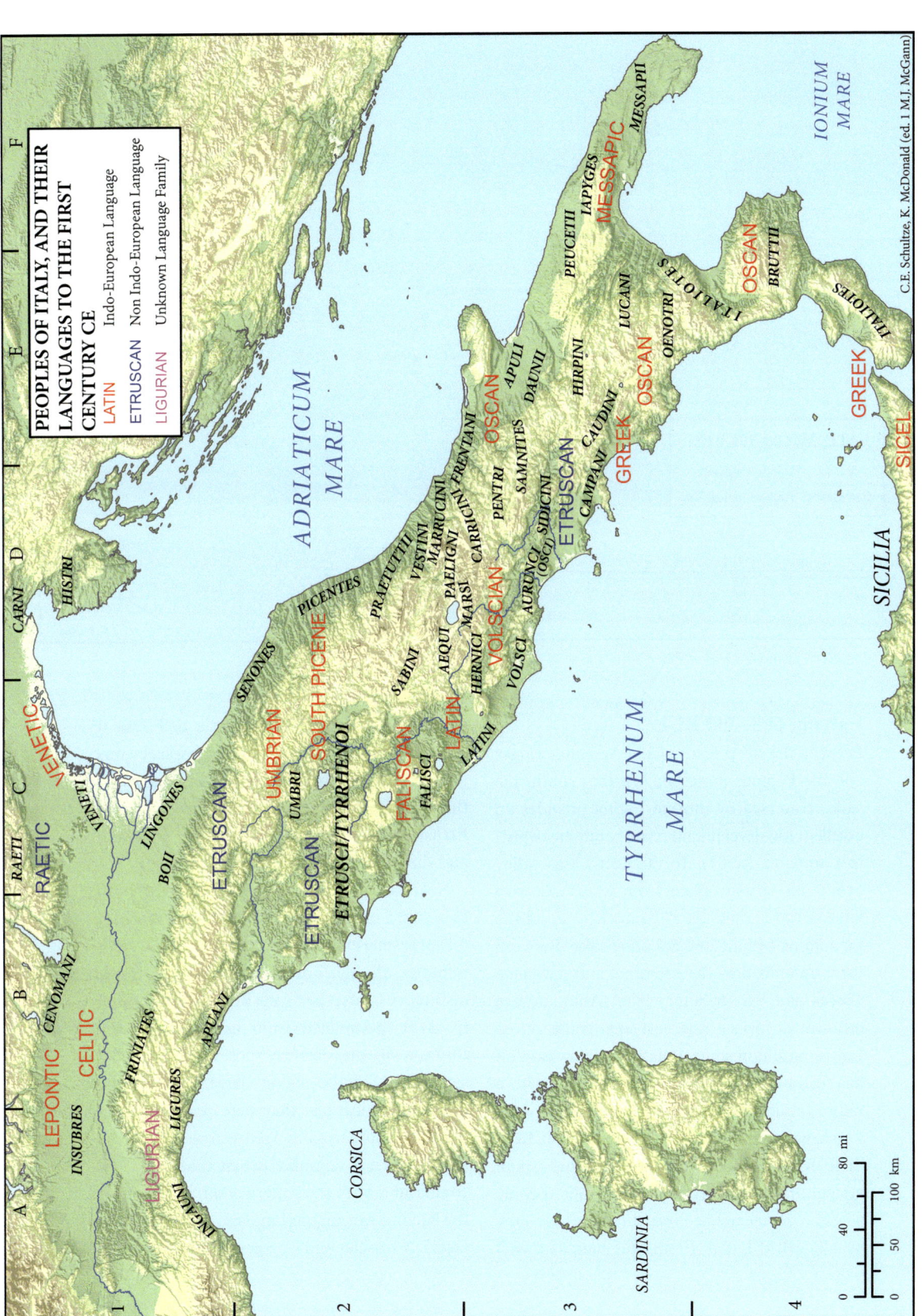

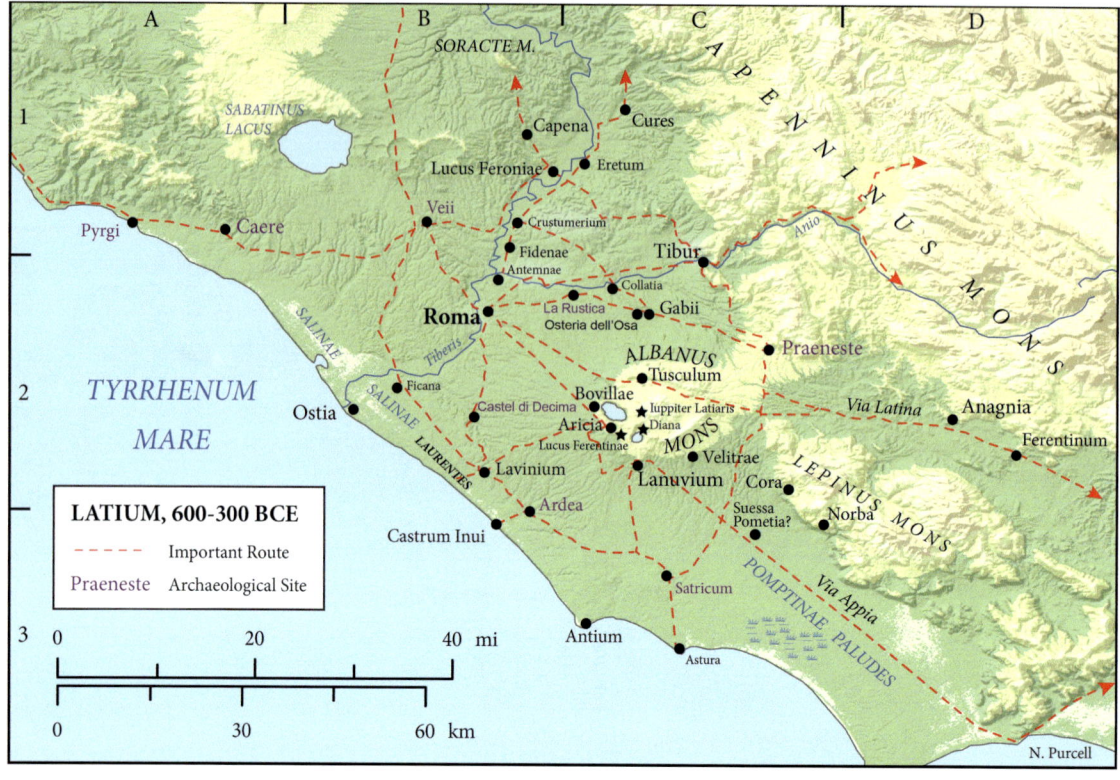

Latium, 600–300 BCE

Between the steep scarp of the Apennine ridges and the Lepinus mountains further south, the valley traversed by the Via Latina provides an excellent low-level inland route south-eastwards to Campania (p. 87). To the north, this valley opens into a wide plain from which rise two large volcanic uplands, Albanus Mons and the mountains beyond the Sabatine lake. Between these uplands flow the perennial and navigable Tiber, and its tributary the Anio, whose headwaters form a rare east-west route across Italy's mountain spine. Relatively heavy rainfall has furrowed the sides of the volcanoes with a radial pattern of deeply incised gullies, between which are many defensive sites. By 600 BCE these were occupied by the numerous small agricultural settlements of an Italic people whose copious archaeological remains are now usually called Latial. From sites such as Castel di Decima, Satricum and Osteria dell' Osa it has become clear that their urban society was prosperous and complex. It was distinct from, though in constant contact with, the Hellenized Etruscans to the north (p. 81) and in Campania, and the other Italic peoples.

Near the Tiber river – which served both as a route to the interior and as port of entry for overseas cultural influences – the terrain is flatter, though not very fertile. This is the distinctive landscape of the Roman 'Campagna' (p. 117), dominated from an early date by Rome, a city precociously successful among the settlements of the region, largely because of the communications that were possible along the river and across it. Well before 300, Rome had become a complex urban centre (p. 91), comparable with the larger communities across the Mediterranean, and in close touch with the Greek, Etruscan and Carthaginian worlds.

Campania

The map makes Campania's distinctive physical geography immediately apparent. The high limestone ridges of the Apennines and their outliers surround a series of low-lying plains. These, while easily accessible from one to another, are broken up by Mount Vesuvius and the volcanic hills of the Campi Phlegraei ('Burning Fields'), as well as by extensive areas of intractable marshland along the rivers. Otherwise the land is extremely fertile, making it not only the most highly prized arable terrain of ancient Italy, but also some of the most intensively exploited. Throughout antiquity, Capua (near modern Caserta) was one of Campania's most important settlements; its central position is clear. Other towns which controlled access to the region also grew dramatically: Teanum and Nuceria at mountain passes; Sinuessa, Cumae, Puteoli and Pompeii as port towns. Although the relations between the coast and interior were always close, the separation of the ports from the plains by hill or marsh assisted a certain cultural divergence. Despite the predominance of Etruscan and local cultures inland, the Greek colonies (*apoikiai*) of the coast kept their distinctive character; even widespread penetration by Oscan speakers at the end of the fifth century BCE did not end this situation.

Most notably, Puteoli and Neapolis – boosted by the tenacious links of the Campanian ports with the eastern Mediterranean – retained many Hellenic characteristics to the end of the Roman empire. This Hellenism, added to the advantages of wealth, populousness and great natural beauty, attracted the wealthy of Rome to such an extent that the Bay of Naples, and Baiae in particular, became a notorious playground of the elite. So too did Pompeii (p. 123), Herculaneum (p. 124) and Stabiae, three cities destroyed by Vesuvius in 79 CE. Meantime Puteoli remained one of Italy's most important ports. Eventually, as tectonic activity drowned the pleasure palaces and harbour works, and as draining of the Sebethus and Clanius marshes improved communications with the interior, Neapolis succeeded Puteoli as the chief city of the area. Modern Naples enjoys the same primacy.

Roman Expansion in Italy to 241 BCE

Sixth-century Rome was one among several rival city-states in Latium and Etruria. Tradition asserted that its annexation of neighbouring settlements began in the regal period (ended 509 BCE), and that by 495 Rome's citizens were enrolled in four urban and seventeen rural tribes (local areas of domicile). In 493, the Cassian Treaty strengthened Romans' ties of intermarriage and trade exchange with their Latin neighbours, and as a member of the so-called 'Latin League' Rome participated in campaigns against the Aequi and Volsci. Its territory was doubled by the conquest of Etruscan Veii in 396. Veii's land was allotted in 'viritane' grants to individual Roman citizens; these were enrolled in four new tribes in 387. Although the Gallic capture of Rome in 390 marked a setback, the next three decades saw successful Roman encroachment in Etruria and Latium, with two new tribes created in 358.

After winning the Latin War of 341–338 (against Latins, Campanians, Volscians and others), Rome dissolved the Latin League and devised new forms of association and control, ones not necessarily entailing annexation, settlement or even administration – for which Rome was not equipped. Certain existing communities were incorporated on terms that made their inhabitants *cives Romani optimo iure* (Roman citizens with full rights), completely equal to existing Roman citizens, enrolled in Roman tribes, and liable to military service and taxation. In less privileged communities, incorporated *sine suffragio* (without vote), individual citizens possessed the same rights in private law and were liable for military service, but could not vote in Roman elections. The precise gradations of privilege are unclear and changed over time. No doubt there was overlap between the rights and duties of communities without the vote, and those of political units whose relationship with Rome took another form.

The concept of allied states (*socii* or *foederati*) implies the making of a bilateral treaty (*foedus*) with Rome. Their duties and privileges varied greatly, but the chief requirement was to provide troops and pay them. However, when alliances were imposed by Rome after conquest – which normally entailed confiscation of territory – the provision of troops from a reduced economic base was onerous. Moreover, in some (perhaps many) instances, the terms of a community's subordination to Rome were not even recorded in a formal treaty, but stemmed simply from defeat and surrender. Allied and other associated communities were accordingly diverse in origin and social organization – Greek city-states, Italian towns, tribal peoples – as well as in how much independence they retained.

After 338, the last power to resist Roman control of Italy was the Samnites, whose tribes formed a loose confederation in the southern Apennines. Rome had recognized a Samnite sphere in a treaty of 354, and – despite hostilities in 343–341 – the Samnites were Rome's allies again by the time of the Latin War. However, Rome's continuing expansion, and especially the foundation of the colony Fregellae (328), provoked lengthy second and third Samnite wars (327–304, 298–290); 321 saw Rome's humiliating defeat at the Caudine Forks. Since the Samnites had Etruscan, Umbrian and Gallic allies, Rome was often fighting on two fronts. Strategically placed colonies established from around 312 to the early 290s aimed to split up the hostile peoples (see p. 92). Victory at Sentinum (295) gave Rome control over north-central Italy, and by 290 the defeated Samnites were forced into alliance, losing much territory. Between 280 and 272 the Tarentines, other south Italians, and Samnites together made a last unsuccessful stand against Rome with help from King Pyrrhus of Epirus.

Colonization and viritane grants continued meanwhile, together with the creation of new tribes; in 241 their total reached its final figure of thirty-five. The entire peninsula south of Ariminum was now Roman territory, or somehow subject to Rome.

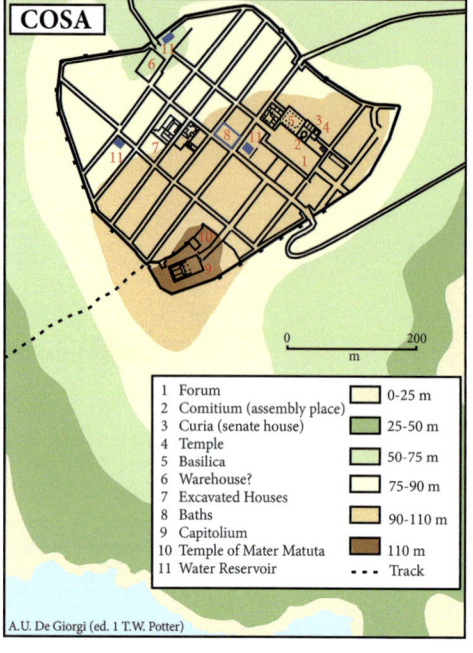

Cosa

The Latin colony of Cosa was founded in 273 BCE in the territory of the Etruscan city of Vulci. Strongly positioned on a limestone hill overlooking the Tyrrhenian Sea, it has been extensively excavated. The walls enclosed some 13 ha of undulating terrain which dictates the irregular shape of its defences. Fifteen towers faced the sea and four more the fertile hinterland; there were three gates. Inside, the streets divided the town into rectangular blocks. The site's unevenness ensured that the forum and associated buildings (which represent at least five main phases of construction) lay off centre, while the Capitolium (with Temple of Jupiter) was situated within its own precinct on an eminence to the southwest. Houses varying in size are attested in most blocks: excavation shows them to have consisted of rooms laid out around a central court. Water storage tanks are also a key feature. A port and fishery complex (not shown here) were developed to the southeast.

Rome by 300 BCE

Around 300 BCE, Rome was a rather scrappy city on defensible hills where paths from the Apennines to salt flats near Ostia crossed the Tiber river (see p. 86). This crossing was bridged – supposedly by a seventh-century king – with the Pons Sublicius. The 'Servian' Walls built in the sixth century enclosed 426 ha, not all inhabited, but more than the area of any other city on the Italian peninsula and an indication of Rome's preeminence by this time. The area included two large valleys rendered more serviceable by massive landfill and sewerage drains and channels: the Cloaca Maxima (not covered throughout until the early 100s) ran from the Subura district through the Forum Romanum, while another channel drained the long straight Circus Maximus valley. The Campus Martius and other land close to the Tiber flooded regularly. Rome's riverside location made water-borne commerce feasible, yet it also exposed the population to malaria and other communicable diseases.

This population – perhaps as many as 200,000 by 300 BCE – mostly lived on the higher hills. According to tradition, those living on the Esquiline and other eastern hills were of Sabine descent, while descendants of the Latin tribes inhabited the other hills. In fact, our scanty information suggests a fairly close-knit and undifferentiated community. The Forum Romanum housed communal political spaces and buildings: citizens assembled in the Comitium and the wider area of the Forum; senators deliberated in the Curia Hostilia (7); speakers harangued from the Rostra (14); some of Rome's enemies were jailed in the Carcer (11). In the Forum and around its edges were *tabernae* accommodating money exchange and commerce (15), also some of Rome's most venerable shrines and temples, such as the Temple of Vesta with Rome's eternal flame (19). The Forum Boarium was for commerce, and the Circus Maximus for entertainment, especially chariot races; both also held religious structures. Rome's citizen army was mustered and trained in the Campus Martius.

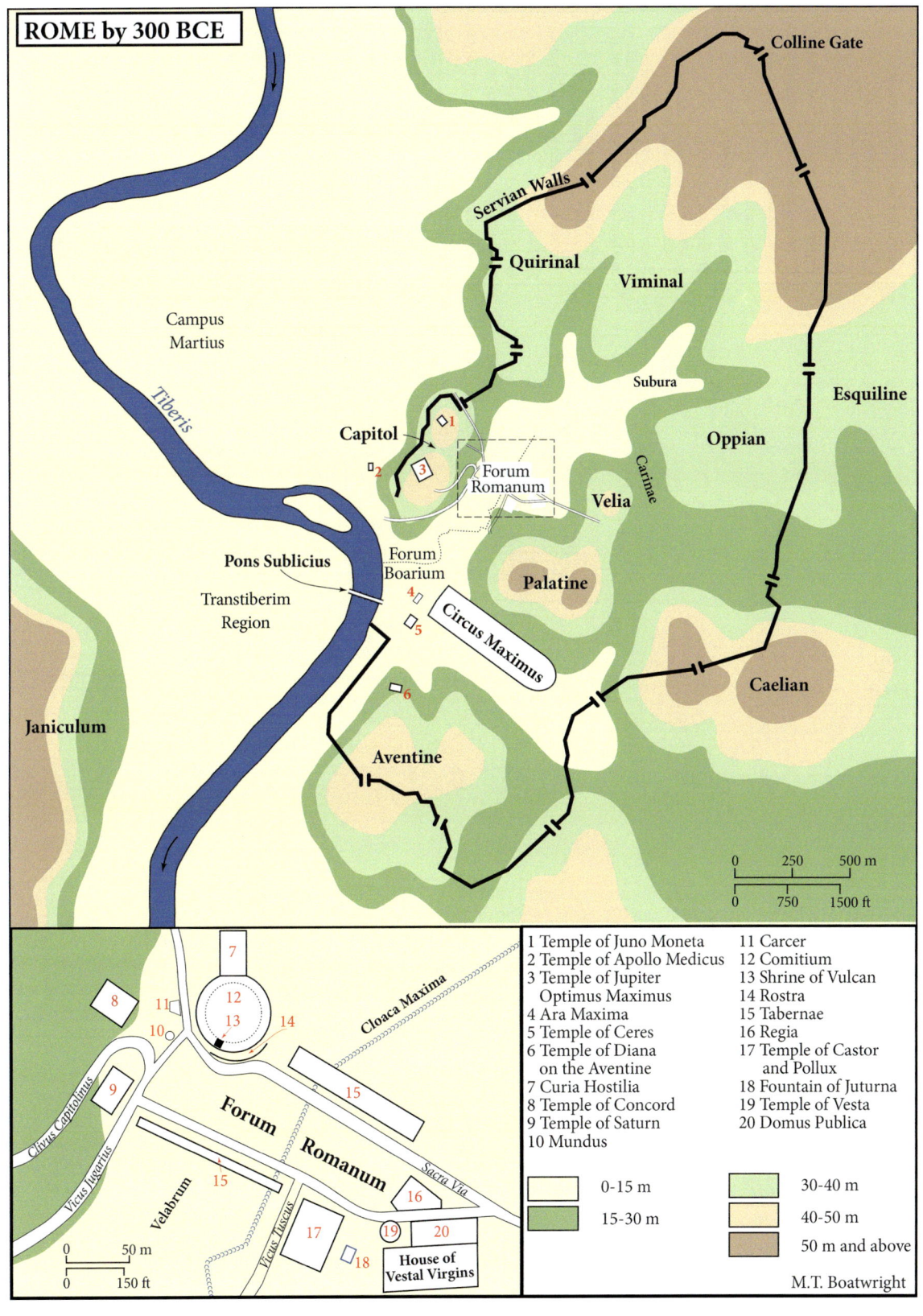

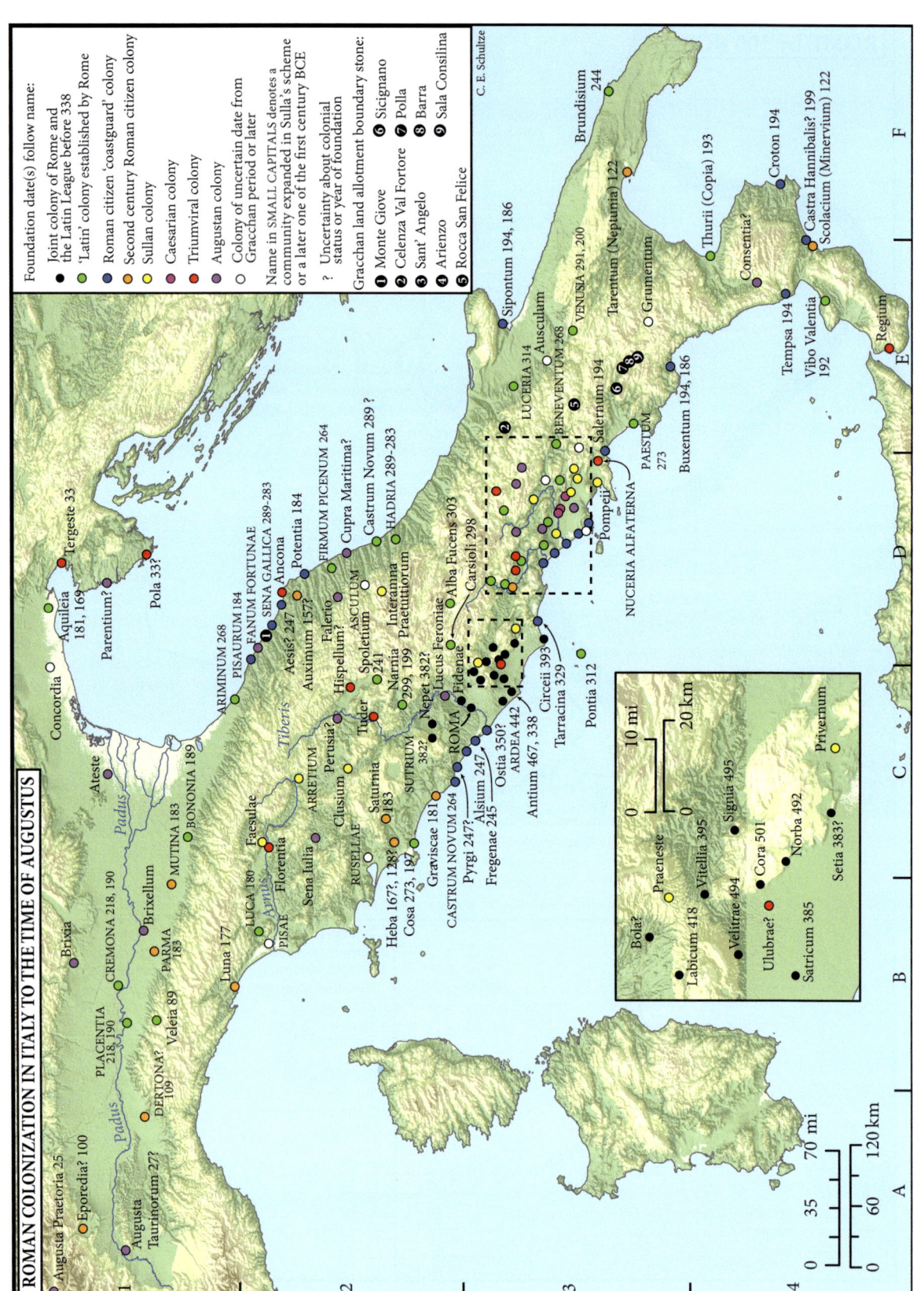

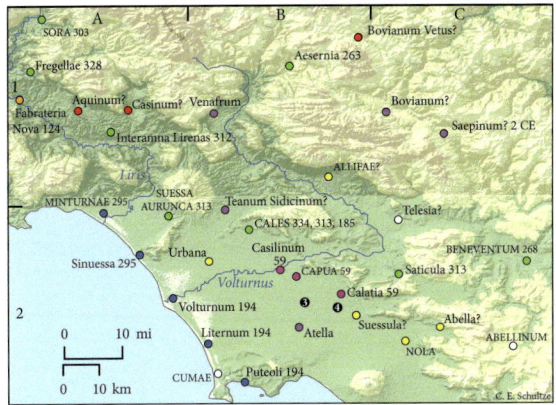

Roman Colonization in Italy to the Time of Augustus

Roman colonies during the Republic were civic communities, each with its own laws and magistrates, located on land often acquired by conquest. An urban centre with markets and administrative and religious buildings served a population living in the town itself and the *territorium* around; the citizens received land allotments and enjoyed rights over common land.

According to tradition, Rome's first colonies (*priscae Latinae coloniae*) in the fifth and fourth centuries BCE were jointly founded with fellow members of the Latin League (see p. 89) All the colonists held the citizenship of their new community, which had Latin status like any existing League member. In fact, these early foundations may have been less enduring, less centrist and formal in their organization, and more diverse in ethnic makeup than later accounts represent them.

Following the League's dissolution in 338, Rome continued to found colonies (the first at Cales in 334), which likewise possessed 'Latin' status although the settlers might not be Latin by origin. These colonies increasingly lay beyond the geographic area of Latium, and contributed to Rome's growing dominance over the peninsula (which was reinforced by road-building). Thus Fregellae (328) controlled a crossing of the Liris river and threatened Samnium; Venusia (291) split up the Hirpini and Lucani after the third Samnite war; Ariminum (268) provided a base for northward operations towards Cisalpine Gaul. Later, Cremona and Placentia (218) thrust far into Gallic territory. Smaller maritime *coloniae civium Romanorum*, whose members retained full Roman citizenship, functioned to guard the coast.

After the Second Punic War (see p. 94), Rome used land expropriated from communities that had defected to Hannibal to found larger 'agrarian' Roman and Latin colonies from the 190s to 170s. Their settlers received land allotments of varying sizes, creating an economic hierarchy; in all probability, some of the former indigenous population remained as an unprivileged class. Land deemed 'public' (*ager publicus*) might also be granted on a 'viritane' basis, whereby plots were assigned to individuals without the establishment of an urban centre.

Then for forty years, there were almost no new colonial foundations. In the Gracchan period (133–121) colonization and viritane allotment resumed, now on public land in Picenum, Campania, Apulia and Lucania. Grid-like centuriation markings, still visible in many areas of Italy, indicate land that was first surveyed and divided, but typically such centuriation is hard to date. Overseas colonies (rare at earlier periods) were also established. After the Social War (91–89), colonization practice changed. First-century programmes involved the dispatch of new settlers (especially veterans) to existing communities, but (particularly under Augustus) not all towns that received settlers were given the title of colonies. Where insufficient public land was available, private property was purchased or (in the civil wars) confiscated.

An idealizing and systematizing picture derived largely from sources of the first centuries BCE and CE presents colonies as miniature Romes or as bastions of empire (or both), protecting Roman territory and facilitating conquest. In reality, they varied greatly, fulfilling diverse functions: as manpower resources and garrisons; as sites of relocation for Rome's surplus poor population and veterans; and as centres of economic exchange and cultural interaction. Moreover, the extent and impact of colonizing settlement in the middle Republic are inseparable from other major factors – incorporation of communities, extension of citizenship, and network of alliances – contributing to the growth of Rome's ascendancy over Italy.

Punic Wars

Rome's struggle with Carthage for supremacy in the western Mediterranean was fought out in three Punic Wars between 264–241, 218–201 and 149–146 BCE. At the outset, Rome was the chief city of Italy, while Carthage, a wealthy maritime power, dominated western Mediterranean trade in metals and other commodities, and had dependencies and trading posts in Africa, Spain, Corsica, Sardinia and western Sicily. The initial encounter occurred in Sicily, when Rome agreed to help the Mamertini (Italic mercenaries who had taken over Messana) against the Carthaginians. Roman aims expanded to include expulsion of the Carthaginians from the entire island, and Rome necessarily became a naval power, building fleets and drawing heavily upon its citizen and allied manpower. Despite a failed expedition to Africa led by Regulus (256–255), and serious losses at sea, Rome persisted with this aim. For the Carthaginians, it was pointless to continue the struggle over Sicily indefinitely. Defeated off the Aegates Islands in 241, they made peace, agreeing to evacuate Sicily and pay an indemnity. In 238, Rome took advantage of Carthage's internal difficulties to force the cession of Sardinia too; subjugation of native populations there and in Corsica preoccupied the Romans for much of the following decade.

The Carthaginians meanwhile concentrated on extending their empire in Spain, until they dominated the south and east coastal area from the Baetis river to the Iberus (Ebro), and gained some control over the tribes of the hinterland. An excuse for Rome to intervene came in 218 when Hannibal captured Saguntum, a city friendly to Rome. He then marched swiftly to Italy via the Alps, hoping that rapid successes would win over Rome's Italian allies. He inflicted several severe defeats upon the Romans, culminating in that at Cannae (216, p. 97). Although much of southern Italy – previously allied to Rome – then joined Hannibal, he was nonetheless unable to undermine Rome's power base in central Italy, or to make effective use of his Gallic allies in the north.

Rome meanwhile avoided major military confrontations – the so-called 'Fabian' strategy, named after the general Fabius Cunctator. Moreover, Roman determination to remain engaged in Spain required Carthage to divert resources there, so that Hannibal never received reinforcements which might have enabled him to force a decisive battle. A Punic-Macedonian alliance in 215 initiated conflict in Macedon which Rome fought by proxy, using Greek allies. The turning point came in 211 with Rome's recapture of Capua and Syracuse. It gradually became clear that Hannibal could not in the long term retain his gains in Italy. Hasdrubal's attempt to reinforce him from Spain met with defeat at the Metaurus river (207). In 203, Hannibal finally left Italy once Scipio Africanus (who had overcome the Carthaginians in Spain between 210 and 206) began operations in Africa itself. In 202, he defeated Hannibal at Zama (p. 97). Peace terms included Punic evacuation of Spain, payment of a large indemnity, and rewards for Rome's African ally, Massinissa of Numidia.

Over the next fifty years, Carthage continued to prosper, though its scope for territorial expansion was severely restricted. In Africa, it had secure tenure only of the land within the 'Phoenician Trenches,' whose exact position is unknown. Not only was territory beyond disputed with Massinissa, but Rome also tacitly encouraged him to encroach on important Punic possessions such as the Emporia district off the Syrtis Minor. In 149, seizing the chance offered by the Carthaginians' voluntary surrender of Utica during hostilities with Massinissa, Rome declared war. The fighting occurred at Carthage and in its hinterland. Punic resistance was stiff. Only in 146, when the city had been sealed off by walls and ditches, and its harbour by a mole, did it fall to Scipio Aemilianus. It was then totally destroyed.

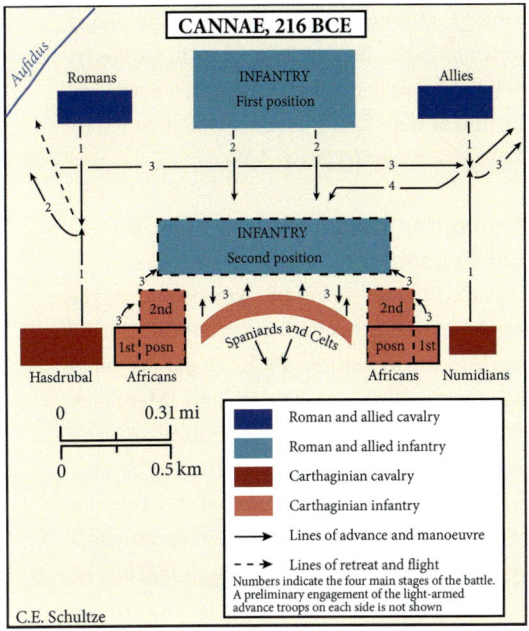
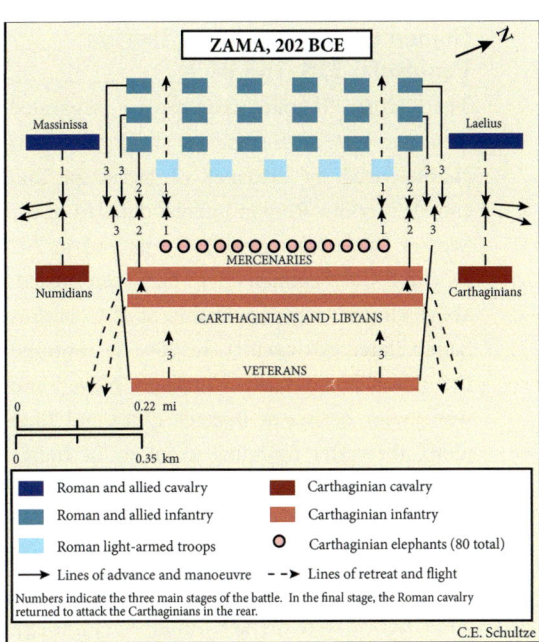

Cannae, 216 BCE

This stunning victory for Hannibal occurred on 2 August 216 BCE. The terrain, on the right bank of the Aufidus river, is fairly smooth and slopes seawards. Roman and allied forces were 6,000 cavalry, 55,000 infantry and 15,000 light-armed troops; corresponding Punic numbers were approximately 10,000, 32,000 and 8,000. After preliminary skirmishing by light-armed troops, the cavalry forces met (stage 1). Hasdrubal on the Punic left wing routed the Roman cavalry facing him (2), then crossed behind the Roman infantry to help against the Italian allied cavalry (3). Hannibal deployed his infantry as a convex crescent; the Roman troops met and pushed back its foremost ranks, but lost formation as they advanced. Meanwhile Hannibal's Africans, stationed left and right, turned to face the Roman flanks, attacking from either side as his Spaniards and Celts fell back (3). The Romans could not redeploy, and suffered further pressure from the regrouped Spaniards and Celts as well as from Hasdrubal's cavalry attacking from behind (4).

Zama, 202 BCE

This decisive battle was fought in autumn 202, probably near Sicca, although Naraggara and Zama Regia have been suggested. The Romans under Scipio Africanus had 23,000 infantry and 6,000 cavalry, while Hannibal had at least 36,000 infantry and 4,000 cavalry. Initially, Scipio positioned light-armed troops to face the charge of Carthaginian elephants (stage 1). He left retreat routes by arranging the Roman infantry maniples in rows with gaps rather than in the usual chessboard formation. Meanwhile, when the cavalry on each wing engaged (1), the Carthaginians were pursued off the field. Then, the front line of Roman infantry successfully attacked Hannibal's first two lines (2), which retreated to the flanks with heavy losses. While the Roman front line closed up, Scipio brought in his second and third lines, which engaged Hannibal's third-line veterans, hitherto kept in reserve (3). Finally, the Roman cavalry returned from pursuit, and from the rear massacred the Carthaginians. Roman losses were relatively light.

Roman Campaigns in the Iberian Peninsula, 218–133 BCE

The large Iberian peninsula, separated from the rest of Europe by the Pyrenees, is characterized by extremes of landscape and climate. Serious Roman interest dates from the Second Punic War (p. 94). By its end in 202 BCE the Carthaginians here had been ousted, above all due to the leadership of P. Cornelius Scipio (later 'Africanus'). In 209, he captured the main Punic base, Carthago Nova, and won major battles at Baecula (208) and Ilipa (206), thereafter founding a colony at Italica near the latter. Romans proceeded to occupy the peninsula's most productive areas: its east coast, and the valleys of the Baetis and lower Ebro rivers. Two provinces, Hispania Citerior and Ulterior, were marked out in 197, although regular exploitation of their populations only began during the 170s. Many new settlements gradually came to be established – at Carteia, Corduba, Gracurris, Tarraco, Valentia and elsewhere.

Until the 130s, Rome's need to protect and stabilize its conquered territory, together with greed for the peninsula's rich variety of natural resources (minerals especially), encouraged persistent efforts at expansion; these were further fuelled by governors' lust for loot and glory. Bitter conflicts with native peoples ensued, culminating in two major struggles from 155: one against an alliance led by the Lusitanian Viriathus until bribery secured his assassination (139), the other against the Celtiberians, whose stronghold Numantia held out until 133 (p. 100). The seemingly endless and unrewarding campaigns alienated Roman conscripts, whose discontent became a powerful trigger for the social and political changes that would eventually undermine the Republic. After 133, with Rome now controlling around two-thirds of the peninsula, conflict was much reduced, although Roman civil wars involving Sertorius in the 70s and Pompeians in the 40s (p. 104) did prove damaging. The rugged north and northwest were finally subdued and annexed by Augustus in the 20s (see p. 138).

Numantia: Roman Siege (133 BCE) and Region

The Celtiberian town of Numantia, in the territory of the Arevaci, was founded during the late third century BCE. It stands on a hill overlooking the Duero and Merdench rivers. Frequently attacked during Rome's second-century Iberian campaigns, it became a notorious focus of Roman efforts between 153 and 133, when five successive attempts by Roman consuls to capture it all failed. The headquarters for their sieges was 7 km to the west at Renieblas, where large Roman camps came to be established. Eventually, in 133, Scipio Aemilianus was able to take Numantia and destroy it after an eight-month siege. He ringed the town with fortified camps connected by a ditch, palisade and stone wall behind them, as described by Appian (*Iberian Wars* 90–93). Some sections of their courses can now only be conjectured, but the entire circuit measures about 9.5 km. After its destruction by Scipio, Numantia was soon rebuilt; it expanded and continued to thrive until the fourth century CE. Scipio's siege-works were investigated by the German archaeologist Adolf Schulten between 1905 and 1912. Thereafter, until 1931, he excavated at Renieblas, where the sequence and dating of the five overlapping Roman camps he identified remain controversial. However, recent excavations reinforce his opinion that Camp III – with a layout that can be related to Polybius' description (Book 6) of the Roman army organized by maniples – was in use during the first half of the second century.

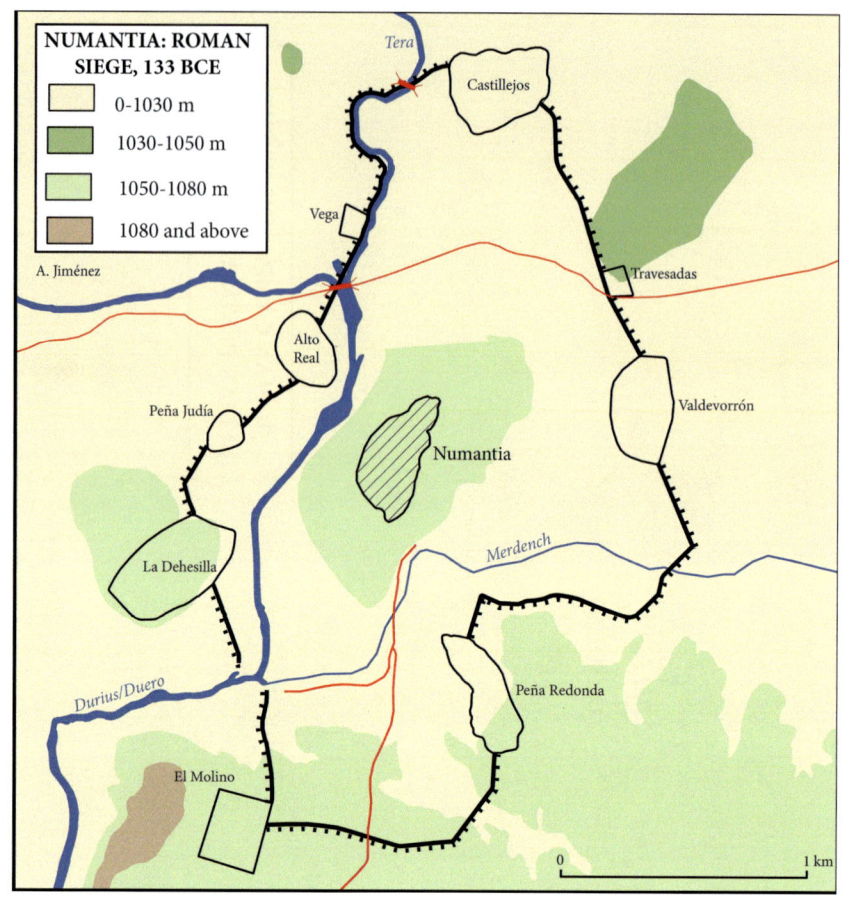

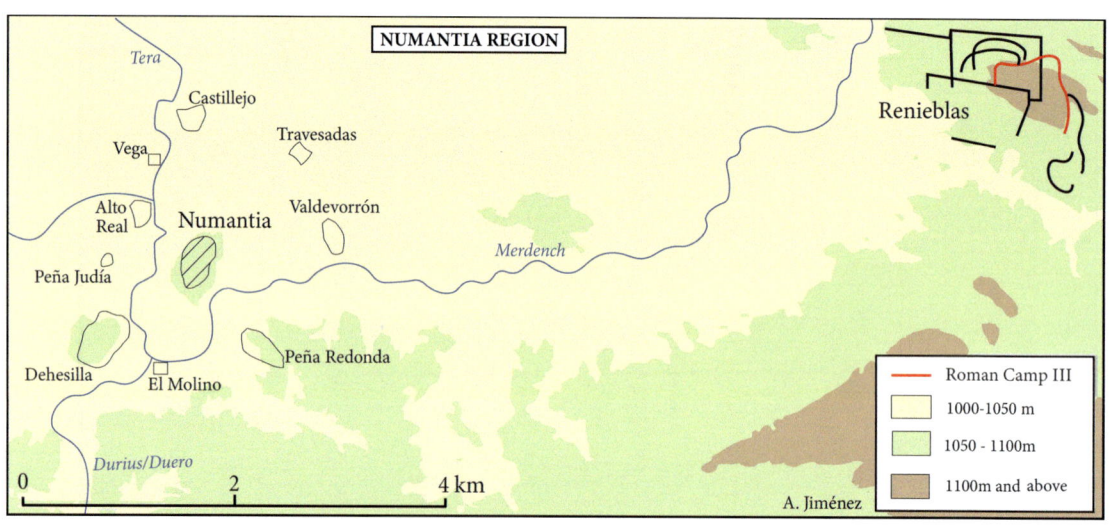

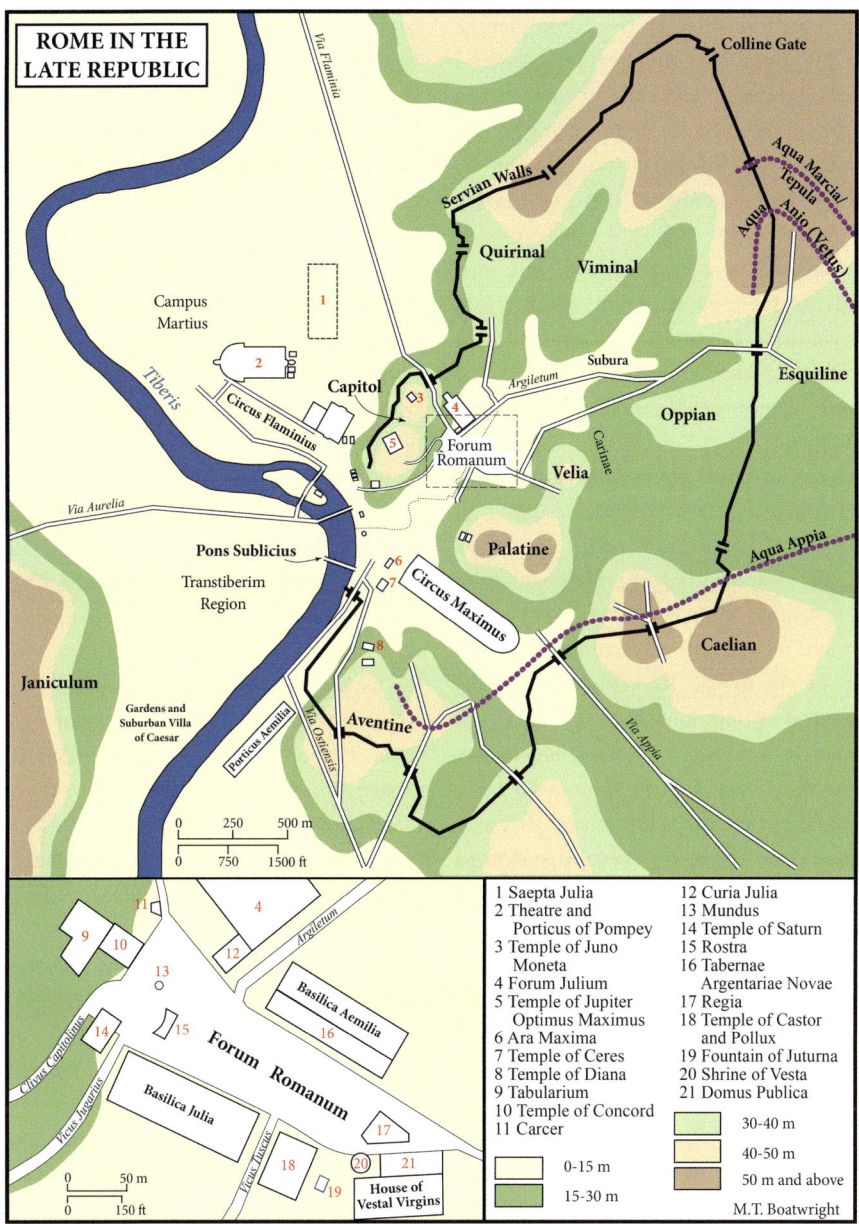

Rome in the Late Republic

By the time of Julius Caesar's victories in the civil war of 49–45 BCE (p. 104), Rome had grown mightily in complexity and population (estimated as some 600,000). Its extent was no longer constrained by the Servian Walls, which had not been maintained and were even breached during civil strife in 82. Major roads – notably the Via Flaminia going north, Appia southeast and Aurelia west – encouraged trade and development as well as facilitating troop movements. They were also the sites for many roadside burials and memorials.

Rome's victorious domination of the Mediterranean world acted to transform the city and make it a magnet for migrants. From the late second century, Roman citizens here were offered monthly grain rations, first at a reduced price and later gratis; consequently, storage buildings like the Porticus Aemilia were constructed, and the Transtiberim region was developed for crews working the grain barges. Politicians curried favour by sponsoring two aqueducts – Aqua Marcia (140s), Aqua Tepula (120s) – that provided fresh water and construction jobs, and also returned to the people some spoils from Rome's victories. Triumphant generals funded numerous temples as thank-offerings to the gods and memorials of their exploits and family names.

Politicking increased in intensity as the gains from successful warfare swelled, resulting in the erection of some monuments – such as Caesar's Basilica Julia (inset) and Saepta Julia (1), where soldiers could be mustered and voters tallied – and the effacement of others. Caesar's repaving of the Forum Romanum obliterated the ancestral Comitium and rendered the Rostra mostly decorative (15); the senate house, rebuilt as the Curia Julia (12), became more imposing. These and other initiatives by Caesar – including a new Forum (4) – broadcast Rome's claims to be a world city, as had the earlier Theatre and Porticus of Pompey (2), where Caesar was assassinated. Even so, Rome during this period was also characterized by extreme wealth disparities, in-fighting among the elite, disorder, jerry-building and fires.

Rome's Empire around 60 BCE

For Rome, acquisition of an empire was a slow, haphazard process, and involvement in its administration always remained limited. Communities continued to manage their local affairs. Not until the 220s BCE were Rome's first gains – Sicily and Sardinia/Corsica – organized, and arrangements made for each to become the regular, annual *provincia* (or 'sphere of action') of a praetor. Two more such praetorships were created for 'Further' (Ulterior) and 'Nearer' (Citerior) Spain in 197. But none was added for Macedonia (whose governor also oversaw Achaea or southern Greece), or for Africa, both annexed in 146, or for Asia, organized in the 120s, or for Gallia Transalpina, to which a governor was being sent regularly by 100. It was therefore necessary for promagistrates to fill these posts, a practice that became the norm for all provincial governorships from the late second century. *Provincia* now comes to have the specific connotation of an administered territory beyond Italy. A promagistrate was regularly assigned to govern Gallia Cisalpina from around 80; usually an ex-consul was chosen, perhaps to avoid ex-praetors abusing the unique opportunity this province offered to solicit votes in future consular elections from its many communities awarded Roman citizenship by the Lex Pompeia (89). Cyrene and Crete, annexed respectively in 74 and 67, were governed as a single province. During the 60s, Pompey's eastern conquests added vast areas: Bithynia/Pontus, Cilicia, Syria.

To the end of the Republic, Rome's hold over most provinces was patchy, and their frontiers were generally ill-defined. In the case of Illyricum Rome even laid claim to the coastal strip, yet seldom sent a governor. In many regions definition of frontiers had little significance when these adjoined the territories of 'client kings,' local rulers recognized by Rome and willing to be loyal allies in return for the benefits of freedom and protection. The most important such friendly states during the late Republic (in Africa and Asia Minor) are marked.

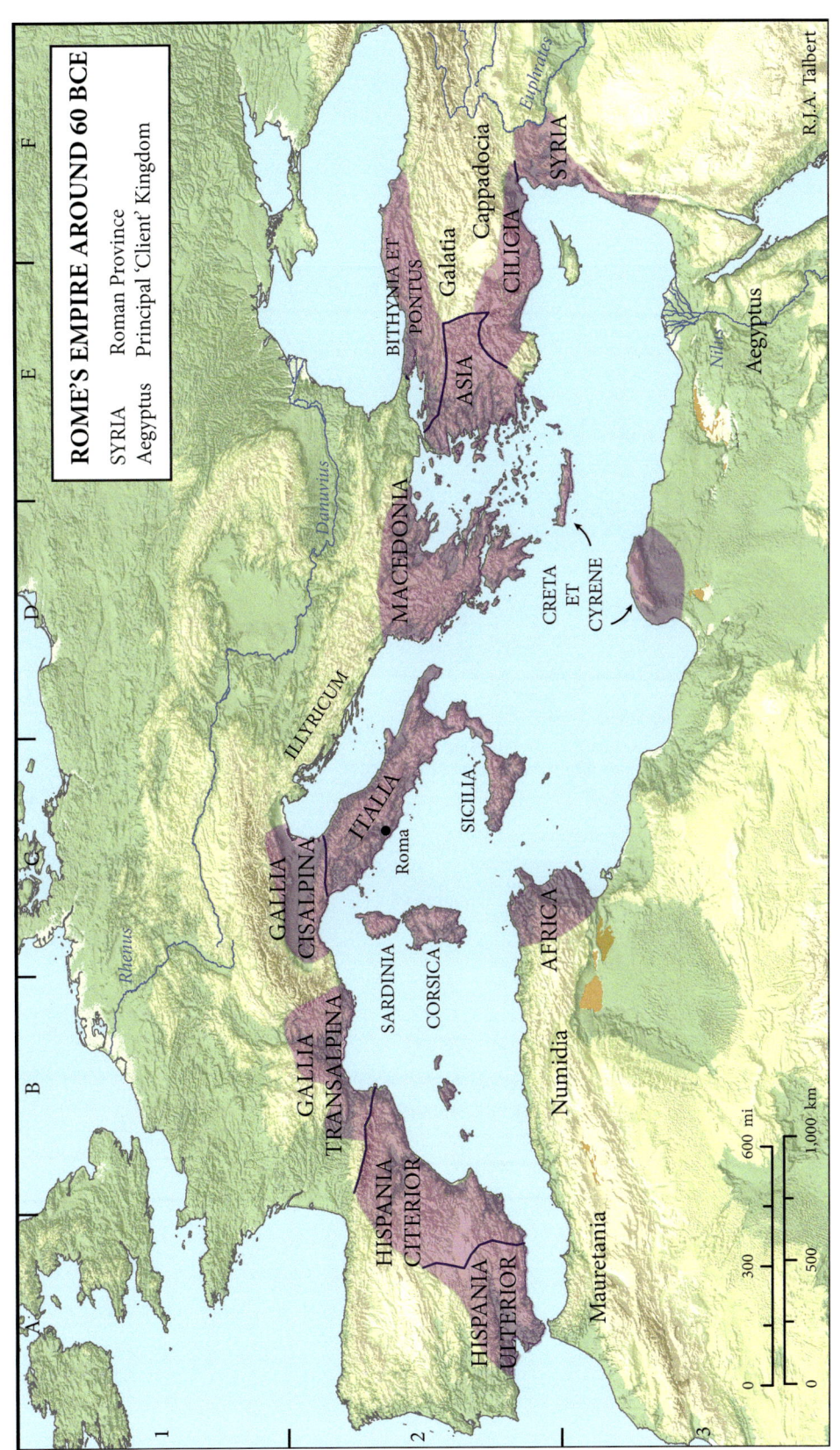

Roman Campaigns, 58–30 BCE

During the 50s BCE Rome's wars in the West and East ended very differently. Julius Caesar's initial aim in 58 was to prevent migration by the Helvetii, but this effort induced him to curb peoples further north on both sides of the Rhine (Rhenus) river. Eventually – after investigating the prospects for an invasion of Britain (Britannia) in 55 and 54 – he subjugated Gaul (Gallia) in its entirety by 51, having overcome his most formidable opponent Vercingetorix (of the Arverni) at Alesia in 52. Meanwhile in the East Crassus' campaign across the Euphrates river from Syria against the Parthians resulted in his catastrophic defeat at Carrhae in 53.

After Caesar precipitated civil war by crossing the Rubicon river into Italy (January 49), it took him five years of intermittent campaigning to impose his authority. He gained Italy in only two months, but Pompey escaped across the Adriatic with an army. Lacking a fleet, Caesar delayed pursuit, and turned to Spain (administered by Pompey's legates) where he overcame superior forces at Ilerda, and then marched south to Corduba which surrendered. Massilia did likewise after a five-month blockade.

In 48, Caesar crossed to Epirus. After a blockade of Pompey's army at Dyrrachium failed, Caesar made for Thessaly and routed superior forces at Pharsalus. Pompey fled to Egypt, only to be assassinated on arrival. Caesar followed, but roused such hostility that he was besieged in Alexandria during winter 48/47, and only relieved in the spring, when Ptolemy XIII was defeated and Cleopatra (now Caesar's mistress) made effective ruler. Caesar then dashed to crush the threat to Asia Minor posed by Pharnaces of Bosphorus, which he did at Zela in a five-day campaign.

After some months in Italy, Caesar returned to campaigning in late 47, because Pompeian forces in Africa – supported by Numidia's King Juba – had grown alarmingly strong. Caesar risked a winter campaign and, after early difficulties at Ruspina, achieved victory within four months. The final battle, at Thapsus, became a massacre. Even so, Pompey's sons regrouped their forces in Spain, where Caesar faced them in March 45. This battle at Munda was his toughest, but its outcome proved decisive; Pompeian casualties were heavy, and of the leaders only Sextus Pompeius survived.

After Caesar's assassination (44) civil war resumed, now between his supporters and his assassins. In 43 heavy fighting occurred in Cisalpine Gaul. Here the governor, Decimus Brutus, was besieged in Mutina by Antony, who was then defeated by forces of both consuls and Octavian at Forum Gallorum and Bononia. However, Antony, Octavian and Lepidus formed a (second) Triumvirate. Meanwhile, the assassins Brutus and Cassius consolidated their hold on the East, but were defeated by Antony and Octavian at Philippi (October 42). Thereafter Octavian in Italy took Perusia by siege during unrest in winter 41/40. Elimination of Sextus Pompeius was his next challenge. Only when his fleet was strengthened by Agrippa, did he eventually defeat Sextus at Naulochos in 36. His subsequent campaigns in Illyricum (35–33) aimed to safeguard northeast Italy.

In the East Antony, who joined himself to Cleopatra, faced two crises. An Illyrian people, the Parthini, was invading Macedonia, while the Parthians were overrunning Syria and threatening Asia Minor. During 39, Antony's lieutenants repulsed all these incursions. But his own retaliatory campaign through Armenia into Parthia in 36 proved disastrous. He failed to capture Phraaspa, capital of Media Atropatene, and could not shake off Parthian harassment. An invasion confined to Armenia in 34 was more successful.

Deteriorating relations between Octavian and Antony led to war in 31. Antony advanced to Greece, where he was defeated on land and sea at Actium (p. 107). Having fled back to Egypt, he was pursued there by Octavian in 30. Antony and Cleopatra committed suicide, leaving Octavian finally without rivals.

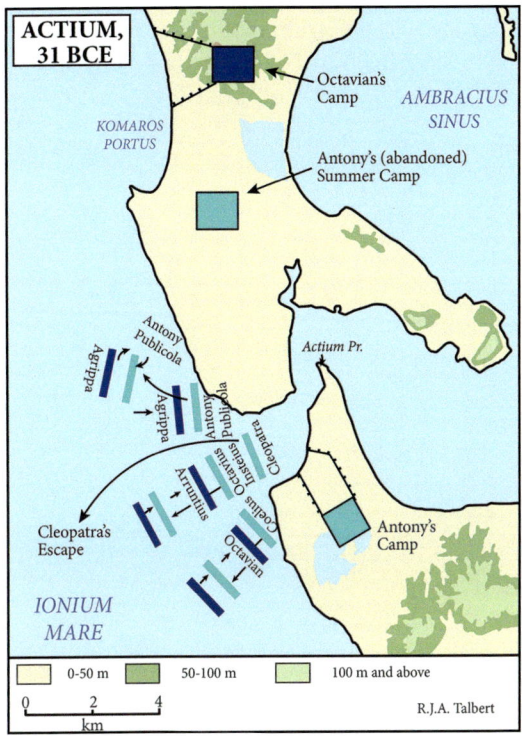

Actium, 31 BCE

Although accounts differ considerably, the battle's outline can be recovered. Fought on the afternoon of September 2nd, it centred around the Straits of Actium, the entrance to the Ambracian Gulf. Here the fleet and army of Antony and Cleopatra were trapped by Octavian's fleet under Agrippa's command. Pressured by disease, hunger and desertions, Antony resolved to break out by sea, not land, with 200 (?) warships in three divisions, conveying 20,000 marines and 2,000 archers. Agrippa with similar support deployed 250 (?) ships, albeit smaller ones, marshalled likewise. Their damaging nimbleness evidently convinced Cleopatra, after only about two hours, that Antony's initiative would fail. By now Agrippa, controlling his left division, had moved it northwards to outflank the division opposite under Antony and Publicola, which in fact also veered north. Cleopatra with her sixty ships (held in the rear) seized the chance to flee through the gap created; Antony followed. Fighting continued indecisively till nightfall, when his fleet, and later army, surrendered.

Augusta Praetoria (Aosta)

Augusta Praetoria was founded in 25 BCE as a colony for 3,000 ex-Praetorian Guardsmen to hold; it has been occupied ever since (today named Aosta). Its walls, over 10 m high, were heavily buttressed along their inner face, an exceptional feature. With twenty square towers and four gates, they remain largely intact, enclosing a rectangle of 724 × 572 m, divided into 16 blocks – a plan still preserved in the town's layout. The (probable) Capitolium was within a north block, possibly with the forum, although it may have been more central. A covered theatre has been found, also an amphitheatre – unusually – inside the walls. Traces of baths remain, but few of housing. The street from East gate to West is on Rome's strategic route from Italy (to the southeast) through the Alps. Hereafter it splits, continuing north by the Great St. Bernard Pass, also west by the Little St. Bernard to reach Lugdunum in Gaul (p. 147).

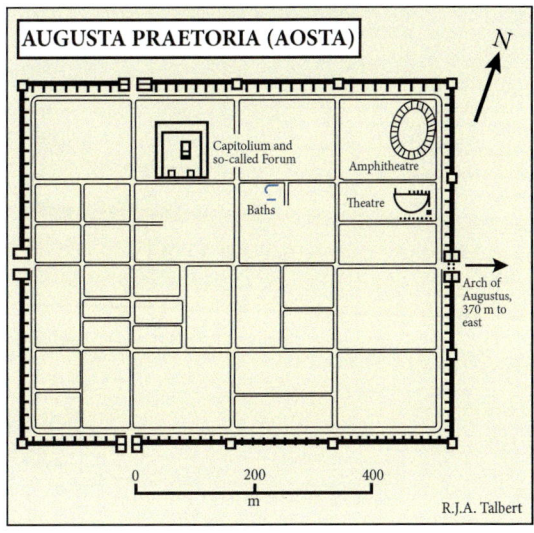

Italy

The Augustan age witnessed the integration of the former Gallia Cisalpina into Roman Italy both juridically and culturally. Earlier, only those regions west of the Apennine watershed or south of the Rubicon river enjoyed the benefits of belonging to Italia – namely, after the Social War (90–89 BCE), Roman citizenship for the local freeborn population, and exemption from direct tax on land (*tributum soli*) for landowners. In the northwest, the Ligurian and Cottian Alps were secured by colonies at Augusta Praetoria (p. 107), Augusta Taurinorum and Augusta Bagiennorum. Similarly, to the east, colonies at Iulia Concordia, Pola, Emona and (a little later) Parentium protected Venetia and Histria. By 6 BCE, after ten years of campaigning, Augustus was able to celebrate the subjugation of forty-five mountain tribes, stretching around the arc of the Alps from the head of the Adriatic to the Tyrrhenian Sea, where Italy's western threshold was marked dramatically by the Tropaeum Augusti monument. By the end of the republican period, the peninsula's highway network was effectively complete. The most frequented overland route from Rome to northern Italy remained the Via Flaminia and Via Aemilia. Via Postumia provided east-west communication across the Po valley, and Via Appia connected Rome to Brundisium, gateway to the eastern provinces. New roads traversing the now pacified Alps were opened up under the Julio-Claudian emperors, connecting the increasingly important cities of Mediolanum, Placentia and Aquileia to the armies based on the Rhine and Danube frontiers. Later, most notably, Trajan funded a new alternative route from Beneventum to Brundisium via Canusium.

The transition from republic to empire transformed the relationship between the Italian population and the Roman state in various ways. After traumatic expropriations by the Triumvirs in the 40s and 30s BCE, and a phase of purchasing land for demobilized soldiers (following the move in 13 to a fully professionalized soldiery receiving cash rewards on retirement), veteran settlement in Italy all but ceased. Its communities were no longer a major recruiting ground for the rank and file of the legions; these forces were now stationed permanently outside Italy. However, the prestigious praetorian and urban cohorts based in Rome did recruit principally from the municipalities of Italy, and the local landowning elite continued to provide the majority of officers. Faltering prosperity in small towns may partly explain Trajan's decision to invest some of his gains from the conquest of Dacia in subsistence allowances for children in selected communities (p. 127). Outside Rome, until around 200 CE when Septimius Severus stationed his new legion II Parthica nearby to the south at Albanum (p. 117, C2), Italy's military garrison was little more than the two imperial fleets; these were based at Ravenna and Misenum, and manned by crews recruited from provincials.

The relative under-policing of the peninsula partly explains the success enjoyed by the notorious brigand Bulla Felix in the south during the early 200s. Not assigned as a province and therefore lacking governors, the peninsula was divided by Augustus into eleven regions for the collection of indirect taxes (on, for example, inheritances and manumissions of slaves) by imperial procurators. Senators served as *curatores* for maintaining sections of the road network. For a time, *iuridici* were appointed to hear cases beyond the competence of municipal courts, although eventually higher jurisdiction came to be divided between the prefect of the city of Rome up to the 100th milestone from it, and the praetorian prefects beyond. Although Italy became a theatre of civil war in the third century, it remained largely insulated from barbarian incursions until a transalpine raid by the Iuthungi (p. 149, C3) grabbed thousands of captives in 260.

Corsica

Surviving ancient texts give this rugged island minimal attention; it was reputed to be a dismal place with wild inhabitants. Greeks from Phocaea made an ill-fated attempt to found a colony at Alalia around 565 BCE, but less than thirty years later Etruscans came to dominate the island. Around the same time, they are said to have founded Nikaia, perhaps on the site of Mariana (see below). Later, part of Corsica came under the control of the Carthaginians, whom Rome ousted in 238; but the new province Sardinia et Corsica was not formally established until 227. Even then, the mountainous interior remained largely unaffected by Roman authority.

Only on the east coast are there productive plains, and it was here alone that urbanization took root. Early in the first century BCE, Roman colonies were founded by Marius at Mariana and by Sulla at Aleria (Greek Alalia). Standard buildings of a Roman provincial city have been excavated at both, although those at Mariana (now including a temple of Mithras) only date to the second century CE or later. No other settlement is mentioned by Pliny the Elder – nor the garrison at Praesidium in the interior – and only a single road (along the east coast) is attested. A detachment of Rome's Misenum fleet was stationed in the sheltered lagoon of Artemidos Limen. Ptolemy – writing around 150 CE – lists (all in Greek) numerous tribal names and two dozen other places, no doubt indigenous hilltop settlements (*oppida*) rather than fully-fledged Roman towns. One of the very few of these so far excavated, at Lourinon, reveals strong stone fortifications and simple rectangular houses.

Honey, milk, meat and red mullet are mentioned among Corsica's products, but its main export was probably timber, with fir, pine and box especially prized for their broad girth. Grey granite was quarried on islets off the south-east coast.

Sicily (Roman)

Sicily became the first of Rome's provinces at the end of the First Punic War (241 BCE). By then, certain celebrated Greek cities – notably Gela, Himera, Selinous (see p. 43) – were extinct, as were some hill towns of the interior. Other such towns were peacefully abandoned during the late third century, once Roman control made defensive capability a secondary concern in the choice of site. These changed circumstances prompted instead a pattern of more dispersed settlement on farms as well as in villages and new market centres. The latter sprang up in the valleys and along the new Roman roads. Archaeology has shown that meantime places such as Megara Hyblaia, Camarina, Morgantina, Heraclea Minoa and Ietas (all mentioned by Cicero or Pliny the Elder) either became extinct between 50 BCE and 50 CE, or dwindled to the size of hamlets. Helorus, Segesta, Soluntum and others barely outlasted the second century CE. However, Augustus founded six Roman colonies. Until his time (late first century BCE), the number of Romans resident in the island had remained small.

Sicily's economic importance stemmed mainly from its production of grain. In addition, wines were widely exported, as were horses, timber, alum and sulphur. The countryside continued to flourish, especially so in the fourth and fifth centuries, according to recent field surveys; this was when the luxury villas at Piazza Armerina and elsewhere were built. Although under Roman rule Latin became the language of government, that of everyday communication undoubtedly remained Greek, and the island retained a distinctly Greek character.

Sardinia

The best anchorages along the island's western and southern coasts were colonized by Phoenicians in the eighth and seventh centuries BCE. These settlements, bolstered by trade and each controlling a fertile hinterland, flourished under Carthaginian control. Relations with the Nuraghic peoples of the interior were often hostile; Carthaginians' spheres of influence never extended far inland. They were ousted by Rome in 238, but further campaigns were necessary before the new province Sardinia et Corsica was formally established in 227. As in Corsica (p. 108), Sardinia's mountainous interior remained largely untamed. Roman forces had to quell repeated native revolts until the end of the second century; even then, brigandage was only suppressed in the first century CE.

Sardinian culture during the last two centuries BCE shows the continuing domination of Punic traditions, with Carthaginian deities still being worshipped, magistrates with mainly Punic names, and many inscriptions still written in Punic. Significant change only came with Augustus: Turris Libisonis was made a Roman *colonia*, and Caralis a *municipium* (with Latin rights). Then Uselis was soon made a *colonia*, and later at least Cornus, Nora and Sulcis *municipia*. Even so, Punic cultural influence long persisted in the coastal cities. The interior stayed unsettled for the first two centuries CE, hence the presence of auxiliary garrisons there (although remains of forts are missing).

Much grain was grown for export, while lead and silver mines in the Metalla district were notably productive. Molaria takes its name from exploitation of the local red-brown lava to make mills which were exported to North Africa and western Sicily. Some pink granite extracted from quarries in the far north was exported to Sicily, Rome and Carthage.

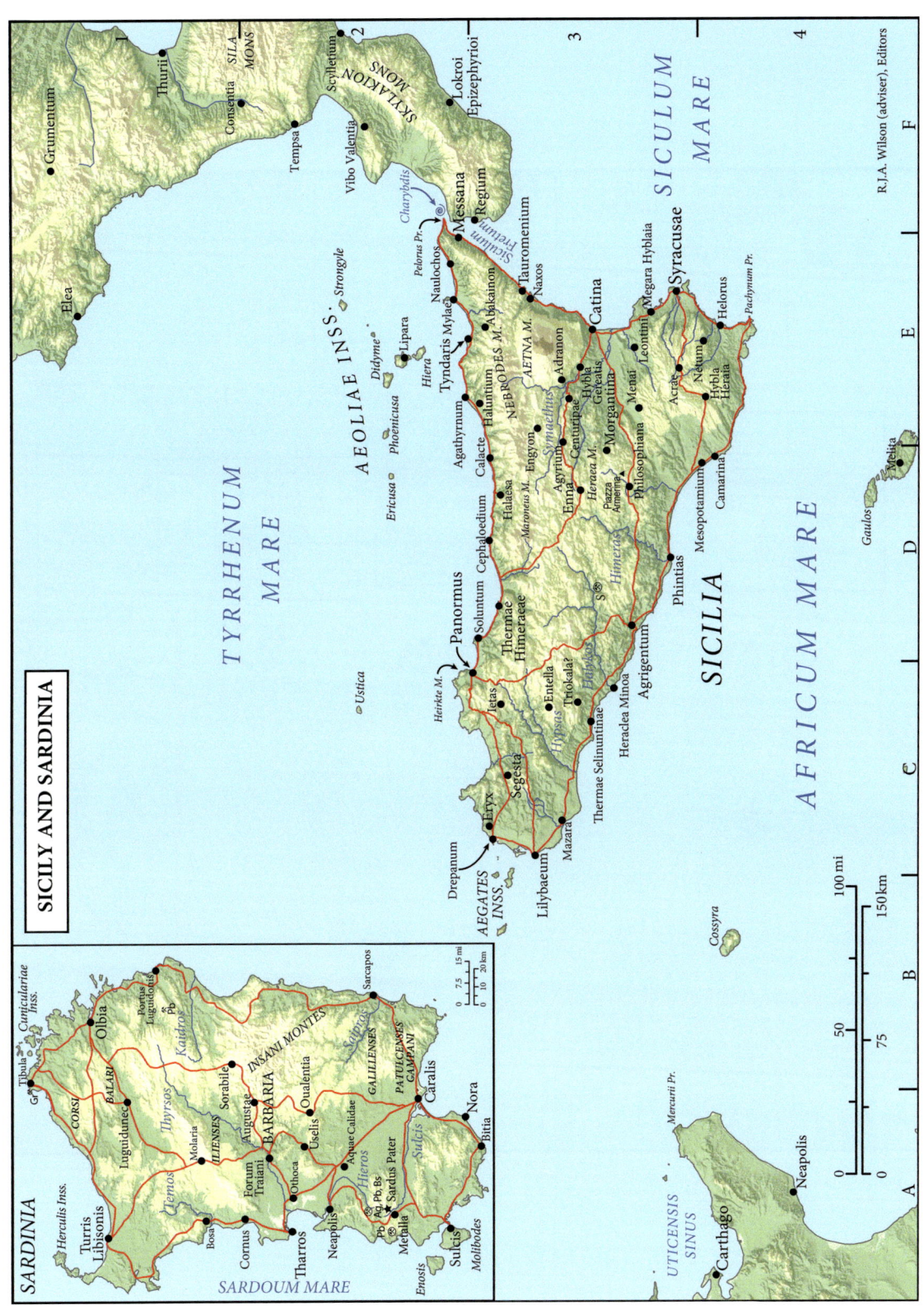

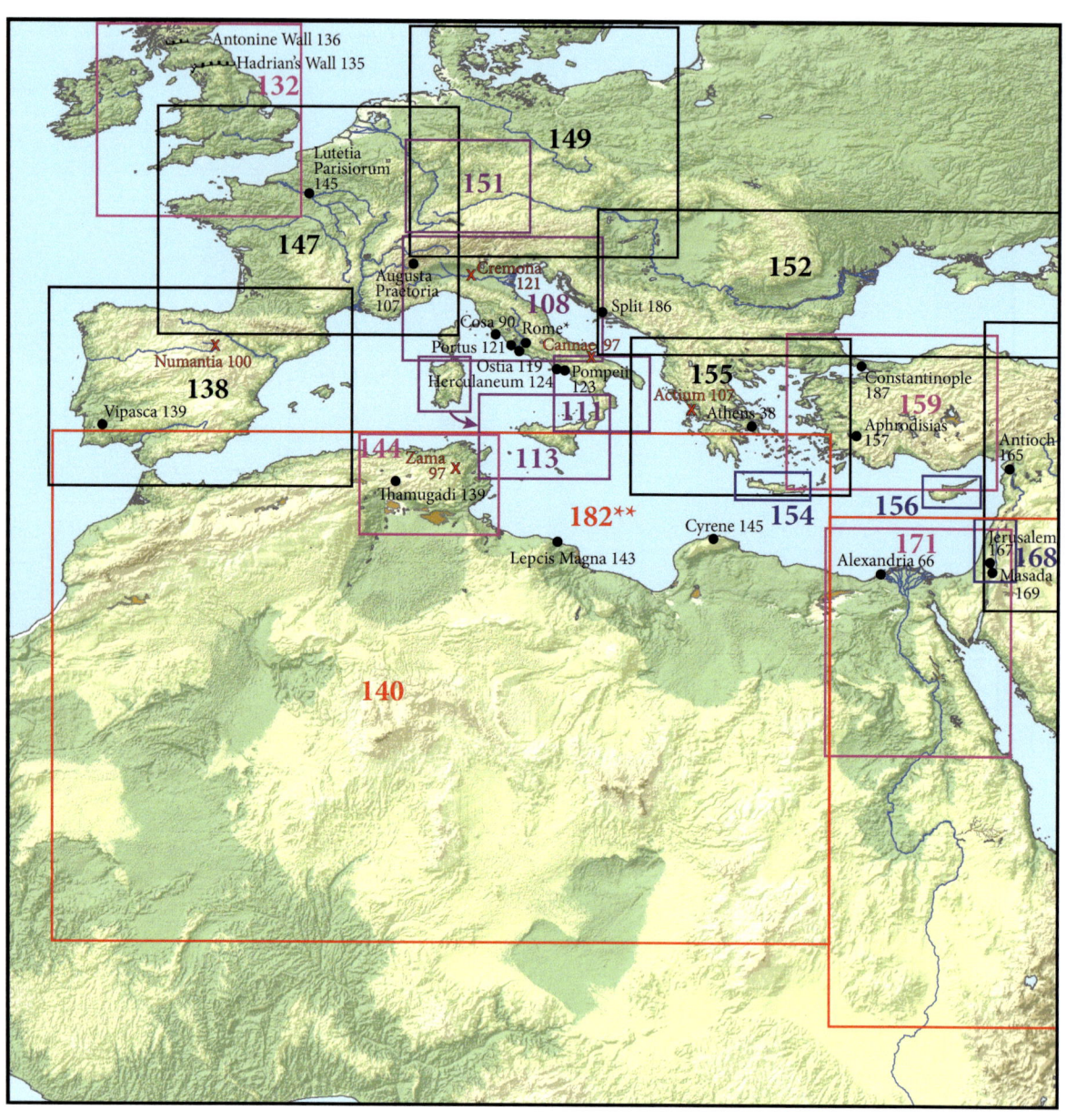

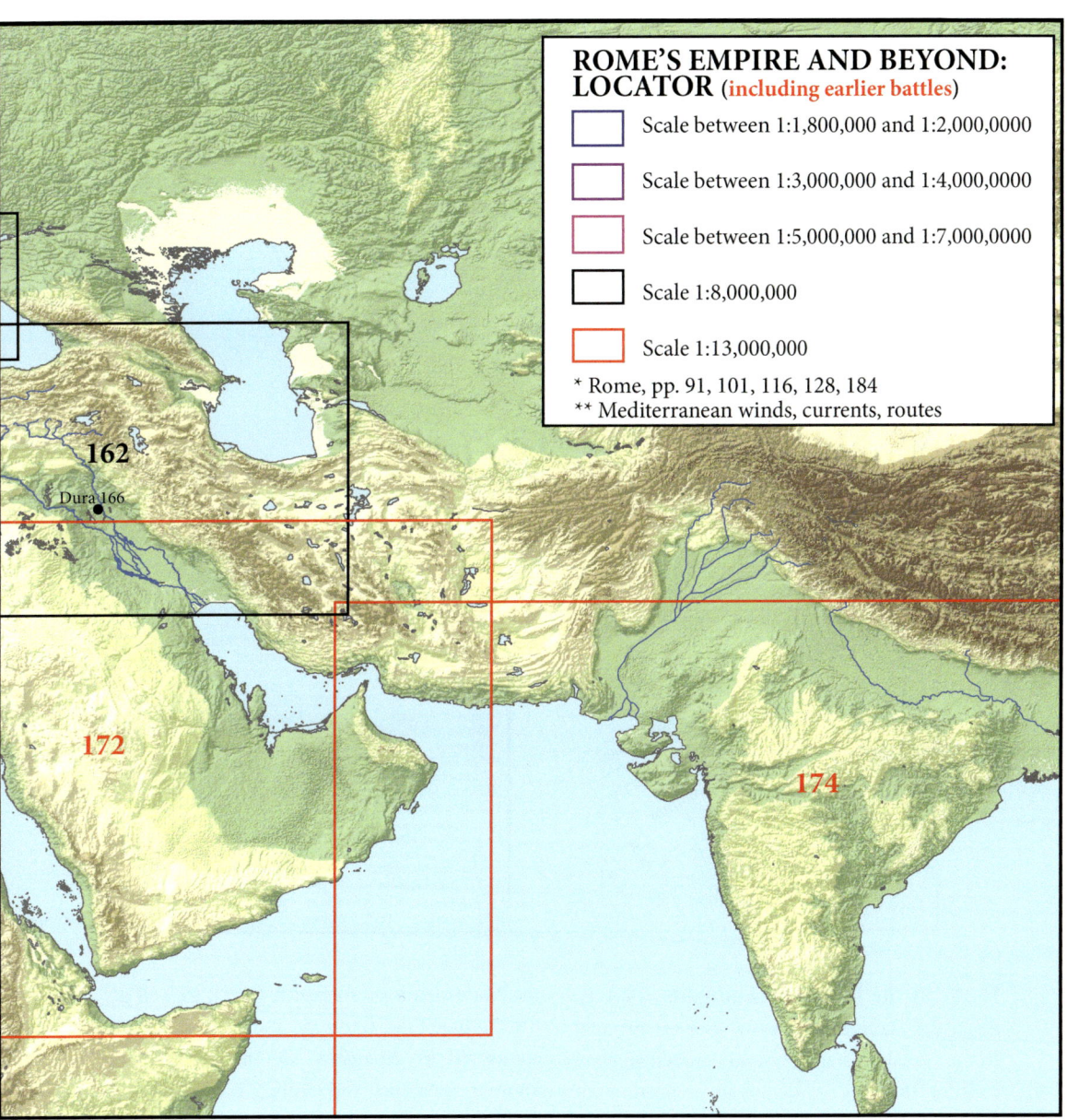

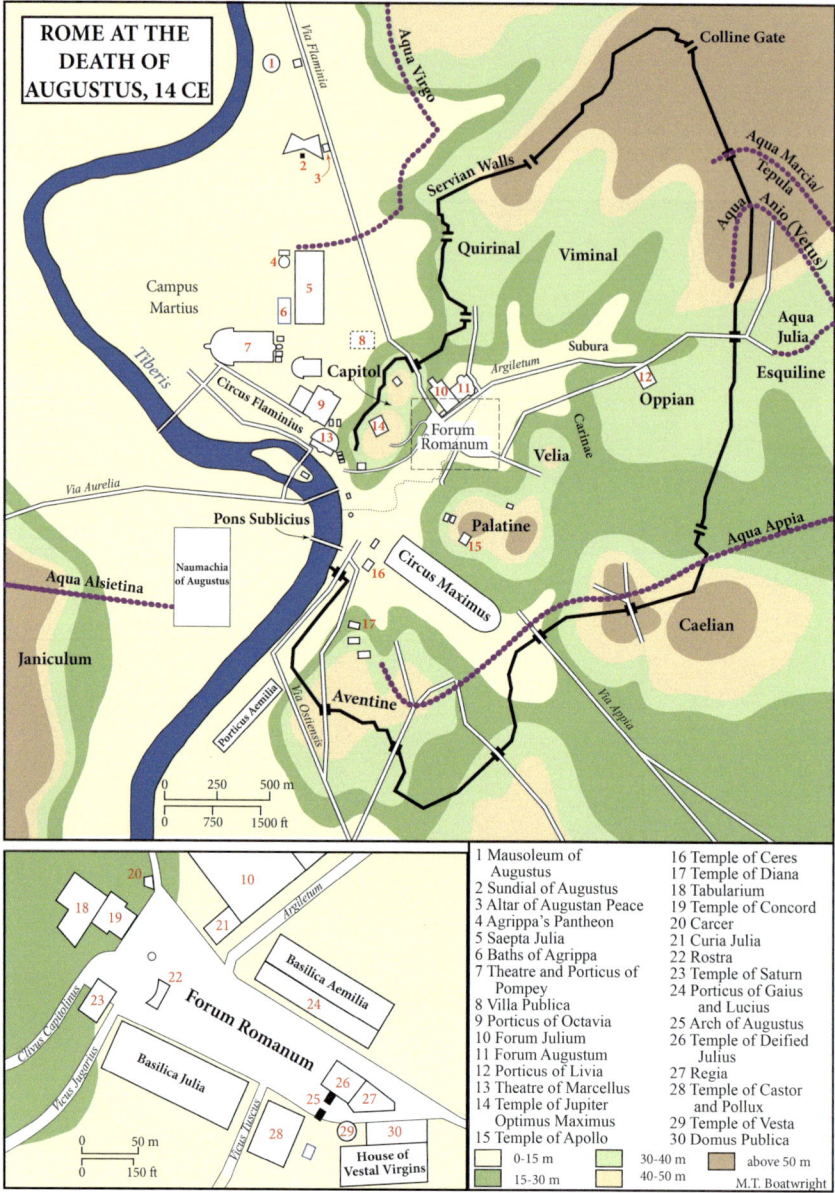

Rome at the Death of Augustus, 14 CE

Augustus' consolidation of power brought Rome greater stability and embellishment, making the city a deliberate reflection of Roman power and control. Although Augustus piously maintained many traditions and restored numerous structures and shrines like the Temple of Jupiter Optimus Maximus on the Capitol (14), public building now became the prerogative of the imperial family. The formerly rather undeveloped Campus Martius showcased the Altar of Augustan Peace (Ara Pacis) and the Mausoleum of Augustus (3, 1), as well as the Pantheon (4), Baths (6) and Aqua Virgo all sponsored by Augustus' son-in-law Agrippa; another aqueduct too (Julia) was Agrippa's work. Augustus' sister Octavia, wife Livia and nephew Marcellus were commemorated in buildings like the Porticus of Octavia (9, a meeting-place, among other functions), Porticus of Livia (12) in Rome's residential hills, and Theatre of Marcellus (13). A further Forum (11) with a temple of Mars Ultor was added beyond that of Caesar. Augustus sited

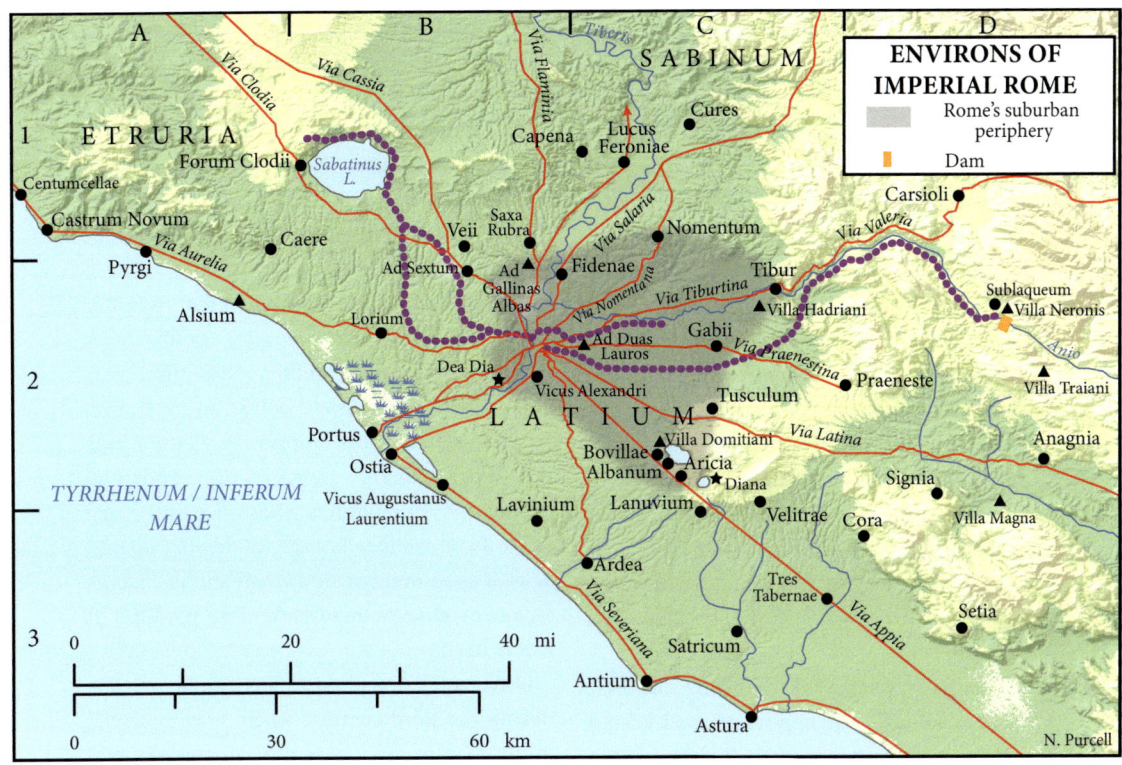

a Naumachia on low-lying ground in the Transtiberim region; its large basin where mock naval battles entertained Rome's masses was served by Aqua Alsietina.

Less visible here are changes affecting daily life, including the job opportunities offered by constant construction and embellishment. Augustus divided Rome into fourteen regions and 265 neighbourhoods (neither shown) to encourage communal ties and – some claim – to achieve tighter supervision of the previously chaotic city. The regions extended outside the Servian Walls. At Augustus' instigation, arrangements were made for regular aqueduct maintenance; measures were also instituted to reduce Tiber flooding. Firefighters were now stationed in seven barracks throughout the regions. A new police force promised greater order, and the imperial family was protected by the Praetorian Guard (for whom, however, there were as yet no barracks). Officials were appointed to oversee the grain supply, its shipping from Egypt and distribution, all in order to eliminate food shortages among a city populace estimated to have grown to at least 800,000 by 14 CE.

Environs of Imperial Rome

For centuries until the early 1900s, much of Rome's Campagna – 50 km or more from side to side – remained virtually uninhabited. Earlier, however, in the imperial period, it became the city's teeming hinterland. It was crisscrossed by a network of local and long-distance roads which gave access to suburban communities, dormitory towns, villas and truck-farming areas; aqueducts crossed it too, bringing water from far afield to the metropolis. The city itself sprawled across a wide area, and its vital port-communities, Ostia and Portus (pp. 119, 120), shared in its social and economic patterns. This unique human landscape was the product of Rome's astonishing success as an imperial capital. Across the region, from the city's suburban fringes or the comfortable slopes below the Apennines to the hunting-parks of the wilder mountains and coastal marshes, emperors owned numerous palatial villas: the most spectacular was one developed by Hadrian below the city of Tibur (modern Tivoli).

Ostia

Ostia and Portus (p. 120) played key complementary roles in the supply of foodstuffs and other goods to imperial Rome about 25 km distant to the northeast. Ostia, a river-port, lay close to the Tiber mouth. Its complex plan betrays a long history of growth and rebuilding. Excavations show it to have been originally established just south of the Tiber in the fourth century BCE as a *colonia maritima* around 2 ha in extent. Its *kardo* and *decumanus maximus* ran through the fortified core (*castrum*), whose east gate (5) remains visible within the later town. With a great increase in trade – handled in conjunction with Puteoli on the Bay of Naples (p. 87) – the port expanded to around 69 ha by the mid-first century BCE, when it was granted the status of a *colonia* and the existing walls were constructed.

Ostia's prosperity peaked during the first two centuries CE. The import of food bound for Rome – supervised by officials of the *praefectus* in charge of the *annona* (grain supply) – depended upon it. It had a 1 ha harbour basin (upper left) – which proved too small for the volume of traffic, and fell out of use during the first century CE – as well as extensive quays running either side of the Tiber. Ostia's commercial role was boosted by the construction and subsequent enlargement of Portus in the mid-first and early second centuries. By the later second century, Ostia encompassed well over 100 ha, boasted a wealth of public monuments, and had a population approaching 40,000. At the centre was a long forum (9) with temples at either end and a basilica (12); there were also suites of large public baths and barracks for the *vigiles* (night-watch). Behind the theatre (3) lay the magnificent *Piazzale delle Corporazioni*, comprising a central temple within a rectangular colonnaded enclosure. Mosaic floors of offices here indicate this to have been a hub for merchants, shippers and others active in commerce at both Ostia and Portus, and in supplying Rome. Large warehouses were built between the *decumanus maximus* and the port installations on the Tiber's south bank, as well as opposite on Isola Sacra (*Trastevere Ostiense*, p. 120); smaller warehouses have been documented south of the *decumanus*.

Throughout were many temples and shrines to various Italic and eastern deities, as well as meeting places (*scholae*) for popular associations, markets (*macella*), grain stores (*horrea*), bakeries, fulling establishments and other lower-level industrial premises. An additional most impressive feature was the extraordinary density of residential occupation, in buildings whose size and scope range from smaller houses to wealthy *domus*, as well as to multi-storey *insula* and *medianum* tenement blocks; these have close parallels at Rome itself.

Ostia entered a period of economic decline during the third century, when its commercial infrastructure was seriously disrupted, and numerous houses and *insula* blocks were abandoned. However, the port revived somewhat in the early fourth century: several public buildings along the *decumanus* at the centre were restored and baths near the seafront constructed, as were high-status mansions – scattered throughout – belonging to imperial officials. Ostia was eventually abandoned by the mid-fifth century.

Portus

Portus Augusti, about 3.5 km north of Ostia (p. 119), was established by the emperor Claudius by 46 CE and formally inaugurated by 64. The main feature was a 200 ha harbour basin enclosed by two large manmade moles projecting into the sea; its primary entrance lay between these either side of a monumental lighthouse (*Pharos*) on a small manmade island. South-east of this basin was a small (1.07 ha) rectangular harbour basin (*Darsena*). Two canals connected Portus to the Tiber and the sea: the northern one seems to have been abandoned quite early, but the southern *Fossa*

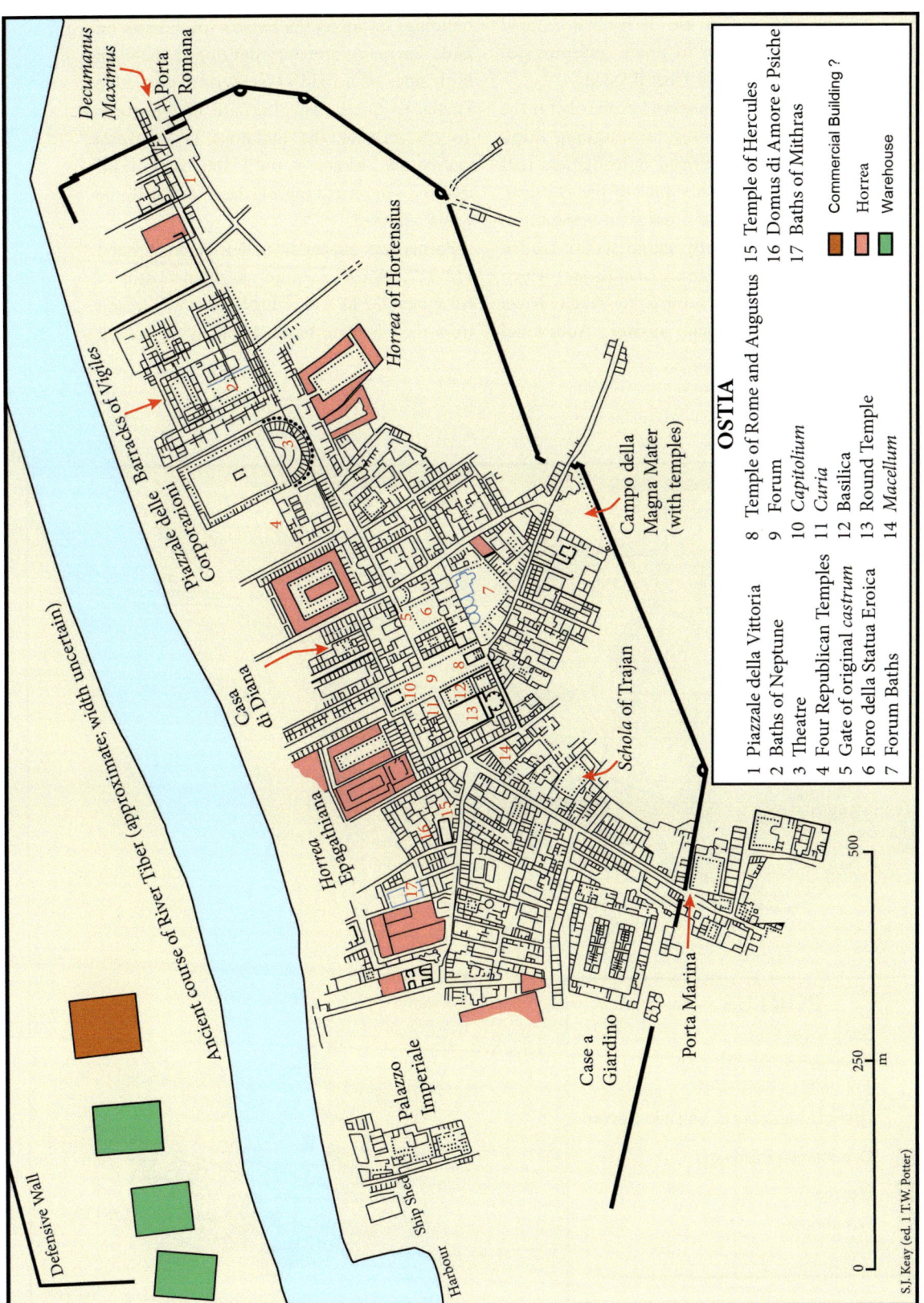

Traiana remained in use. It facilitated rapid movement of cargoes to Rome, and provided relief upriver when the Tiber flooded.

The Claudian basin served primarily for the anchorage and mooring of sea-going ships. Cargoes were transhipped onto lighters that passed via an internal canal to the *Darsena*, where unloading and storage in warehouses followed. Subsequently, cargoes were loaded onto smaller boats (*naves caudicariae*) which used the *Canale Traverso* to reach *Fossa Traiana* and continue upriver. Additional buildings lay along the *Fossa*'s south bank on Isola Sacra. A cemetery developed there on both sides of a road (*Via Flavia*) connecting Portus to Ostia from the late first century. To the east of the buildings lay a *statio marmorum*, where – until the early third century – imported marble destined for Rome was stockpiled.

Portus was expanded under Trajan around 112–117, when a third harbour basin – hexagonal, 32 ha – was dug a short way inland from the Claudian basin. It raised the overall

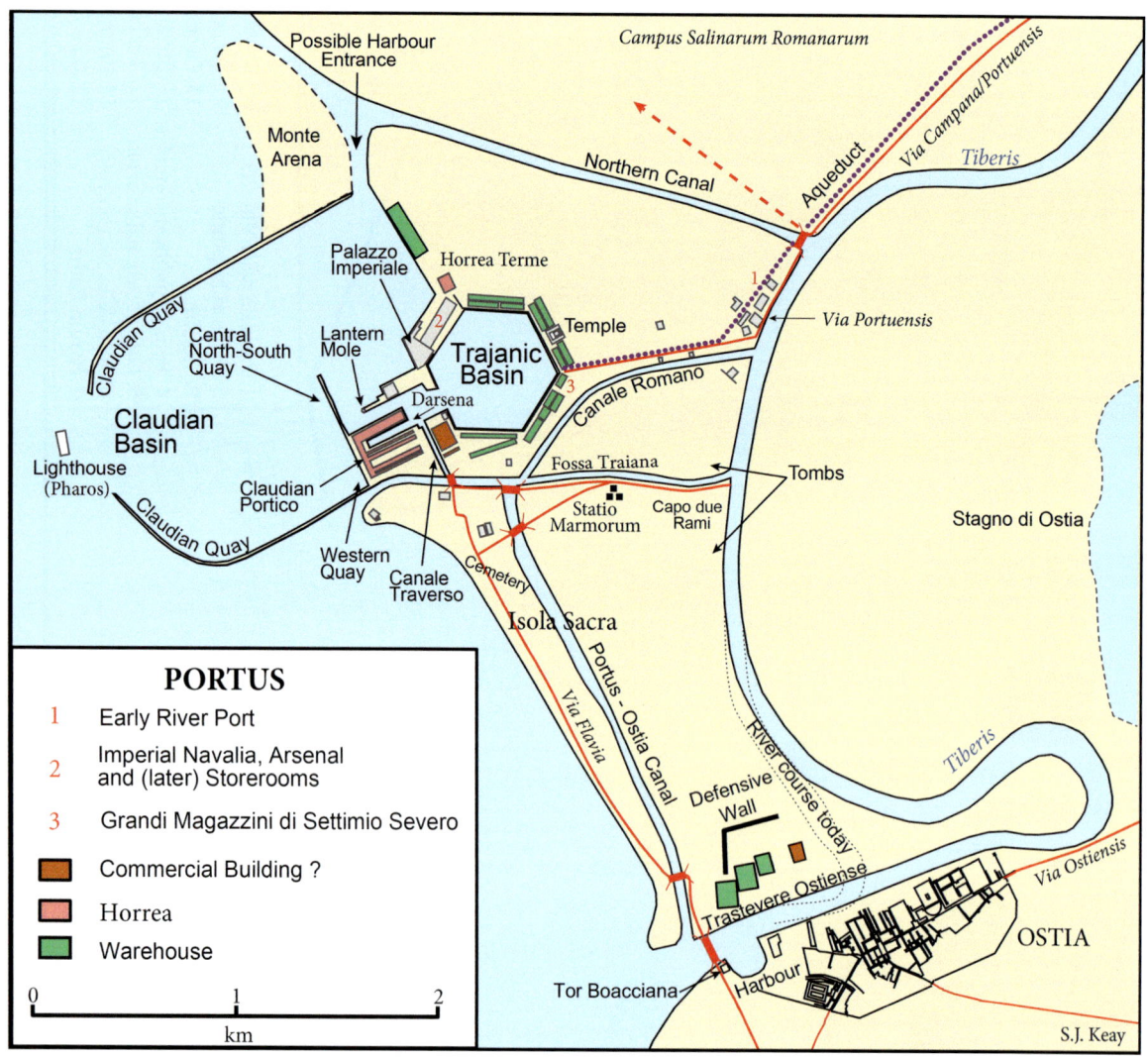

basin capacity to about 233 ha, one of the largest in the Mediterranean. Trajan dug a third canal, *Canale Romano*, from *Fossa Traiana* to the Tiber; it skirted the hexagon's south-east side, which became a key transhipment area. A fourth canal as wide as 90 m has recently been detected, running towards Ostia across Isola Sacra from near the junction of *Canale Romano* and *Fossa Traiana*.

The topography of Portus was determined by its infrastructure in a way that Ostia's was not. An imperial maritime villa of late Trajanic date – the *Palazzo Imperiale*, centrally situated between the Claudian and Trajanic basins – was probably used by imperial officials under the *praefectus annonae*. Adjacent was an imperial arsenal (*navalia*), later converted into storerooms (2). The so-called *Grandi Magazzini di Settimio Severo* (3) were probably a base for monitoring the flow of goods through the port. Oblong warehouses proliferated around the hexagonal basin, while a massive 10-ha complex for storing grain was built in the south-east corner of the Claudian basin.

Portus was thus carefully planned to control shipping, transfer and storage of cargoes, and payment of dues. There were several temples and a few baths, but nothing like the range of amenities typical for a city – such as Ostia boasted. Also, given the apparent absence of houses, Portus lacked a large stable population. During the sailing season numbers perhaps reached 10,000–15,000, with many commuting daily from Ostia. Portus underwent extensive development during the early third and fourth centuries, and around 340 gained urban status. Recent work suggests that it continued to supply Rome until the mid-fifth century.

Second Battle of Cremona, 69 CE

This crucial civil war battle for Cremona occurred on the plain about 8 km east towards Bedriacum. Tacitus' account (*Histories* 3.15–25) and the preservation of Roman centuriation make it possible to identify the location. Although the Flavians were already stretched – the cavalry by clashes with squadrons from Cremona's Vitellian garrison, the infantry by a long march – during the afternoon they demanded an immediate assault. Their commander Antonius Primus first refused, but decided otherwise on learning that the garrison was now swelled to 35,000 legionaries (against his 25,000); the newly arrived Vitellians had just marched 45 km, but were also eager to engage. Antonius chose his ground astride the Via Postumia, and the Vitellians rashly risked a night encounter (24–25 October), which proved confused and indecisive. But once the moon rose behind the Flavians (by 10 pm), they gained from its light; at dawn, news (false) that they were receiving reinforcements energized them for a final thrust which dispersed the Vitellians.

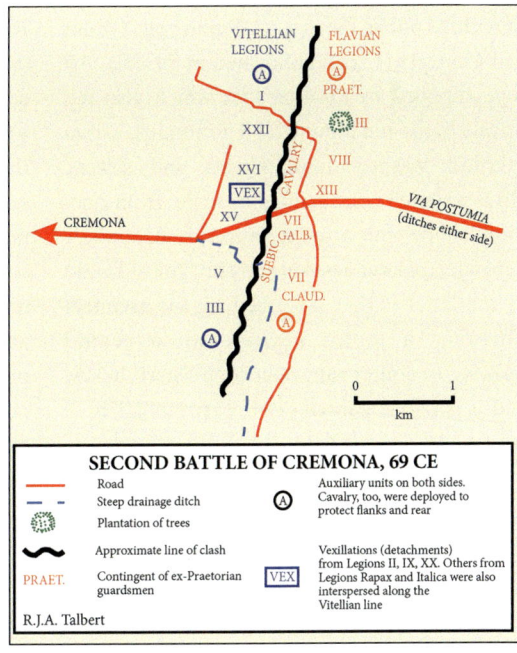

Pompeii

Pompeii in Campania (p. 87) was the leading city and port in the eastern part of the Bay of Naples, measuring some 1,200 × 720 m within its walls. Roughly two-thirds of Pompeii has now been liberated from the thick mantle of volcanic deposits which enveloped it in August 79 CE, when Mt. Vesuvius to the west erupted. Buildings from several centuries have emerged, the oldest a Greek Doric temple of the sixth century BCE, part of an early nucleus underlying the Triangular Forum. However, most structures belong to the second century and later.

There are three main areas of public buildings. First, the one just mentioned, with a large theatre (16) and small covered one (Odeon) nearby, as well as a temple of Isis (between 16 and 17). Second, to the west, an unusually long forum with a Corinthian temple – the Capitolium – at one end (1); around were more temples, a cloth hall, judicial basilica, market, and three other halls (municipal offices?). Third, at the city's eastern edge, an amphitheatre built around 80 BCE and Great Palaestra, a large enclosure surrounding a swimming pool. There were three public baths too – Suburban, Forum and Central (11, still unfinished in 79 CE). All were supplied by an aqueduct which also fed private baths and innumerable fountains, whose overflow washed down streets and sewers. Houses varied considerably in scale, from one-room shops with a room above, to elaborately decorated palatial residences. The typical layout of the latter is that described by the architect Vitruvius: a roofed *atrium* with a central opening to collect rainwater in a cistern below, and a peristyle garden court surrounded by a colonnade.

Pompeii became prosperous through trade and agriculture, although establishments producing lava millstones, cloth and fish sauce also developed here. By 79, with a population of some 20,000, Pompeii was expanding considerably, to the west in particular, where sections of the old circuit wall were obliterated.

Herculaneum

West of Pompeii and directly below Mt. Vesuvius, Herculaneum lies buried beneath no less than 15 m of volcanic mud from the eruption in 79 CE. In consequence, only a relatively small part has so far been excavated. Nonetheless, Herculaneum's area would seem to have been quite modest, perhaps 320 × 370 m, with a population of around 5,000. The preservation of wood and other organic materials here is excellent, so that many buildings have yielded an extraordinary quantity of detailed information. *Decumani* (east-west streets) and *cardines* (north-south streets) divided the city into blocks (*insulae*). To the north was a particularly wide *decumanus*, closed off to vehicular traffic; it may have served as the forum. On its north side there is thought to have been a basilica, while to the east was a palaestra with a large pool at the centre of its peristyle court. A theatre is known from old excavations in the north-west area.

Herculaneum dates back to the sixth century BCE at least, but the houses now visible belong mainly to the final centuries of the Roman Republic. Many are laid out around an *atrium* in the Italic style, but their plans vary considerably. Some have porticoes in front, while a great many possessed a second or even third storey. Attached to the houses were shops selling wine, grain, metalwork, glassware and more; one even still has its painted sign. To the south, at the edge of the early city, were some much grander houses – with peristyles, gardens and other rooms – affording panoramic views out to sea; they date mainly to the Augustan period and later. To the south-east lay an extensive complex of baths and religious buildings (7–9). The famous, and immense, Villa of the Papyri was situated just west of the city. Early excavators used tunnelling techniques to retrieve numerous papyrus scrolls discovered here. Part of the villa has now been uncovered, but it mostly remains underground.

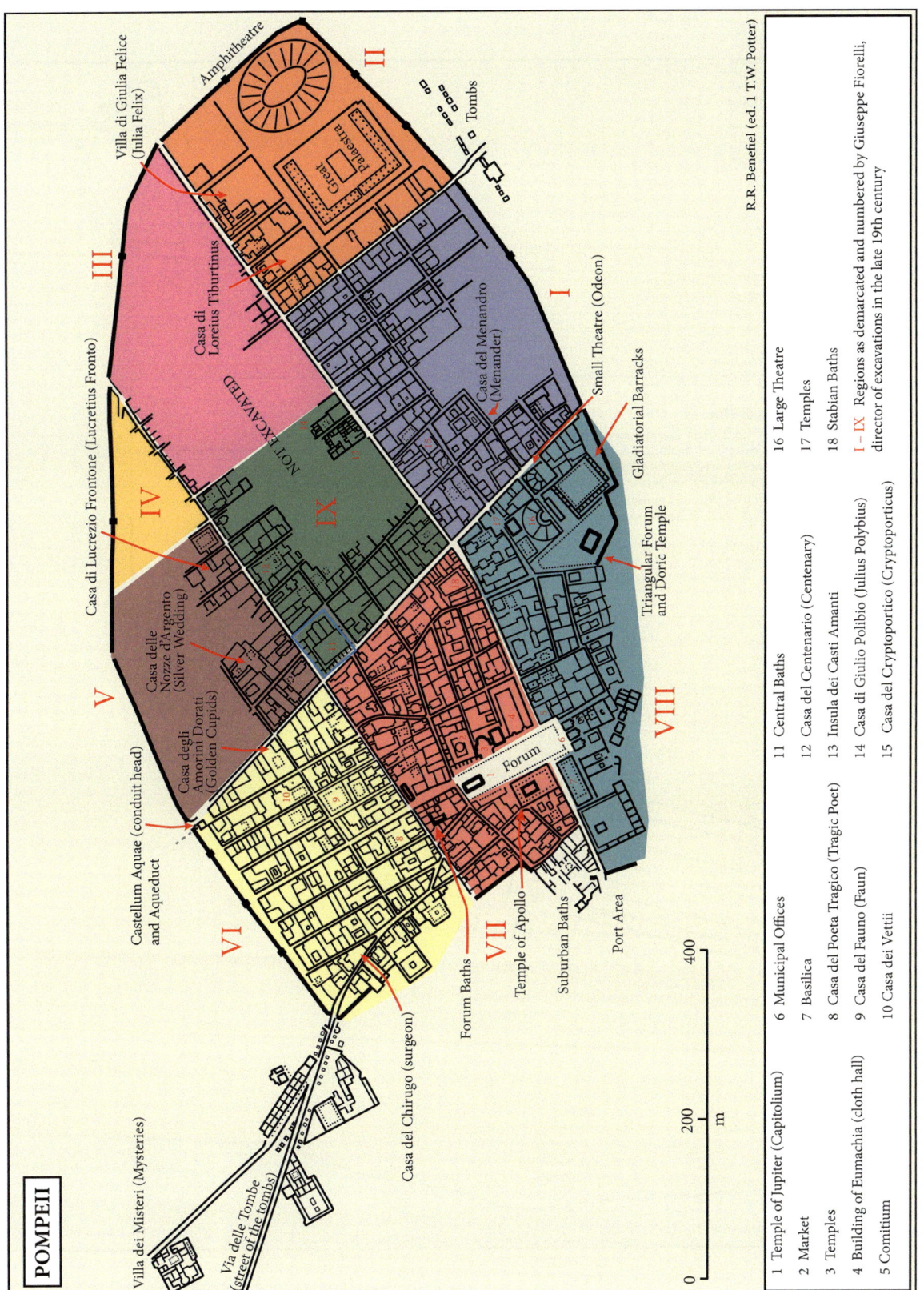

HERCULANEUM

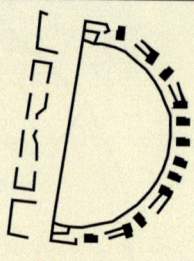
Theatre

Principal Houses
1. Casa del bicentenario (bicentenary)
2. Casa del mosaico di Nettuno e Anfitrite (mosaic of Neptune and Amphitrite)
3. Casa del mobilio carbonizzato (carbonized furniture)
4. Casa Sannitica (Samnite house)
5. Casa del tramezzo in legno (wooden partition)
6. Casa del scheletro (skeleton)
7. Casa del atrio mosaico (mosaic atrium)
8. Casa dei cervi (stags)
9. Casa della gemma (gem)
10. Casa del rilievo di Telefo (relief of Telephus)

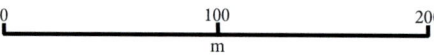

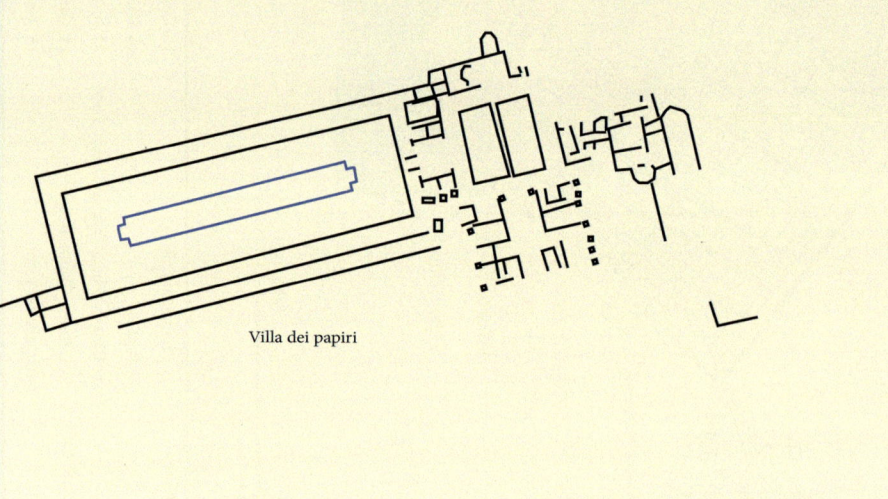
Villa dei papiri

Italian Towns with Alimentary Schemes

Alimentary schemes (*alimenta*) for the support of boys and girls are known from the mid-first century CE onwards. Private benefactors took the initiative first, but Nerva and Trajan came to sponsor a major scheme throughout Italy, best documented in substantial inscribed records from Veleia and Ligures Baebiani. The emperors offered capital, though in all other respects their schemes were locally based in each participating community, and designed to operate with the minimum of future adjustment. Larger local landowners accepted perpetual loans from the emperor amounting to approximately 8% of the valuation made of their property; the interest they paid at the low rate of 5% furnished cash for modest monthly support grants. The method by which children were chosen for inclusion in a scheme is unknown. They were not orphans primarily, it seems, nor necessarily from the poorest families. Claims made that the emperors' scheme was in fact initiated in order to provide smaller landowners with working capital do not convince, but still its real aims remain obscure. Arguably, these were a mix of philanthropy and concern for a supposed population decline which might affect legionary recruitment. The imperial *alimenta* were perhaps extended a little by later second-century emperors, and they continued functioning into the third century. No doubt they strengthened an emperor's image and a community's links with him, but their practical benefit was never great.

Evidence for *alimenta* is almost exclusively epigraphic. Perhaps the spread of the fifty or so communities from which indications have emerged reflects merely the random survival of relevant testimony (references to a local *quaestor alimentorum* and the like). Yet a suspicion lingers that the emperors' scheme was seldom extended to remoter or poorer areas. Evidence for private schemes is slight, although the arrangements for one set up by Pliny the Younger at Comum are described in his *Letter* 7.18.

Rome at the Death of Trajan, 117 CE

The density of Rome's population probably peaked at this time, with perhaps around one million residents occupying a built-up area of some 15 km^2. In its centre emperors continued to construct monumental public buildings to accommodate official functions and represent imperial ideology. Trajan's Forum (11) – built with loot and slaves won in his Dacian wars – displayed statues of abject conquered 'barbarians' and gloriously victorious Romans, while its Column's frieze narrated the campaigns. Alongside his Forum Trajan erected a market complex, and elsewhere immense Baths (15). Earlier, to the northeast, Tiberius had built huge barracks for the Praetorian Guard. Claudius completed two aqueducts (Aqua Claudia, Anio Novus) begun by Caligula. After a catastrophic fire in 64 CE wiped out three of the city's regions and damaged all but four of the other eleven, Nero sequestered an extensive area for himself in order to develop a palatial 'Golden House' (*Domus Aurea*) with its own park and lake. However, the Flavians Vespasian and Titus repurposed the land for public benefit, erecting an amphitheatre (Colosseum) and bath complex (17, 16). Vespasian also restored the Temple of Jupiter on the Capitol (14) – destroyed by fire in 69 – and built a Temple of Peace (inset). Domitian's initiatives included a stadium (2) with a concert hall adjacent (5), and a temple to his deified father and brother (8). Nerva added a further Forum (inset) between that of Julius Caesar and the Temple of Peace.

More than ever, Rome was now a city made vibrant and exciting by its forums, baths, entertainments, immigrants and visitors from across the known world. Even so, extreme wealth disparities persisted. The super-wealthy had hilltop *horti* (villas with a park and gardens) on the outskirts (see p. 117), while the poor were crammed into unsanitary tenements (*insulae*) in low-lying, malarial areas along the flood-prone banks of the Tiber.

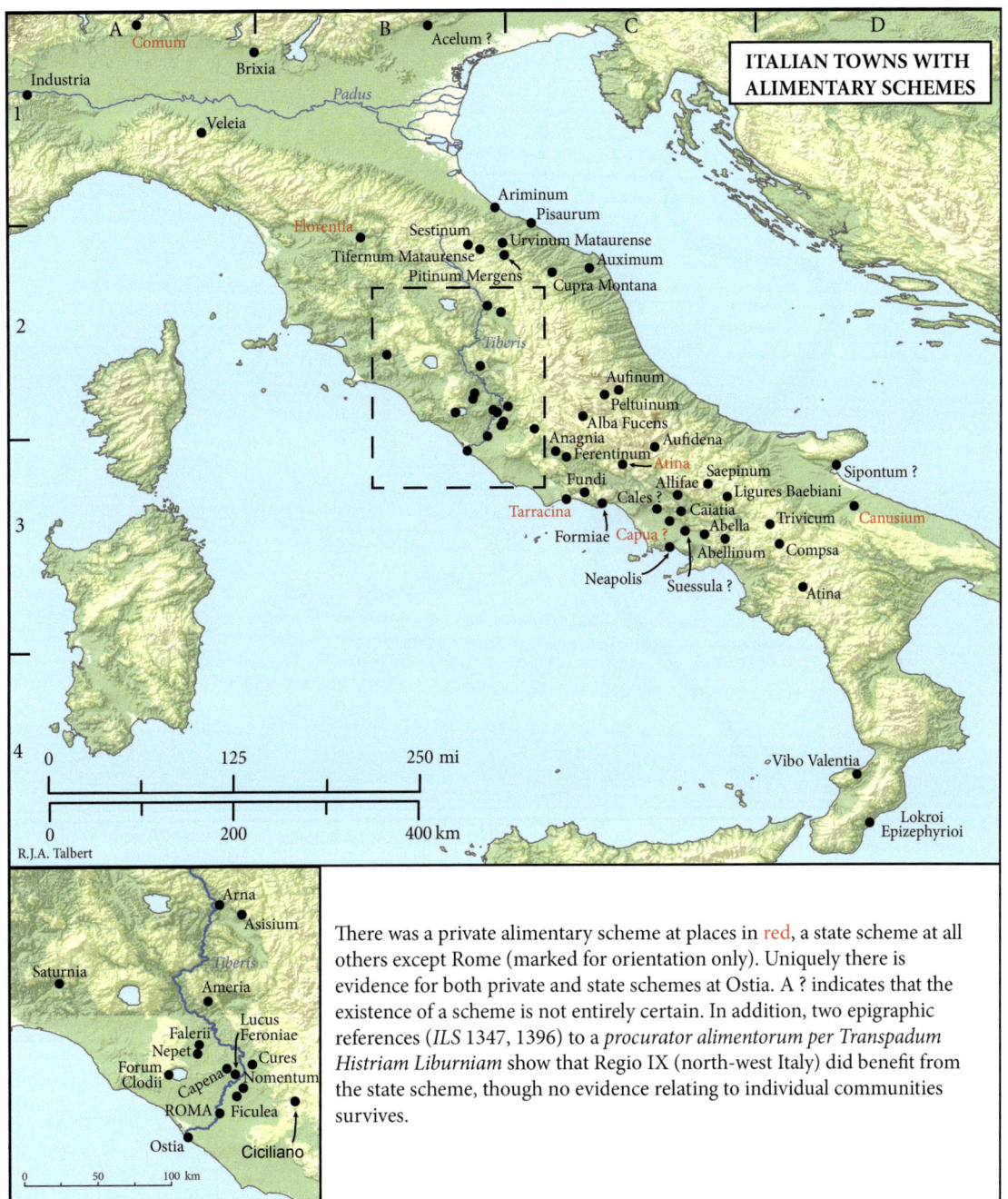

ITALIAN TOWNS WITH ALIMENTARY SCHEMES

There was a private alimentary scheme at places in red, a state scheme at all others except Rome (marked for orientation only). Uniquely there is evidence for both private and state schemes at Ostia. A ? indicates that the existence of a scheme is not entirely certain. In addition, two epigraphic references (ILS 1347, 1396) to a *procurator alimentorum per Transpadum Histriam Liburniam* show that Regio IX (north-west Italy) did benefit from the state scheme, though no evidence relating to individual communities survives.

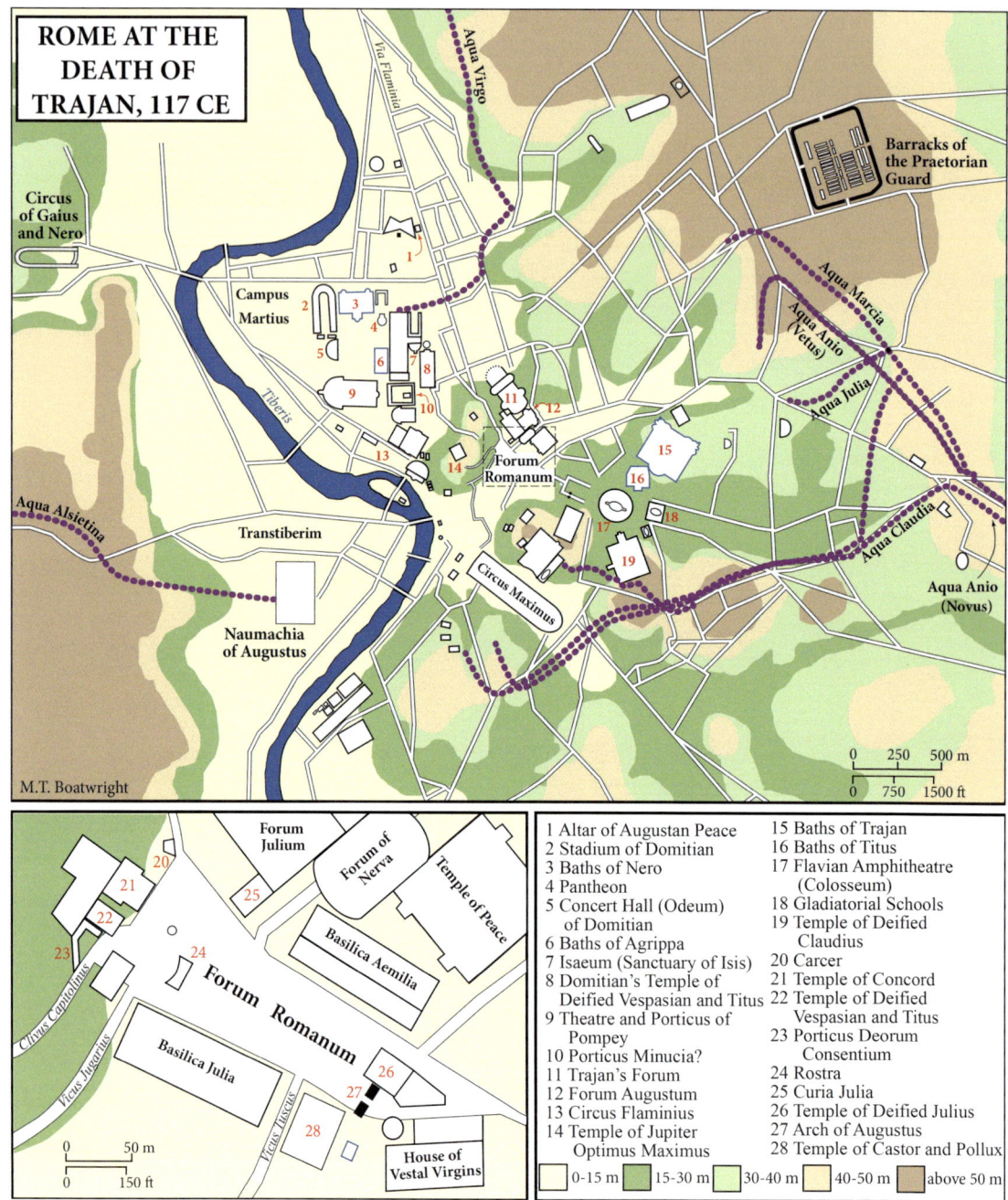

Rome's Empire around 60 CE

During the 120 years between 60 BCE (p. 103) and 60 CE Rome's empire was impressively extended and consolidated. Though it was Julius Caesar who conquered Gaul in its entirety during the 50s BCE and subsequently enlarged the province of Africa, the expansion was above all the achievements of Augustus. During his Principate Egypt was annexed (30 BCE), while Spain, Gaul and the Alps were all pacified and organized (by 13 BCE). However, persistent efforts to subdue Germany and push Roman control as far as the Elbe river (Albis) failed; the Rhine river (Rhenus) was therefore made the frontier in this region, and heavily garrisoned. Arguably, Augustus' greatest contribution to the consolidation of the empire was to link its western and eastern sections by subduing all the territory up to the Danube river (Danuvius) along its whole course; this frontier, too, was strongly garrisoned. By Augustus' death in 14 CE much of the empire was indeed, as Tacitus says (*Annals* 1.9), "bordered by the ocean or by long rivers." In the East, the Euphrates river formed part of the frontier, yet this was less secure and less sharply defined than in the West, with extensive areas still left in the hands of friendly 'client kings' (though Galatia had been annexed in 25 BCE), and with no substantial garrison. For a variety of reasons – political and financial, as well as military – Augustus had no wish to station many legions in the East, and he feared no pressing danger from there. For all its size, the neighbouring Parthian empire was normally weak and divided, while most of its monarchs respected Roman concern that kings of Armenia (a mountainous region bordering both empires) should swear allegiance to the emperor.

Tiberius did incorporate the former 'client kingdom' of Cappadocia within the empire in 17 CE. Otherwise, however, having already earned military glory over many years, as emperor he mostly followed Augustus' advice against expansion. Claudius, by contrast, lacking any prior such record, proved more ambitious. During the 40s he could boast of the incorporation of 'client states' on each of the three continents – Mauretania in Africa, Thrace in Europe, Lycia and Judaea in Asia – while also emulating and surpassing Julius Caesar by initiating the conquest *trans Oceanum* ("over the Ocean") of Britain. In 60, Roman forces there faced a native rebellion. At the same time the eastern legions needed reinforcements to combat an unusually strong and aggressive Parthian monarch, Vologeses I, who was refusing to recognize even Rome's nominal claim to Armenia.

From 27 BCE, governors were appointed by two different methods, depending on whether a province belonged (in legal fiction) to the share 'of the people' (public), or to that 'of Caesar' (imperial). It remained the case that most governors were still senators, men who during their careers might be sent to both public and imperial provinces. For the public ones, proconsuls chosen by lot continued to govern for fixed one-year terms, as in the Republic; all were ex-praetors, except those for Africa and Asia, who were senior ex-consuls. By 14 CE, only one of the twenty-seven legions remained under a proconsul's command (in Africa), and it, too, was removed in 39. For most imperial provinces, the governors were senators acting as the emperor's legate – officially of praetorian rank, although some (in heavily garrisoned provinces especially) were ex-consuls. The emperor appointed all these governors, and they served until he recalled them; a term of around three years became the norm. Similarly, further provinces within the imperial share were administered by *equites* in the emperor's service holding the title of either prefect (in Egypt most famously), or – combining civil, military and financial responsibilities – procurator (often in annexed 'client kingdoms').

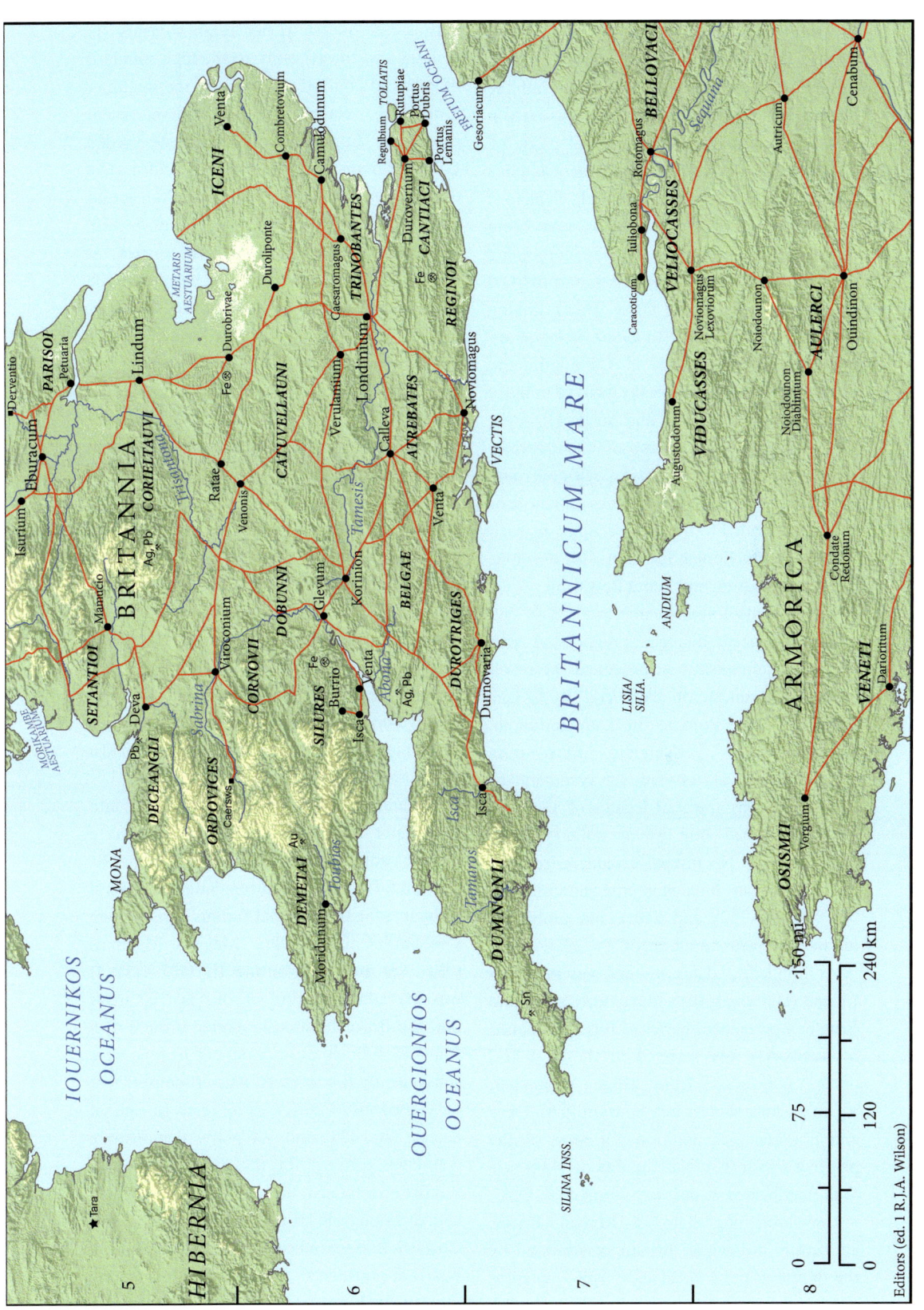

Britain

Thanks to intensive research and excavation, Britain is among the best studied of all the Roman empire's provinces. It was annexed in 43 CE on completion of the initial phase of invasion, after which the emperor Claudius processed into Camulodunum with elephants. By 47, control of the lowlands was being consolidated south-east of the diagonal joining the rivers Sabrina and Trisantona, and marked by the strategic road ('Fosse Way') linking Isca (C7) with Lindum. *Coloniae* of legionary veterans were established at Camulodunum, Glevum and Lindum, while the focus of military campaigning moved west and north. However, as in Gaul (p. 147), most of the province was organized as *civitates*, self-governing communities controlling territories that more or less corresponded to the area occupied by each tribe before the Roman invasion – for example, Calleva Atrebatum and Venta Belgarum.

Roman control nearly came to an early end when exploitative financial practices as well as abusive administration provoked the revolt of Boudica, queen of the Iceni. In 61 she annihilated the Romans in Camulodunum, Londinium and Verulamium. Even once internal peace was restored, the command of Britain, held by imperial legates of consular status, remained one where military glory could be won. Northward expansion reached the Caledonian highlands intermittently (in the 80s, 140–150s and 210s), but ambitions for the complete conquest of the island were never fulfilled, and no attempt was made on Ireland (Hibernia). Instead, to protect lowland Britain, a permanent buffer of forts garrisoned by auxiliaries was required to the west and north, controlled from three permanent legionary fortresses at Isca Silurum (C6), Deva and Eburacum; in addition, for most of the province's history, it was the line of Hadrian's Wall that formed its northern frontier (p. 135).

The flourishing state of Romano-British agriculture in lowland Britain is witnessed by the thousand or so villas and farms located to date. The mosaics, painted plaster and lavish bath suites of the richer establishments (in country and town) testify to the high standard of material comfort achieved by the wealthier propertied classes. Urban development continued: Londinium – which superseded Camulodunum as the key administrative centre after Boudica's revolt – received grand public buildings for Hadrian's visit in 122. The civilian settlement beside the fortress at Eburacum – Septimius Severus' base from 208 till his death in 211 – was raised to the status of a *colonia*. Although Britain formed part of the breakaway Gallic Empire (260–274) and hosted the usurpers Carausius and Allectus (286–296), it was relatively untouched by the insecurity of the third century. Despite the destruction during strife caused by the 'barbarian conspiracy' in 367, it enjoyed a period of economic prosperity that lasted till the fifth century. Not least because Septimius Severus' one-time rival Clodius Albinus had used the three-legion command of Britain as his springboard to imperial power, under Caracalla (211–217) the single province was split: now a consular legate governed Britannia Superior (centred on Londinium) with two legions, while Britannia Inferior (centred on Eburacum) had a praetorian legate with one.

In Late Antiquity, the island was split into four (later five) provinces organized into a diocese administered from Londinium. Its substantial military resources launched several claimants for the imperial throne, among them Constantine I (in 306), Magnus Maximus (383–388) and Constantine III (407–411). It was the administration of this last claimant that the Britons famously ejected around 410. Imperial authorities in mainland Europe were subsequently too weak to reassert control, but St. Germanus of Auxerre's missions to combat heresy (in 429 and 446/447) demonstrate continued concern for the moral welfare of the Britons. Indeed, the survival of the British church alongside British languages (Welsh, Cornish, Breton) indicates that Christianization was more advanced than Latinization among most of the Romano-British population.

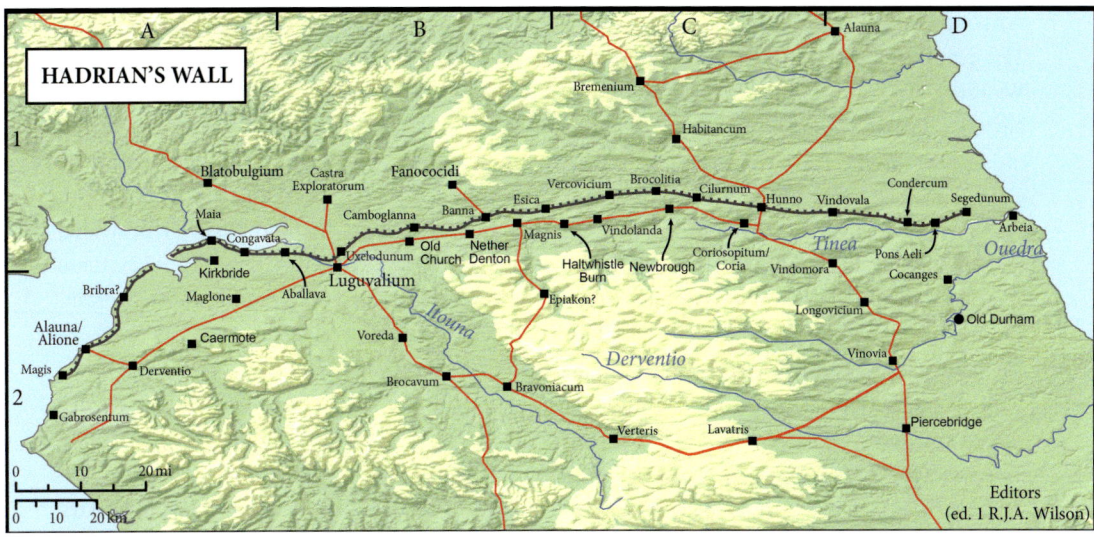

Hadrian's Wall

Gnaeus Iulius Agricola first grasped the strategic potential of a line running from the Tinea river to Britain's west coast: while governor (77–84 CE), he built a road ('Stanegate') from Coriospitum/Coria to Luguvalium with several forts along it. Vivid testimony to the everyday life of auxiliary soldiers in them has emerged from wooden writing-tablets found at Vindolanda. After the Romans' withdrawal from southern Caledonia around 105, the 'Stanegate' served as the frontier; probably now, it was extended to west and east, and further forts were built along it. Hadrian, however, addressed the frontier problem more boldly by erecting 'Hadrian's Wall,' a continuous 118-km barrier from coast to coast north of the 'Stanegate' – in stone 3 m thick from Pons Aeli to the Itouna river, and in turf onwards to the west coast. All along the barrier, at intervals of one Roman mile, were placed fortified gateways ('milecastles') – stone in the eastern sector, turf and timber in the western – with smaller stone towers spaced out between each. An impressive V-ditch was dug just north of the barrier, except where crags rendered it superfluous. The main garrisons were to remain in the 'Stanegate' forts.

After inspection by Hadrian, drastic modifications were made around 124. Forts were now placed on the Wall itself, originally twelve, later sixteen. To expedite this change, the stone Wall was reduced to 2.5 m thickness, and its course extended to Segedunum for better eastwards coverage. Most idiosyncratic of all, a continuous flat-bottomed ditch ('Vallum'), with earth mounds on either side, was dug just south of the Wall, thus delineating the military zone starkly; the only crossing-points were now at control gates opposite each fort. Even though this 'Vallum' was soon partly filled in, both its construction and the decision to move the main garrisons up to the Wall itself no doubt reflect hostile local responses to the very idea of erecting any barrier.

Also integral to Hadrian's frontier was the system of stone watch-towers, timber palisade and timber fortlets which continued down the west coast to Magis and possibly further. Likewise essential to frontier defence were the northern outpost forts at Blatobulgium, Castra Exploratorum and Fanococidi; others, including Habitancum, were built later. Hadrian's frontier was essentially complete by around 128. It was to be temporarily superseded by the 'Antonine Wall' during the 140s and 150s (p. 136), but thereafter it again became – and remained – Rome's frontier, with its western sector now rebuilt in stone.

Antonine Wall

Ten years after the completion of Hadrian's Wall (p. 135), Antoninus Pius ordered an advance further north and the building of another Wall – only 59 km long – from Carriden westwards to Old Kirkpatrick. Inscribed distance slabs commemorate its construction by the legions II Augusta, VI Victrix and XX Valeria Victrix (based at Isca, Eburacum and Deva, respectively) between 139 and 142 CE. As finally completed, the Wall was of turf on cobblestone foundations, with a thickness of 4.5–5 m. It was guarded by more forts (17+) than on Hadrian's Wall (twice as long); as there, these were garrisoned by auxiliary soldiers. About 7 m north of the Antonine Wall a formidable ditch was dug, approximately 12 m wide and at least 3.5 deep; however, to the south there was no ditch like Hadrian's Vallum. Nor were there structures resembling turrets (apart from six platforms at high points, perhaps used for signalling), and only occasional fortlets, such as Watling Lodge guarding the passage of the northward road. A fort at Bishopton (and fortlets) protected the Wall to the west; to the east (p. 132), there were garrisons at Cramond and Inveresk, while Alauna and Victoria served as northern outpost forts.

After an active service life of under twenty years, the Antonine Wall was gradually abandoned and demolished between 158 and 163. There was no subsequent activity at its forts, although others in southern Caledonia were retained as outposts for Hadrian's Wall.

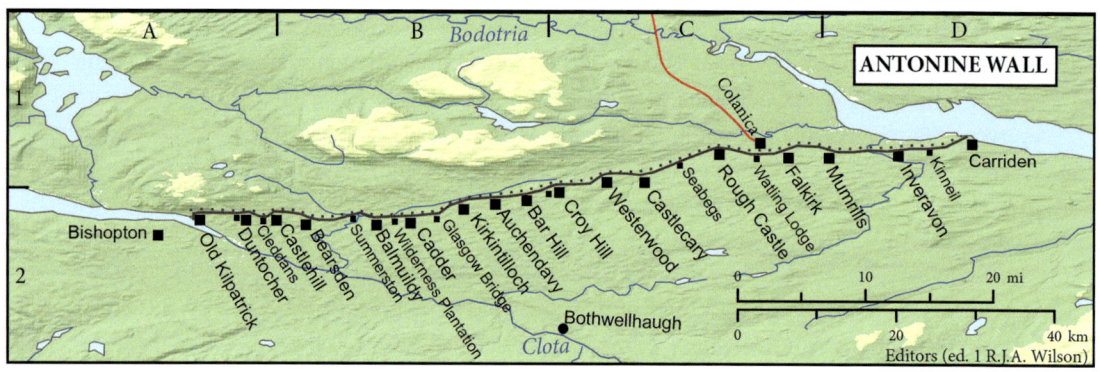

Iberian Peninsula

In his reorganization after completing Rome's conquest of the entire Iberian peninsula during the 20s BCE (p. 99), Augustus created three provinces: Baetica (the fertile and densely populated south), governed by a proconsul; Tarraconensis (covering the Iberus river valley, central plateau and wild north-west) and Lusitania (encompassing the Tagus river and Upper Anas river basin), each governed by an imperial legate. Thereafter, for the most part, the peninsula enjoyed prolonged internal stability; a single mention of fighting against the Astures in Nero's reign is unique. The three legions assigned here by Augustus were reduced by Vespasian to one – VII Gemina, based at the place named after itself, today León.

The fullest surviving descriptions of the peninsula under Roman rule are those of Strabo dating to Augustus' time and the early years of Tiberius, and of Pliny the Elder in the Flavian period. Pliny rates Spain second only to Italy in productivity. Both authors indicate the impressive number of new *coloniae* founded by Julius Caesar and Augustus, and of existing towns granted either colonial or some lesser Roman status. Emerita Augusta, established in 25 BCE for legionary veterans, is one outstanding example of the former group; among the latter, the ancient Phoenician foundation of Gades, awarded Roman municipal status by Caesar, prospered sufficiently to boast as many as 500 men qualifying for equestrian status according to Strabo. Much survives (on bronze inscriptions) of the municipal charters of Salpensa, Malaca and particularly Irni, drawn up in Domitian's reign. Although his father Vespasian had bestowed Latin rights upon every community in the Spanish provinces, it is important to keep in mind that a stark contrast persisted between the south – rich, urban, Romanized – and the rest of the peninsula, where cities were few in frequently harsh environments, and tribal organization persisted along with native customs and languages. Nonetheless, while many Spaniards may indeed have been "obscure people with barbaric names," as Pliny put it, the number of educated men from here who rose to make their mark at Rome in the first and early second centuries CE is remarkable. They sprang not only from the Italian émigré settler elite of Baetica (the philosopher Seneca, and emperors Trajan and Hadrian), but also from Romanized native communities in Tarraconensis (the poet Martial and orator Quintilian).

The sources of Spain's wealth were diverse. It was rich in herds and crops, especially wheat, vines, olives, flax. Fish were caught on a large scale, both for pickling and for the manufacture of *garum*, the salty fish sauce which added zest to every Roman meal. In Rome itself, the manmade hill of discarded jars (*amphorae*), Monte Testaccio, attests to the enormous quantity of Baetican olive oil imported there. Most valuable of all, however, were Spain's minerals – gold, silver, lead, tin, iron and copper: the last was mined over extensive areas, principally at Rio Tinto and Vipasca (p. 139). Most mines came to be owned by the state. Export of all Spanish products was facilitated by navigable rivers and a well-developed highway network.

The peninsula was harmed successively by Moorish invasions, widespread banditry, and the effects of the empire-wide civil wars of the 190s. For a period after 260, it formed part of Postumus' breakaway Gallic Empire. In Late Antiquity, Emerita Augusta became the centre of the Spanish diocese, which also encompassed Mauretania Tingitana (p. 188). The choice of Iliberri (Elvira) for holding a church council indicates the early flourishing of Christianity (p. 192). The strong Nicene views of the emperor Theodosius (379–395), from central Spain, had a far-reaching impact on the religious history of the Greek East. From 409, the peninsula suffered waves of barbarian settlement. Roman civil administration ceased to function by 472.

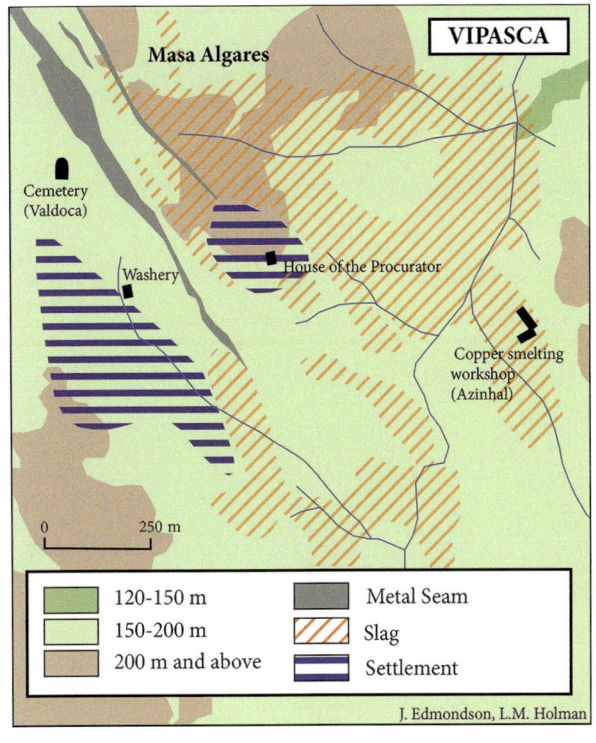

Vipasca

The *Metallum Vipascense* (at modern Aljustrel, Portugal) was probably the largest producer of copper in the Iberian Pyrites Belt during Roman times; silver was also extracted. Exploitation lasted from the late first century BCE to the fifth CE, peaking between the early first and late third CE. Our understanding of operations is enhanced by two second-century sets of rules (on bronze plaques) stipulating terms – one for leasing concessions to provide services (such as baths, fullery, shoemaking) within the mining community; the other for state contracts to exploit shafts. These were dug into the Algares gossan down to 118 m, with horizontal galleries then cut outwards; items found there include wooden props and ladders, iron tools and esparto-grass buckets. Excavations near the 'House of the Procurator' show that the settlement extended at least 1.2 km; almost 500 burials have been found in its Valdoca cemetery. In the 1860s, Roman slagheaps with residue from copper production extended over 44 km^2, but today are reduced to about 8 km^2 because slag has been re-smelted or reused as construction material. A copper smelting workshop operated at Azinhal throughout the first century CE.

Thamugadi (Timgad)

In the late nineteenth century French archaeologists uncovered here the remarkably complete remains of a Roman colony on a site unoccupied during the previous millennium. Founded by Trajan in 100 CE, it was strategically placed on the road between Theveste and Lambaesis (p. 144), the base of Legio III Augusta in which the first settlers had served. The camp-like core is a square grid, with walled sides 355 m long and blocks divided into four quarters by intersecting main streets. Population growth led to development both within the core (the theatre dates to around 160) and beyond, particularly to the west and north, where numerous baths were built. Around 200, both a Capitolium temple and a triple imperial arch (3, erroneously associated with Trajan) were erected. During the fourth century Thamugadi became a stronghold of the Donatists (schismatic Christians). It was also then that a public library was built where there had been a private house (1).

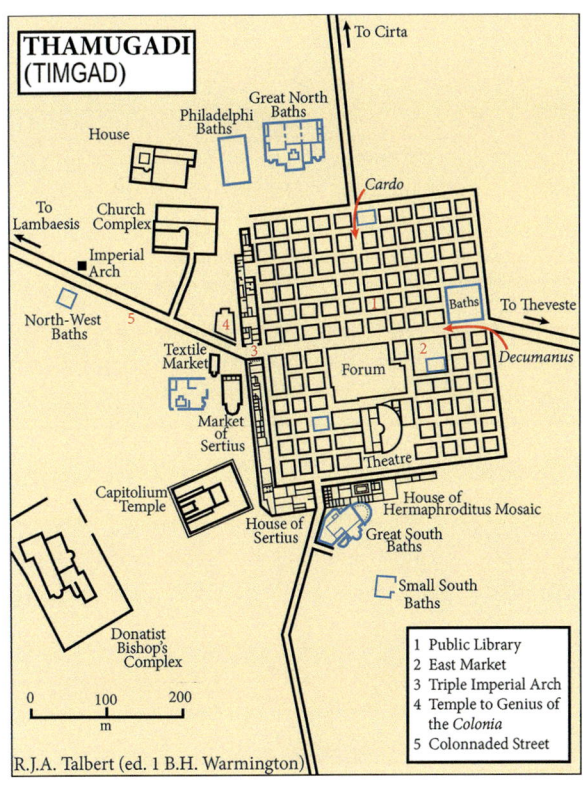

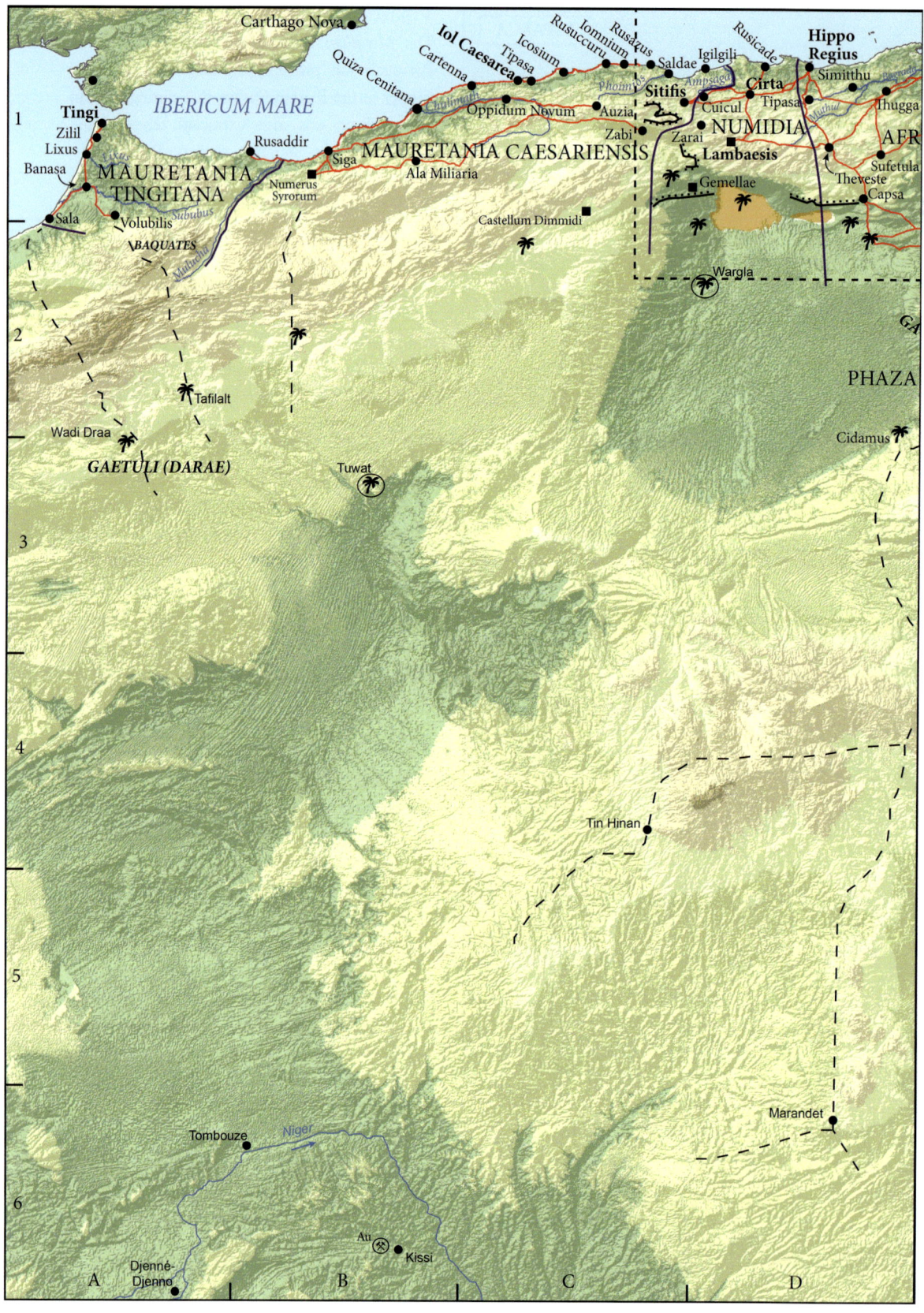

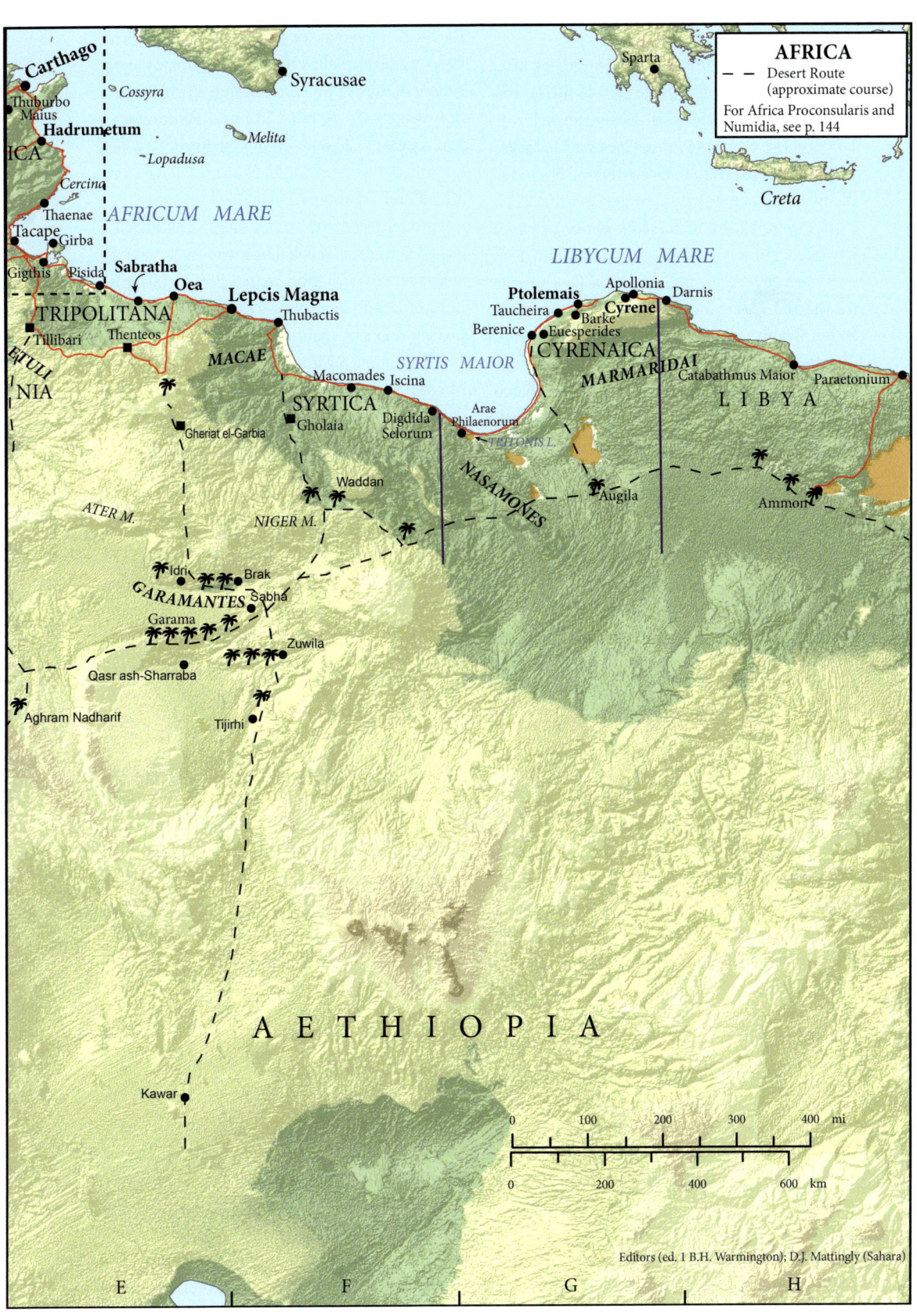

Africa (Rome's provinces)

Rome acquired its first province in Africa after the destruction of Carthage in 146 BCE; this comprised a relatively small area governed from Utica (p. 144, C1). In 46 Julius Caesar added a new province created from the kingdom of Numidia; the two were combined by Augustus around 27. 'Africa' in this form remained a public province governed from Carthage, now refounded as a *colonia* by Augustus. In 39 CE, Caligula transferred command of the province's single legion from the proconsul to a *legatus Augusti* of praetorian rank. For all practical purposes he took charge of Numidia – not designated as a separate province until 196 – as well as the military zone on the desert fringes eastwards to the border with Cyrenaica. In 42/43, the client kingdom of Mauretania was annexed and split into two provinces, Mauretania Caesariensis and Mauretania Tingitana, separated by mountains (with no through road); both were governed by equestrian procurators. No serious threats were envisaged: the African garrison amounted to just one legion with numerous auxiliaries, in all about 28,000 men.

During the Punic period, urban life had developed at numerous coastal sites; these survived the destruction of Carthage. Development was subsequently boosted by considerable immigration from Italy under Caesar and Augustus. Several *coloniae* (such as Madauros, p. 144, B1) were founded, and there was much private settlement. The restriction of nomadic and pastoral movements opened wide areas to intensive agriculture; the intermittent *fossatum Africae* barriers (C1-D1) regulated the flow of transhumance at the desert fringe.

Tribal structures broke down rapidly in some areas (though not in the mountains), so that some 400 or more indigenous communities, mostly mere villages, came to be recognized by Rome as having local administrative responsibilities. With increased wealth, many developed into Roman *municipia* during the second century. Some, like Lepcis Magna (p. 143) and Hadrumetum, were old Phoenician settlements; others, like Thugga, Thubursicum Numidarum, Thuburbo Maius and Mactaris, were indigenous (p. 144).

By 200 CE the density of urban life in northern Proconsularis rivalled that of Italy. In most cases the population of these communities probably did not exceed 10,000, but Cirta and Hadrumetum had perhaps 30,000, and Carthage – which became the western Mediterranean's largest city after Rome – perhaps 250,000.

Throughout North Africa there were extensive imperial estates; much land, too, was held by absentee owners. But many provincials also prospered, and increasingly they are found in the highest ranks of the imperial administration. In 193, Septimius Severus, an African from Lepcis Magna, rose to be the first emperor not of Italian descent. In Late Antiquity, the proconsular territory was restricted, as the provinces Byzacena and Tripolitana were carved out of the south and east of the old province; together with Numidia and Mauretania Caesariensis (which was split in two), these formed the diocese of Africa under a *vicarius* based at Cirta. A further notable feature of North Africa is the speed with which Christianity spread there – faster than in any other Latin-speaking region (see p. 192). Many of the most important early Christian writers in Latin – among them Tertullian, Cyprian, Lactantius, Augustine – were Africans. However, the consequences of Diocletian's persecutions split African Christians into bitterly opposed Donatist and Catholic factions.

While Latin culture advanced further west, Cyrenaica retained the Hellenic character stemming from its settlement by Greeks in the seventh century BCE (p. 18). During the Roman period, immigration from Italy was slight. Following its annexation in 74 BCE, Cyrenaica formed a proconsular province jointly with Crete. This linkage was only broken around 300 CE, when Cyrenaica was divided into Libya Superior and Libya Inferior. Greek ways of life continued in the coastal cities, the term Pentapolis being applied to Apollonia, Cyrene (p. 145), Ptolemais, Taucheira and Berenice. Serious damage was caused during a revolt by Jewish inhabitants in 115–117, but the province suffered no major military problem until the fourth century, when desert tribes came to exert intense pressure on its cultivated areas.

Africa (south of Rome's provinces)

North Africa in antiquity may be best known for its regions close to the Mediterranean, but it was also in large measure shaped by its deep Saharan hinterland. Contrary to the impression given by ancient sources, this vast desert's inhabitants were not just periodically belligerent nomads. In particular, archaeological research into the central Saharan people known as the Garamantes has now revealed hundreds of oasis farming villages and several sites meriting recognition as towns. Some of these oases already existed in the early first millennium BCE, although the peak of settlement and Garamantian civilization came in the early first millennium CE, when the Garamantes form a recognizable state.

Oases had originated even earlier in Egypt's western desert, and most modern ones in the eastern Sahara can be demonstrated to have had ancient origins. Further oases seem to have already existed alongside Roman frontier works where these followed close to the desert's edge across modern Algeria, Tunisia and Libya. Further west, investigations in the main Moroccan oases of the Tafilalt and Wadi Draa have also produced evidence of pre-Islamic oasis formation during the first millennium CE. Deeper into the Sahara there are other major oasis groups – Tuwat and Wargla among them – where unequivocally pre-Islamic evidence has not yet been identified, but in time may emerge.

The early steps of establishing trans-Saharan trade and contact occurred in the pre-Islamic period, with the Garamantes certainly exercising influence along central and eastern routes. Finds that can be linked to the Roman and Garamantian worlds at sites like Marandet, Tin Hinan, Kissi (near a major gold field), Tombouze (near Timbuktu) and Djenné-Djenno offer hints to the routes followed, although the map reflects the many uncertainties. Black Africans were an important element in many Saharan communities, intermixed with Berbers (Mediterranean Africans); Ptolemy (*Geog.* 4.8.3) at least seems to imply that the Aethiopes lay south of the Garamantes.

Lepcis Magna

Although the Old Forum area (9) at Lepcis (or Leptis) was evidently settled by Phoenicians during the seventh century BCE, the earliest visible remains only date to the first century BCE. By then, profiting from the export of local crops (olive oil especially), a thriving city had developed. The Chalcidicum sanctuary (6), market (7) and theatre were all built soon after, and the street grid extended and shifted so that the coast road could be its *decumanus*; hence the addition of 'Magna' to the city's name now. Development continued through the second century CE, with a further boost at its end when the emperor Septimius Severus spent lavishly on his birthplace. His projects – never fully completed – included a forum (4), basilica (3), colonnaded street (2), arch and enlarged harbour. During the fourth century, however, decline began, caused by earthquakes and nomads' raids. By the time that Italian archaeologists initiated professional investigation in 1920, Lepcis had lain abandoned for around a millennium.

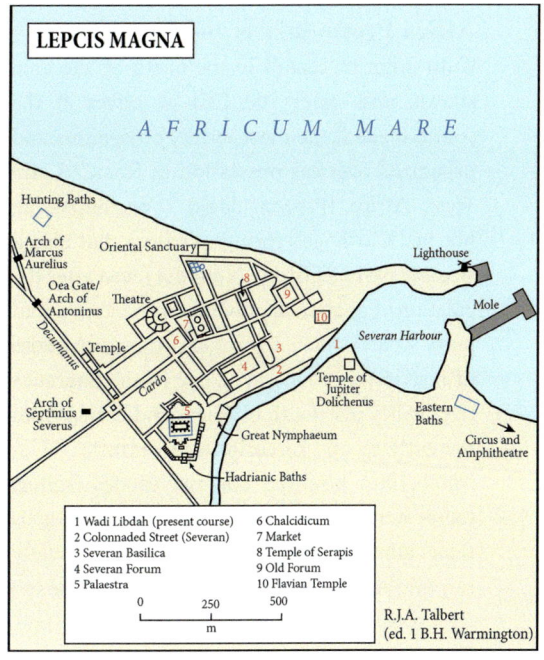

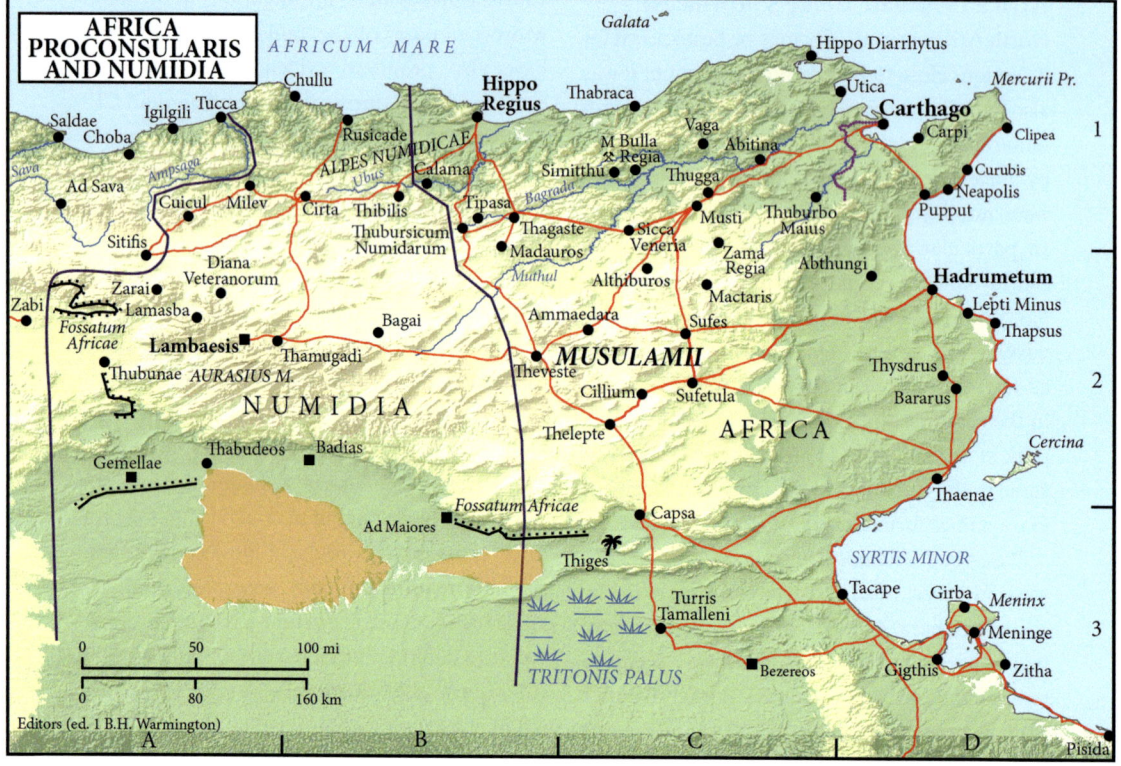

Africa Proconsularis and Numidia

Cultivation of cereals in the north of the area shown, and (after 100 CE) of olives in the south, made it the most fertile, prosperous and urbanized overseas possession in Rome's Latin West. Africa (Proconsularis) – encompassing not just Carthage's former territory, but also a sizeable part of historic Numidia (even after the creation of a separate province there) – produced more senators than any other province. A series of inscriptions found in a zone of the Bagradas river valley just south of Vaga, and dating from the early second to early third centuries, gives insight into how the imperial estates (*saltus*) there were managed. Of special interest is their administration by procurators directly responsible to the emperor, acting in liaison with a *conductor* (chief lessee) for each estate. These texts preserve regulations encouraging tenants' cultivation of marginal land (*subseciva*) according to an enactment of the first century CE termed the *lex Manciana*: this allowed for tenancies of small marginal plots to be sold back to the estate if found to be uneconomic.

Steady advance of the settled zone can be traced in the progressive relocations westwards of the legion III Augusta's base from Ammaedara to Theveste to Lambaesis, adjacent to which was planted the veteran *colonia* of Thamugadi (Timgad, p. 139) in 100. The success of the *lex Manciana* in encouraging the progressive development of settled agriculture in lands at the fringe is confirmed by the fact that the same regulations are repeatedly cited several centuries later in the 'Albertini Tablets' of 493–496, a cache of documents from the Jebel Mrata 65 km west of Capsa and around 300 km southwest of the Bagradas river valley. The literary output of Fabius Planciades Fulgentius and of Corippus/Gorippus during the sixth century demonstrate the continued vitality of Africa's Latin culture into the Byzantine period.

Cyrene

Cyrene was founded from Thera around 630 BCE (see p. 18). It lies 8 km inland, with a road leading to its port, Apollonia, 19 km distant. The acropolis, where the original colonists settled, remains largely unexplored. The city visible today is predominantly Roman, although it retains the layout developed by Ptolemaic rulers, as well as some remodelled structures of the Hellenistic period. It was then that long fortification walls were built, encircling two hills which rise to 620 m, separated by a valley descending to the northwest. Modern Shahhat encroaches on the site to the east and south, so the best-explored areas are the Street of Battus and Apollo's sanctuary to the northwest. The public and private buildings along this street show how

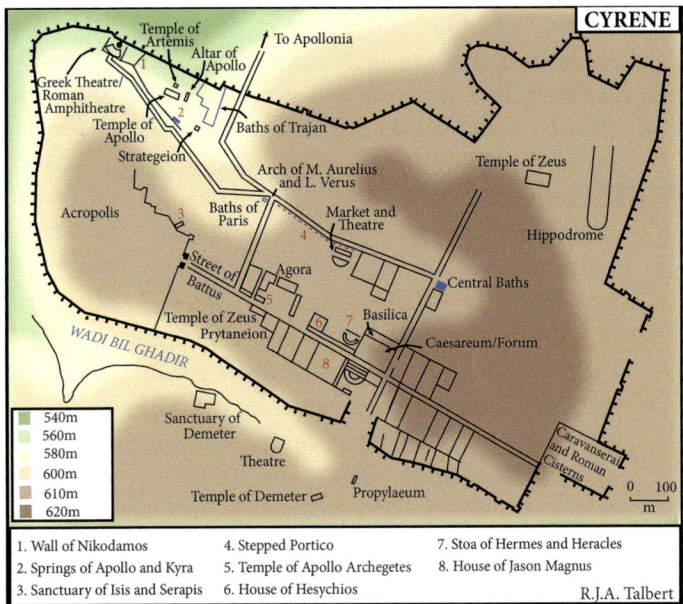

Cyrene thrived as a provincial capital. However, recovery after widespread destruction during the Jewish revolt of 115–117 CE was slow, and lasting damage was caused by earthquakes in 262 and 365.

Lutetia Parisiorum (Paris)

Lutetia Parisiorum (today Paris, France) was a typical midsize northern Gallic *civitas*-capital, with a population of perhaps 6,000. It succeeded a Celtic *oppidum* settlement on the Île de la Cité, an easily defended site controlling an important route across the Sequana (Seine) river. However, continuity of settlement was only assured when Romans built a road which crossed the river here. The Romano-Gallic city's centre lay on the left bank. Its layout reflects local acceptance of Greco-Roman ideas of urbanization, with a street grid and substantial buildings for administration, entertainment and relaxation. Especially notable are the central forum complex – including an open area with a surrounding portico, a great hall and temple – and baths. The city was unwalled, a tribute to secure conditions during the Principate. In regular Roman fashion, cemeteries were located beyond its sacred boundary. Although the Later Roman and medieval city retreated to the Île de la Cité, suburban habitation clearly continued on the left bank.

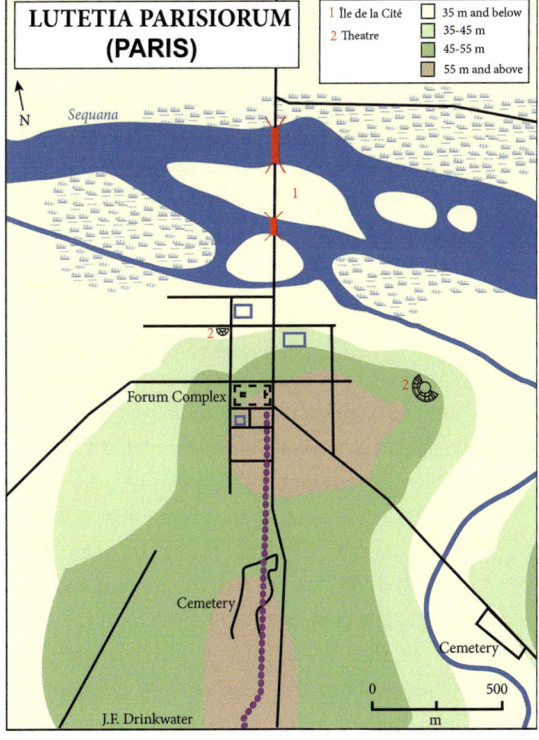

Gaul

Rome first gained a foothold across the Alps in southern Gaul during the late second century BCE by intervening to help Massilia against the Salluvii. War with the Allobroges extended Roman territory to Lake Lemannus (Geneva). Aquae Sextiae was established as a garrison town and a *colonia* was founded at Narbo Martius, both of them linked to Rome's provinces in Spain by the Via Domitia. Feuds left the northern Gallic tribes blind to the threat posed by Rome in the south, as well as to possible consequences of the appearance of Germanic peoples in the north. Julius Caesar, however, readily exploited the 'German threat' to justify Roman intervention and subsequent conquest of Gallia Comata ('Long-haired Gaul') up to the Rhine river between 58 and 51 (p. 104). Once dictator, he established veteran *coloniae* at Narbo, Arelate, Forum Iulii and Baeterrae. Augustus followed his example, founding more *coloniae* in Narbonensis, as the old province now became known. Thus began the intensive Romanization of the provincial society that eventually produced the Flavian general Gnaeus Iulius Agricola and the forebears of Tacitus and Antoninus Pius. To the northeast, Caesar founded three *coloniae* – Raurica, Noviodunum (Iulia Equestris), Lugdunum – to block Germanic invasion. However, a new defensive line was soon established along the Rhine; supporting its garrison became Gaul's prime responsibility.

Under Augustus, while Narbonensis remained a public province governed by proconsuls, Caesar's conquests were divided into three new provinces under imperial legates – Lugdunensis, Aquitania, Belgica – whose shared provincial assembly (*concilium Galliarum*) met at Condate outside Lugdunum, the hub of the road network. Augustus founded no new *coloniae* in the north. Instead, the old tribes were organized as *civitates* (civic communities) and given single centres of administration ('*civitas*-capitals' such as Augustodunum), but otherwise left alone. Thus the 'Three Gauls' developed a Gallo-Roman culture rather than a Roman one. Augustus also began the subjugation of the western Alps, which improved communications between Gaul and Italy, and led to the creation of three further provinces, all governed by equestrian procurators: Alpes Graiae et Poeninae, Alpes Cottiae, Alpes Maritimae.

Following the failure of Augustus' advance to the Elbe river, and the return of the frontier to the Rhine, the military zones Germania Inferior and Germania Superior were carved out of Belgica and Lugdunensis; during the late first century CE both were reclassified as provinces governed by legates of consular status. Germania Superior included the only permanent Roman acquisition across the Rhine, the *Agri Decumates*, an area annexed to shorten the northern frontier. The second century saw the development of an impressive overland boundary (p. 151). Legions came to be stationed at Castra Vetera, Bonna, Mogontiacum and Argentorate. Together with associated auxiliaries, and naval personnel at Gesoriacum and Claudia Ara Agrippinensium, they amounted to a formidable garrison. Its needs prompted improvement of road and river communications, while soldiers' spending power stimulated the economy. Increased wealth was reflected in urbanization, not only in *coloniae* and *civitas*-capitals, but also in spontaneous agglomerations around military bases and along main routes. Prosperity, and perhaps a growing population, are also seen in the widespread appearance of substantial Romanized farmhouses and villas, around Samarobriva, for example.

During the mid-third century, Gaul suffered badly from barbarian incursions across the Rhine. From 260 to 274 the legions here sustained a breakaway imperial government. Although the Agri Decumates were abandoned, order was eventually restored, and Augusta Treverorum became the regular base of an imperial court for a century from the late 200s. It remained the seat of the Gallic Prefecture (encompassing the Gallic, British and Spanish dioceses) until this was moved to Arelate in the early fifth century, after civil war and Germanic invasion broke the all-important Rhine frontier. Even after 476, the Gallic field army briefly formed a Roman rump state sandwiched between the Visigoths to the south and Franks to the north.

Germany

Normally, the rivers Rhine and Danube marked the northern limit of Roman expansion in western and central Europe. By the late first century BCE, the Celtic-speaking peoples of the region (living both north and south of the rivers) were at different levels of political, social and economic development. In the West, Julius Caesar reached the Rhine in 55. In 15, Augustus initiated a series of campaigns to annex the lands between it and the Elbe (Albis), building fortresses on the Rhine's west bank (including Noviomagus, Castra Vetera, Novaesium and Mogontiacum), and bases in the Lippe (Lupia) valley further east. However, his forward policy was reversed after the Germans' ambush and massacre of three legions under P. Quinctilius Varus in the Teutoburgiensis Saltus (9 CE); thereafter, the Rhine was made the frontier. By 90, the rump of Augustan Germania – two narrow military zones on the west bank – became the provinces of Germania Inferior and Superior governed by imperial legates.

In Augustus' time, after the Alpine tribes had been subjugated (p. 147), the Vindelici and the kingdom of Noricum were overrun up to the Danube. It was Claudius who instituted two provinces here, Raetia and Noricum, governed initially by equestrian procurators. Because this region was situated between Germania Superior and Pannonia – both well garrisoned – neither legionary troops nor imperial legates were required until the late second century.

Claudius reinforced the river frontiers with new forts. However, in 69–70 the civil conflicts and Batavian revolt caused widespread destruction, prompting Vespasian to overhaul the defensive systems. On the Danube he rebuilt the Claudian forts; east of the Upper Rhine, he linked Mogontiacum and Augusta Vindelicum by new roads, and fortified the Upper Neckar (Nicer). The defensive system linking the Upper Rhine and Danube was progressively developed over the next century (p. 151).

Under threat of attack by the Marcomanni, in 179 Raetia was protected by a new legionary base at Reginum; soon afterwards, Lauriacum did the same for Noricum. Germanic raids all along the frontier progressively threatened the security of provincial life, especially after 233. The Romans' retreat in 260 to the old front lines along the Upper Rhine and Danube allowed the Alamanni to move into the Agri Decumates. From the late 200s, new strongpoints were built along both the rivers and several main routes in the hinterland. Even so, Rome's position had to be repeatedly bolstered by imperial campaigns through the 300s.

It was the army that caused rapid Romanization in these frontier provinces: urbanization and the intensive exploitation of natural resources are amply documented by archaeology. Veteran *coloniae* such as Claudia Ara Agrippinensium and Augusta Raurica were founded, and many lesser towns sprang up. Most forts, too, had dependent civilian settlements, some of considerable importance. Villa estates in the countryside supported a prosperous upper class, while marginal land was farmed by a sizeable peasant population.

In Late Antiquity, administrative responsibility for the Rhine and Upper Danube areas was split between the prefectures of Italy and the Gauls, and between three dioceses (Gaul, Italy, Pannonia). Although imperial travel between Rhine and Danube was generally via northern Italy, Julian did pass north of the Alps on his way east to confront Constantius II in 360. After the disastrous breach of the Rhine frontier in 406/407, the defences of Germania Inferior seem never to have recovered fully. The *Life of St. Severinus* provides a vivid account of the piecemeal disintegration of the Roman garrison and the decline of urban life along the Danube in Raetia Secunda and Noricum Ripense during the second half of the fifth century. While the lowlands were largely abandoned to Germanic settlers, Latin culture proved more tenacious in the high Alpine region of Raetia Prima around Curia.

Rhine-Danube *Limes*, 40–260 CE

The *Agri Decumates*, a triangle of land between the upper Rhine (Rhenus) and Danube (Danuvius) rivers, formed a vulnerable re-entrant into Roman territory. Rome maintained firm possession here only between the late first and mid-third centuries CE. After Augustus' failure to annex Germany up to the Elbe (Albis) river, the Rhine and Danube served as the frontier. Initially, major bases at Mogontiacum (B2), Argentorate (A3) and Vindonissa (B4) were supported by forts in the Rhine valley and south of the Danube. It was in this latter area that Claudius created the first frontier line (Latin *limes*) by constructing forts between Brigobannis (B4) and Oberstimm (E3). Next, the Flavian emperors extended this chain eastwards with forts in the Reginum area (E3). During the same period, forts were constructed along the Upper Neckar (Nicer) river north of Arae Flaviae (B3), and a road was built east of the Rhine from Mogontiacum to Augusta Vindelicum (D3).

Trajan and Hadrian then constructed a line with forts to the northwest and northeast beyond the Rhine from Mogontiacum; they did the same in the mid-Neckar area, as well as considerably north of the Danube, where Claudius' line had kept south of it. These initiatives protected much previously underexploited fertile land, which attracted numerous migrants. From around 160 a further line was constructed – often running dead straight, with lookout towers and wooden palisade – south of the Main (Moenus) river and east of the Neckar, all the way from Miltenberg (C2) to Abusina on the Danube (E3). From this time too, elsewhere many wooden forts and palisades were rebuilt in stone. However, the lines beyond the Rhine and Danube came under increased pressure from Germanic peoples from the 230s. In 254, the Raetian sector was breached, prompting the Iuthungi to raid Italy in 260. The subsequent standoff between Gallienus and Postumus' breakaway Gallic Empire compelled the *limes* troops to pivot round to face each other, leaving the Agri Decumates exposed and its settlers forced to evacuate.

Danube–Black Sea

Until the late first century BCE, Rome's interests in Europe east of Italy were largely confined to the Histria peninsula (p. 109, F2) and the occupation of Macedonia. However, Roman control was extended to the Danube river as a result of Augustus' campaigns down the Savus river valley, together with the conquest of Dalmatia's interior and the route to the Danube down the Margus river valley. Before Augustus' death (14 CE), three imperial provinces – Dalmatia, Pannonia, Moesia – had been created. Of these, Moesia was to be divided later by Domitian, Pannonia by Trajan. When Dacia was annexed at the beginning of the second century, it was sometimes governed as a single province, at other times as two or even three.

Towns – both Macedonian foundations and Greek colonies – only existed on the periphery of the new conquests, on the Aegean coast of Thrace and on the Black Sea. New autonomous communities (*coloniae* of Roman veterans and *municipia*) were founded under Augustus and Tiberius, notably in Liburnia (p. 109, G3) and northern Macedonia, providing civilian administration for newly conquered territory. In addition, the *coloniae* guaranteed a military reserve at strategic centres vacated by the legions after the initial phase of conquest. By the mid-first century CE, all along the Dalmatian coast numerous towns had been established.

In the interior, the pace of urbanism was much slower. Native administration was maintained in central Pannonia and Moesia, regularly supervised by centurions detached from their legions. The first urban foundation on the middle Danube – Claudius' *colonia* at Savaria – lay on the 'Amber road,' the route north from Italy to the legionary fortress at Carnuntum. Savaria's citizens included both veterans and Italian traders eager to exploit the major military markets on the Danube. Later in the first century, Siscia and Sirmium (the former founded with discharged sailors) were established to strengthen the development of the Savus valley;

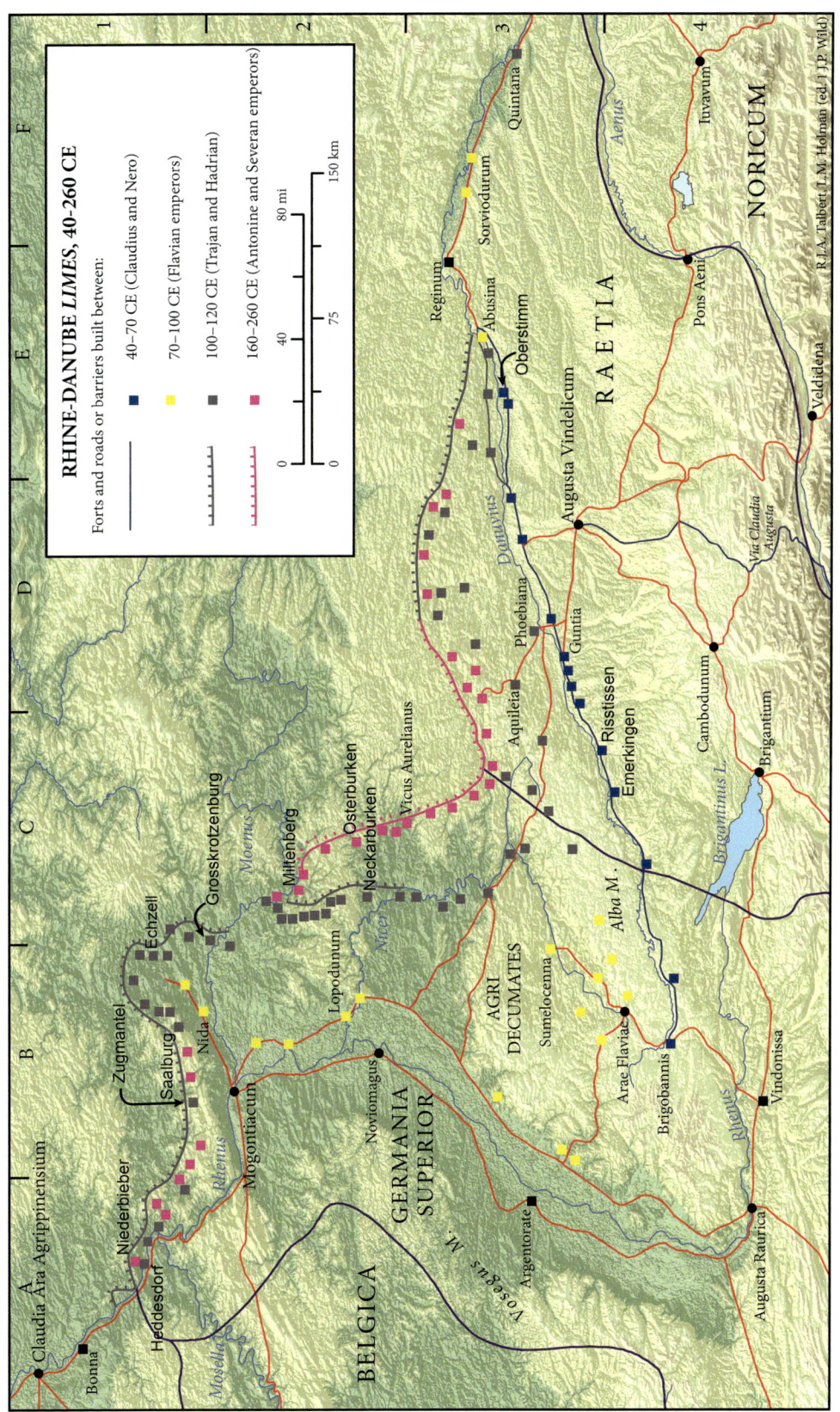

it formed a second important route through Pannonia, leading south-east to the Danube at Singidunum. Sufficiently Romanized native communities were also granted urban status under the Flavians, among them Andautonia and Scarbantia. In Moesia, tribal administration was maintained, and Romanization proved more difficult. The only *colonia* here was Scupi, founded by Domitian, a mixed community of veterans drawn from all four Moesian legions.

The greatest impetus to urban development came from the conquest and annexation of Dacia in 106. Three new *coloniae* were founded: Poetovio in Pannonia (p. 109, H1), Ratiaria in Moesia Superior, Oescus in Moesia Inferior. Hadrian granted civic status to native settlements in Pannonia's interior, such as Cibalae and Bassiana. Close to the legionary fortresses on the Danubian frontier, substantial civilian settlements (*canabae*) formed from a mix of veteran soldiers, native traders and foreign immigrants. Hadrian raised several to municipal status, notably Carnuntum, Aquincum and Viminacium.

Further east, urban development was slower. Thrace, annexed by Claudius, had few urban centres inland. Although Vespasian did found a *colonia* at Deultum, such initiatives were mainly left to Trajan. While Pautalia, Serdica and Augusta Traiana could claim native origins, his foundations at Nicopolis ad Nestum, Nicopolis ad Istrum and Marcianopolis (the latter two north of the Haemus range) were all new creations. In the case of Nicopolis ad Istrum at least, its citizens were mostly civilians from Asia Minor and military veterans from the Danubian garrisons. Hadrian founded only one more city in Thrace, Hadrianoupolis (Adrianople). Otherwise, this province's landscape remained largely one of villages remote from the towns; these latter commanded extensive territories exploited through subsidiary market centres.

Similarly, the conquest of Dacia was not followed by the creation of towns on the scale of Augustus' programme in Dalmatia or the Flavian one in Pannonia. The establishment of Ulpia Traiana Sarmizegetusa as a *colonia* only three years after the conquest was a political decision; it demonstrated Rome's power, not an intention to engage with the local population. Unlike in other western provinces, no native names appear on cities' inscriptions here; most of the richer citizens came from regions to the south or from Asia Minor. Hadrian added only two new towns, Drobeta on the Danube and Romula in the Alutus river valley, both south of Dacia's heartlands.

The second century witnessed the most prosperous period in the development of the Danubian provinces. Towns of the interior were provided with temples, *fora* and lavishly decorated public buildings. By contrast, country farms were generally small, lacking the luxury of villas in Gaul or Africa. Mining, though an imperial monopoly, encouraged the growth of settlements in Moesia Superior and western Dacia; these gained municipal rights by the third century. Ampelum, the centre of gold mining in Dacia, attracted skilled miners from Dalmatia. Moesia Superior was exploited especially for its lead and silver, western Thrace for gold, northern Dalmatia for iron.

Military centres that attracted substantial civilian settlements in Dacia (such as Porolissum, Napoca and Potaissa) and in Moesia Inferior (Durostorum, Tropaeum Traiani, Troesmis) received civic rights, as did the native settlements of Margum, Horreum Margi and Naissus along the Margus river valley in Moesia Superior. From the early third century, awards of the title *colonia* to existing settlements become increasingly common: Potaissa in Dacia and Aquincum in Pannonia Inferior were so honoured. Not long afterwards, however, the barbarian invasions commenced, bringing devastation to the region's provinces and ending nearly two centuries of economic and urban development.

After rule by Mithridates VI of Pontus in the early first century BCE and then a long period of internal power struggles, Bosphorus (p. 34) eventually stabilized as a Roman client kingdom whose rulers proudly proclaimed themselves "friends of Caesar and of the Roman people." It flourished in the second century CE, but was damaged by Goths around 250, and destroyed by Huns in the 370s.

Greece

After 146 BCE, Rome governed peninsular Greece through the proconsul of Macedonia, whose main concerns lay north of the Via Egnatia, a strategic route linking the Adriatic Sea with the Aegean and the Bosphorus. Athens was heavily penalized by Sulla for supporting Mithridates in 88. Only in 46 was the separate province Achaia created. Its proconsul was based at Corinth, now refounded by Caesar as a Roman *colonia*; hereafter it overshadowed Athens in political and economic terms. After Roman armies had already made a marked impact on Greece during the civil wars (p. 105), this was intensified permanently in the triumviral period by six veteran colonies in Macedonia, including Dyrrachium, Pella and Philippi, all key locations; Augustus founded another colony at Patrae. Early in the second century CE, Nicopolis, a Greek city also founded by him to commemorate his victory at Actium (p. 107), became the leading community of a new province, Epirus, governed by an equestrian procurator.

Although the Greek cultural world was now centred on Alexandria (p. 66) and Asia Minor, Athens remained a destination for foreign students, including Cicero and the future emperors Hadrian and Julian; the city hosted schools of philosophy into the sixth century. Nero's enthusiasm for Hellenic culture culminated in his tour of Greece's festivals in 66. Hadrian's philhellenism led to substantial building schemes at Athens and the focusing of his new religious confederation, the Panhellenion, there. Pausanias' mid-second-century *Guide to Greece* reinforces the impression of Achaia as essentially an open-air museum. Its peace was shattered by incursions from beyond the Danube river by Costoboci (p. 153, E1) who sacked Eleusis (p. 36, A4) in 170/171, and later by Heruli (p. 149, D1) who badly damaged Athens in 267. In Late Antiquity, the region's supremacy passed to Thessalonica, where the route between Italy and Constantinople met that from the Danube to the Aegean. During the fourth century the diocese of Macedoniae was generally subordinate to Italy, as were the jurisdictions of the ecclesiastical hierarchy into the Middle Ages.

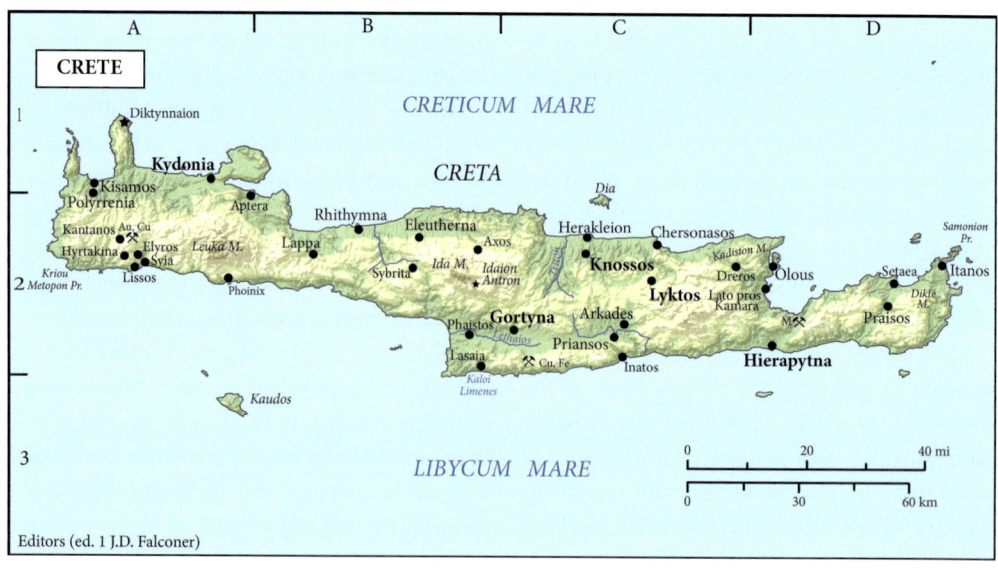

Editors (ed. 1 J.D. Falconer)

Crete

Following the collapse of Minoan civilization (p. 9) and subsequent Dorian settlement in the eighth century BCE, Crete in the seventh century became a prosperous island of independent cities, where the arts flourished sufficiently to influence developments throughout the Greek world. Communities of archaic Crete were also the first in Greece to introduce written law codes.

Such prosperity evidently came to an abrupt end in the sixth century. Thereafter, Crete never again occupied such a dominant position in either the historical or archaeological record. From the fifth century until the Roman conquest in 69–67, the island suffered frequent inter-city wars, in which the larger communities of Kydonia, Knossos, Gortyna and Hierapytna fought to increase their power over the weaker ones. During this period, settlement was concentrated in walled cities occupying strong positions on hilltops.

The Roman conquest was carried out by Q. Caecilius Metellus, following accusations that the Cretans were guilty of piracy and were helping Mithridates VI of Pontus in his fight against Rome. After the annexation, Gortyna became the provincial capital, and Crete was combined with Cyrene to form a single province, governed by a proconsul of praetorian rank – an arrangement which continued until the early fourth century CE, when the island became a separate province in the diocese of Moesiae (p. 189). Close social and economic ties to Italy were forged when in 36 BCE Capua was compensated for territory lost to veteran settlers with valuable land taken from Knossos; after 27 BCE, that city was refounded as Colonia Iulia Nobilis, perhaps receiving Capuan settlers. Because the Principate brought peace, settlements in low-lying and coastal areas became more common. The building of country villas during the second and third centuries CE indicates some prosperity. Knossos seems to have been largely abandoned after the major earthquake in July 365 that caused a tsunami to strike Alexandria (p. 66); Herakleion – more easily defensible – then became the major centre on the island's north coast.

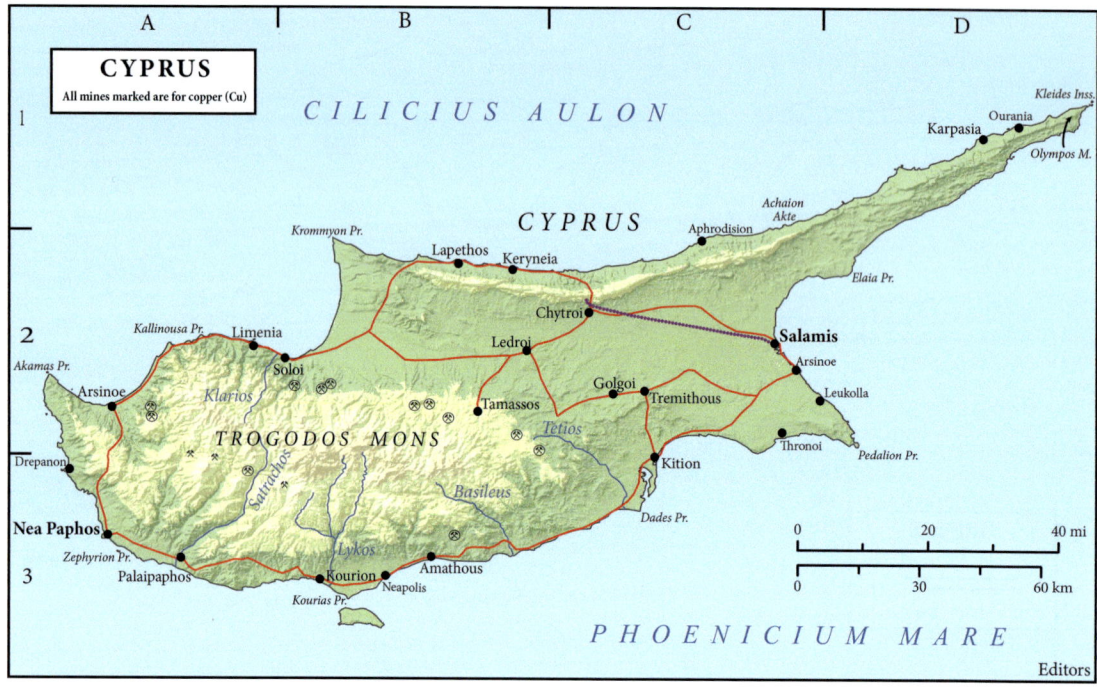

Cyprus

Annexation of Cyprus for the Roman people in 58 BCE at the instigation of the populist tribune Clodius followed two-and-a-half centuries of Ptolemaic rule. The island was first administered with Cilicia (as during Cicero's governorship, 51–50). Julius Caesar and Antony returned it to Egyptian rule, but Octavian claimed it permanently for Rome after his victory at Actium (31). From 22 onwards it was a separate public province, governed by a proconsul of praetorian rank, and divided into four districts centred around Nea Paphos, Salamis, Amathous and Lapethos. Nea Paphos, famous for its temple of Aphrodite, was developed as the administrative capital, where the provincial council (*koinon*) also met. Salamis, however, with its harbour and fertile hinterland was the largest and most cosmopolitan city, and the main commercial centre. It exported the island's principal products – copper, timber, grain – and was well situated to exploit trading opportunities with Syria, Judaea and Egypt. Copper was mined (under state control) mainly in the northwest between Arsinoe and Soloi, and in the rugged interior around Tamassos.

The island did suffer occasional earthquake damage, and it was also convulsed by its sizable Jewish population at the time of Jewish risings throughout the East in 115–117 CE, prompting Trajan to dispatch detachments of Legio VII Claudia to restore order. Even so, archaeological findings along with meagre literary and epigraphic evidence do confirm the impression that under Roman rule Cyprus was a quiet, comparatively prosperous backwater. By the time of Diocletian's tetrarchy (293–305), *praesides* of equestrian rank governed the island, and by the mid-fourth-century Paphos had yielded its primacy to Salamis, rebuilt after an earthquake with aid from Constantius II (337–361) and renamed Constantia in his honour. Although for civil administration the province was made part of the diocese of Oriens, its church leaders vigorously resisted ecclesiastical domination from Antioch and were successful in claiming independent (autocephalous) status for Cyprus.

Aphrodisias

Aphrodisias, a classical-style urban community, only developed in the valley-floor of the Morsynos river (tributary of the Maeander) after a nearby hilltop settlement, Plarasa, moved to synoecize with the sanctuary of Aphrodite there around 100 BCE. The latter was sufficiently famous to attract both Sulla and Julius Caesar. Loyalty to Rome in the Mithridatic War, and later to Caesar's cause, was rewarded with privileges that were repeatedly confirmed by emperors in communications proudly engraved on its theatre's so-called 'archive wall.' Monumentalization advanced rapidly during the first century CE: the theatre and new temple were financed by an imperial freedman, and an imperial cult complex (Sebasteion) was lavishly decorated with sculpted reliefs celebrating the Julio-Claudians' conquests. The excellent local marble was used throughout, and it also facilitated the development of a notable school of sculpture.

The urban centre boasted three impressive public areas: the main political space, North Agora, situated between (to the north) the extensive temple precinct and (to the south) the portico-lined South Agora or 'urban park' (for leisure), featuring a grand pool surrounded by palm trees. Not only the monumental stadium, but also the Aphrodisian origin of (T. Aurelius) Alexander, head of the School of Peripatetic philosophy at Athens around 200, are testimony to the city's vitality as a Greek cultural centre; meantime, two sets of public baths, and adaptation of one end of the stadium to serve as an arena, reflected the popularity of Roman pastimes. Local wealth produced Roman senators by the mid-third century, including at least one proconsul of Asia. Around 303 the city became metropolis of the new province Caria. Later, despite (or because of) Christianization, important elements of the sculptural heritage were relocated to the Civil Basilica. At the same period, the city's cemeteries were plundered for stone to construct an imposing walled circuit. Aphrodite's temple was eventually repurposed as a cathedral around 500. After being sacked by Persians in the early 600s, the site was mostly abandoned. American excavations since 1961 continue to uncover it.

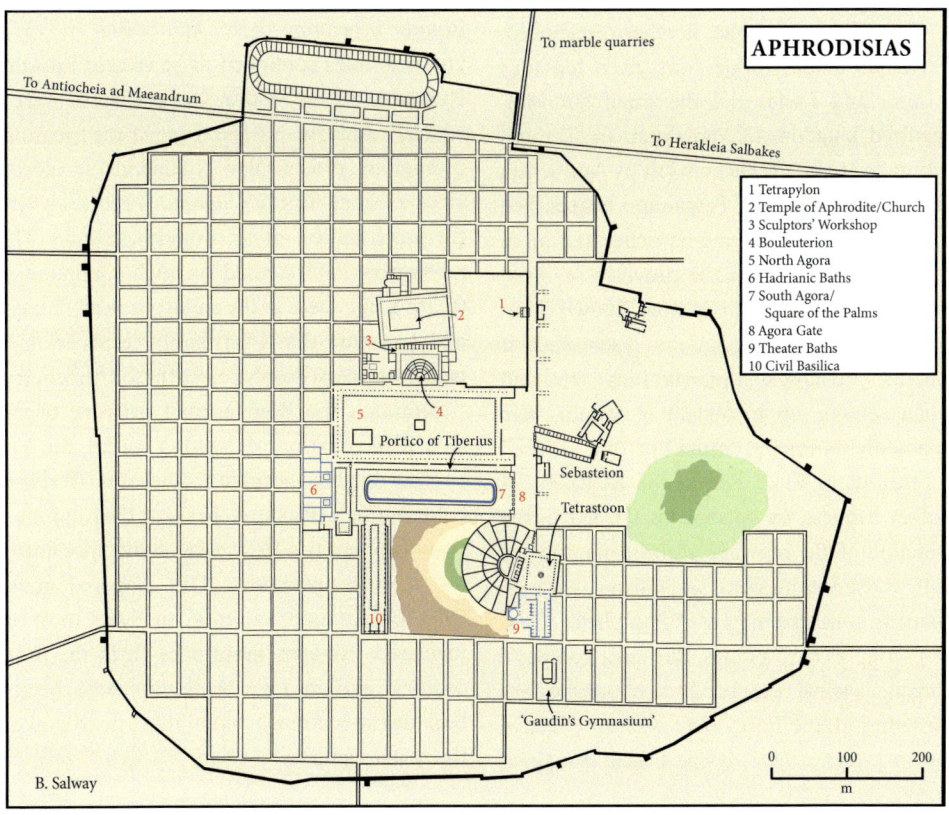

Asia Minor

Asia Minor's geographical centre – in ancient terms Phrygia, Galatia, Lycaonia and western Cappadocia – consists of a rolling plateau at 1,100 m altitude, drained by the Sangarius and Halys rivers and by lakes of varying salinity; rainfall is low, winters severe. This plateau is bounded to the north by the Paphlagonian mountains; their wooded northern slopes drop to a narrow coastal plain. Southwards, the Taurus range begins in Lycia, runs roughly parallel to the coast and finally, east of the Cilician Gates, merges into the mountain mass 300 km wide which separates the Pontic coast from the Cilician and north Syrian plains (p. 162). Westwards, the plateau and Pisidian mountains are broken by large river valleys, notably those of the Maeander, Hermus and Sangarius: these made Lydia, Mysia and Bithynia the richest parts of Asia Minor.

Serious Roman interest began here with the war against Antiochus III. Victory in 190 BCE left Rome as arbiter of the peninsula (p. 72). The Seleucids were generally confined to Cilicia, while native kings were retained in control of Cappadocia and the northern seaboard. Of Rome's allies, Rhodes was given territory in Caria and Lycia, and the small but well-organized kingdom of Pergamum (p. 77) was encouraged to fill the vacuum left by Antiochus.

In 133 Attalus III of Pergamum bequeathed his kingdom to Rome, and its richer and more accessible parts became the province of Asia. The system of taxation is now known from inscribed customs regulations discovered at Ephesus. Economic opportunities attracted Italian settlers, up to 80,000 of whom were supposedly massacred in the uprising inspired by Mithridates VI of Pontus (88 BCE). In 74 another bequest, by Nicomedes III, led to the formation of the province of Bithynia. On the south coast the province of 'Cilicia' – which originally consisted mainly of Pamphylia – had been set up to curb pirates. But until Pompey's campaign against them in 67 and his subsequent reordering of the East, there was no effective Roman presence here; hence Cilicia remained nominally Seleucid territory. After the defeat of Mithridates by Pompey, most of his kingdom was added to Bithynia.

Next, in 25, Amyntas of Galatia bequeathed his kingdom – including much newly captured territory that was ethnically Pisidian, Phrygian, Lycaonian and Isaurian – to form the basis of a new province of Galatia governed by an imperial legate. Cappadocia was taken over in 17 CE. Initially it was controlled by a procurator, later attached to Galatia, and finally made a separate imperial province by Trajan. The Lycian federation was annexed by Claudius, while Vespasian reinstated the province of Cilicia, which for over a century had formed part of Syria.

In more developed areas, Greek-style cities were usually the main unit of local government; elsewhere, the tribe continued to govern. There were also large imperial estates, such as the Praedia Considiana, that never acquired city status. Roman *coloniae* were rare, apart from a group founded by Augustus to hem in the turbulent Pisidians. Hellenization of the peninsula's interior was encouraged under Roman hegemony (note Aphrodisias, p. 157), and new cities continued to be created into the Byzantine period. Within the province of Asia – which became (with Africa) one of the two most prestigious proconsular commands – certain cities acted as district (*conventus*) centres where the proconsul on circuit would hear cases. The missionary Paul focused on such communities (p. 160), but it was in the countryside of Phrygia and Lycaonia that Christianity seems to have penetrated most deeply before the fourth century.

Although the Roman road network began as a regularization of existing routes, the Via Sebaste at least (linking Augustus' Pisidian colonies), as well as stretches near the Euphrates river frontier (p. 162), were built specifically for military purposes. The diagonal route from Byzantium/Chalcedon to Syria took on increased strategic importance from the third century, and in Late Antiquity Asia Minor became the economic and military heartland of the eastern empire.

Paul's Journeys

The journeys outlined here are the four made by the Christian missionary Paul during the mid-first century CE, as defined and described in the New Testament *Acts of the Apostles*. Only the last (from Jerusalem to Rome) is narrated in detail, and during it uniquely Paul travels as a Roman prisoner. For the other journeys, it is seldom apparent how he proceeded on land (walking, riding, in vehicle?), with what servants if any, where he lodged, or how long he paused at stopping-points; a few lengthy stays are specified, such as eighteen months at Corinth during the second journey. Both *Acts* and Paul's own *Letters* refer to journeys, or the prospect of them, elsewhere too. At the moment of conversion he was on his way to Damascus, and earlier he had travelled extensively from Jerusalem in order to persecute. He says that immediately after conversion he went to 'Arabia,'

without elaborating on where this means. Later, writing from Corinth to Christians in Rome, he mentions a longstanding hope that he might visit them en route to Spain. *Before* the journey he eventually made to Rome, he claims to have been shipwrecked three times, cast adrift on open sea for a night and day, and to have suffered from rivers, robbers and many others. No account of these episodes survives. At least, what we do learn underlines the remarkable freedom of movement by land and sea that Rome made feasible during Paul's time. One indication that many exploited it is the complement of 275 with him on a ship which finally limped to landfall on Malta after encountering severe autumn storms southwest of Crete. But this near-death experience in turn underlines that travellers – on land, especially those without any official Roman rank or function – were still exposed to multiple hazards.

Syria–Persian Gulf

In antiquity, 'Syria' denoted the fertile strip along the Mediterranean's entire eastern shore from the Taurus mountains to Egypt. It was held by Seleucids prior to Roman annexation by Pompey in 63 BCE. Its southern regions (Judaea and Arabia) were initially left as client kingdoms (pp. 168, 172). In Roman parlance, 'Syria' came to be associated with the disparate northern region, to which Commagene was added from 72 CE.

Behind the narrow coastal plain there lie two parallel chains of mountains, broken at several points, and separated by valleys where the Orontes river flows northwards, the Jordan southwards. Eastwards, beyond the mountains, a vast desert gives Syria no defined border; to the north, the middle course of the Euphrates river marked the frontier. Prosperity derived from vines, olives, fruit and vegetables; the weaving of linen and wool were important, too, together with dyeing. Also lucrative were silk and other luxuries imported by caravan across the desert. This trade, on which Rome imposed an unusually high duty of 25%, encouraged the growth of communities on the desert fringe (especially Damascus), and at oases (especially Palmyra), as well as seaports on the Mediterranean coast. Otherwise, Syria remained under-urbanized and rural, with the village as the centre of local life. Mostly the population continued to speak varieties of Aramaic and was little influenced by Greco-Roman culture.

Given its strategic importance to Rome, Syria was governed by senior ex-consuls in command of a substantial garrison, much of it recruited locally. The capital, Antioch, ranked among the empire's greatest cities (p. 165). Around 200, Septimius Severus divided the province into two – to the north, Syria Coele with two legions, governed from Antioch by a consular legate; to the south, Syria Phoenice with one legion, governed from Tyrus by a praetorian legate.

East of Syria lay another part of the Seleucid inheritance, the Parthian empire. The attractive area closest to Rome's empire, the northwest of the Mesopotamian plain, was ruled by Parthian vassals, the princes of Osrhoene, from their capital at Edessa. The Parthian capital itself, Ctesiphon on the Tigris river, lay far to the south, and Parthia's realm extended beyond the Caspian Sea into central Asia. Although Parthia potentially posed a grave threat to Roman interests, in practice it was for long so weak and divided that Rome seldom sought any permanent commitment beyond the Euphrates. However, Septimius Severus' Parthian War did lead to the annexation of Osrhoene and to the creation of a province of Mesopotamia; by the 230s it stretched as far as Hatra, bringing Roman troops within striking distance of Ctesiphon.

Septimius' advance also provided a base for domination of Armenia. The strategic situation of this mountainous, undeveloped land had always made the allegiance of its rulers a matter of concern to both Parthia (with its close cultural links to Armenians) and Rome. From the Flavian period, Armenia was monitored from the frontier road linking legionary bases at Samosata, Melitene and Satala. However, despite various attempts, Rome failed to hold any of the country and could usually exert influence there only by diplomacy. To the south, Roman expansion undermined the Parthian Arsacids, who in 224 were displaced by the more aggressive Sasanian Persians. They repeatedly overran Roman Syria in the third century; Shapur I even captured the emperor Valerian in 260. Thereafter, Rome's authority was only restored thanks to the efforts of its Palmyrene allies.

In the fourth century, Antioch regularly hosted an imperial court, and became the secular and ecclesiastical centre of the diocese of Oriens. Armenia's early conversion to Christianity brought it progressively within the Roman sphere of influence, while to the south the Romans came to rely increasingly on Arab tribal federations for the security of the Syrian frontier. In the seventh century, the region was the key theatre for the last great war of antiquity: this so exhausted both Romans and Persians that they quickly succumbed to the forces of Islam emerging from Arabia.

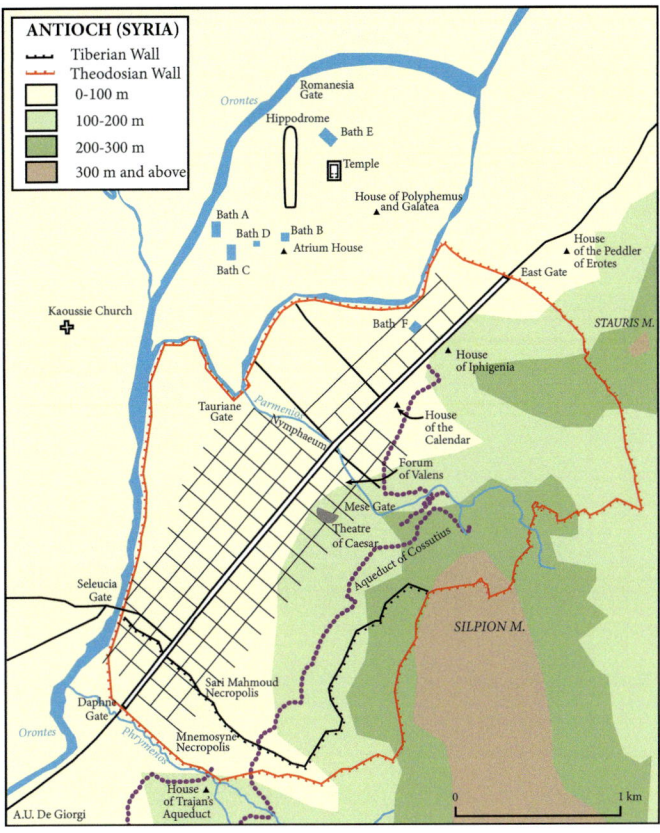

Antioch

Syrian Antioch on the Orontes river – strategically situated between the Mediterranean and the Orient – was a major city during ancient and medieval times, one that has remained continuously occupied (today Antakya in Turkey). It was a Seleucid foundation (302 BCE), then royal capital, and during the fourth century CE Rome's eastern capital. However, earthquakes and fires, as well as constant runoff from Mounts Silpion and Stauris, have mostly buried its ancient phase. Only recently have numerous research initiatives started to bring into focus the agencies that shaped it in fundamental ways. In particular, it is now accepted that the enclosing wall underwent eight construction phases between the Hellenistic and Crusader periods, and determined the location of water supply systems; aqueducts drew from springs at Daphne and on Mount Silpion. The island in the Orontes – no longer visible, and of uncertain extent – accommodated the residence of king Antiochus III; this was later superseded by the palace of Gallienus and Diocletian. As the site of a temple and hippodrome (presumably inaugurated by Q. Marcius Rex in the late 60s BCE), as well of many baths excavated during the 1930s, the island could be regarded as the city's centre, at least until the earthquake of 458 CE.

Elsewhere, the long main colonnaded street (*cardo*) – celebrated by the fourth-century orator Libanius – survives to this day, though buried under several metres of sediment, as shown by explorations in the 1930s. Its siting assists not only reconstruction of the city's grid plan, but also tentative placement of several important structures, including the theatre of Caesar, the forum of Valens, and the main gates that led out to the city's hinterlands. A few richly decorated houses of Roman and Late Roman date have been found on the island, and others on the slopes of Mounts Silpion and Stauris. However, Antioch's residential areas are still not known, nor is the location of any church in the city.

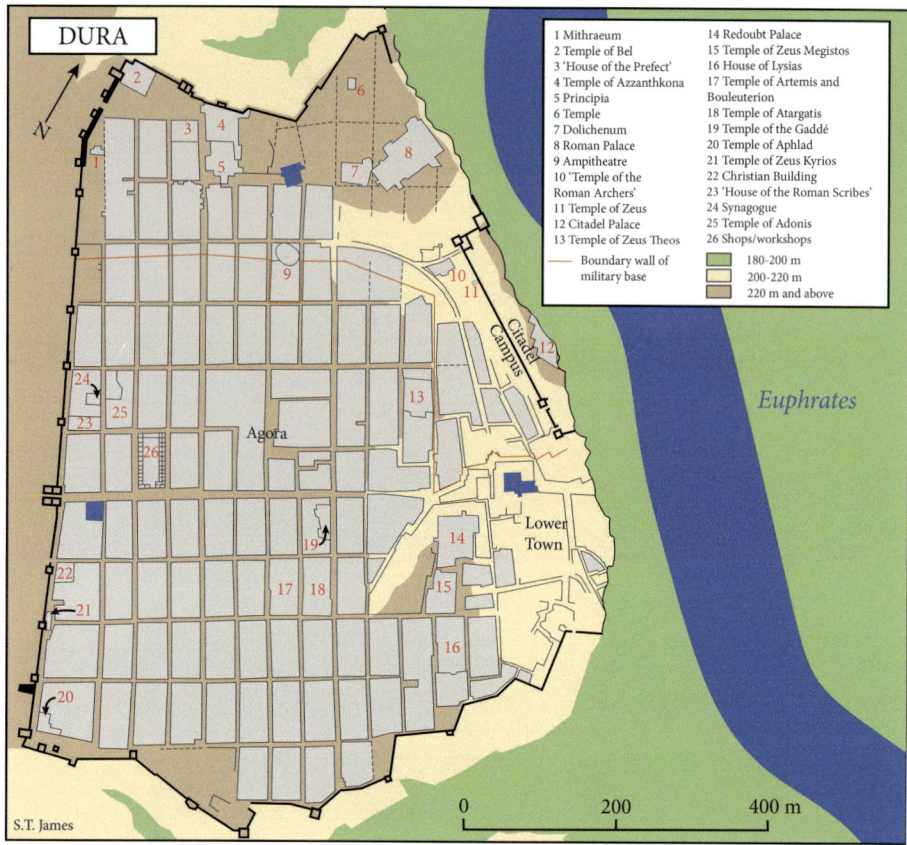

Dura

A place known as Dura – 'stronghold' in Old Babylonian – was chosen for Europos, a Macedonian military colony founded around 300 BCE. Situated on cliffs overlooking the Euphrates river and Mesopotamia beyond, it lay midway between the Seleucid capitals of Seleucia on the Tigris and Syrian Antioch (p. 68). During the second century, it became a constitutionally Greek city with a walled area exceeding 55 ha. Its population was culturally diverse, with an Aramaic-speaking majority ruled by an elite of *Europaioi*, nominally Macedonian but actually of mixed descent. Dura retained its Greek façade under Arsacid hegemony from around 113 BCE to the mid-second century CE. While it lay on the important Euphrates trade route between Arsacid Babylonia and Roman-ruled Syria, its main economic base was the agricultural potential of the river valley, for which it was the administrative centre.

After brief Roman occupation during Trajan's reign, Dura reverted to Arsacid Parthian control until the 160s, when it again fell to Rome. Now housing a large garrison, it achieved the status of Roman *colonia*, although the troops themselves were Syrians; meantime the population became even more diverse, including Jewish and Christian communities (cf. 24, 22). Because Dura is barely mentioned in historical sources, its story – following its identification in 1920–1922 – stems almost entirely from excavation. The remains recovered largely represent the Late Arsacid urban fabric: mostly a Hellenistic street grid built up with Mesopotamian-style houses and multiple sanctuaries generally of courtyard form, constructed in plastered rubble and mudbrick. Under Rome the military sequestered the northern part, converting civilian housing for soldiers' families, and erecting a headquarters (5), amphitheatre (9) and (across the city) several bathhouses shared with the civilian population. Dura was besieged and destroyed by Sasanian Persians around 256, then permanently abandoned.

JERUSALEM ON THE MADABA MOSAIC MAP

Jerusalem/Aelia Capitolina, Second and Third Centuries CE

Steep-sided valleys protect Jerusalem to the east, south and west. The plan shows it after refoundation as Aelia Capitolina by the emperor Hadrian around 130 CE and before fourth-century Christianization. Much is conjectural, primarily because dense occupation since antiquity continues to limit archaeological investigation. The street grid was laid out after Rome's destructive storming of the city during the Jewish revolt of 66–70; the Tenth Legion's camp was also established then, although even its location remains controversial. Again, it is likely but unproven that Hadrian erected a temple of Jupiter approximately where the Jewish temple had stood on the Temple Mount. The two main streets proceeding south from the column (date and purpose unknown) near the Northern Gate were evidently colonnaded, as seen here in the vignette of the city on the sixth-century Madaba mosaic map (oriented East). Pre-Roman structures for channelling and storing water – aqueducts, dam walls, cisterns, pools – continued in use.

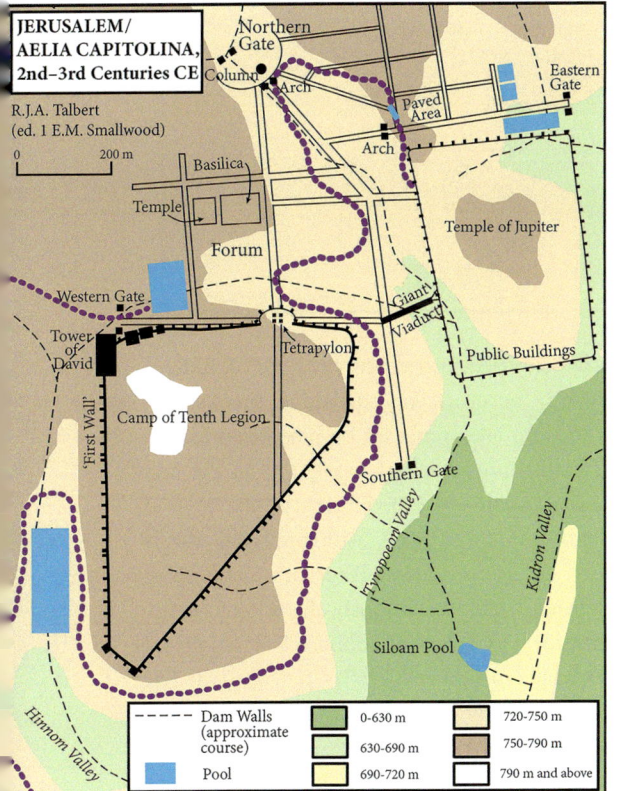

Judaea

When the Jews under the Hasmonaean dynasty achieved political independence from Seleucid Syria in the mid-second century BCE (p. 74), their territory consisted of Iudaea only, cut off from the sea by the line of Greco-Syrian (formerly Phoenician) coastal cities. Rapid territorial expansion followed. By the death of Jannaeus in 76, Jewish dominions comprised Galilaea (with its considerable Jewish population before annexation), Samaria (home to a schismatic form of Judaism), Idumaea (which was forced to accept Judaism), Peraea, the coastal cities, and some other Greco-Syrian cities to the north across the Iordanes (Jordan) river.

In 63, when Pompey turned Judaea under its last Hasmonaean king into a Roman client kingdom, the Jews' cities in northern Transjordan were removed from their control and linked with others as the semi-autonomous Dekapolis. The Idumaean Herod the Great, placed on the throne by Rome in 40, subsequently had Oulatha, Paneas and extensive territory to the north-east added to his kingdom. When he died

in 4, it was divided between three of his sons: Archelaus ruled Iudaea and Idumaea until 6 CE, when his oppression provoked his subjects to seek annexation by Rome; consequently, the province of Judaea was established, governed by equestrian prefects. Philip ruled the northeastern territories till his death in 34. Antipas ruled Galilaea, Samaria and Peraea until deposed in 40.

Next, in 37, Herod Agrippa, a grandson of Herod the Great, was appointed king of Philip's former territory, then absorbed Antipas' in 40, and in 41 Rome's province Iudaea. However, on Herod Agrippa's death in 44 his kingdom was converted into a new province of Judaea, initially governed by equestrian procurators, who were later replaced by praetorian legates after this province was nearly lost in the first Jewish revolt (66–70). During it, the Second Temple was destroyed, with profound effects for Judaism. Later, Hadrian's antisemitic policies – most notoriously the refounding of Jerusalem as Aelia Capitolina, a Roman *colonia* dedicated to Jupiter (p. 167) – provoked the Bar Kochba revolt of 132–135. Afterwards, Jews were banned from the city, and the province, now under consular legates, was renamed Syria Palaestina.

Masada

Masada is a rock plateau rising 360 m from the narrow plain between the Dead Sea and the Judaean mountains, with access only from the east by the dangerous 'Snake Path.' Not until the 1960s did Israeli archaeologists thoroughly investigate the remains here. Supposedly strengthening an earlier fortress (no longer traceable), in the late first century BCE Herod the Great built a double (casemate) wall – creating space for storage and lodging – around the cliff edge except at the northern tip, where the precipices are almost vertical. Here, on three descending rock terraces, he made a small private palace. On the plateau itself, larger palace complexes were built, together with residences for staff and visitors. Numerous cisterns – mostly in the cliffs, fed by an aqueduct from a wadi to the west and by occasional rain – enabled the fortress to withstand a long siege. During the Jewish revolt of 66–70 CE, refugee rebels occupied Masada. Eventually, in 73 Roman forces enclosed it within a circuit wall (except where the terrain made this impossible) and eight camps (A–H). They then used a projecting rock bastion on the west as an assault ramp, raising it with stone and timber to the level of the wall, which they breached with battering rams. The reliability of the only surviving account of the siege – by Josephus, *Jewish War* 7.275–406 – is controversial.

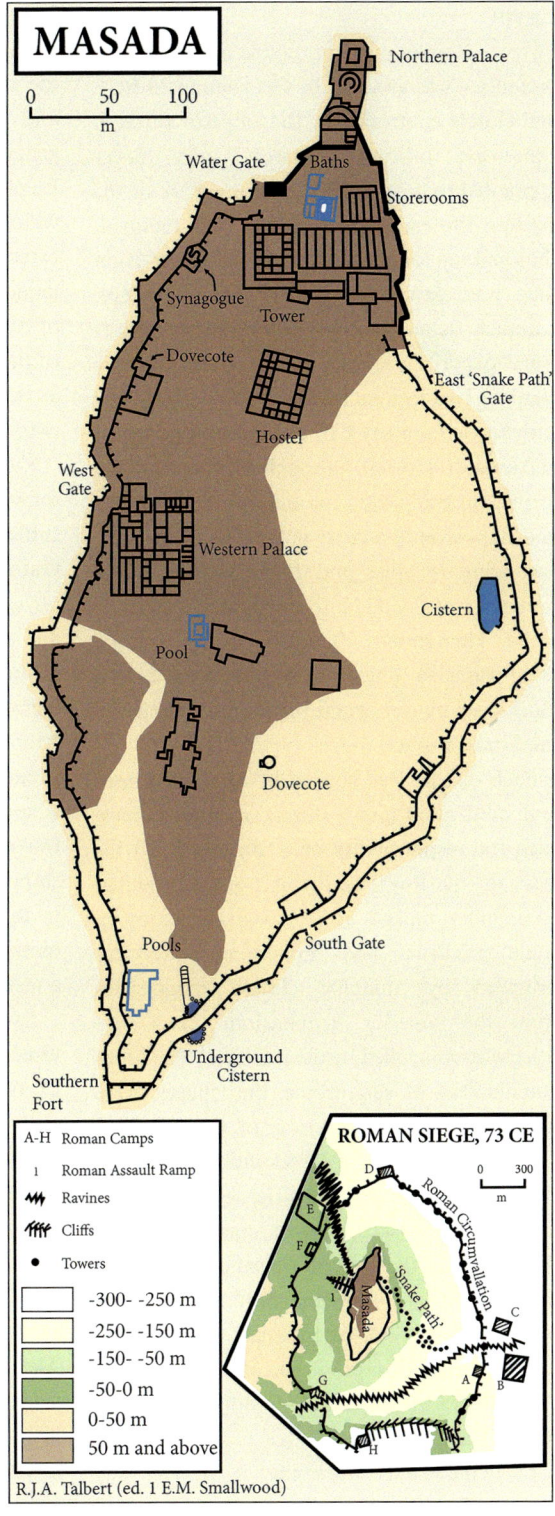

R.J.A. Talbert (ed. 1 E.M. Smallwood)

Egypt

Egypt – Rome's most profitable and populous province – was annexed by Octavian in 30 BCE and closely controlled by the emperor through equestrian officials; senators were never appointed to posts there. The framework of the existing Ptolemaic organization was retained, thus making for a tighter degree of supervision than was exercised over any other province. Uniquely detailed insight into daily life derives from papyrus records preserved in the dry climate. Two legions (reduced to one from the early second century CE) and a fleet were based at Alexandria (p. 66), although soldiers from the former were deployed throughout the province, and ships from the latter policed the Nile river. For administrative and fiscal purposes, the province was divided into three large districts – Delta, Heptanomia, Thebais; to the last of these was also joined the frontier zone of the Dodekaschoinos beyond the natural barrier of the First Cataract.

Each district was headed by an *epistrategus*, and subdivided into a dozen or more nomes, each the responsibility of a *strategus* and his assistant the Royal Scribe. A nome's principal community ranked as a *metropolis*, enjoying some privileges and limited civic services provided by annually elected magistrates from the superior 'gymnasium' class, but otherwise controlled by the *strategus*. The other communities of each nome, the villages, were wholly under the supervision of the *strategus*. The limited number of Greek cities lay outside the nome structure, and in every respect formed the most privileged communities of the province: the capital Alexandria, with its mixed Greek and Jewish population and by far the best harbour on the coast of the Delta, ranking as the most privileged of all; Naucratis; Ptolemais Hermiou; and Antinoopolis founded by Hadrian.

Like the lands adjoining it, Egypt was almost all desert. The only fertile areas were the marshy lands of the Delta (where papyrus was principally grown), the country around Lake Moeris (modern Fayum), and a narrow strip on either side of the Nile. In consequence, the river was the focus of the whole province, and its annual inundation was vital to general prosperity: the level was predicted at Elephantine Island from a 'Nilometer,' or gauge, which survives. The flooding – at its greatest extent during October – both refertilized the land and watered crops. Regular maintenance of dykes, embankments and canals was so vital to the country's economy that five days' labour at this work was required annually from every man of lower status.

Rome valued and exploited Egypt above all for its agricultural produce – chiefly cereals in sufficient quantities to fill whole convoys of vessels (see p. 182), but in addition vegetables, olives, vines and flax. Animals were raised, and there was also some quarrying and mining (notably for gold in the southeast). Highly lucrative, too, was the province's trade with Arabia and India through its Red Sea ports. Luxury goods landed there (and attracting a special duty of 25% of their value) were transported by caravan to the Nile, and then shipped to Alexandria for re-export elsewhere in the empire. The manufacture of perfumes, ointments and medicines was well developed as a result.

Two key changes brought Egypt into the Greco-Roman mainstream: the conversion of the *metropoleis* into self-governing Greek cities under Septimius Severus around 200, and the suppression of Egypt's separate coinage under Diocletian (296). The foundation of Constantinople (p. 187) brought profound socio-economic realignment, for example, enabling Egypt's wealthy landowners to enter the senatorial order of the New Rome. Alexandria maintained its intellectual leadership in the Greek world. Its Christian bishops were frequently at the forefront of international theological controversy, while evangelization of the peasantry went hand-in-hand with the development of a new alphabetic form of Egyptian, 'Coptic.'

Arabia

In Ptolemy's *Geography* (around 150 CE), the Arabian peninsula is divided into two: Arabia Deserta and Arabia Eudaemon or Felix. They approximate Saudi Arabia and Yemen today, and reflect the distinction between the nomadic or transhumant society of tribal groups (later known as Saracens) who herded camels, sheep and horses and harvested the dates from palms, and the urbanized communities occupying areas able to sustain sedentary agriculture. Although Arabia Felix was famous for producing incense, Greco-Roman interest in the peninsula was chiefly as a conduit for trade with India; hence Hellenistic settlements were established on the islands Icarus and Tylos in the Persian Gulf. Control of this trade motivated the (unsuccessful) expedition of Aelius Gallus sent by Augustus against the Sabaeans of Arabia Felix. Ultimately, Rome's suppression of piracy in the Red Sea (hence the distant outpost at Ferresanus Portus) boosted direct commerce not only between Egypt and India (see below), but also down east Africa's coast as far as Rhapta (p. 53).

The other significant area of sedentary agriculture lay in the Transjordan region, where in the second century BCE there emerged the Nabataean kingdom – with its capital Petra – also known as Arabia Petraea. Already Hellenized, it was annexed in 106 CE as the Roman province Arabia, governed first by imperial *legati*, later (from 260s) by equestrian *praesides*. A military highway, Via Nova Traiana, was constructed from the highlands on the frontier with Syria (p. 162), through Bostra and Petra, down to Aelana/Aila. Although the highway marked the edge of the cultivable area, both the Nabataeans and the Romans maintained forward stations in the desert: a northerly one at Dumatha, far down the Wadi Sirhan, on the caravan route from the Persian Gulf via Gerra; and a southerly one at Egra, on the western route from Arabia Felix via Macoraba and Iathrippa. It was from the cosmopolitan environment of these trading communities – where Jews, pagans and Christians all interacted – that Islam sprang in the late sixth century.

India

The Mauryas, beginning with Chandragupta (324/321–300/297 BCE), were the first major dynasty to establish hegemony over almost the entire subcontinent from their capital Palibothra in the Ganges river valley. Pushing back the Seleucids, they extended their rule not only southwards but also westwards beyond the Indus river (p. 69). The Mauryan ruler Ashoka (268–232), best known for the Buddhist-inspired edicts that he had inscribed in multiple languages (including Greek and Aramaic) in different locations around his empire, maintained diplomatic ties with the Seleucids, Ptolemies and other Hellenistic kings. By around 180 the empire had declined for various reasons including political weakness, fiscal crises and top-heavy administration. Parthian conquest of Babylonia in the 140s cut off direct communication between India and the Mediterranean world through the Persian Gulf. At this time too, the Greco-Bactrian kingdom that had survived on India's north-west frontier was obliterated by invaders from central Asia (see p. 65).

Direct travel from Egypt to India via the Red Sea was hindered by the peoples of south Arabia, but their monopoly on the Indian Ocean trade was challenged by the discovery around 100 BCE of open-sea routes from there to India exploiting the monsoon winds, as described in the anonymous *Periplus of the Red Sea*. The discovery opened up trade links between the Roman world and western India. These expanded following Rome's annexation of Egypt in 30 BCE, with chief exchange points at Barbarikon and Barygaza, as well as Tyndis, Muziris and Nelkynda in the Chera, Chola and Pandya kingdoms of south India; also in Taprobane. Roman exports included linen, coral, glass, base metals, pottery, wine and quantities of gold and silver coins. In exchange were imported luxuries such as perfumes, spices (especially pepper), gems, ivory, exotic woods and textiles (including Chinese silk).

Excavations at Arikamedu and elsewhere suggest that direct trade contacts were reduced from the third century CE. In Late Antiquity, Christianity did reach India, but through Persian Christians bringing the East Syriac rite rather than directly from the Roman world.

Rome's Empire around 211 CE

Efforts to extend the empire between 60 CE (see p. 130) and 211 were just as vigorous as those of the Julio-Claudian period. It now sprawled further than ever over three continents through diverse landscapes and climates. However, by no means everything gained could be held. After the client kings of Pontus and Commagene died in 64 and 72, respectively, the opportunity was taken to extend and consolidate the eastern provinces; more legions were assigned here, and new locations were chosen for their bases. Germany's two military zones were reclassified as provinces (Germania Superior and Inferior), and territory forming a dangerous re-entrant angle between the Rhine and Danube rivers – the *Agri Decumates* – was annexed; the frontier was thereby shortened, and the garrison reduced (p. 151). In Britain, the conquest of England and Wales was completed. During the 80s, forces under Gnaeus Iulius Agricola even penetrated deep into Scotland, but this initiative was not maintained. At the same time, the Danube frontier came under intense pressure from peoples north of the river. Additional commands were created by dividing the provinces of Pannonia and Moesia. Even so, the situation was stabilized only after two campaigns by Trajan (101–102, 105–106): these resulted in the annexation of Dacia to protect the lower Danube area.

In the East, the frontier was further strengthened with the annexation of Nabataea as a new province, Arabia Petraea, in 106. Five years later, Trajan made Parthian interference his pretext for attempting to gain full control of Armenia, which Nero's legate Gnaeus Domitius Corbulo had overrun around 60 in order to install a client king. In 113/114 Trajan was similarly successful, but he then rashly ventured further, sweeping as far south as the Persian Gulf (p. 173) by 115. Such gains soon proved too much to hold: rebellion here, and unrest elsewhere in the empire, prompted their immediate abandonment by Hadrian in 117. Rejecting Trajan's aggression, his goal was to consolidate the empire and its frontiers, even to the extent of building a wall to mark the northern limit of Britannia province (pp. 132, 135). His successor, Antoninus Pius, permitted a modest advance to a shorter line further north, where a turf wall was built and held for a brief period (p. 136).

The general peace that continued into the 160s was then shattered first in the East, where Parthia once again seized Armenia. It was recovered only after a long struggle, and as protection part of Upper Mesopotamia was now kept under Roman control (p. 166). Next, from 170, Marcus Aurelius' struggle to repulse the German peoples who swept across the Danube deep into the empire led him to attempt the subjugation of central and southeast Europe north of the river. He might have succeeded, had not a bid for the Principate made in the East by Gaius Avidius Cassius forced him to rush there. In 177, after the bid's failure, Marcus returned to the Danube and continued his efforts there until his death in 180. However, his son and successor Commodus then preferred to abandon the struggle and negotiate peace treaties.

Septimius Severus, who emerged as the victor in the civil wars of the 190s, attacked Parthia in retaliation for its support of a rival, and extended Roman control of Mesopotamia, which he made a new province. In North Africa, the security of the desert frontier was improved. However, Septimius' efforts to extend the province Britannia far north of Hadrian's Wall failed, and were abandoned after his death at Eburacum in 211. By raising three new legions, he brought the total above thirty for the first time in over two centuries. He also departed from the principle that none should be stationed in Italy by basing one at Castra Albana just southeast of Rome, intending it to serve as a reserve or 'field army,' without responsibility for a designated area.

Circuit of the Roman Empire by Aurelius Gaius, 285–299 CE

On a remarkable inscription the Christian veteran Aurelius Gaius – from Pessinous in Galatia – records with pride what he describes as his circuit of the empire. In fact, he ranged more widely still, serving under the tetrarchs Diocletian, Galerius and Maximian. Damage to the stone has deleted some of the places and peoples named, and left others unclear; it is also difficult to date the successive moves with certainty. The reconstruction followed for compiling this modern outline of the 'mental map' that Gaius records is by Kevin Wilkinson. Inevitably, however, much must be inferred from other evidence, and many points remain controversial.

Gaius probably served first along the Danube, making the first three of his four forays into Sarmatia between 285 and 294 CE under Diocletian's command. The circuit proper evidently begins in late 294 when, under Galerius, he travels from the province of Asia as far south as 'India' (in fact the Blemmyes' territory, beyond the first Nile cataract), east into Mesopotamia, and north against the Carpi. Next, under Diocletian again, from late 295/early 296 he moves westwards to Pannonia; probably also at this stage, he makes the forays mentioned against Goths (twice) and Germans. Then, transferred to Maximian's army, from mid-296 he moves from Noricum south-west as far as Mauretania, followed by a return eastwards to the province of Africa. Here his record of the circuit ends. Thereafter in all likelihood he accompanied Maximian to Italy by early 299, and later that year made his fourth foray into Sarmatia under Galerius' command. He was then discharged after fifteen years or more of soldiering, and settled at Kotiaeion (west of Pessinous).

Etesian Winds and Sea Currents
Sea Routes in Diocletian's Edict on Prices

Diocletian's Edict on Maximum Prices is a uniquely important document for understanding not only the priorities and ambitions of the Roman government, but also the question of the Roman world's economic integration. With the copy inscribed at Aphrodisias (p. 157) now pieced together, the full extent of the text emerges, including the enlarged and revised additional version of the last chapter on the cost of transporting goods by water. Issued in 301 CE, along with regulations revaluing the coinage, the edict aimed to control inflation in retail prices for goods and services, explicitly to preserve the purchasing power of soldiers' wages. Although the Christian polemicist Lactantius makes it clear that the measure was a failure, the extensive list of goods and prices provides precious insight into the world of the Roman economy. That the intention to regulate prices went in practice well beyond the normal needs of soldiers in the marketplace can be gauged from the list's comprehensiveness: it includes some 1,400 items. Priorities are revealed by its ordering, and care has been taken in the layout of the Aphrodisias copy to reflect logical groupings of material: Chapters 1–7, food and wages (248 entries); 8–48, leather, timber and materials (349 entries); 49–56, cloth and clothing (418 entries); 57–68, gold, silver, slaves, beasts, marbles, pigments (241 entries); 69–70, water transport, detailing over fifty sea routes within the Mediterranean and Black Sea.

The Mediterranean certainly facilitated long-distance transport. There has been much debate about how far the cycle of government taxation and spending stimulated production for long-distance trade that tapped the relatively low costs of water-borne freighting. The pattern and efficiency of maritime transport were in fact subject to numerous variables. For example, navigation by the stars enabled large grain ships returning to Alexandria from Rome to sail continuously and on a direct course; their speed was further accelerated by the seasonal (etesian) winds that blew steadily from between the north-west and north-east during the summer, combined with the stronger west to east current in the same season. Conversely, prevailing currents and winds dictated a more circuitous route for the journey in the opposite direction; and winter storms and cloudy skies effectively confined these larger ships' period of activity to between April and October. Modern computer simulation – factoring in data on currents and seasons – has confirmed the supposition that built into the maxima in the edict is a rough calculation of a maximum of one denarius per day for the transport of one *castrensis modius* of a given item.

In general, environmental conditions favoured the development of largely separate spheres of seaborne circulation to the east and west of Sicily respectively. It has been observed that a list of destinations organized alphabetically in Greek (Alexandria, Anatolē, Asia, Libyē, etc.) lies behind the order of the first version of the maritime transport list (Alexandria, Oriens, Asia, Africa, etc.). This is consistent with the presumption that the edict was almost certainly compiled at Diocletian's court somewhere in the Greek East (Antioch or Alexandria). The revised version sought to correct that limited perspective, and to give the edict greater universality by promoting the Rome routes to the head of this list. It also specified that different rates were to apply to *species fiscales* (fiscal goods) and *onera fiscalia* (fiscal cargoes), confirming that the published lists relate to the open market and not the state economy. Accordingly, it is interesting to find prices for through routes from Alexandria to Baetica and Lusitania. The presence elsewhere in the edict of far-flung 'origin brands' – for example, of cloaks from places as distant as Gallia Belgica (the *civitates* of the Treveri, Ambiani and Nervii, p. 147) and Britain – is testimony to the globalization of fashions. Such features suggest that, despite the disruptions of the third century, the economic world of the edict features a considerable degree of long-distance integration.

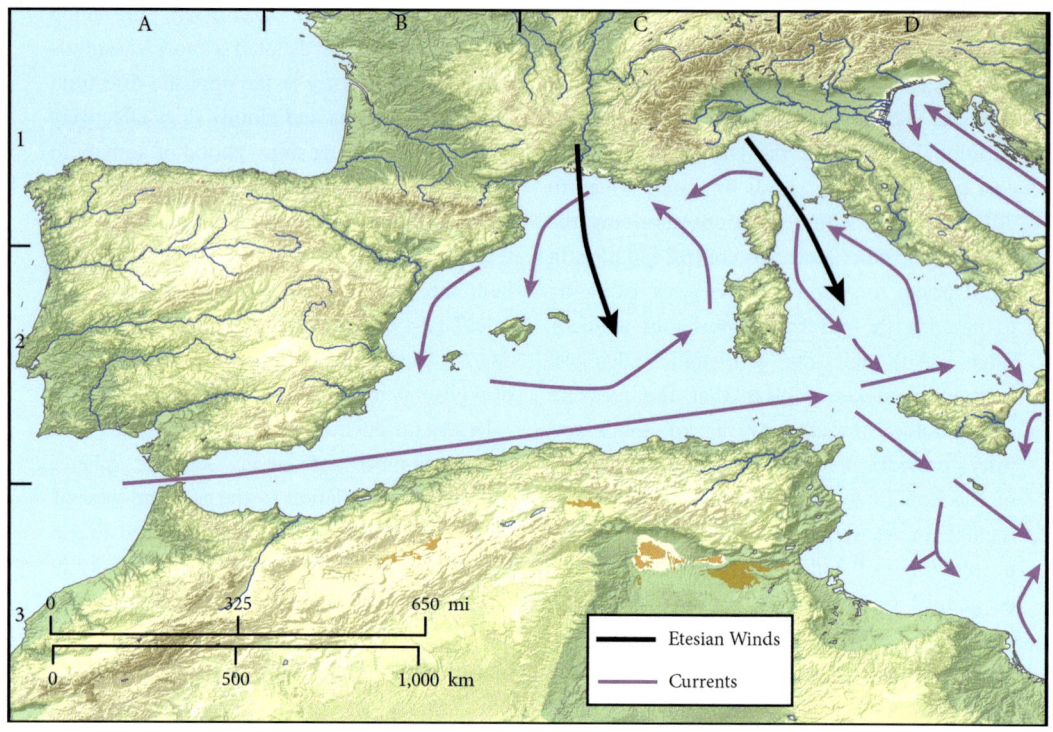
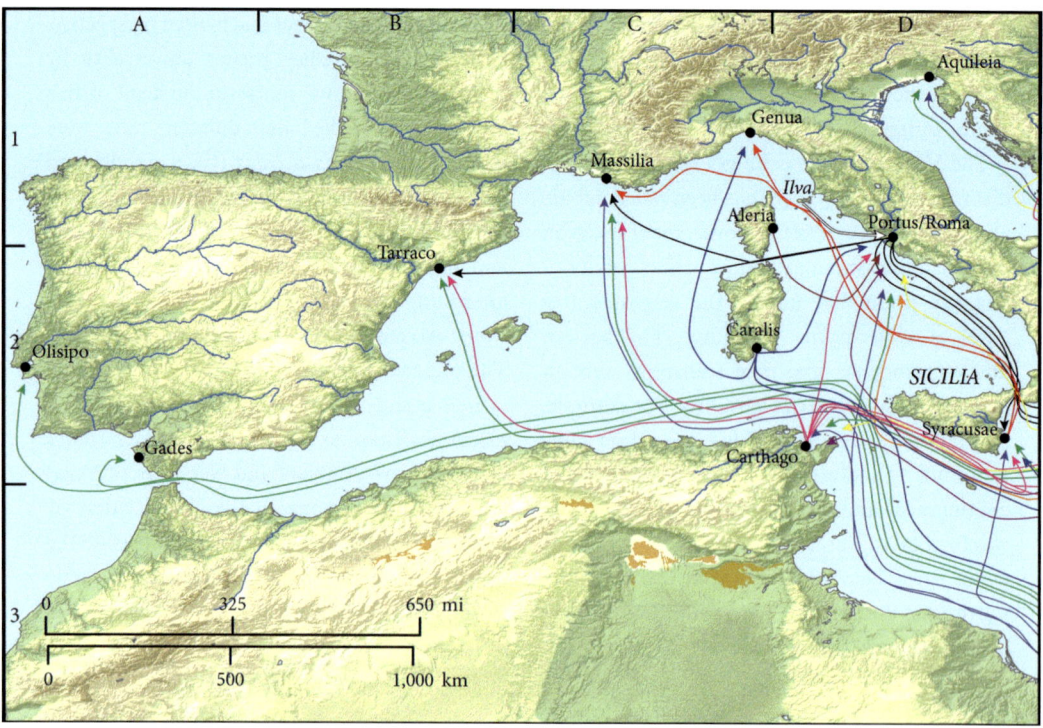

183

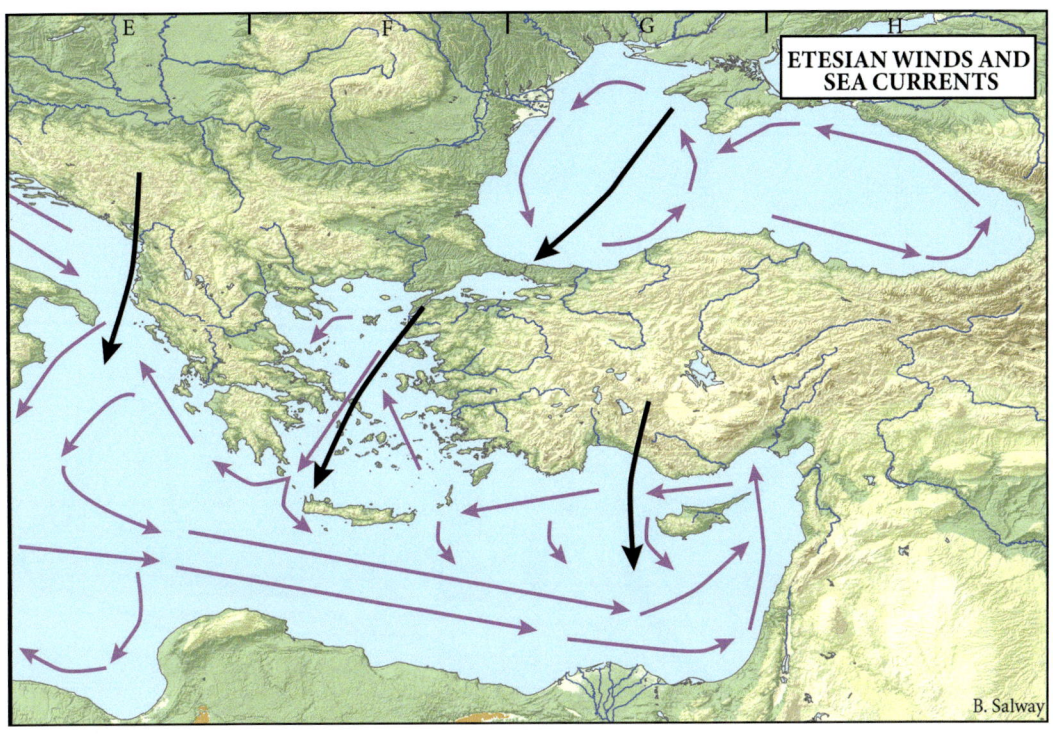

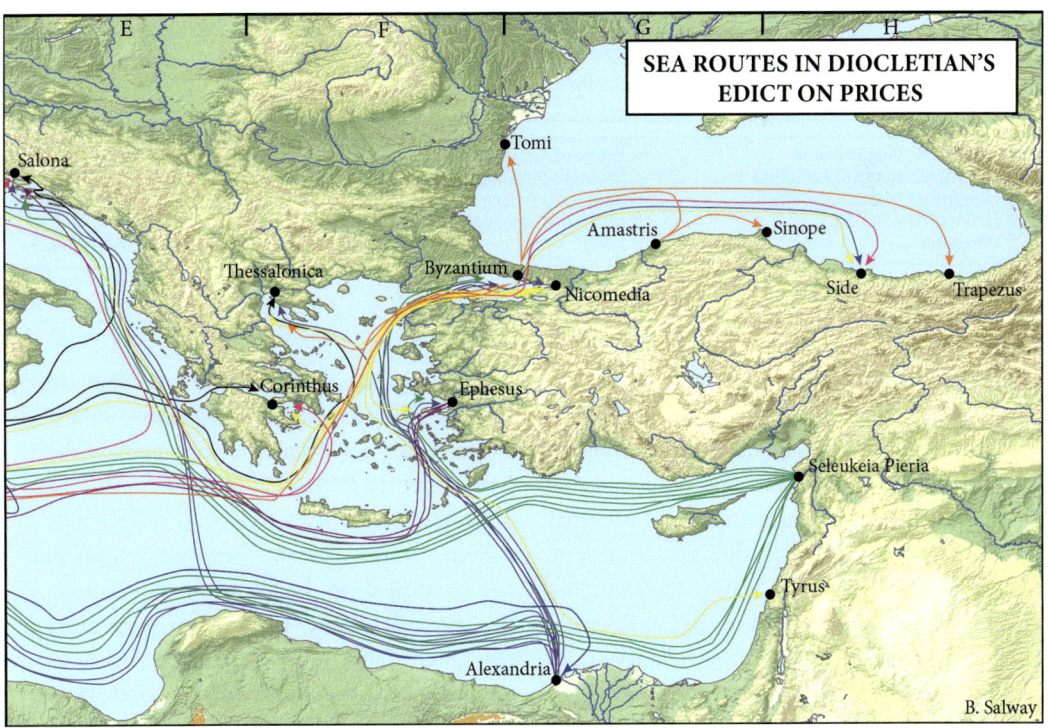

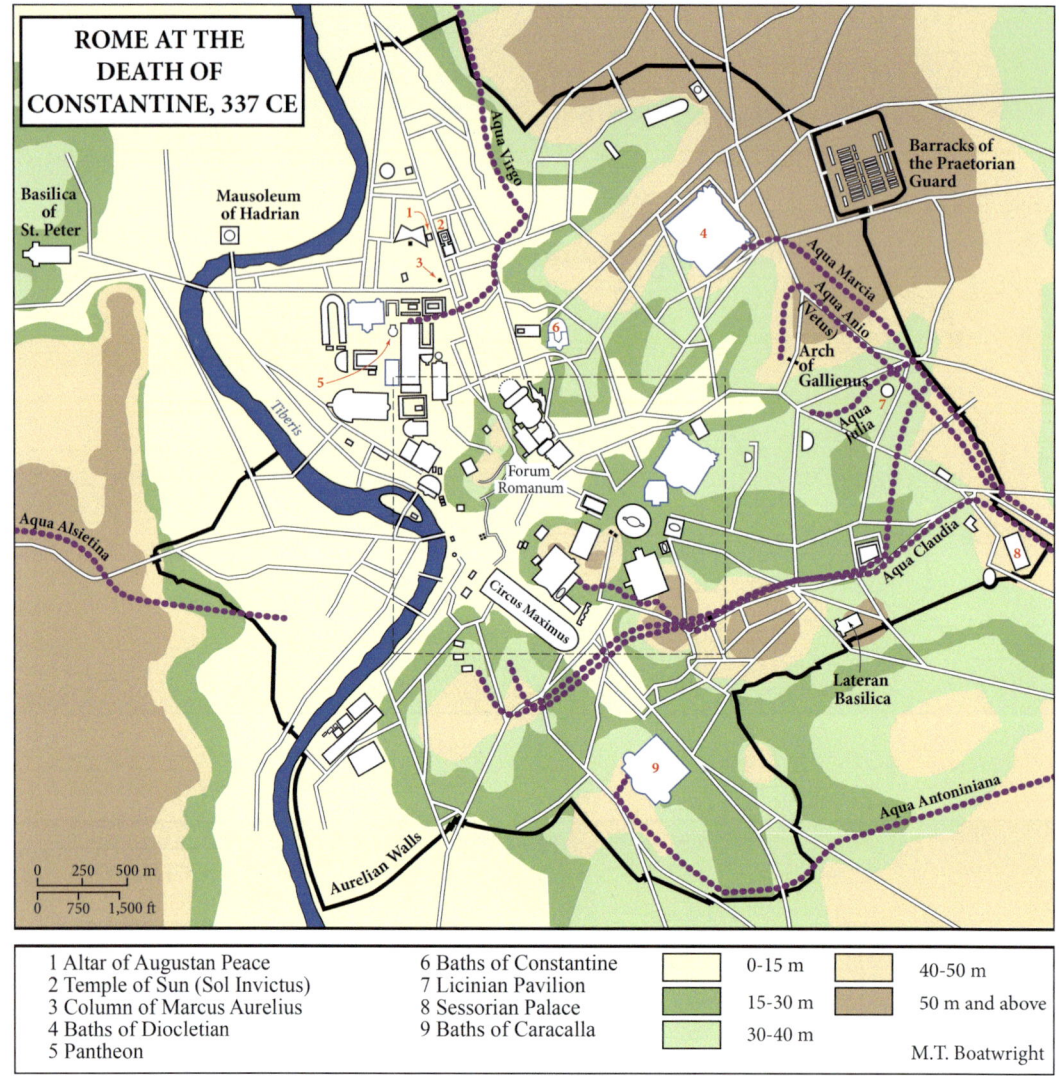

1 Altar of Augustan Peace	6 Baths of Constantine
2 Temple of Sun (Sol Invictus)	7 Licinian Pavilion
3 Column of Marcus Aurelius	8 Sessorian Palace
4 Baths of Diocletian	9 Baths of Caracalla
5 Pantheon	

Elevation: 0-15 m, 15-30 m, 30-40 m, 40-50 m, 50 m and above

M.T. Boatwright

Rome at the Death of Constantine, 337 CE

The ever more numerous public buildings visible here mask the undeniable, but unquantifiable, drop in Rome's population that had occurred by 312 CE, when Constantine won control of the city from Maxentius. During the preceding century, few emperors had resided in Rome as they were called elsewhere by military crises (note p. 180), and the apparatus of government followed them. During the early 270s, growing insecurity had even induced Aurelian to build a massive 19-km-long defensive wall: it encompassed 1,400 ha, and incorporated the barracks of the Praetorian Guard as well as the Transtiberim region.

Even while absent, however, emperors had continued to build in Rome. Hadrian was especially active, funding not only many renovations but also new commissions such as a school, the Athenaeum (right, 1), Temple of Venus and Rome (right, 14) and his Mausoleum

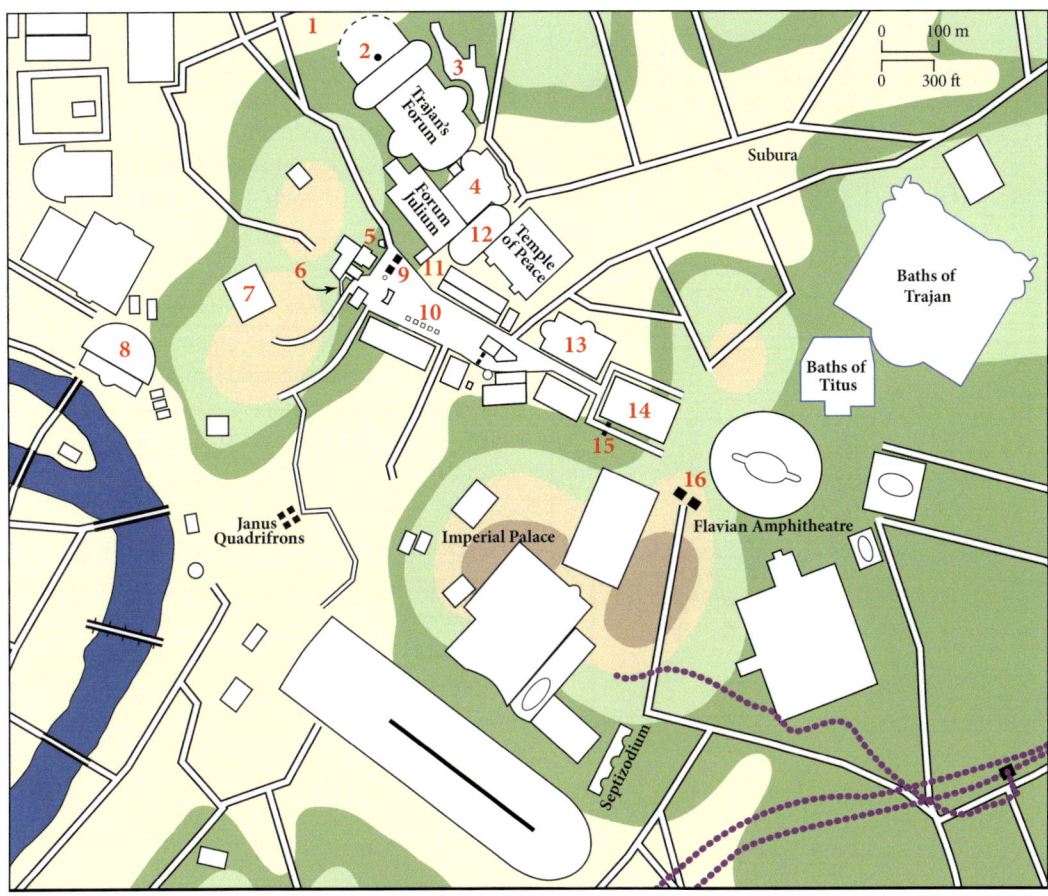

1 Athenaeum
2 Column of Trajan
3 Trajan's Markets
4 Forum Augustum
5 Carcer
6 Porticus Deorum Consentium
7 Temple of Jupiter Optimus Maximus
8 Theatre of Marcellus
9 Arch of Septimius Severus
10 Five Column Monument of Diocletian
11 Curia Julia (rebuilt under Diocletian)
12 Forum of Nerva (Forum Transitorium)
13 Basilica of Maxentius and Constantine
14 Temple of Venus and Rome
15 Arch of Titus
16 Arch of Constantine

across the Tiber (left). His flood control work in the Campus Martius made it possible to site the Column of Marcus Aurelius (left, 3) and other Antonine monuments there. The ever-popular Flavian Amphitheatre (right), Circus Maximus and other spectacle buildings were repeatedly renovated. Septimius Severus restored the Temple of Peace (right) after a fire, and displayed there a detailed city plan on marble, 12 m tall × 18. Caracalla, Diocletian and Constantine all sponsored large baths outside the centre (left, 9, 4, 6), and Constantine completed the basilica begun by Maxentius (right, 13). Less massive structures include the Arch of Septimius Severus (right, 9), his decorative Septizodium (right), Diocletian's Five-Column Monument in the Forum Romanum (right, 10), and the Arch of Constantine erected by Senate and People to commemorate his victory (right, 16). Constantine's adherence to Christianity left lasting and conspicuous proof in his empire-wide church-building programme: in Rome, this included the Basilica of St. Peter and the Lateran Basilica (both left).

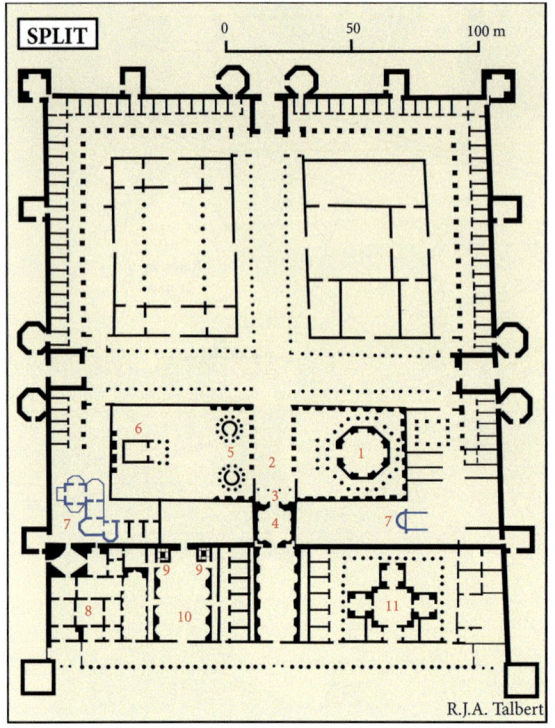

Split

Around 300 CE, the emperor Diocletian commissioned a palatial fortified villa at Spalatum (near Salona) as a retirement residence. Today its substantial remains form the urban core of Split in Croatia. Because the site slopes to the seashore, the villa's lower part has a basement level, still well preserved; this plan reconstructs the main level from what lies below. Two wide colonnaded streets intersected to divide the villa. How the northern half was used is uncertain – perhaps barracks, staff quarters, workshops. The southern half, however, was Diocletian's space. An impressive peristyle (2) led to a monumental porch (3) and circular vestibule (4). West of the peristyle was a temple (6) and shrines (5); east of it, Diocletian's mausoleum (1). Next lay baths on either side (7), then a range including imperial private quarters (8), apsed reception hall (10) from which stairs descended to the basement (9), and dining suite (11).

Constantinople

After defeating Licinius in 324 CE, Constantine I (306–337) began to rebuild and extend the ancient city of Byzantium on the Bosphorus as a new capital. He dedicated it under his own name on 11 May 330. Constantinople was proclaimed to be a New Rome, with an imperial palace, an imperially organized grain supply drawing on the surplus of Egypt, and (later) its own senate. Constantine expanded some pre-existing structures, such as the hippodrome and Baths of Zeuxippos (14), and added many more, including a circular forum with a porphyry column (6), atop which stood a statue of the Christian emperor nude and with attributes of the Sun God. The city's monuments were laid out along a central road, the Mese, which divided at the Philadelphion to head due west along the Via Egnatia, and north-west towards Hadrianoupolis (Adrianople) and the Danube river.

Constantine's new walls expanded the city's land area to 6 km^2, but this was at least doubled when more were built by Theodosius II around 413, providing the city with nearly impregnable defences not breached until the 1400s. Its population swelled to around 300,000 by the mid-fifth century, a growth made possible by increased water supplies brought from afar by the Aqueduct of Valens (completed 373), as well as by the construction of multiple cisterns. To ensure grain imports, four harbours (lettered A–D) were dug by 400. Theodosius I (379–395) rebuilt the Forum Tauri, and Arcadius (395–408) added yet another imperial forum. Constantine may have built as few as two churches, St. Eirene

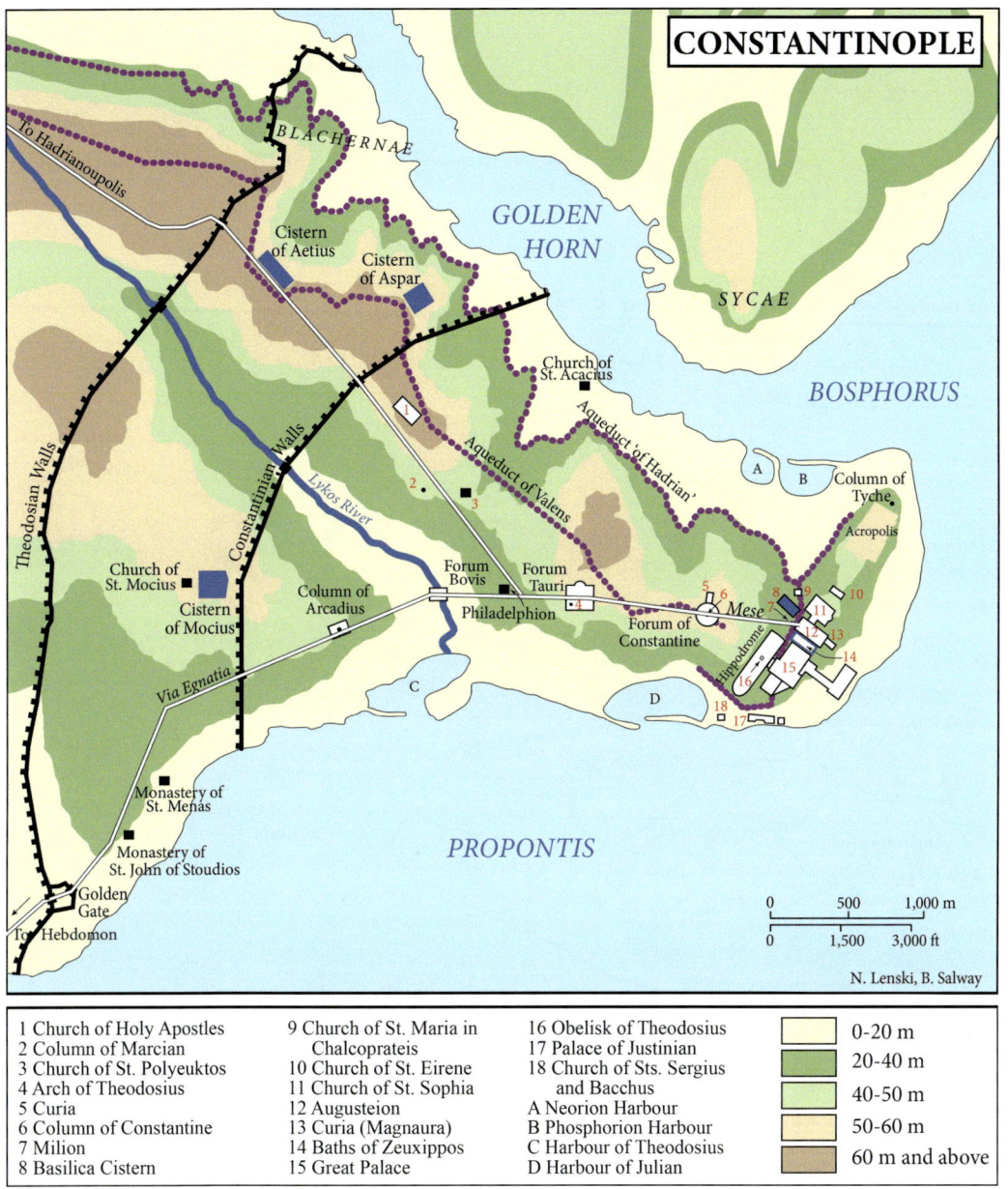

(10) and Holy Apostles (1), but his son Constantius II (337–361) added a church of St. Sophia (11); Justinian (526–565) later rebuilt it to become the domed masterpiece that still stands. Further churches and monasteries were added by emperors and private citizens as befitted a city whose Patriarch was already declared second in authority to the Pontiff of Rome by 381.

Rome's Empire around 314 CE

By the death of Septimius Severus in 211 CE, there were about forty-five provinces (reckoning Italy as one). He had divided Syria in two, and his son Caracalla then divided Britannia – a three-legion province – likewise. Subdivision and territorial reorganization continued throughout the third century, although the mechanics and motivations varied. It can hardly have been for political reasons (such as motivated Caracalla and his father) that a new procuratorial province of Pontus was established around 230, separate from Bithynia and incorporating the coastal region of Cappadocia; around 250 it was enlarged when the cities of the Paphlagonian *koinon* were transferred to it. At the same time, the regions of Phrygia and Caria were carved out of the great proconsular province of Asia as a new imperial province governed by consular legates. In this area and many others, by the end of the century such senatorial governors had been replaced by *praesides* of equestrian rank; then a further stage of subdivision created separate provinces of Phrygia and Caria around 303. In the Balkans, following the evacuation of Rome's trans-Danubian territories by Aurelian (270–275), the refugee population and name of Dacia were assigned to a new province south of the river, where the future emperor Constantine was born; it amalgamated slices of Moesia Superior and Inferior with part of Thrace. Around the same time, it seems to have been a petition by local cities that led to Novem Populi being carved out from Aquitania. It was also Aurelian who began the provincialization of Italy, although dignity was preserved by employing the term *regiones* (not *provinciae*) and referring to their governors as *correctores*.

This process accelerated under Diocletian (284–305) as part of his wide-ranging concern to tighten up civil administration. By 314, when a summary record (with slips) of the empire's provincial organization survives in a manuscript at Verona, the number of provinces had risen to approximately 101, including the *regiones* of Italy, now all reduced to tributary status. The map is based on this 'Verona List.' However, provincial boundaries are often uncertain (particularly so in Britain), and the identification of capitals is by no means always secure. A few of the new provinces proved short-lived – the two Numidias created in 305 were reunited by the end of 314 – but over the next century the trend was towards further subdivision.

Under Diocletian's arrangements, senators now only governed the much-reduced proconsular Africa and Asia and some of the Italian *regiones*; otherwise, each province was under an equestrian *praeses*. From the sole reign of Gallienus (260–268) onwards, senators also no longer served as tribunes in the army, as legionary commanders, or as legates of provinces with legionary garrisons. Instead, armies were placed under *duces* of equestrian status, whose commands might straddle several civil provinces. Constantine favoured the hitherto small 'field armies' (*comitatenses* as opposed to *limitanei*, 'frontier forces'), whose commanders came to be known as *magistri peditum* and *equitum* by the 340s.

To facilitate administrative coordination of so many more governors, the provinces were grouped into twelve 'dioceses.' In the 320s Constantine divided the diocese of Moesiae into two, styled Daciae and Macedoniae, separating the Latin-speaking provinces north of Epirus Nova and Macedonia from the Greek-speaking areas to the south. In the 380s, Egyptian and Libyan provinces were hived off from the diocese of Oriens (administered from Syrian Antioch) to form their own diocese. Each diocese was ruled by an equestrian *vicarius* (deputy to the praetorian prefects), and had one or more *rationales* and *magistri* to handle those financial affairs that fell outside the praetorian prefects' responsibilities.

The new civil administration formed the blueprint for the hierarchical organization of the Christian church: see p. 191.

Christianity by the Early Fourth Century

As with other forms of religion, it is impossible to map the Christian beliefs of individuals. The best which may be done is to chart the spread of organized churches, that is to say, of groups of Christians sufficiently numerous and stable to have regular meeting places for worship. In practice, this means plotting on a map those places which are known – or may on reasonable evidence be assumed – to have had a bishop by the period in question. Here the period is defined as the time of Christianity's emergence to full toleration and active imperial support during the reign of Constantine: he controlled Gaul and Britain from 306 CE, Italy and Africa from 312, and the whole empire from 324 until his death in 337. At this stage, Christians were possibly somewhere around 10% of the population.

This procedure has its drawbacks. First, there is little doubt that individual Christians could be found in almost every town in the empire at a fairly early date; indeed, writing in about 200, Tertullian was able to claim that Christians were to be found even in parts of Britain inaccessible to the Romans. But any attempt to map the presence of individuals from scanty literary or archaeological evidence would be so random as to prove meaningless. Not even the record of a martyrdom at a given city is necessarily proof of an *organized* Christian community there.

Second, the evidence for the existence of bishoprics is itself far from complete. Most useful here are the lists of bishops who attended, or accepted the decisions of, church councils – held at Carthage in 256, Elvira (Iliberri) around 306, Rome in 313, Arles (Arelate) in 314, Nicaea in 325 and Serdica in 343 – though with all these lists it should be noted that difficulties of topographical identification often arise. The Council of Nicaea seems to have been attended by the majority of eastern bishops, so that our picture of bishoprics for the eastern provinces may be taken as relatively complete. But some of the other councils were more localized; thus it is from the signatures recorded at the councils of Carthage and Elvira that the clusters of bishoprics in Africa and southern Spain emerge. Detailed studies of Serdica mean that information on Gaul is relatively good; yet evidence for the Danubian provinces remains thin. It is certain, too, that there were many more bishoprics in Italy than can be located: sixty Italian bishops apparently attended a council held at Rome in 251, although no list survives. Records of councils may be supplemented to some degree from literary sources, in particular Eusebius' *History of the Church*. So far as possible, all the place names given by Eusebius have been marked on the map, along with other cities where councils were held, or which assume significance in early Christian history for different reasons.

Important findings emerge from the picture which results. Little progress had been made in evangelizing the non-Roman world. In the early fourth century, Christianity was still more widespread in the eastern provinces than in those of the west apart from Africa. And it was predominantly an urban religion: hence the new meaning which the word *paganus*, 'villager,' was to acquire. Bishoprics were urban; their territory generally corresponded to the civil territory of the city. A hundred years later, virtually all the cities of the empire had gained bishoprics, but the process was far from complete at the date of this map.

Christians had already begun to develop some forms of higher jurisdiction by the early fourth century: the bishop of a provincial capital was coming to outrank his fellow provincial bishops, and to be known as the metropolitan (or 'archbishop') of his province. Equally, the Council of Nicaea recognized that the bishops of Rome and Alexandria had statuses not confined to the province of the empire where the city of each was situated.

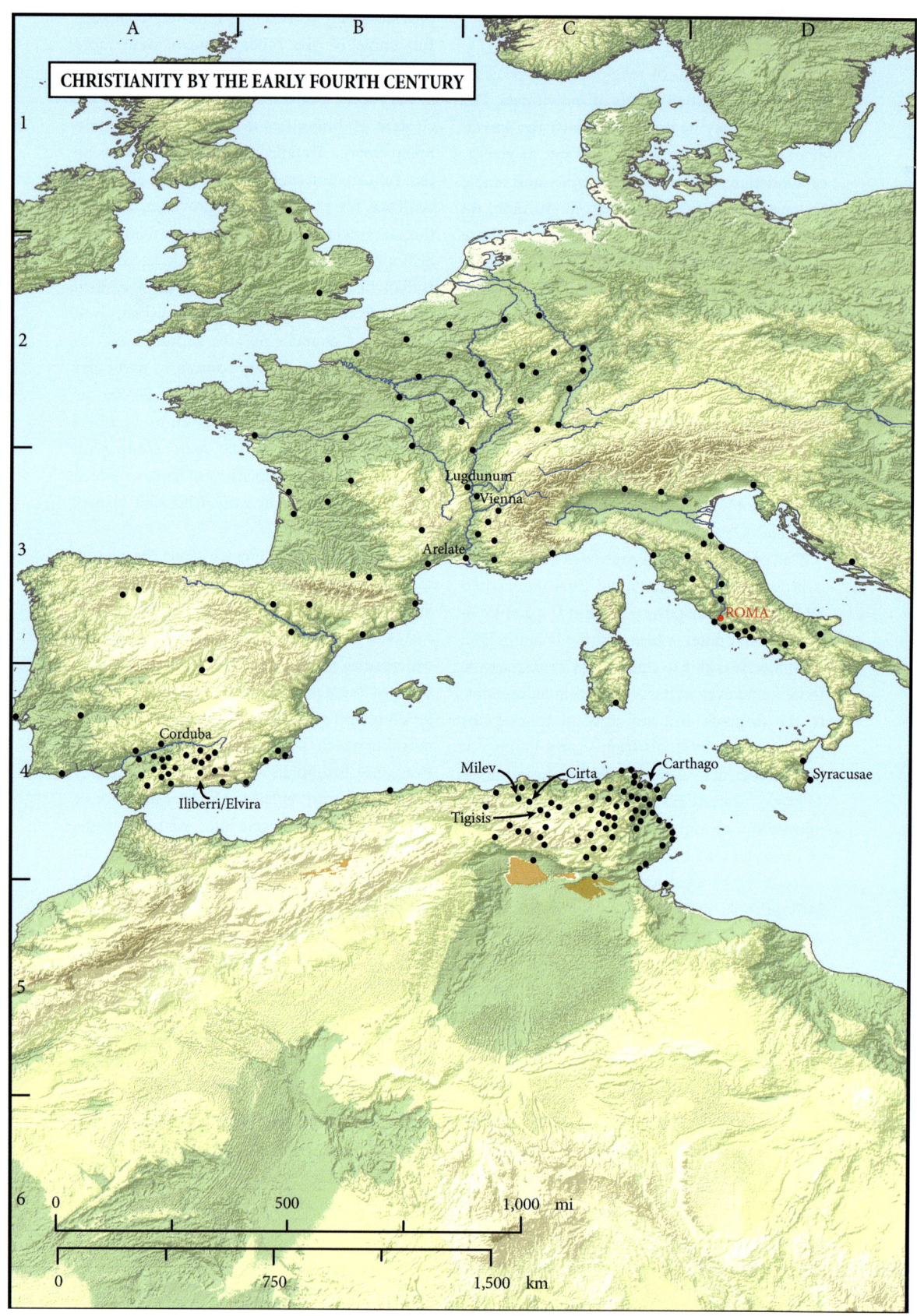

Roman World on Two Portable Sundials

Romans were most concerned to know the time of day (which spanned sunrise to sunset and was divided into twelve hours; hence hours varied in length by season). Typically, they checked fixed sundials, but small bronze portable ones were also produced. The most versatile of these, including the two here, could be adjusted to function at any latitude. For users' convenience, they might also incorporate a set of names, each listed with its latitude figure in the format devised by Ptolemy around 150 CE. Either Greek or Latin is used for these names, which are always cities or regions/provinces (never peoples or physical features), even ones situated beyond the Roman empire.

Mostly the names seem an individual's choices rather than a workshop's standard compilation, so they offer revealing glimpses of where mattered most to different owners. Observe the minimal duplication in the sets here, with twenty-eight and twenty-three names respectively. Ordering of names varies: by latitude in instances such as this Latin one (diameter 10.4 cm), a surface find on a villa site near Samarobriva Ambianorum (modern Amiens, France) in Roman Belgica (p. 147). But note that Belgica's placement in the list uniquely interrupts its latitudinal sequence; evidently in the owner's worldview Belgica – possibly their home province – is inseparable from Lugdunensis and Aquitania. By contrast in the Greek instance here (diameter 7.55 cm), unearthed in excavations at Aphrodisias (p. 157), the sequence of names reflects a Mediterranean *periplus* (circular tour), one imagined perhaps rather than actually undertaken.

Because longitude does not affect a sundial's functioning, figures for it are never listed; this map, therefore, relies on longitude figures calculated today. However, it places the two sundials' names at the latitudes listed on them, even when the figures – drawn from various sources no longer identifiable – are inaccurate. Note the substantial difference in the case of Cappadocia (34, 39.5).

VIGNACOURT

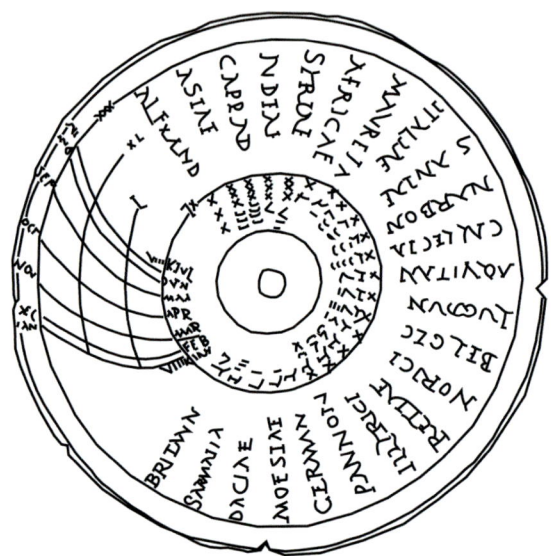

APHRODISIAS

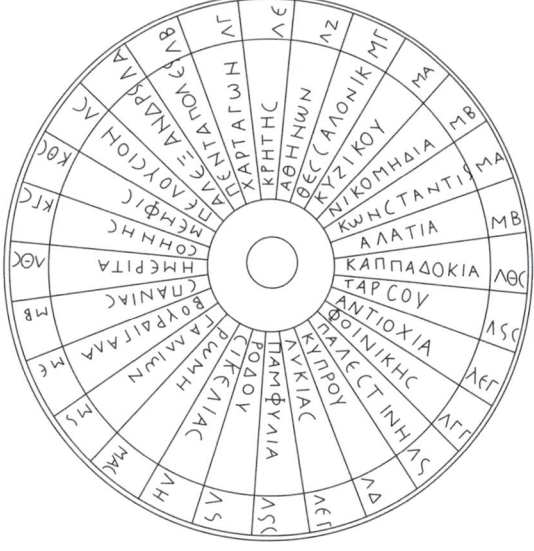

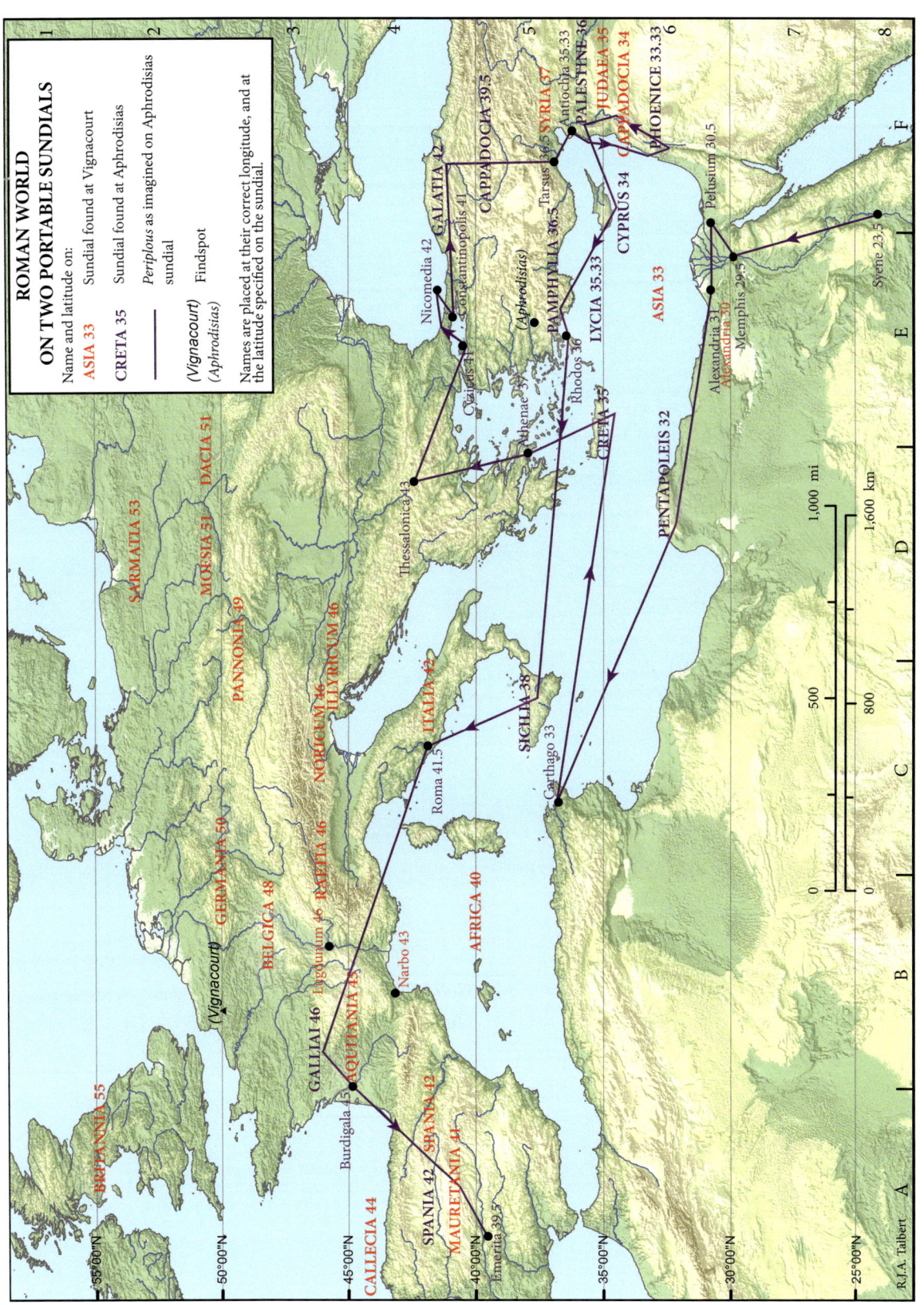

Barbarian Invasions of the Roman Empire, 370–500 CE

During the late fourth and fifth centuries CE, the Roman empire lost control of the western territories from which its origins sprang. Debate about this development is intense and ongoing. According to the traditional view, the collapse of Roman power was caused by 'barbarian invaders' – peoples who entered imperial territory from the outside, organized their assaults around new ethnic and political structures, and brought about major social changes within their new 'barbarian kingdoms.' However, more recent scholarship questions these assumptions, arguing that the number of persons who migrated during this period was modest, that they were organized as armies with little ethnic cohesion, and that the changes resulting from the fragmentation of Roman power stemmed from natural social evolution rather than from the introduction of new national identities. This map nonetheless offers a schematic view closer to the traditional one. Taken as a whole, it shows four important trends:

First is the impact of the Huns, a nomadic steppe people from central Asia. Their arrival in eastern Europe during the 370s unleashed a stream of migration into Roman territory by Germanic peoples on the lower Danube river, Goths especially. This began in 376 with the movement into Scythia Minor of a Gothic group that later (in 410) sacked the city of Rome; thereafter, as Visigoths, it moved further west to establish its own independent kingdom in Aquitania (418). Some of the Hun invaders settled north of the lower Danube; from here, in the 440s, they menaced eastern Roman territories under the leadership of Attila. A few years later he marched west into Gaul, but was defeated in battle by a coalition of Roman and Visigothic forces at the Campi Catalauni (451). Shortly thereafter, Attila died and Hunnic power on the middle Danube collapsed. As a result, there emerged a powerful new Gothic group, consisting of those formerly under Hunnic control. It eventually (by 493) took control over Italy, and ruled there under its own Ostrogothic leadership until Justinian's armies destroyed this kingdom (by 554).

Second, at the end of 406, there occurred major migrations across the Rhine frontier by Vandals, Suebi and Alans, who thereafter together took over the Iberian peninsula. The Vandals and Alans in due course made the crossing into North Africa; they seized Carthage by 439, and ruled there until displaced by Justinian's forces a century later (534). The Vandals' departure from Spain made way for the Visigoths, who gradually occupied Tarraconensis. Eventually, they took over the entire peninsula when forced out of western Gaul after suffering defeat by the Franks in 507.

Third, many non-Roman peoples of the Rhine river basin – especially Alamanni, Burgundians and Franks – moved only short distances across the river into former Roman territory. Here they established independent states, all of which came to be dominated by Frankish power by the early 500s.

Fourth, the Saxons of northern Germany initially entered Britain as much to trade as to raid, but gradually assumed power here; after 410, Rome had largely abandoned Britain. Thus altogether Roman imperial control of the West dissolved over the course of a century. Power in these western territories shifted from rulers who followed southern European cultural ways to ones who followed northern patterns, even while often maintaining unbreakable ties to the Roman past (see further p. 200).

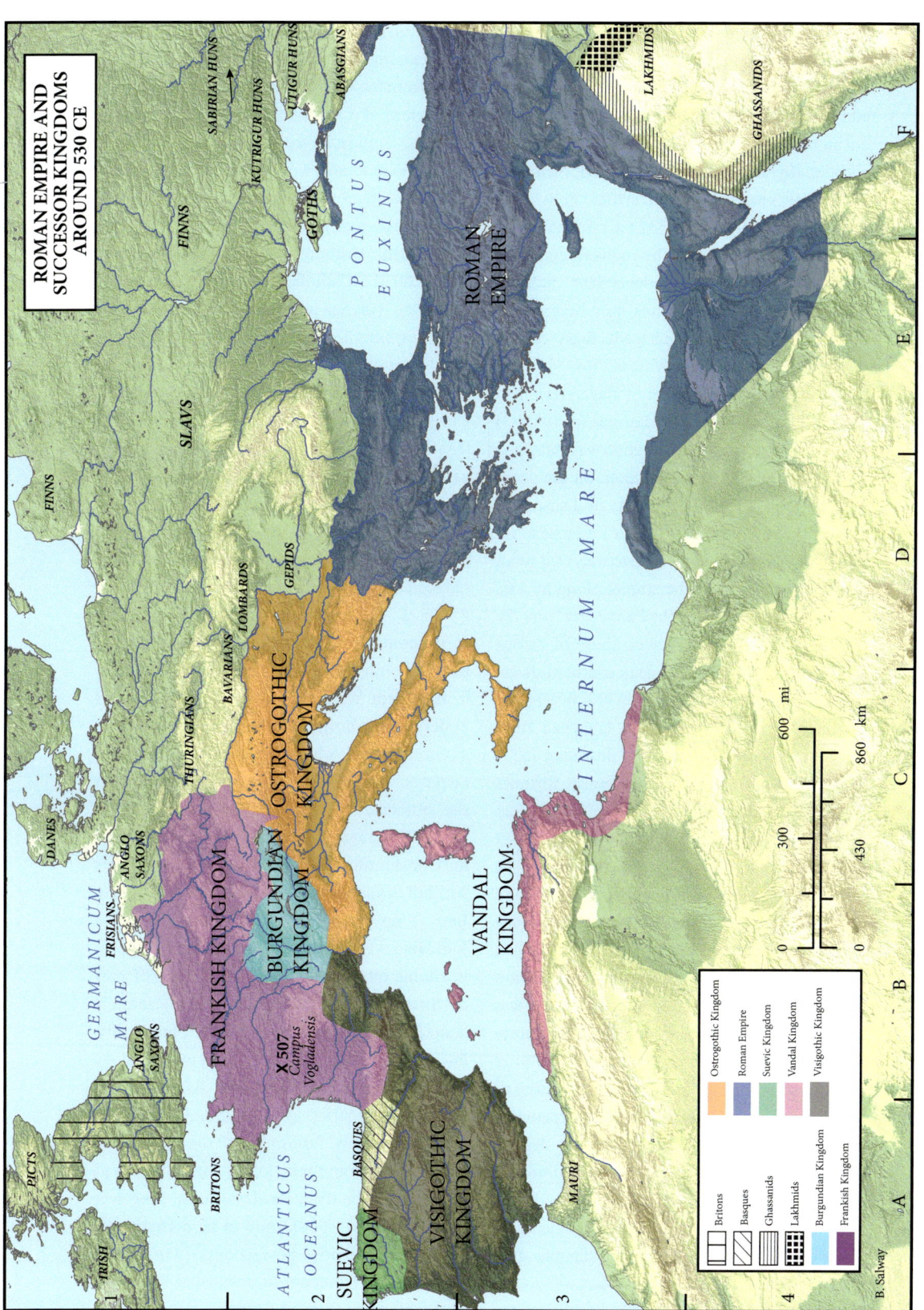

Roman Empire and Successor Kingdoms around 530 CE

Diocletian's experiment with polycentric administration focused on provincial nodes strung out along the empire's East-West communications corridor (Syrian Antioch, Nicomedia, Sirmium, Milan, Trier) was essentially recreated in dynastic form by Constantine (306–337 CE). Julian's brief reign (361–363) aside, rule by multiple emperors operating parallel but independent judicial, financial and military systems now became the norm. Failure to co-ordinate effectively caused the death of the emperor Valens (364–376) and the Goths' devastating defeat of the eastern field army at Hadrianoupolis/Adrianople (p. 197, F3) in 378. In this instance, the situation was stabilized with help from the West. However, on the death of Theodosius (379–395) hostility and suspicion between the military and civilian leaderships (in Milan and Constantinople respectively) led to an entrenched division of the empire along an axis separating the dioceses of the Pannoniae from the Daciae in Europe, and likewise those of Africa and Egypt on the Mediterranean southern shore.

The geopolitical situation in 530 – just before campaigns of reconquest were launched from Constantinople by the emperor Justinian (527–565) – starkly illustrates the divergent fortunes of the eastern and western halves of the Roman world in the fifth century. Although the empire of Constantinople had been threatened by Hunnic inroads in the Balkans around 440, and was distracted by its own civil war when the last emperor was deposed in Italy (476), the Roman state in the East survived essentially intact into the sixth century, not least because peace was maintained on its eastern front with the assistance of Arab allies. By contrast, the former territories of the western empire were occupied by a series of kingdoms whose Germanic rulers perpetuated the Roman cultural legacy to varying degrees (p. 198). At one extreme, the highly acculturated Ostrogothic regime in Italy preserved the structures of civilian administration, including elements stretching back to the Republic (the senate in Rome and the appointment of one of the consuls annually); it even re-established the Praetorian Prefecture of Gaul in Provence. At the other extreme, former Roman Britain – which had fallen from imperial control after separating from the regime of Constantine III (407–411) based at Arles – gradually reverted to its pre-Roman state as Saxon settlers encroached from mainland Europe. Some of the Romano-British population took refuge across the Channel in Armorica (henceforth Brittany), while its churchmen transplanted Catholic-Orthodox Christianity across the Irish Sea with notable success.

Meanwhile, the Mediterranean kingdoms were ruled by groups that, although rapidly Latinized, had been evangelized to the Arian variant of Christianity, which helped to keep them distinct from their Nicene subjects. In contrast, greater assimilation of subject and ruler was facilitated by the Catholicism of the Franks, who took the lead in Gaul after defeating the Visigoths at Campus Vogladensis (Vouillé) in 507; they reduced the Visigothic kingdom north of the Pyrenees – formerly centred on Toulouse – to a rump around Narbonne. In the face of political fragmentation, Nicene Christianity in the Latin West became increasingly unified under the authority of the bishops of Rome, a development which contrasted with bitter disputes within the Eastern Church over the outcome of the Council of Chalcedon (452). Theological initiatives by the emperors in Constantinople tended to alienate Rome without conciliating divisions in the Greek East. Thus reconquests – of Africa from the Vandals in 533, of Italy from the Ostrogoths in a long, bitter struggle (535–554), and of part of Spain from the Visigoths (552) – severely dented the fortunes of Arian Christianity, but did not contribute to increasing harmony among the Nicene Churches. Although the territorial integrity of Byzantine Italy was soon irreparably fractured by the Lombards' arrival from Pannonia (568), the empire was able to recover from its devastating long war with Persia (603–628), only to be permanently deprived of the prize possessions of Oriens and Egypt by the Islamic movement that swept out of Arabia from the mid-630s.

Further Reading

(in addition to standard reference works such as the *Oxford Classical Dictionary* and Wiley Blackwell *Encyclopedia of Ancient History*)

A place name denotes the press of the university so named as publisher, with these exceptions: Ann Arbor/Michigan, Austin/Texas, Baltimore/Johns Hopkins, Berkeley/California, Chapel Hill/University of North Carolina, Philadelphia/Pennsylvania. For other well-known publishers in the ancient field, place of publication is omitted.

Abbreviations

ASCSA	American School of Classical Studies at Athens
BNP	*Brill's New Pauly*
BSA	British School at Athens
BSR	British School at Rome
CAH	*Cambridge Ancient History*
EAB	M. Whitby, H. Sidebottom, eds., *The Encyclopedia of Ancient Battles*, Wiley Blackwell, 2017
JHS	*Journal of Hellenic Studies*
JRA	*Journal of Roman Archaeology*
JRS	*Journal of Roman Studies*
PBSR	*Papers of the British School at Rome*

Books Referenced by Author and Date Only

A.B. Bosworth, *Conquest and Empire: The Reign of Alexander the Great*, Cambridge, 1988

A.R. Burn, *Persia and the Greeks*, ed. 2, Duckworth, 1984

C.J. Butera, M.A. Sears, *Battles and Battlefields of Ancient Greece: A Guide to Their History, Topography and Archaeology*, Pen and Sword, 2019

E.H. Cline, ed., *The Oxford Handbook of the Bronze Age Aegean (ca. 3000–1000 BC)*, Oxford, 2010

A.E. Cooley, ed., *A Companion to Roman Italy*, Wiley Blackwell, 2016

F. De Angelis, *Archaic and Classical Greek Sicily. A Social and Economic History*, Oxford, 2016

G.D. Farney, G.J. Bradley, eds., *The Peoples of Ancient Italy*, De Gruyter, 2018

P. Green, *Alexander of Macedon, 356–323 BC: A Historical Biography*, Berkeley, 2013

N.G.L. Hammond, *Studies in Greek History*, Oxford, 1973

—— *The Genius of Alexander the Great*, Duckworth, 1997

—— and G.T. Griffith, *A History of Macedonia II*, Oxford, 1979

C. Hignett, *Xerxes' Invasion of Greece*, Oxford, 1963

D. Kagan, *New History of the Peloponnesian War*, Cornell, 2013

J.F. Lazenby, *The Defence of Greece, 490–479 BC*, Aris and Phillips, 1993

—— *The Peloponnesian War: A Military Study*, Routledge, 2004

F.S. Naiden, *Soldier, Priest and God. A Life of Alexander the Great*, Oxford, 2019

—— and R. Talbert, eds., *Mercury's Wings: Exploring Modes of Communication in the Ancient World*, Oxford, 2017

W.K. Pritchett, *Studies in Ancient Greek Topography*, Berkeley, vols. 1 (1965), 2 (1969), 4 (1982)

I. Worthington, *By the Spear: Philip II, Alexander the Great, and the Rise and Fall of the Macedonian Empire*, Oxford, 2014

Egypt and the Near East, 1200–500 BCE

M. Van De Mieroop, *A History of the Ancient Near East, ca. 3000–323 BC*, ed. 3, Wiley Blackwell, 2016

D.C. Snell, ed., *A Companion to the Ancient Near East* [including Egypt], ed. 2, Wiley Blackwell, 2020

M. Van De Mieroop, *A History of Ancient Egypt*, ed. 2, Wiley Blackwell, 2021

Troy: Citadel and Lower Town

C.W. Blegen, *Troy and the Trojans*, Thames and Hudson, 1963

T. Bryce, "The Trojan war." In Cline (2010) 475–482

P. Jablonka, "Troy." Ibid. 849–861

C.B. Rose, *The Archaeology of Greek and Roman Troy*, Cambridge, 2013

Neolithic and Bronze Age Greece and the Aegean, Crete, Cyprus

C.W. Shelmerdine, ed., *The Cambridge Companion to the Aegean Bronze Age*, Cambridge, 2008

Cline (2010)

A.B. Knapp, *The Archaeology of Cyprus: From Earliest Prehistory through the Bronze Age*, Cambridge, 2013

E.H. Cline, *1177 BC: The Year Civilization Collapsed*, Princeton, 2014

Knossos

S. Hood, W. Taylor, *The Bronze Age Palace at Knossos: Plan and Sections*, BSA Suppl. 13, 1981

S. Hood, D. Smyth, *Archaeological Survey of the Knossos Area*, BSA Suppl. 14, 1981

C. Macdonald, "Knossos." In Cline (2010) 529–542

J.C. McEnroe, *Architecture of Minoan Crete*, Austin, 2010

J.W. Shaw, *Elite Minoan Architecture. Its Development at Knossos, Phaistos, and Malia*, INSTAP, 2015

Mycenae: Citadel and Outside

E.B. French, *Mycenae: Agamemnon's Capital*, Stroud: Tempus, 2002

S.E. Iakovides, E.B. French, *Archaeological Atlas of Mycenae*, Archaeological Society at Athens, 2003

Homer's World
Mainland Greece in Homer's Epics

J.V. Luce, *Celebrating Homer's Landscapes: Troy and Ithaca Revisited*, Yale, 1998

J. Latacz, *Troy and Homer: Towards a Solution of an Old Mystery*, Oxford, 2004

S. Saïd, *Homer and the* Odyssey, Oxford, 2011

D. Nakassis, "Homeric geography." In C.O. Pache, ed., *The Cambridge Guide to Homer*, 267–277. Cambridge, 2020

Iron Age Greece

A.M. Snodgrass, *The Dark Age of Greece: An Archaeological Survey of the Eleventh to the Eighth Centuries B.C.*, Edinburgh, 2000

I.S. Lemos, *The Protogeometric Aegean. The Archaeology of the Late Eleventh and Tenth Centuries BC*, Oxford, 2002

J.N. Coldstream, *Geometric Greece 900–700 BC*, ed. 2, Routledge, 2003

O. Dickinson, *The Aegean from Bronze Age to Iron Age*, Routledge, 2006

Greek Colonization, 800–500 BCE

J. Boardman, *The Greeks Overseas: Their Early Colonies and Trade*, ed. 4, Thames and Hudson, 1999

R.G. Osborne, *Greece in the Making, 1200–479 BC*, ed. 2, Routledge, 2009, 105–123

Archaic Greece

R.G. Osborne, *Greece in the Making, 1200–479 BC*, ed. 2, Routledge, 2009

J.M. Hall, *A History of the Archaic Greek World, ca. 1200–479 BCE*, ed. 2, Wiley Blackwell, 2014

Persian Empire, 550–330 BCE

J. Wiesehöfer, *Ancient Persia: From 550 BC to 650 AD*, Tauris, 1996, 1–101

P. Briant, *Cyrus to Alexander. A History of the Persian Empire*, Eisenbrauns, 2002

M. Waters, *Ancient Persia: A Concise History of the Achaemenid Empire, 550–330 BCE*, Cambridge, 2014

B. Jacobs, R. Rollinger, eds., *A Companion to the Achaemenid Persian Empire*, Wiley Blackwell, 2021

Persepolis

A. Mousavi, *Persepolis: Discovery and Afterlife of a World Wonder*, De Gruyter, 2012

R. Stoneman, *Xerxes: A Persian Life*, Yale, 2015, 160–180

Marathon, 490 BCE

Hignett (1963) 55–74; Hammond (1973) 170–250; Burn (1984) 236–257; Lazenby (1993) 45–80; P. Krentz, *The Battle of Marathon*, Yale, 2010; Butera, Sears (2019) 3–17

Persian Wars

Burn (1984); Lazenby (1993); P. Green, *The Greco-Persian Wars*, Berkeley, 1996; G. Cawkwell, *The Greek Wars: The Failure of Persia*, Oxford, 2005, 87–125; R.B. Strassler, ed., *The Landmark Herodotus, The Histories*, New York: Pantheon, 2007

Thermopylae, 480 BCE: Ephialtes' Route

Hignett (1963) 105–148, 356–378; Pritchett (1982) 176–210; Lazenby (1993) 130–142; P. Cartledge, *Thermopylae. The Battle That Changed the World*, Woodstock, NY: Overlook, 2006; Butera, Sears (2019) 49–63

Artemision, 480 BCE

Hignett (1963) 149–192; Pritchett (1969) 12–18; Burn (1984) 394–402; Lazenby (1993) 117–130, 138–140, 148–150; Butera, Sears (2019) 67–83

Salamis, 480 BCE

Hammond (1973) 251–310; Burn (1984) 436–475; Lazenby (1993) 151–197; B. Strauss, *The Battle of Salamis: The Naval Encounter That Saved Greece – and Western Civilization*, New York: Simon and Schuster, 2004; Butera, Sears (2019) 19–33

Plataea, 479 BCE

Hignett (1963) 289–344, 418–438; Pritchett (1965) 103–121; Burn (1984) 503–546; Lazenby (1993) 217–247; Butera, Sears (2019) 85–107

Greece and the Aegean
Classical Greece

P.J. Rhodes, *A History of the Classical Greek World, 478–323 BC*, ed. 2, Wiley Blackwell, 2010

S. Hornblower, *The Greek World, 479–323 BC*, ed. 4, Routledge, 2011

Cimmerian Bosphorus

J. Hind, "The Bosporan kingdom." In *CAH*² VI (1994) 476–511

G.R. Tsetskhladze, "A survey of the major urban settlements in the Kimmerian Bosporus." In T.H. Nielsen, ed., *Yet More Studies in the Ancient Greek Polis*, 39–81. Steiner, 1997

Olympia

D.C. Young, *A Brief History of the Olympic Games*, Blackwell, 2004

J.M. Barringer, *Olympia: A Cultural History*, Princeton, 2021

Attica

C.W.J. Eliot, *Coastal Demes of Attika: A Study of the Policy of Kleisthenes*, Phoenix Suppl. V, 1962

J.S. Traill, *The Political Organization of Attica*, Hesperia Suppl. XIV, 1975

Id., *Demos and Trittys*, Toronto: Athenians, 1986

Athens

J. Travlos, *Pictorial Dictionary of Ancient Athens*, New York: Praeger, 1971

J.M. Hurwit, *The Athenian Acropolis*, Cambridge, 1999

J. McK. Camp II, *The Athenian Agora: Site Guide*, ed. 5, ASCSA, 2010

J. Neils, D. Rogers, eds., *The Cambridge Companion to Ancient Athens*, Cambridge, 2021

Delphi

M. Scott, *Delphi: A History of the Center of the Ancient World*, Princeton, 2014

Sparta

N.M. Kennell, *Spartans: A New History*, Wiley Blackwell, 2010

W. Cavanagh, "An archaeology of ancient Sparta." In A. Powell, ed., *A Companion to Sparta*, 61–92. Wiley Blackwell, 2018

Miletus

V.B. Gorman, *Miletos, The Ornament of Ionia: A History of the City to 400 B.C.E.*, Ann Arbor, 2001

A.M. Greaves, *Miletos: A History*, Routledge, 2002

Priene

K. Ferla, ed., *Priene*, ed. 2, Harvard, 2005

Halicarnassus

S. Hornblower, *Mausolus*, Oxford, 1982

https://www.carlsbergfondet.dk/da/Forskningsaktiviteter/Forskningsprojekter/Andre-forskningsprojekter/Poul_Pedersen_The_Danish_Halikarnassos_Project

Akragas

De Angelis (2016) 73–93, 106–116

Greek and Punic Sicily

R.J.A. Talbert, "The Greeks in Sicily and South Italy." In L.A. Tritle, ed., *The Greek World in the Fourth Century*, 137–165. Routledge, 1997

R.J.A. Wilson, "Hellenistic Sicily, c. 270–100 BC." In J. Prag, J. Quinn, eds., *The Hellenistic West*, 79–119. Cambridge, 2013

De Angelis (2016)

Athenian Empire

R. Meiggs, *The Athenian Empire*, Oxford, 1972 [for the location of all tribute payers and new assessments in 425, see Maps I(i)-I(vi)]

L.J. Samons II, *The Empire of the Owl. Athenian Imperial Finance*, Steiner, 2000

P. Low, ed., *The Athenian Empire*, Edinburgh, 2008

J. Ma et al., eds., *Interpreting the Athenian Empire*, Duckworth, 2009

Greek Dialects around 450 BCE

C.D. Buck, *The Greek Dialects*, Chicago, 1955

R.D. Woodard, ed., *The Ancient Languages of Europe*, Cambridge, 2008, 50–72

E.J. Bakker, ed., *A Companion to the Ancient Greek Language*, Wiley Blackwell, 2010, 200–212

Peloponnesian War, 431–404 BCE

R.B. Strassler, ed., *The Landmark Thucydides*, New York: Free Press, 1996; G. Cawkwell, *Thucydides and the Peloponnesian War*, Routledge, 1997; Lazenby

(2004); R.B. Strassler, ed., *The Landmark Xenophon's Hellenika*, New York: Pantheon, 2009; Kagan (2013)

Pylos/Sphacteria, 425 BCE
Pritchett (1965) 6–29; J.B. Wilson, *Pylos 425 B.C.*, Aris and Phillips, 1979; Lazenby (2004) 67–79; Kagan (2013) 218–259; Butera, Sears (2019) 301–317

Syracuse (and Athenian Siege, 415–413 BCE)
De Angelis (2016) 62–125
EAB (2017) 345–365

Explorers
J.S. Romm, *The Edges of the Earth in Ancient Thought: Geography, Exploration, and Fiction*, Princeton, 1992

J.B. Friedman, K.M. Figg, eds., *Trade, Travel, and Exploration in the Middle Ages: An Encyclopedia*, Garland, 2000

D. Buisseret, ed., *The Oxford Companion to World Exploration*, Oxford, 2007

D.W. Roller, *Ancient Geography: The Discovery of the World in Classical Greece and Rome*, Tauris, 2015

Anabasis (Spring 401 to Winter 400/399 BCE)
R.D. Barnett, "Xenophon and the Wall of Media," *JHS* 83 (1963) 1–26

J.W.I. Lee, *A Greek Army on the March: Soldiers and Survival in Xenophon's Anabasis*, Cambridge, 2007

S. Brennan, D. Thomas, *The Landmark Xenophon's Anabasis*, New York: Pantheon, 2021

Leuctra, 371 BCE
Pritchett (1965) 49–58; J.K. Anderson, *Military Theory and Practice in the Age of Xenophon*, Berkeley, 1970, 192–220; J. Buckler, *The Theban Hegemony, 371–362 B.C.*, Harvard, 1980, 46–69; Butera, Sears (2019) 139–155

Second Athenian League
F.H. Marshall, *The Second Athenian Confederacy*, Cambridge, 1905

J.L. Cargill, *The Second Athenian League: Empire or Free Alliance?* Berkeley, 1981

Chaeronea, 338 BCE
Hammond (1973) 534–557; Hammond, Griffith (1979) 596–603; J.T. Ma, "Chaironeia 338: Topographies of commemoration," *JHS* 128 (2008) 72–91; Worthington (2014) 85–90; Butera, Sears (2019) 157–164, 171–176

Growth of Macedonian Power, 359–336 BCE
J.R. Ellis, *Philip II and Macedonian Imperialism*, Thames and Hudson, 1976; Hammond, Griffith (1979) 203–698; I. Worthington, *Philip II of Macedonia*, Yale, 2008; Worthington (2014)

Alexander's Campaigns, 334–323 BCE
Bosworth (1988); Hammond (1997); P. Briant, *Alexander the Great and his Empire: A Short Introduction*, Princeton, 2010; J. Romm, ed., *The Landmark Arrian, The Campaigns of Alexander*, New York: Pantheon, 2010; Naiden (2019)

Granicus River, 334 BCE
N.G.L. Hammond, "The Battle of the Granicus River," *JHS* 100 (1980) 73–88; Bosworth (1988) 40–44; Green (2013) 395–412; Worthington (2014) 144–148

Issus, 333 BCE
Bosworth (1988) 59–62; Hammond (1997) 86–90; Green (2013) 226–235; Naiden (2019) 71–75

Tyre, 332 BCE
Bosworth (1988) 65–67; N. Marriner et al., "Holocene morphogenesis of Alexander the Great's isthmus at Tyre in Lebanon," *Proceedings of the National Academy of Sciences* 104 (2007) 9218–9223; Worthington (2014) 173–178

Gaugamela, 331 BCE
E.W. Marsden, *The Campaign of Gaugamela*, Liverpool, 1964; P.A. Brunt, *Arrian* I, Loeb (1976) Appendix 9; Bosworth (1988) 80–85; Hammond (1997) 103–110; Green (2013) 288–296; Naiden (2019) 118–122

Hydaspes River, 326 BCE
N.G.L. Hammond, *Alexander the Great, King, Commander and Statesman*, Noyes, 1980, 204–212; A.M. Devine, "The battle of Hydaspes: A tactical and source-critical study," *Ancient World* 16 (1987) 91–113; Bosworth (1988) 126–130; P.H.L. Eggermont, *Alexander's Campaign in Southern Punjab*, Peeters, 1993; Hammond (1997) 164–167; Green (2013) 322–332

Alexandria Oxiana (Ai Khanoum)
L. Martinez-Sève, "Ai Khanoum after 145 BC: The post-palatial occupation," *Ancient Civilizations from Scythia to Siberia* 24 (2018) 354–419

Ead., "Recherches récentes sur la Bactriane et la Sogdiane à l'époque hellénistique." In R. Oetjen, ed.,

New Perspectives in Seleucid History, Archaeology and Numismatics: Studies in Honor of Getzel M. Cohen, 348–374. De Gruyter, 2020

Alexandria
J. McKenzie, *The Architecture of Alexandria and Egypt, c. 300 BC to AD 700*, Yale, 2007

A. Abdo, *Alexandria Antiqua: A Topographical Catalogue and Reconstruction*, Archaeopress, 2022

Hellenistic World
M.M. Austin, *The Hellenistic World from Alexander to the Roman Conquest*, Cambridge, 1981

G. Shipley, *The Greek World after Alexander 323–30 BC*, Routledge, 2000

P. Thonemann, *The Hellenistic Age*, Oxford, 2016

M. Canepa, "Cross-cultural communication in the Hellenistic Mediterranean and western and south Asia." In Naiden, Talbert (2017) 249–272

Pergamum
BNP Pergamum

Delos
BNP Delos

N. McGilchrist, *McGilchrist's Greek Islands 6. Mykonos and Delos*, London: Genius Loci, 2011, 35–126

J.-C. Moretti et al., *Exploration archéologique de Délos XLIII: Atlas*, Ecole Française d'Athènes, 2015

Etruria and Etruscan Expansion
J.M. Turfa, ed., *The Etruscan World*, Routledge, 2013

C. Smith, *The Etruscans: A Very Short Introduction*, Oxford, 2014

Early Italy and Its Neighbours
Peoples of Italy
E. Isayev, "Italy before the Romans." In Cooley (2016) 2–32

K. Lomas, *The Rise of Rome. From the Iron Age to the Punic Wars, 1000 BC–264 BC*, London: Profile, 2017

Farney, Bradley (2018)

Languages of Italy to the First Century CE
J. Clackson, G.C. Horrocks, *The Blackwell History of the Latin Language*, Blackwell, 2007, 37–76

R. Wallace, *Zikh Rasna: A Manual of the Etruscan Language and Inscriptions*, Ann Arbor, MI: Beech Stave, 2008

N. Zair, "The languages of ancient Italy." In Farney, Bradley (2018) 127–148

Latium, 600–300 BCE
P.S. Lulof, C.J. Smith, eds., *The Age of Tarquinius Superbus: Central Italy in the Late 6th Century BC*, Peeters, 2017

G. Bradley, *Early Rome to 290 BC*, Edinburgh, 2020, 263–304

Campania
M. Frederiksen, *Campania*, BSR, 1984

M. Zarmakoupi, *Designing for Luxury on the Bay of Naples: Villas and Landscapes (c. 100 BCE-79 CE)*, Oxford, 2014

R.R. Benefiel, "Regional interaction." In Cooley (2016) 441–458

Roman Expansion in Italy to 241 BCE
R. Scopacasa, "Rome's encroachment on Italy." In Cooley (2016) 35–56

F. Carlà-Uhink, *The "Birth" of Italy: The Institutionalization of Italy as a Region, 3rd–1st Century BCE*, De Gruyter, 2017

G.J. Bradley, J. Hall, "The Roman conquest of Italy." In Farney, Bradley (2018) 191–214

Cosa
A.M. McCann, *The Roman Port and Fishery of Cosa: A Short Guide*, Rome: American Academy, 2002

G. Poggesi, M.A. Turchetti, *Cosa, Orbetello: Itinerari Archeologici* [text in Italian and English], Firenze: Pegaso, 2016

E. Fentress, P. Perkins, "Cosa and the *Ager Cosanus*." In Cooley (2016) 378–400

Rome by 300 BCE; in the Late Republic; at the Death of Augustus, 14 CE; at the Death of Trajan, 117 CE; at the Death of Constantine, 337 CE
G.S. Aldrete, *Floods of the Tiber in Ancient Rome*, Baltimore, 2007

A. Claridge, *Rome. An Oxford Archaeological Guide*, ed. 2, Oxford, 2010

P. Erdkamp, ed., *The Cambridge Companion to Ancient Rome*, Cambridge, 2013

A. Carandini, *The Atlas of Ancient Rome: Biography and Portraits of the City*, Princeton, 2017

G. Bradley, *Early Rome to 290 BC*, Edinburgh, 2020, 138–191

Roman Colonization in Italy to the Time of Augustus
L. Keppie, *Colonisation and Veteran Settlement in Italy, 47–14 B.C.*, BSR, 1983

G. Bradley, J.-P. Wilson, eds., *Greek and Roman Colonization: Origins, Ideologies and Interactions*, Classical Press of Wales, 2006

Punic Wars

A. Goldsworthy, *The Fall of Carthage: The Punic Wars 265–146 BC*, London: Cassell, 2003

B.D. Hoyos, ed., *A Companion to the Punic Wars*, Wiley Blackwell, 2011

Cannae, 216 BCE

G. Daly, *Cannae: The Experience of Battle in the Second Punic War*, Routledge, 2002, 25–45

EAB (2017) 704–711

Zama, 202 BCE

EAB (2017) 790–796

Roman Campaigns in the Iberian Peninsula, 218–133 BCE

J.S. Richardson, *Hispaniae: Spain and the Development of Roman Imperialism, 218–82 B.C.*, Cambridge, 1986

L.A. Curchin, *Roman Spain: Conquest and Assimilation*, Routledge, 1991

Numantia: Roman Siege, 133 BCE and Region

A. Jimeno, "Conquest and Romanization in Celtiberia Ulterior: Numantia as paradigm." In L. Abad Casal et al., eds., *Early Roman Towns in Hispania Tarraconensis*, 172–183. JRA, 2006

M.J. Dobson, *The Army of the Roman Republic: The Second Century BC, Polybius and the Camps at Numantia, Spain*, Oxbow, 2008

A. Jiménez et al., "Renewed work at the Roman camps at Renieblas near Numantia (2nd–1st c. B.C.)," *JRA* 33 (2020) 4–35

Rome's Empire around 60 BCE

D.C. Braund, *Rome and the Friendly King: The Character of the Client Kingship*, Croom Helm, 1984

A. Lintott, *Imperium Romanum: Politics and Administration*, Routledge, 1993

F. Drogula, *Commanders and Command in the Roman Republic and Early Empire*, Chapel Hill, 2015

Roman Campaigns, 58–30 BCE

J. Osgood, *Caesar's Legacy: Civil War and the Emergence of the Roman Empire*, Cambridge, 2006

K. Raaflaub, ed., *The Landmark Julius Caesar*, New York: Pantheon, 2017

Actium, 31 BCE

EAB (2017) 978–982

Butera, Sears (2019) 361–380

Augusta Praetoria (Aosta)

BNP Augusta 3

Corsica

R.J.A. Wilson, "Sicily, Sardinia and Corsica." In *CAH*² X (1996) 434–448

J. Cesari, ed., *Corse antique*, Guides archéologiques de la France 45, 2010

Italy

M.H. Crawford, "Italy and Rome from Sulla to Augustus." In *CAH*² X (1996) 414–433

N. Purcell, "Rome and Italy." In *CAH*² XI (2000) 405–443

Cooley (2016)

Sicily (Roman)

R.J.A. Wilson, *Sicily under the Roman Empire. The Archaeology of a Roman Province, 36 BC–AD 535*, Aris and Phillips, 1990

L. Pfuntner, *Urbanism and Empire in Roman Sicily*, Austin, 2019

L. De Ligt, "The impact of Roman rule on the urban system of Sicily." In id., J. Bintliff, eds., *Regional Urban Systems in the Roman World, 150 BCE–250 CE*, 217–280. Brill, 2020

Sardinia

S.L. Dyson, R.J. Rowland, *Archaeology and History in Sardinia from the Stone Age to the Middle Ages: Shepherds, Sailors & Conquerors*, Philadelphia, 2007

R.J.A. Wilson, "Becoming Roman overseas? Sicily and Sardinia in the Later Roman Republic." In J. DeRose Evans, ed., *A Companion to the Archaeology of the Roman Republic*, 485–504. Wiley Blackwell, 2013

Environs of Imperial Rome

B.S. Frizell, A. Klynne, eds., *Roman Villas around the Urbs: Interaction with Landscape and Environment*, Swedish Institute in Rome, 2005

T.C.A. de Haas, G.W. Tol, eds., *The Economic Integration of Roman Italy: Rural Communities in a Globalizing World*, Brill, 2017

Ostia
Portus
R. Meiggs, *Roman Ostia*, ed. 2, Oxford, 1973

S. Keay et al., *Portus: An Archaeological Survey of the Port of Imperial Rome*, BSR, 2005

C. Pavolini, "A survey of excavations and studies on Ostia (2004–2014)," *JRS* 106 (2016) 199–236

S. Keay, "The role played by the Portus Augusti in flows of commerce between Rome and its Mediterranean ports." In B. Woytek, ed., *Infrastructure and Distribution in Ancient Economies*, 147–192. Austrian Academy of Sciences, 2018

Second Battle of Cremona, 69 CE
K. Wellesley, *The Year of the Four Emperors*, Routledge, 2000, 141–150

EAB (2017) 1013–1015

Pompeii
Herculaneum
J. Berry, *The Complete Pompeii*, Thames and Hudson, 2007

A. Wallace-Hadrill, *Herculaneum: Past and Future*, London: Frances Lincoln, 2011

A.E. and M.G.L. Cooley, eds., *Pompeii and Herculaneum: A Sourcebook*, ed. 2, Routledge, 2014

R. Laurence, "Pompeii and the *Ager Pompeianus*." In Cooley (2016) 401–416

Italian Towns with Alimentary Schemes
G. Woolf, "Food, poverty and patronage," *PBSR* 58 (1990) 197–228

Rome's Empire around 60 CE
F. Millar et al., *The Roman Empire and Its Neighbours*, ed. 2, Duckworth, 1981

*CAH*² X (1996): E.S. Gruen, "The expansion of the empire under Augustus," 147–197; R.J.A.Talbert, "The senate and senatorial and equestrian posts," 324–343; A.K. Bowman, "Provincial administration and taxation," 344–370; L. Keppie, "The army and the navy," 371–396

A.R. Birley, *The Roman Government of Britain*, Oxford, 2005, 3–9

Britain
D. Mattingly, *An Imperial Possession: Britain in the Roman Empire, 54 BC–AD 409*, Allen Lane, 2006

P. Salway, *Roman Britain: A Very Short Introduction*, ed. 2, Oxford, 2015

Historical Map and Guide to Roman Britain, Ordnance Survey, 2016

Hadrian's Wall
R.S.O. Tomlin, *Britannia Romana: Roman Inscriptions and Roman Britain*, Oxbow, 2018, 83–118

D.J. Breeze, *Hadrian's Wall: A Study in Archaeological Exploration and Interpretation*, Archaeopress, 2019

M. Symonds, *Hadrian's Wall: Creating Division*, Bloomsbury, 2021

Antonine Wall
R.S.O. Tomlin, *Britannia Romana: Roman Inscriptions and Roman Britain*, Oxbow, 2018, 119–154

D.J. Breeze, W.S. Hanson, eds., *The Antonine Wall: Papers in Honour of Professor Lawrence Keppie*, Archaeopress, 2020

D.J. Breeze, *The Antonine Wall*, Origin, 2022

Iberian Peninsula
S.J. Keay, *Roman Spain*, British Museum, 1988

J.S. Richardson, *The Romans in Spain*, Blackwell, 1996

M. Kulikowski, *Late Roman Spain and its Cities*, Baltimore, 2004

G. Bravo, *Nueva historia de la España antigua: una revisión crítica*, Madrid: Alianza, 2011

Vipasca
C. Domergue, *La mine antique d'Aljustrel (Portugal) et les tables de bronze de Vipasca*, Paris: de Boccard, 1983

J. Edmondson, "Mining and production of precious metals in Roman Lusitania (1st century B.C.–3rd century A.D.)," *Madrider Mitteilungen* 61 (2020) 166–191

Thamugadi (Timgad)
J.-M. Blas de Roblès, C. Sintès, P. Kenrick, *Classical Antiquities of Algeria: A Selective Guide*, London: Society for Libyan Studies, 2019, 185–221

Africa (Rome's provinces)
S. Raven, *Rome in Africa*, ed. 3, Routledge, 1993

D.J. Mattingly, *Tripolitania*, Batsford, 1995

J. Conant, *Staying Roman: Conquest and Identity in Africa and the Mediterranean, 439–700*, Cambridge, 2012

R.B. Hitchner, ed., *A Companion to North Africa in Antiquity*, Wiley Blackwell, 2022, 117–371

Africa (south of Rome's provinces)

D.J. Mattingly et al., eds., *Trade in the Ancient Sahara and Beyond*, Cambridge, 2017

K. Bickford Berzock, ed., *Caravans of Gold, Fragments in Time: Art, Culture, and Exchange across Medieval Saharan Africa*, Princeton, 2019

M. Sterry, D.J. Mattingly, eds., *Urbanisation and State Formation in the Ancient Sahara and Beyond*, Cambridge, 2020

Lepcis Magna

P. Kenrick, *Libya Archaeological Guides: Tripolitania*, London: Silphium, 2009, 86–140

Africa Proconsularis and Numidia

E.W.B. Fentress, *Numidia and the Roman Army: Social, Military, and Economic Aspects of the Frontier Zone*, British Archaeological Reports, 1979

D. Cherry, *Frontier Society in Roman North Africa*, Oxford, 1998

M.S. Hobson, *The North African Boom: Evaluating Economic Growth in the Roman Province of Africa Proconsularis (146 B.C.–A.D. 439)*, JRA, 2015

Cyrene

P. Kenrick, *Libya Archaeological Guides: Cyrenaica*, London: Silphium, 2013, 148–254

Lutetia Parisiorum (Paris)

D. Busson, *Atlas du Paris antique: Lutèce, naissance d'une ville*, Paris: Parigramme, 2019
https://archeologie.culture.fr/paris/en/early-roman-city

Gaul

J.F. Drinkwater, *Roman Gaul: The Three Provinces 58 B.C.–A.D. 260*, Croom Helm, 1983

A. King, *Roman Gaul and Germany*, British Museum, 1990

C. Goudineau, "Gaul." In CAH^2 X (1996) 464–502, and XI (2000) 462–495

Germany

G. Alföldy, *Noricum*, Routledge and Kegan Paul, 1974

J.D. Creighton, R.J.A. Wilson, eds., *Roman Germany: Studies in Cultural Interaction*, JRA, 1999

S. James, S. Krmnicek, eds., *The Oxford Handbook of the Archaeology of Roman Germany*, Oxford, 2015

Rhine-Danube *Limes*, 40–260 CE

C.R. Whittaker, *Rome and its Frontiers: The Dynamics of Empire*, Routledge, 2004

S. Matešić, C.S. Sommer, eds., *At the Edge of the Roman Empire: Tours along the Limes in Southern Germany*, Deutsche Limeskommission, 2015

M. Kemkes, "The *Limes*." In S. James, S. Krmnicek, eds., *The Oxford Handbook of the Archaeology of Roman Germany*, 166–197. Oxford, 2015

Danube–Black Sea

J.J. Wilkes, "The Danubian and Balkan provinces." In CAH^2 X (1996) 545–585; and "The Danube provinces." In CAH^2 XI (2000) 577–603

W.S. Hanson, I.P. Haynes, eds., *Roman Dacia: The Making of a Provincial Society*, JRA, 2004

J.J. Wilkes, "The Roman Danube: An archaeological survey," *JRS* 95 (2005) 124–225

D. Mladenović, *Urbanism and Settlement in the Roman Province of Moesia Superior*, Archaeopress, 2012

J. Valeva, E. Nankov, D. Graninger, eds., *A Companion to Ancient Thrace*, Wiley Blackwell, 2015

BNP Regnum Bosporanum III

Crete

I.F. Sanders, *Roman Crete: An Archaeological Survey and Gazetteer of Late Hellenistic, Roman and Early Byzantine Crete*, Aris and Phillips, 1982

R.J. Sweetman, *The Mosaics of Roman Crete: Art, Archaeology and Social Change*, Cambridge, 2013

J.E. Francis, A. Kouremenos, eds., *Roman Crete: New Perspectives*, Oxbow, 2016

Greece

C. Habicht, *Pausanias' Guide to Ancient Greece*, Berkeley, 1985

S.E. Alcock, *Graecia Capta: The Landscapes of Roman Greece*, Cambridge, 1993

R.M. Rothaus, *Corinth: The First City of Greece*, Brill, 2000

Cyprus

V. Karageorghis, *Cyprus from the Stone Age to the Romans*, Thames and Hudson, 1982

E. Hussein, *Revaluing Roman Cyprus: Local Identity on an Island in Antiquity*, Oxford, 2021

Aphrodisias

K.T. Erim, *Aphrodisias: City of Venus-Aphrodite*, New York: Facts on File, 1986

R.R.R. Smith, *Roman Portrait Statuary from Aphrodisias*, von Zabern, 2006

R.R.R. Smith, *The Marble Reliefs from the Julio-Claudian Sebasteion*, von Zabern, 2013

http://aphrodisias.classics.ox.ac.uk

Asia Minor
S. Mitchell, *Anatolia: Land, Men, and Gods in Asia Minor*, Oxford, 1993

M. Cottier et al., eds., *The Customs Law of Asia*, Oxford, 2008

C. Marek, *In the Land of a Thousand Gods: A History of Asia Minor in the Ancient World*, Princeton, 2016

Paul's Journeys
BNP Paul, the Apostle

Syria–Persian Gulf
M.H. Dodgeon, S.N.C. Lieu, *The Roman Eastern Frontier and the Persian Wars (A.D. 226–363): A Documentary History*, Routledge, 1991

F. Millar, *The Roman Near East, 31 BC–AD 337*, Harvard, 1993

G. Greatrex, S.N.C. Lieu, *The Roman Eastern Frontier and the Persian Wars, Part II. AD 363–630*, Routledge, 2002

T.B. Mitford, *East of Asia Minor: Rome's Hidden Frontier*, Oxford, 2018

T. Kaizer, ed., *A Companion to the Hellenistic and Roman Near East*, Wiley Blackwell, 2021

Antioch (Syria)
A.U. De Giorgi, A.A. Eger, *Antioch. A History*, Routledge, 2021

Dura
J.A. Baird, *Dura-Europos*, Bloomsbury, 2018

S.T. James, *The Roman Military Base at Dura-Europos, Syria: An Archaeological Visualisation*, Oxford, 2019

Jerusalem/Aelia Capitolina, 2nd–3rd Centuries CE
M. Piccirillo, E. Alliata, eds., *The Madaba Map Centenary 1897–1997: Travelling Through the Byzantine Umayyad Period*, Jerusalem: Studium Biblicum Franciscanum, 1999

S. Weksler-Bdolah, *Aelia Capitolina – Jerusalem in the Roman Period*, Brill, 2020

Judaea
P. Schäfer, *The History of the Jews in the Greco-Roman World*, revised ed., Routledge, 2003

M. Goodman, *Rome and Jerusalem: The Clash of Ancient Civilizations*, Allen Lane, 2007

Masada (and Roman Siege, 73 CE)
J. Magness, *Masada: From Jewish Revolt to Modern Myth*, Princeton, 2019

Egypt
S.E. Sidebotham, *Berenike and the Ancient Maritime Spice Route*, Berkeley, 2011

C. Riggs, ed., *The Oxford Handbook of Roman Egypt*, Oxford, 2012

R.S. Bagnall, ed., *Roman Egypt: A History*, Cambridge, 2021

Arabia
G.W. Bowersock, *Roman Arabia*, Harvard, 1983

S.T. Parker, *Romans and Saracens: A History of the Arabian Frontier*, American Schools of Oriental Research, 1986

F. Millar, *The Roman Near East, 31 BC–AD 337*, Harvard, 1993, 387–436

G. Fisher, ed., *Arabs and Empires before Islam*, Oxford, 2015

India
M. Canepa, "Cross-cultural communication in the Hellenistic Mediterranean and western and south Asia." In Naiden, Talbert (2017) 249–272

M.A. Cobb, *Rome and the Indian Ocean Trade from Augustus to the Early Third Century CE*, Brill, 2018

F. De Romanis, *The Indo-Roman Pepper Trade and the Muziris Papyrus*, Oxford, 2020

D.G.J. Shipley et al., *Geographers of the Ancient Greek World*, Cambridge, 2023, no. 24 (*Periplus of the Red Sea*)

Rome's Empire around 211 CE
F. Millar, *Rome, the Greek World, and the East*, Chapel Hill, 2004, 160–245

A.A. Barrett, ed., *Lives of the Caesars*, Blackwell, 2008, 107–227

D.S. Potter, ed., *A Companion to the Roman Empire*, Wiley Blackwell, 2009

Circuit of the Roman Empire by Aurelius Gaius, 285–299 CE
K.W. Wilkinson, "Aurelius Gaius (*AE* 1981.777) and imperial journeys, 293–299," *Zeitschrift für Papyrologie und Epigraphik* 183 (2012) 53–58

Etesian Winds and Sea Currents
Sea Routes in Diocletian's Edict on Prices
B. Salway, "Sea and river travel in the Roman itinerary literature." In R. Talbert, K. Brodersen, eds., *Space in the Roman World: Its Perception and Presentation*, 43–96. Münster: LIT, 2004

C.E.P. Adams, "Transport." In W. Scheidel, ed., *The Cambridge Companion to the Roman Economy*, 218–240. Cambridge, 2012

W. Scheidel, "Explaining the maritime freight charges in Diocletian's Prices Edict," *JRA* 26 (2013) 464–468

M.H. Crawford, *Diocletian's Edict on Maximum Prices at the Civil Basilica in Aphrodisias*, Wiesbaden: Reichert, 2022

Split
S. McNally, "The palace of Diocletian at Split." In J.N. Beresford-Peirse, ed., *Croatia: Aspects of Art, Architecture and Cultural Heritage*, 48–59. London: Frances Lincoln, 2009

Constantinople
R. Krautheimer, *Three Christian Capitals: Topography and Politics*, Berkeley, 1983

L. Grig, G. Kelly, eds., *Two Romes: Rome and Constantinople in Late Antiquity*, Oxford, 2012

J. Harris, *Constantinople: Capital of Byzantium*, ed. 2, Bloomsbury, 2017

Rome's Empire around 314 CE
T.D. Barnes, *The New Empire of Diocletian and Constantine*, Harvard, 1982

N. Lenski, ed., *The Cambridge Companion to the Age of Constantine*, Cambridge, 2005

Christianity by the Early Fourth Century
R.L. Mullen, *The Expansion of Christianity: A Gazetteer of Its First Three Centuries*, Brill, 2004

M. Kulikowski, "Christianity." In Naiden, Talbert (2017) 229–246

Roman World on Two Portable Sundials
R. Talbert, "Communicating through maps: The Roman case." In Naiden, Talbert (2017) 340–362

Id., *Roman Portable Sundials: The Empire in Your Hand*, Oxford, 2017

Barbarian Invasions of the Roman Empire, 370–500 CE
P. Heather, *The Fall of the Roman Empire: A New History of Rome and the Barbarians*, Oxford, 2006

G. Halsall, *Barbarian Migrations and the Roman West, 376–568*, Cambridge, 2007

M. Maas, ed., *The Cambridge Companion to the Age of Attila*, Cambridge, 2015

N. Di Cosmo, M. Maas, eds., *Empires and Exchanges in Eurasian Late Antiquity: Rome, China, Iran, and the Steppe, ca. 250–750*, Cambridge, 2018

Roman Empire and Successor Kingdoms around 530 CE
Y. Hen, *Roman Barbarians: The Royal Court and Culture in the Early Medieval West*, Palgrave Macmillan, 2007

W. Pohl et al., eds., *Transformations of Romanness: Early Medieval Regions and Identities*, De Gruyter, 2018

F.K. Haarer, *Justinian: Empire and Society in the Sixth Century*, Edinburgh, 2022

Gazetteer

Note: In principle, this concise gazetteer comprises a single, alphabetic listing of every ancient and modern name marked on the maps, together with the modern country where it was located as of January 1, 2022; its modern name or location there where applicable; and the page number and grid-square letter/number. Descriptors such as fl. (river), Ins. (island), province (Roman) or T. (temple) omitted on the map may be added for clarification. Where a symbol accompanies a name on the map, the grid-square listed is the one where that symbol can be found. Otherwise the grid-square listed is the one where the name begins.

Only the name itself of each battle- and city-plan is listed (with page number **bolded**), but not any of the names on it.

The listing for a name marked on numerous maps normally offers only several instances, not all. **Bolding** of a page number draws attention to a map that may prove especially informative.

Modern names appear in *italic* type. The abbreviations used for modern countries are expanded below. No statement concerning the status of any country is intended here; the same applies to any apparent failure to take into account the course of a boundary correctly. Where an ancient name – either certainly (as in the case of many mountain ranges and rivers), or probably (as often with peoples) – should be associated with more than two modern countries, no attempt is made to state any of them.

Further information about names is most readily provided by pleiades.stoa.org

Modern Countries (in alphabetical order of their abbreviations)

AFG Afghanistan	GIN Guinea	QAT Qatar
ALB Albania	GRE Greece	ROM Romania
ALG Algeria	HUN Hungary	RUS Russia
AND Andorra	IND India	SAN San Marino
ARM Armenia	IRE Ireland	SAU Saudi Arabia
AUS Austria	IRN Iran	SLE Sierra Leone
AZE Azerbaijan	IRQ Iraq	SOM Somalia
BAH Bahrain	ISL Iceland	SPN Spain
BAN Bangladesh	ISR Israel	SRB Serbia
BFA Burkina Faso	ITL Italy	SRI Sri Lanka
BGM Belgium	JOR Jordan	SUD Sudan
BOS Bosnia and Herzegovina	KUW Kuwait	SVK Slovakia
BUL Bulgaria	LBY Libya	SVN Slovenia
CMR Cameroon	MKD North Macedonia	SWE Sweden
CRO Croatia	MLI Mali	SWI Switzerland
CYP Cyprus	MLT Malta	SYR Syria
CYX Territory outside the control of Cyprus	MNE Montenegro	TAJ Tajikistan
	MOL Moldova	TAN Tanzania
CZE Czech Republic	MOR Morocco	TKM Turkmenistan
DEN Denmark	NER Niger	TKY Turkey
DJI Djibouti	NET Netherlands	TUN Tunisia
EGY Egypt	NOR Norway	UAE United Arab Emirates
ERT Eritrea	OMN Oman	UKG United Kingdom
ETH Ethiopia	PAK Pakistan	UKR Ukraine
FRA France	POL Poland	UZB Uzbekistan
GEO Georgia	POR Portugal	VAT Vatican City
GER Germany	PSE Palestinian Territories	YEM Yemen

Abai GRE *Palaiokhori Exarkhou* 6C3, 71C2
Abakainon ITL *Abacano* 113E3
Aballava UKG *Burgh-by-Sands* 135B1
Abantes GRE 14E2
Abarnahara 22C3
Abasgians 199F2
Abdera GRE *Avdira* 19E2, 31E1, 71D1, 152D4
Abdera SPN *Adra* 94B4, 138C4
Abella ITL *Avella* 83D3, 89E3, 93C2, 127C3
Abellinum ITL *La Civitá* 93C2, 127C3
Abila JOR *Khirbet el Kafrein* 168C4
Abila Dekapoleos JOR *Tell Abil* 74E3, 168D2
Abiria IND 175E2
Abitina TUN *Chouhoud el-Batin* 144C1
Abona fl. UKG *Avon* 133C6
Abonouteichos TKY *Inebolu* 159E1
Aborras fl. SYR/TKY *Habur* 162C3
Abritus BUL *Razgrad* 152D3
Abthungi TUN *Henchir-es-Souar* 144D2
Abusina GER *Eining* 151E3
Abydos EGY *el-Araba el-Madfuna* 2C6
Abydos TKY *Maltepe* 13D1, 30A6, 71E1, 159A2
Acarnania GRE *Akarnania* 30B3, 48B3, 59B3, 155B2
Acci SPN *Guadix* 99C3, 138C3
Acelum ITL *Asolo* 109E2, 127B1
Acerrae ITL *Acerra* 87B2, 89D3
Acesinus fl. UKR *upper Ingulets* 153G1
Achaea GRE 18D5, 21B2, 30C4, 48B4
Achaea Phthiotis GRE 30C3, 59C3
Achaia (province) GRE 131E4, 155B2, 179E4, 189E4
Achaia (region) GEO/RUS *NW Caucasus* 162C1
Achaion Akte CYX 156C1
Acharnai GRE *Menidi* 33E5, 36B3, 48D4
Achelous fl. GRE *Akheloos* 14B1, 21A2, 30B3, 155B1
Acheron fl. GRE *Akheron* 14B1, 30A3
Achilleion GRE 6B3
Achilleion TKY *Beşika Burnu* 30A6
Achilleos Dromos UKR *Tendrovskaya Kosa* 153F2
Acholla TUN *Ras Botria* 95F5
Aciris fl. ITL *Agri* 111C1
Acitodunum FRA *Ahun* 147C3
Acquarossa ITL 81C5
Acrae ITL *Palazzolo Acreide* 18B3, 113E3
Actium GRE *Aktion* 32A4, 71B2, 105B3, **107**
Actium Pr. GRE *Akra Akri* 30A3
Ad Duas Lauros ITL *Centocelle* 117C2
Ad Gallinas Albas ITL *Prima Porta* 117B2
Ad Maiores ALG *Henchir Bessariani* 144B3
Ad Sava ALG *Hammam du Guergour* 144A1
Ad Sextum ITL 117B2
Adada TKY *Karabaulo* 159D3
Adamas fl. IND *Subarnarekha* 175H2
Adana TKY *Adana* 2C2, 73E5, 159F4, 163G2
Adane YEM *Aden* 172D6
Addua fl. ITL *Adda* 108C1
Adedou Kome YEM *Hudayda* 172D5
Adiabene IRQ 162D3
Adılcevaz TKY 3F2
Adisathron M. IND *Sahyādri hills* 175E3
Adisdara IND *Ramnagar?* 175F1
Adora PSE *Dura* 168B5

Adouli ERT *Azouli?* 172C5
Adramiton Chora YEM *Hadramaut* 173E5
Adramyttion/Adrammytium TKY *Ören* 31G2, 54A2, 71F2, 159A2
Adranon ITL *Monte Adranone* 43B3
Adranon ITL *Adrano* 43E3, 113E3
Adriaticum Mare *Adriatic Sea* 83D2, 95G2, 109F3, 152A3
Adur Gushnasp IRN *Takht-i Suleiman* 163E4
Adys TUN 94A6
Aecae ITL *Troia* 95G3
Aeclanum ITL *Mirabella Eclano* 89E3, 109G6
Aedui FRA 147D3
Aegae TKY *Nemrut Kale* 31G3
Aegaeum Mare *Aegean Sea* 13C2, 31E3, 71D2, 155C2
Aegates Inss. ITL *Isole Egadi / Aegadian Is.* 94B5, 113B3
Aegeae TKY *Yumurtalık* 163G2
Aegina Ins. GRE *Aigina* 14E3, 36A6, 155C2
Aegyptium Mare 171C1
Aegyptus EGY *Egypt* 53C3, 68B4, 131F5, **171**
Aegyptus Herculia (province) EGY 189G5
Aegyptus Iovia (province) EGY 189G5
Aelana JOR *Aqaba* 75D5, 162A6, 171D2
Aelaniticus Sinus *Gulf of Aqaba* 171D3
Aelia Capitolina ISR *Jerusalem* **167**, 168C5, 179G5
Aemilia ITL/SAN 108D3
Aemilia et Liguria ITL/SAN 188D3
Aeminium POR *Coimbra* 138A2
Aenaria Ins. ITL *Ischia* 87A3
Aenis GRE 59B3
Aenona CRO *Nin* 109G3
Aenus fl. AUS/GER *Inn* 108C1, 149C4, 151F4
Aeoliae Inss. ITL *Isole Eolie/Aeolian Is.* 111A3
Aeolis TKY 19E4, 31G3, 49F3, 159A2
Aequi ITL 85D2
Aequum Tuticum ITL *S. Eleuterio* 83E3
Aesernia ITL *Isernia* 93B1, 109G6
Aesipos fl. TKY 31H2
Aesis ITL *Iesi* 92D2, 109F4
Aesontius fl. ITL/SVN *Isonzo/Soča* 109F2
Aethiopia 53D3, 60B4, 141F5, 172B5
Aetna M. ITL *Etna* 94C5, 113E3
Aetolia GRE *Aitolia* 13B2, 30B3, 59B3
Aetos GRE 6A3
Africa (diocese) 188B5
Africa (province) 103C2, 130D5, 140D1, 178D5
Africa (region) 53B2
Africa Proconsularis **144**, 188C4, 196C4
Africum Mare 95F5, 113C4, 141E1
Agatha FRA *Agde* 18A4
Agathokleous Inss. YEM *Berbera and 'Abd al-Kuri* 173F6
Agathyrnum ITL 113E2
Agedincum FRA *Sens* 147D2
Ager Campanus ITL 87B2
Ager Falernus ITL 87A2
Aghram Nadharif LBY 141E4
Agia Eirene GRE 16D3
Agiation FRA *Ajaccio* 108B5
Aginnum FRA *Agen* 147C4
Agnone ITL 89D3

Agora TKY *Bolayır?* 30B6
Agri Decumates GER 130C2, 147F2, 149B3, 151B3
Agrianes BUL 59B1
Agrigentum ITL *Agrigento* 94B6, 113D3
Agrinion GRE *Vrakhori* 33B5
Agrippias PSE *Teda* 168A5
Agruvium MNE *Kotor* 152A3
Agryle GRE 36B4
Aguntum AUS *Dölsach* 109E1, 149D4
Agyrion/Agyrium ITL *Agira* 43E3, 113E3
Aiane GRE *Aiani* 6B2, 32B3
Aidepsos GRE *Loutra Aidepsou* 32D4
Aigai GRE *Akrata* 33C5
Aigaion Antron GRE *Psykhro/Diktaian cave* 16E4
Aigaleos M. GRE *Aigaleos* 36B4
Aigeai GRE *Vergina* 16B1, 30C2, 59C2, 71C1
Aigeira GRE *Vitrinitsa* 33C5
Aigila Ins. GRE *Antikythera* 33D8
Aigilia GRE *Phoinikia* 36C5
Aigina GRE *Aigina* 21C2, 30D4, 45A3
Aigion GRE *Aigion* 6B3, 14C2, 33C5, 71B2
Aigition GRE *Strouza* 48C3
Aigospotamos TKY *Cumalı?* 30B6, 49F2
Aigosthena GRE *Porto Germano* 33D5
Aigousa Ins. ITL *Favignana* 43A2
Aigousai Nesoi ITL *Isole Egadi/Aegadian Is.* 43A2
Aila JOR *Aqaba* 75D5, 162A6, 171D2
Aineia GRE *Nea Michaniona* 32D2, 45A1
Ainis GRE 27B2
Ainos TKY *Enez* 13D1, 31F1, 71E1, 152D4
Ainos M. GRE *Ainos* 33A5
Aiolou Nesoi ITL *Aeolian Is.* 43E1
Airai TKY *Aşağı Demirci* 45C2, 49F4
Aisepos fl. TKY *Gönen Çay* 13E1
Aitne Oros ITL *Mt. Etna* 43E2
Aixone GRE *Glyphada* 36B5
Aizanoi TKY *Çavdarhisar* 159C3
Akalan TKY 2D1
Akamas Pr. CYP *Cape Arnaoutis* 156A2
Akanthos GRE *Ierissos* 18D2, 30D2, 48D2
Ake/Akko ISR *Tell Accol Acre* 2C4, 74D3, 168B2
Akesines fl. PAK 61H3
Akhmim EGY 2B5
Akila YEM *Khor Ghurayrah (Shaykh Sa'id)?* 172D6
Akmonia TKY *Ahat Köy* 159C3
Akovitika GRE 6B5
Akra Leuke SPN 94C4
Akraba PSE *'Aqrabah* 168C4
Akragas ITL *Agrigento* 18A3, **42,** 43C3
Akrai ITL *Palazzolo Acreide* 43E3
Akritas Pr. GRE *Akritas* 33B7
Akrothooi GRE 45B1
Akrotiri GRE 7E9
Akte GRE *Akte/Athos peninsula* 31E2, 32F2
Akte *(in Attica)* GRE *Akte* 36B4
Al Mina see Posideion
Ala Miliaria ALG *Bénian* 138E4, 140B1
Alabanda TKY *Araphisar* 31H4, 72B5, 159B3
Alaca Höyük TKY 2C1
Alaisa ITL *Tusa* 43D2
Alalaiou Inss. ERT *Dahalak* 172C5

Alalia FRA *Aleria* 18B4, 108C5
Alamanni GER/SWI 149B3, 196C2
Alanoi/*Alans* RUS/UKR 162D1, 197G1
Alarodioi TKY 22D2
Alassa CYP 9B2
Alauna UKG *Ardoch* 132C3
Alauna UKG *Maryport* 132C4, 135A2
Alauna UKG *Learchild* 135D1
Alauna fl. UKG *Aln* 132D4
Alba Fucens ITL *Albe* 83D2, 92D2, 109F5, 127C2
Alba M. GER *Schwäbische Alb* 147F2, 149B4, 151C4
Albanos fl. AZE/RUS *Samur* 163F2
Albanum ITL *Albano* 117C2
Albanus M. ITL *Monte Cavo* 86C2
Albingaunum ITL *Albenga* 108A3, 147F4
Albintimilium ITL *Ventimiglia* 108A4, 147F4
Albis fl. GER *Elbe* 130D2, 149D2, 178D1
Alburnus Maior ROM *Roşia Montană* 152C1
Alcántara SPN 138B3
Alepotrypa cave GRE 6B5
Aleppo SYR *see* Beroia
Aleria FRA *Aleria* 83B2, 108C5, 178D3, 182C1
Alesia FRA *Alise-Ste.-Reine* 104B1, 147D2
Aletrium ITL *Alatri* 89D3
Alexandreion PSE *Sartaba* 168C4
Alexandria (= Cufis) AFG *Kandahar* 53E2, 61G3, 69G3
Alexandria (= Arachotos) AFG *Kalat-e-Ghilzai?* 69H3
Alexandria *(in Bactria)* AFG *Balkh* 61G2
Alexandria EGY *Iskandariya* 53C2, **66,** 68B3, 74A4, 171B2
Alexandria *(in Carmania)* IRN 61F3
Alexandria IRQ *Jebel Khayabir* 60D3, 69E4
Alexandria (= Rhambakia) PAK *Khandewari?* 61G4, 174C1
Alexandria *(Indus/Chenab confluence)* PAK 61G3
Alexandria *(on Akesines fl.)* PAK 61H3
Alexandria TKM *Erk Kala/Gyaur Kala* 61F2, 69G2
Alexandria ad Issum TKY *Esentepe* 60C2, 73F5, 163G2
Alexandria ad Latmum TKY *Karpuzlu* 60B2
Alexandria Ariorum AFG *Herat* 53E2, 61F2, 69G3
Alexandria Eschate TAJ *Khojend* 53F2, 61G2, 69H2
Alexandria Oxiana AFG *Ai Khanoum* 61G2, **65,** 69H2
Alexandria Troas TKY *Eskistanbul* 60A2, 71E2, 159A2
Alikanas GRE 6A4
Alinda TKY *Karpuzlu* 159B3
Alione UKG *Maryport* 135A2
Alişar Höyük TKY 2C2
Allia fl. ITL 83C2
Allifae ITL *S. Angelo d'Alife* 83D3, 93B1, 95G3, 127C3
Allobroges FRA/SWI 94D1, 147E3
Alluniere ITL 81C5
Alontas fl. GEO/RUS *Terek* 163E1
Alope GRE *Melidoni/Ag. Aikaterini* 48C3
Alopeke GRE *Katsipodi* 36B4
Alopekonnesos TKY 30A6
Aloros GRE *Kypsele?* 32C2
Alpes Carnicae ITL/SVN 109F2
Alpes Cottiae *(province)* FRA/ITL 108A3, 130C3, 147E3, 178C3
Alpes Graiae et Poeninae *(province)* 108A1, 130C3, 147E3, 178C3

Alpes M. *Alps* 95E1, 108A2, 147F3, 149C4
Alpes Maritimae *(province)* FRA/ITL 108A3, 130C3, 147E4, 178C3
Alpes Numidicae ALG 144B1
Alpheios fl. GRE *Alpheios* 13B2, 21B3, 30B4
Alsium ITL *Palo* 92C3, 117A2
Althiburos TUN *Fej El Tamar* 144C2
Altıntepe TKY 3E2
Altinum ITL *Quarto di Altino* 109E2
Alutus fl. ROM *Olt* 152D2
Alzyeia GRE *Kandila* 33A5
Amanus M. TKY *Nur Dağları* 2D2, 163H2
Amardos fl. IRN *Safid Rud* 3G2, 163F3
Amaseia TKY *Amasya* 73E3, 162A2, 189G4
Amastris TKY *Amasra* 72D3, 131G3, 159E1, 179G3
Amathe SYR *Hama* 2D3, 74E2
Amathous CYP 2C3, 156B3
Amathous JOR *Amta* 168C3
Ambelikou CYX 9A1
Amber Is. SWE 53C1
Ambiani FRA 147C2
Amblada TKY *Hisartepe* 159D3
Ambracia GRE *Arta* 21A2, 32A4, 71B2, 155B1
Ambracius Sinus GRE *Ambracian Gulf* 30A3
Ambracus GRE *Phidokastro* 30B3
Ameglia ITL 83B1
Amenanos fl. ITL *Giudicello* 43E3
Ameria ITL *Amelia* 89C2, 109E5, 127A5
Amiata, M. ITL 81C4
Amida TKY *Diyarbakır* 162C3, 189H4
Amisus TKY *Samsun* 19G4, 68C2, 162A2
Amiternum ITL *S. Vittorino* 89C2, 109F5
Ammaedara TUN *Haidra* 144C2
Ammon EGY *Aghurmi, Siwa* 53C2, 60A3, 141H3
Ammon JOR 2D4
Amnias fl. TKY *Göksu* 2C1, 159F1
Amnisos GRE 9C2, 13D4
Amorgoi GRE 45C3
Amorgos Ins. GRE *Amorgos* 21D3, 31F5, 56D4, 159A4
Amorion TKY *Hisar Köy* 159D3
Ampelum ROM *Zlatna-Pătrînjeni* 152C2
Amphiareion GRE *Mavrodilesi* 36C2
Amphilochia GRE 30B3
Amphipolis GRE *Amphipolis* 30D1, 48D1, 71D1, 155C1
Amphipolis SYR *Jebel Khaled, Kara Membidj* 73G6
Amphissa GRE *Salona* 16B2, 30C3, 48C3
Ampsaga fl. ALG *Oued el Kebir* 140C1, 144A1
Amsanctus ITL 89E3
Amyklai GRE *Slavochorion* 14D3, 16B3, 33C7
Amyzon TKY *Mazın Kalesi* 71F3
Ana IRQ 3E3
Anactorium GRE *Ag. Petros* 21A2, 30B3, 48B3
Anagnia ITL *Anagni* 83D3, 86D2, 117D2, 127C3
Anagrana SAU *Nagran/Najran* 172D5
Anagyrous GRE *Vari* 36C5
Anaia TKY *Kadikalesi* 49G4
Anaphe (Ins.) GRE *Kastelli* 31F6, 56D4
Anaphlystos GRE *Ag. Georgios* 36D6
Anapos/Anapus fl. ITL *Anapo* 43E3, 48A6
Anas fl. POR/SPN *Guadiana* 94B3, 99B3, 138C3
Anatolia TKY 2B2

Anazarbos TKY *Anavarza Kalesi* 163G1
Anchialus BUL *Pomorie* 153E3, 193F3
Ancona ITL *Ancona* 83D2, 89D1, 92D2, 109F4
Ancyra TKY *Ankara* 2C1, 60B2, 72D4, 159E2
Andania GRE *Kallirhoe* 71B3
Andautonia CRO *Šćitarjevo* 109H2, 152A2
Andecavi FRA 147B3
Andematunnum FRA *Langres* 147E2, 149A4
Andium Ins. UKG *Jersey* 133D7, 147B2
Andros (Ins.) GRE *Andros* 19E5, 31E4, 71D3, 155C2
Anemurium TKY *Eski Anamur* 159E4
Angles 196B1
Anglo Saxons 199B1
Anio fl. ITL *Aniene* 86C1, 117D2
Ankara TKY *see* Ancyra
Ankyra TKY *Boğaz Köy* 159B3
Ankyronpolis EGY *El-Hiba* 75A6
Anourogrammon SRI *Anurādhapura* 175F6
Anshan IRN *Tal-i Malyan* 3H4
Antaiopolis EGY *Qaw el Kebir* 171B4
Antandros TKY *Devren/Avcılar* 27E2, 31G2, 49F2
Antarados SYR *Tartous* 74E2
Antemnae ITL *Monte Antenne* 86B2
Anthedon GRE *Loukisia* 14E2, 33E5
Anthedon PSE *Teda* 168A5
Anthela GRE *Anthili* 21B2
Anthemous GRE 59C2
Anticaria SPN *Antequera* 138C4
Antigoneia ALB *Lekli?* 71A1
Antigoneia GRE *Mantineia* 71C3
Antigoneia GRE *SE Thessalonica* 71C1
Antigoneia TKY *Eskistanbul* 71E2
Antilibanus M. LEB/SYR *Jebel esh-Sherqi* 162A5
Antinoopolis EGY *Sheik Ibada* 171B3
Antiocheia ad Cragum TKY *Güney Köy* 72D6
Antiocheia Chrysaoron TKY *Araphisar* 71F3
Antiocheia Persidos IRN *Bushir* 69E4, 173F2
Antiochia IRQ *Jebel Khayabir* 69E4
Antiochia TKM *Erk Kala/Gyaur Kala* 69G2
Antiochia TKY *Antakya* 73F6, 131H4, 163G2, **165**
Antiochia SYR/TKY *Nusaybin* 73H5
Antiochia *(N Pisidia)* TKY *Yalvaç* 72C4, 159D3, 161G2, 189G4
Antiochia ad Chrysorhoam JOR *Jerash* 74E4
Antiochia ad Cydnum TKY *Tarsos* 68C2, 73E5
Antiochia ad Maeandrum TKY *Aliağaçiftliği* 72B5, 159B3
Antiochia ad Pyramum TKY *near Kızıltâhta* 73E5
Antiochia ad Sarum TKY *Adana* 73E5
Antipatreia ALB *Berati* 71A1
Antipatris ISR *Ras el-Ain/Rosh Ha-Ayin* 161H4, 168B4
Antiphrai EGY *Marina el-Alamein, el-Bahrein* 171A2
Antipolis FRA *Antibes* 18B4, 108A4
Antirrhion Pr. GRE 33B5
Antissa GRE *Skalokhori/Obriokastro* 31F3, 49F3, 56D2
Antitaurus M. TKY 162A3
Antium ITL *Anzio* 83C3, 86C3, 109E6, 117C3
Antonine Wall UKG **136**
Antron GRE *Glyphai/Akhilleion* 14D2
Anxanum ITL *Lanciano* 109G5
Anydros M. GRE *Xerovouni* 36C5

Aornos rock PAK *Pir Sar?* 61H2
Aous fl. ALB/GRE *Vijosë/Aoos* 30B2, 59A2, 152B4, 155B1
Apaisos TKY 13E1
Apamea SYR *Qalaat el-Moudiq* 68C3, 74E2, 162A4
Apamea TKY *Dinar* 68B2, 72C5, 159C3, 193F4
Apamea TKY *Mudanya* 72B3, 159B2
Apamea TKY *Keskince* 73G5
Apenninus M. ITL *Appennines* 83B1, 108C3
Aperopia Ins. GRE *Dokos* 33E6
Aphetai GRE *Platania/Kato Yeoryios* 27C2
Aphidna GRE *Kotroni* 36C3
Aphrodisias TKY *Geyre* 7H8, **157**, 159B3, 195E5
Aphrodision CYX 156C2
Aphrodito EGY *Atfih* 75B5, 171B3
Aphroditopolis EGY *Kom Isgaw* 75B7, 171B4
Aphroditopolis EGY *Gebelen* 171C5
Aphytis GRE *Aphytos* 32E3, 45A1
Apokopa M. IND *Aravalli Mts.* 175E2
Apollonia ALB *Pojan* 18D4, 71A1, 105E2, 152B4
Apollonia GRE *on Cape Pirgos Apollonias* 32F2
Apollonia GRE *SW Amphipolis* 59C2, 71C1, 160D1
Apollonia ISR *Apollonia-Arsuf* 74D4, 168B4
Apollonia LBY *Marsa Susa* 141G2
Apollonia TKY *NE Pergamum* 71F2
Apollonia TKY *Uluborlu* 72C5, 159C3
Apollonia ad Maeandrum TKY 72B5
Apollonia ad Rhyndacum TKY *Apolyont* 159B2
Apollonia Pontica BUL *Sozopol* 19F4, 59F1, 68B2, 153E3
Apollonia Salbakes TKY *Medet* 159B4
Apollonopolis Magna EGY *Edfu/Idfu* 75C8, 171C5
Apollonopolis Parva EGY *Qus* 171C4
Appia TKY *Pınarcık* 159C3
Aproi TKY *Germeyan* 153E4
Apsaros GEO *Gonio* 162C2
Apsos fl. ALB *Semeni* 152B4, 155A1
Aptera GRE *Megala Khorafia* 154A2
Apuani ITL 85B1
Apuli/Apulia ITL 85E3, 109H6
Apulia et Calabria ITL 188D3
Apulum ROM *Alba Julia* 152C2, 179E3
Apurytai? AFG/PAK 23H3
Aquae Calidae ALG *Hammam Righa* 138E4
Aquae Calidae ITL *Sardara* 113E2
Aquae Flaviae POR *Chaves* 138A2
Aquae Sextiae FRA *Aix-en-Provence* 147E4, 188C3
Aquae Statiellae ITL *Acqui Terme* 108B3
Aquae Terebellicae FRA *Dax* 138D1, 147B4
Aquae Vescinae ITL *Terme di Suio* 87A1
Aquileia ITL 92D1, 109F2, 182D1, 188D3
Aquileia GER *Heidenheim* 151D3
Aquilonia ITL *on Monte Vairano* 89E3
Aquilonia ITL *Lacedonia* 89E3, 109H6
Aquincum HUN *Budapest* 149F4, 152B1, 179E2
Aquinum ITL *Aquino* 89D3, 93A1, 109F6
Aquitani/Aquitania FRA *Aquitaine* 104B2, 138E1, 147C3, 178B3
Aquitanica I *(province)* FRA 188B3
Aquitanica II *(province)* FRA 188B3
Aquitanicus Sinus FRA/SPN *Bay of Biscay* 138C1, 147A4

Ara Ubiorum GER *Köln/Cologne* 147E1, 149A3
Araba SUD *Wad Ban Naqa* 172B5
Arabia 22C4, 162C6, **172–73**
Arabia *(province)* 162A5, 179G5, 189G5
Arabia Petraia 171D2
Arabicus Sinus *Red Sea* 172C3
Arabis fl. PAK *Hab* 174C1
Arachosia AFG 23G4, 61G3, 69G4
Arachotos AFG *Kalat-e-Ghilzai?* 69H3
Arados SYR *Rouad* 74E2, 162A4
Arae Flaviae GER *Rottweil* 147F2, 149B4, 151B4
Arae Philaenorum LBY *Graret Gser et-Trab* 141G2
Araithyrea GRE 14D3
Aram 2D3
Arar fl. FRA *Saône* 147D3
Ararat M. TKY 3F2
Ararene SAU *al-'Ara'ir* 172D5
Arausio FRA *Orange* 147D4
Araxes fl. *Aras/Arax* 3F1, 54D2, 162D2
Araxos Pr. GRE *Araxos* 33B5
Arba Ins. CRO *Rab Is.* 109G3
Arbeia UKG *South Shields* 135D1
Arbela IRQ *Arbil/Erbil* 3F3, 60D2, 162D4
Arbela ISR *Horvat Arbell/Khirbet 'Irbid* 168C2
Arbita M. PAK *Kirthar Mts.* 174C1
Arboukale SPN *El Alba de Villalazán?* 99B2
Arcadia GRE *Arkadia* 13B2, 30C4, 47B3
Arcadians GRE 14C3
Archaiopolis GEO *Nokalakevi* 162C1
Archanes GRE 9C2
Archelais PSE *Khirbet Beiyudat* 168C4
Archelais TKY *Aksaray* 159F3
Ardashir Khurra IRN *Fīrūzābād* 173F2
Ardea ITL *Ardea* 81D6, 86B2, 92C3, 117C3
Ardiaei MNE 59A1
Arduenna Silva BGM/GER *Ardennes* 147E1, 149A3
Are YEM *Urr Mayhan* 173E5
Areia AFG 23F3, 61F2, 69G3
Arelate FRA *Arles* 147D4, 188C3, 192C3
Arene GRE 14C3
Arethousa SYR *Restan* 74E2
Arethousa GRE *near Khalkis?* 56C3
Arevaci SPN 99C1
Argaios M. TKY 159F3
Argarikos Sinus IND/SRI *Palk Bay* 175F5
Argentarius M. ITL *Monte Argentario* 81B5, 108D5
Argentomagus FRA *Saint-Marcel* 147C3
Argentorate FRA *Strasbourg* 130C2, 147F2, 149B3, 151A3
Argilos GRE 27C1, 32E2, 48D1
Arginoussai Inss. TKY *Makronisi* 49F3
Argishtihinili ARM 3F1
Argissa/Argoura GRE *Argissa Magoula* 6B2, 14C1, 32C3
Argolis GRE *Argolid* 30C4
Argos GRE *Argos* 13B2, 33D6, 71C3, 155B2
Argos GRE *Hrupista* 32B2
Argos Amphilochikon GRE *Ag. Ioannes* 30B3, 48B3
Argostoli GRE 6A4
Argoura *see* Argissa
Argyruntum CRO *Starigrad* 109H3

Arhontiko GRE 6B1
Ariake IND 175E2
Ariaratheia TKY *Pınarbaşı* 73F4
Ariaspai 61F3
Ariassos TKY *Üçkapı, Bademağaç* 159C4
Aricia ITL *Ariccia* 81D5, 86C2, 89C3, 117C2
Arienzo ITL 93B2
Arikamedu IND *Pondicherry* 53F3, 175F5
Ariminum ITL *Rimini* 81D3, 89C1, 109E3, 127B1
Arin-Berd see Erebuni
Arisbe TKY *Musakoy?* 13D1, 30A6, 45C1
Arkades GRE *Kefala* 154C2
Arkesine GRE 71E3
Armant EGY 2C6
Armavir ARM 3F1
Armenia 3E2, 22C2, 68C2, 162C2
Armenia Minor *(province)* TKY 189H4
Armenoi GRE 9B2
Armorica FRA *Brittany* 53A1, 133C8, 147A2, 196A2
Arna ITL *Civitella d'Arno* 127A4
Arnon fl. JOR *Wadi Mujib* 168C5
Arnus fl. ITL *Arno* 81B3, 89A1, 92B2, 108D4
Aromata Emporion SOM 173F6
Arouaia M. IND 175F5
Arpad SYR 2D2
Arpi ITL 83E3, 89F3, 95G3
Arpinum ITL *Arpino* 83D3, 89D3, 109F6
Arrabona HUN *Győr* 149F4, 152A1
Arretium ITL *Arezzo* 81C3, 89B1, 95F2, 109E4
Arsameia TKY *Gerger Kale* 162B3
Arsanias fl. TKY *Murat Su* 3E1, 162B3
Arsennaria ALG *Sidi bou Ras* 138E4
Arsinoe CYP *Polis tis Khrysokhou* 74B2, 156A2
Arsinoe CYX 156C2
Arsinoe EGY *Medinet el-Fayum* 171B3
Arsinoe EGY *Kum el-Qolzum/Suez* 53C2, 75B5
Arsinoe GRE 71C3
Arsinoe TKY *Selçuk* 71F3
Arsinoe TKY *Gelemiş* 72B6
Arsinoe TKY *Maraş Harabeleri* 72D6
Arslan tepe TKY 2D2
Artaxata ARM 68D2, 162D2
Artemidos Limen FRA *Etang de Diane?* 108C5
Artemis Brauronia GRE *Brauron* 16D3, 33E6, 36D4
Artemision GRE *Ag. Georgios* 27C2, **28**, 32D4
Artigi SPN *Castuera?* 138B3
Arupium CRO *Prozor* 109H3
Arverni FRA 94C2, 147C3
Arwad SYR 2D3
Arykanda TKY *Aykırca* 159C4
Arzawa TKY 2B2
Asabon M. OMN/UAE *Hajar Mts.* 173G3
Ascalon ISR *Ashkelon* 74D4, 168A5, 171D1
Asciano ITL 81C4
Asculum ITL *Ascoli Piceno* 83D2, 89D2, 92D2, 109F5
Asea GRE 6B4, 16B3, 33C6
Ashdod ISR *Tel Ashdod* 2C4, 74D4
Ashqelon ISR *Ashkelon* 2C4, 74D4, 168A5
Ashur IRQ *Qal'at Sherqat* 3F3
Asia *(province)* TKY 103E2, 131F4, 155D1, 179F4
Asiana *(diocese)* TKY 189F4

'Asiatic Ethiopians'? PAK 23G4
Asinaeus Sinus GRE *Gulf of Messene* 33C7
Asine GRE *Koroni* 30C5, 48D5
Asine GRE *Tolon* 14D3, 16C3, 33D6
Asisium ITL *Assisi* 109E4, 127A4
Askania L. TKY *İznik Gölü* 13F1, 159C2
Askra GRE *Pyrgaki-Episkopi* 21B2
Asomatos GRE 7G9
Asopos GRE *Plytra* 33D7
Asopos fl. GRE *in Boeotia* 30D4, 33E5
Asopos fl. GRE *Sicyon area* 14D3
Aspadana IRN 69E3, 163G5, 173F1
Aspendos TKY *Belkis* 72C5, 159D4
Aspledon GRE *Avrokastro/Polyyria* 14D2
Asseria CRO *Podgrade* 109H3
Assinaros fl. ITL *Fiume di Noto* 43F4, 48A6
Assiros GRE 6C1
Assos TKY *Beyramkale* 31G2, 45C2, 71E2, 159A2
Assyria IRQ/SYR 3E3, 22D3, 162C4
Astaboras fl. SUD *Atbara* 172B5
Astakos GRE 33A5, 48B3
Astakos TKY *Baş İskele* 19F4, 45F1
Asthala Ins. PAK *Astalu* 53E3
Astigi SPN *Écija* 99B3, 138B3
Astura ITL *Torre di Astura* 86C3, 117C3
Asturia SPN 138B1
Asturica Augusta SPN *Astorga* 138B2
Astypalaia (Ins.) GRE *Astypalaia* 31G5, 45C3, 56E4, 159A4
Aswan EGY 2C6
Asyut EGY 2B5
Atabyrion M. GRE 31H6
Atalante GRE 48C1
Atalante Ins. GRE *Talandonisi* 48C3
Atarneus TKY *Kale Tepe* 13E2, 31G3, 59E3, 71F2
Atella ITL 87B2, 89D3, 93B2
Ater M. LBY *Hamada el-Hamra* 141E3
Aternum ITL *Pescara* 109G5
Atesis fl. ITL *Adige* 108D1, 149C4
Ateste ITL *Este* 81C1, 83C1, 92C1, 108D2
Athamania GRE 59B3
Athena Itonia GRE *Philia Karditsis* 16B2
Athenae GRE *Athinal/Athens* 13C2, 30D4, **37–38,** 45B3, 155C2
Athenai Diades GRE *Yialtra Kastelli/ Loutra* 56C2
Athmonon GRE *Amarousion* 36C3
Athos (M.) GRE *Akte peninsula/Agion Oros* 13C1, 27D1, 32F3, 155C1
Athribis EGY *Tell Atrib* 2B4, 75B5, 171B2
Athroula YEM *Baraqish* 172D5
Atina ITL *Atina* 89D3, 109F6, 127C3
Atina ITL *Atena Lucana* 111B1, 127D3
Atintanes ALB 59A2
Atlanticus Oceanus *Atlantic Ocean* 53A1, 138A4, 147A3, 178A2
Atlas M. MOR 53A2
Atrax GRE *Aliphaka/Koutsokhero* 32C3
Atrebates FRA 147C1
Atrebates UKG 133D6
Atropatene IRN/TKY 68D2
Attalea TKY *Antalya* 72C5, 159D4

Attaleia TKY *near Sindirgi* 71F2
Attene SAU 173E3
Attica GRE *Attiki* 21C2, 30D4, **36**
Attidium ITL *Attiggio* 109E4
Atuatuca BGM *Tongres/Tongeren* 147E1, 149A3
Aualites DJI *Assab* 172D6
Aualites Sinus *Gulf of Aden* 173E6
Auara JOR *Humayma* 162A6
Auchendavy UKG 136B2
Aufidena ITL *Castel di Sangro* 83D3, 89D3, 109F6, 127C3
Aufidus fl. ITL *Ofanto* 109H6
Aufinum ITL *Ofena* 109F5, 127C2
Augila LBY *Gialo* 141G3
Augusta Bagiennorum ITL *Bene Vagienna* 108A3
Augusta Euphratensis *(province)* TKY/SYR 189H4
Augusta Libanensis *(province)* SYR 189H5
Augusta Praetoria ITL *Aosta* 92A1, **107,** 108A2, 147E3
Augusta Raurica SWI *Augst* 147F2, 149B4, 151A4
Augusta Taurinorum ITL *Torino/Turin* 92A1, 108A2, 147F3
Augusta Traiana BUL *Stara Zagora* 152D3
Augusta Treverorum GER *Trier* 147E2, 149A3, 188C2, 196C1
Augusta Vindelicum GER *Augsburg* 130D2, 149C4, 151D3, 188D2
Augustae ITL *Austis* 113A2
Augustobriga SPN *Talavera la Vieja?* 138B3
Augustodorum FRA *Bayeux* 133E7, 147B2
Augustodunum FRA *Autun* 147D3
Augustonemetum FRA *Clermont-Ferrand* 147D3
Augustoritum FRA *Limoges* 147C3
Aulerci FRA 133E8
Aulis GRE *Mikro Vathy/Ag. Nikolaos* 13C2, 30D4
Aurasius M. ALG *Aurès Mts.* 144A2
Aurunci ITL 85D3
Ausaritis YEM *Wusr* 173E5
Ausculum ITL *Ascoli Satriano* 89F3, 92E3
Auser fl. ITL *Serchio* 108C3
Ausetani SPN 94C3, 99E2
Autariatae BOS 59A1
Autricum FRA *Chartres* 133F8, 147C2
Auximum ITL *Osimo* 92D2, 109F4, 127C2
Auxoume ETH *Aksum* 172C5
Auzia ALG *Sour-Ghozlan* 138F4, 140C1
Avaricum FRA *Bourges* 147C3, 188B3
Avaris EGY *Qantir?* 2C4
Aveia ITL *Fossa* 89D2
Avens fl. ITL *Velino* 109E5
Aventicum SWI *Avenches* 147E3, 149A4
Avgi GRE 6A1
Axia ITL *Castel d'Asso* 81C5
Axiakes fl. UKR *Tiligul* 153F1
Axima FRA *Aime* 147E3
Axios fl. GRE/MKD *Axios/Vardar* 13B1, 30C1, 48C1, 152C4
Axos GRE *Axos* 21C4, 71D4, 154B2
Ayanis TKY *Ağartı Kalesi* 3F2
Ayia Marina GRE 6A2
Ayia Triada GRE 9B2
Ayios Athanasios GRE 6C1

Ayios Mamas GRE 6C2
Ayios Vasileios GRE 6C5
Azali HUN 152A1
Azania 173E6
Azatiwataya TKY 2D2
Azotos ISR *Tel Ashdod* 74D4, 161H4

Babylon EGY *Fostat/Cairo* 171B2
Babylon IRQ *Tell Amran* 3F4, 22D3, 68D3, 162D5
Babylonia IRQ 3F4, 60D3, 163E6
Baclanaza SAU *Tabūk* 172B2
Bactra AFG *Balkh* 23G2, 61G2, 69G2
Bactria AFG 23G2, 61G2, 69G3
Bademağaci TKY 7I9
Bademgediği Tepe TKY 7G8
Badias ALG *Badès* 144B2
Baecula SPN *Bailén* 94B4, 99C3
Baelo SPN *Bolonia* 138B4
Baeterrae FRA 147D4
Baetica *(province)* SPN 130A4, 138B3, 178A4, 188A4
Baetis fl. SPN *Guadalquivir* 99B3, 130A4, 138C3, 178A4
Baetulo SPN *Badalona* 138E2
Bagacum FRA *Bavay* 147D1
Bagai ALG *Ksar Baghai* 144B2
Bagaudae FRA 196B2
Bagis TKY *Güre* 159C3
Bagradas fl. ALG/TUN *Oued Medjerda* 94A6, 104C3, 140D1, 144B1
Baiae ITL *Baia* 87B2
Baitokaike SYR *Hosn Soleiman* 74E2
Baklatape TKY 7G8
Balari ITL *Berchidda* 113A1
Balatonoi FRA 108B6
Balawat IRQ 3F3
Balboura TKY *Çölkayağı* 72B5, 159C4
Baliares Inss. SPN *Mallorca, Menorca* 99F2, 138E2
Baliaricum Mare *Balearic Sea* 99E2, 138E2
Balissus fl. SYR/TKY *Balikh* 162B4
Balmuildy UKG 136B2
Bambyke SYR *Membidj* 74F1
Banabasi IND *Banavasi* 175E4
Banasa MOR *Sidi Ali bou Jenoun* 138B4, 140A1
Banna UKG *Birdoswald* 135B1
Bannatia UKG *Dalginross* 132B3
Bantia ITL *Banzi* 89F3
Baquates MOR 140A2
Bar Hill UKG 136B2
Barakes Sinus IND *Gulf of Kutch* 174C2
Bararus TUN *Henchir-Rougga* 144D2
Barbaria ITL *Gennargentu* 113A2
Barbarikon PAK 174D2
Barbesula fl. SPN *Guadiaro* 99B4
Barcino SPN *Barcelona* 138E2
Bargylia TKY *Varvıl* 31H5, 71F3, 159B4
Barium ITL *Bari* 83F3, 111C1
Barke LBY *el-Merg/al-Marj* 18D6, 22A3, 141G2
Barra ITL 92E3
Barygaza IND *Broach* 53F3, 175E3
Basileioi UKR 153G2
Basileus fl. CYP *Vasilikos* 156B3
Basilika Therma TKY *Terzili Hamam* 159F2

Basques SPN 199A2
Bassiana SRB *Donji Petrovci* 152B2
Bastam IRN 3F2
Bastarnae MOL/UKR 153E1
Bastetani/Bastetania SPN 99D3, 138D3
Bata RUS *Novorossiysk* 34C3
Batavi NET 147E1, 149A2
Bathinus fl. BOS *Bosna* 152A2
Batiai GRE *Kastri* 59B3
Batnae TKY *Suruc* 162B3
Bauli ITL *Bacoli* 87B2
Bavarians 199C1
Bayrakli (Smyrna) TKY *Izmir* 7G8
Bearsden UKG 136B2
Bedriacum ITL *Calvatone* 108C2
Beer Sheva ISR *Bir es Saba* 2C4, 161H4, 168B6
Begorritus L. GRE *Vegoritida* 30B1
Behbeit el-Hagar EGY 2B4
Belbina Ins. GRE *Chelmos* 33E6
Belerion Pr. UKG 53A1
Belgae *N Gaul* 104C1
Belgae UKG 133D6
Belgica *(province)* 130C2, 147D2, 178B2, 195B3
Belgica I *(province)* 188C2
Belgica II *(province)* BGM/FRA 188B2
Belloi SPN 99D2
Bellovaci FRA 133F7
Benacus L. ITL *Garda* 108C2
Benearnum FRA *Lescar* 138D1, 147B4
Beneventum ITL *Benevento* 87C2, 89E3, 109G6
Berenice EGY *Bender el-Kebir/Medinetel-Haras* 53D3, 68C5, 75D8, 172B3
Berenice JOR *Tabaqat Fahl* 74D3
Berenice LBY *Benghazi* 95H6, 141G2, 193E5
Berenicidis M. EGY *Gebel Zebara* 171D5
Bergalei ITL/SWI 108C1
Bergastrum SPN 138D3
Bergidum Flavium SPN *Cacabelos* 138B2
Bergistani SPN 99E2
Bergomum ITL *Bergamo* 108C2
Bergoule TKY *Lüleburgaz* 153E4
Beroe BUL *Stara Zagora* 59D1
Beroia GRE *Veroia* 32C2, 71B1, 155B1, 160D1
Beroia SYR *Alep/Aleppo* 2D3, 73F6, 163H2
Berosaba ISR *Bir es Saba* 168B6
Berytus LEB *Beirut* 02D3, 74D3, 162A5
Bessi BUL 105E2
Beth Govrin ISR *Bet Jibrin* 168B5
Bethar PSE *Battir* 168B5
Bethel PSE 2C4
Bethlehem PSE *Beit Lahm* 168B5
Bethletepha ISR *Beit Nattif* 168B5
Bethoron PSE *Beit Ur* 168B4
Bethsaida ISR *et Tell/el 'Araj* 168C2
Beth-Shan ISR 2C4
Bettolle ITL 81C4
Beycesultan TKY 7I8
Bezereos TUN *Sidi Mohammed ben Aissa* 144C3
Bibracte FRA *Mont Beuvray* 104B1, 147D3
Bikni, M. IRN 3G3
Bilbilis SPN *Cerro de la Bámbola* 138D2

Billaios fl. TKY *Filyos Çay* 2C1, 159D1
Bisanthe TKY *Tekirdağ* 31H1, 71F1
Bishapur IRN *Shapur* 173F2
Bishopton UKG 136A2
Bistua Nova BOS *Bugojno* 152A3
Bithia ITL *Punta di Chia* 94A5
Bithynia TKY 2B1, 22B2, 68B2, 159C2
Bithynia et Pontus *(province)* TKY 103E2, 131G3, 179F3
Bithynion TKY *Bolu* 72C3, 159D2
Bitia ITL *Punta di Chia* 113A3
Bittigo M. IND *Malayagiri* 175E5
Bituriges FRA *N Burdigala* 147B3
Bituriges FRA *SE Caesarodunum* 147C3
Bizye TKY *Vize* 153E4
Blatobulgium UKG *Birrens* 135A1
Blaundos TKY *Sülmenli* 159C3
Blemmyes EGY/SUD 171C6, 172B4
Blera ITL *Blera* 81C5
Bodotria Aestuarium *Firth of Forth* 132C3
Bodotria fl. UKG *Forth* 132B3, 136B2
Boeotia GRE *Boiotia* 21B2, 30C4, 48C3
Boeotians GRE 14E2
Boğazköy TKY 2C1
Boiai GRE *Neapolis* 33D7
Boibe L. GRE 14D1, 30C2
Boii ITL 85C1, 95F2, 108D3
Bola ITL 92B3
Bolbe L. GRE *Volve* 30D1
Bolbitinon Stoma EGY 171B1
Boliskos GRE 49F3
Bonna GER *Bonn* 130C2, 147E1, 151A1, 178C2
Bononia BUL *Vidin* 152C3
Bononia ITL *Bologna* 92C1, 104C2, 108D3
Boresti UKG 132C3
Bormiskos GRE 48D2
Borsippa IRQ *Birs Nimrud* 3F4
Borysthenes UKR *Parutino* 19F3, 68B1, 153F1
Borysthenes fl. *Dnieper* 19G3, 153G1
Bosa ITL *Bosa* 113A1
Bosphorus RUS/UKR *Kerch'* 34B2, 68C1, 131G3, 153H2
Bosphorus TKY *Boğaziçi* 19H1, 53C2, 153E4, **187**
Bostra SYR *Busra esh-Sham* 74E3, 162A5, 172B1, 179G5
Bothwellhaugh UKG 136C2
Boubastis EGY *Tell Basta* 2B4, 75B5, 171B2
Boubon TKY *Ibecik* 72B5, 159C4
Bouchetion GRE *Rogous* 59B3
Boukephala PAK *Jalilpur?* 61H3
Bouprasion? GRE 14C2
Bousiris EGY *Abu Sir Bana* 02B4, 74B4
Boutadai GRE 36B4
Bouthroton ALB *Butrinti* 30A2
Bouto EGY *Kom el-Farain* 02B4, 74A4, 171B2
Bovianum ITL *Boiano* 89E3, 93C1
Bovianum Vetus ITL 93B1
Bovillae ITL *Frattocchie* 86C2, 117C2
Bracara Augusta POR *Braga* 138A2, 188A3
Bradanus fl. ITL *Bradano* 111C1
Brak LBY 141F3

Branchidai TKY *Didim* 31G5, 159A4
Bravoniacum UKG *Kirkby Thore* 135B2
Brea GRE 45A1
Bremenium UKG *High Rochester* 135C1
Breuci CRO 152A2
Bribra? UKG *Beckfoot* 135A2
Brigaecium SPN *Dehesa de Morales* 138B2
Brigantes UKG 132D4
Brigantinus L. GER/SWI *Bodensee/Lake Constance* 151C4
Brigantium AUS *Bregenz* 147F2, 149B4, 151C4
Brigantium SPN *La Coruña* 138A1
Brigetio HUN *Szőny* 149F4, 152A1, 179E2
Brigobannis GER *Hüfingen* 151B4
Britannia UKG *Great Britain* 53A1, **132–33**, 147B1, 195A2
Britannia *(province)* UKG *Great Britain* 178B2
Britanniae *(diocese)* UKG *Great Britain* 188B2
Britannicum Mare *English Channel* 133C7, 147A2
Brittany see Armorica
Brixellum ITL *Brescello* 92B1, 108C3
Brixia ITL *Brescia* 81A1, 92B1, 108C2, 127A1
Brocavum UKG *Brougham* 132C4, 135B2
Brocolitia UKG *Carrawburgh* 135C1
Brouzos TKY *Karasandıklı* 159C3
Bructeri GER 147E1, 149A2
Brundisium ITL *Brindisi* 83F3, 92F3, 111D1, 152A4
Bruttii/Bruttium ITL 85E4, 111C3
Brygindara GRE 45D4
Bulla Regia TUN *Hammam-Darradji* 94A6, 144C1
Burdigala FRA *Bordeaux* 130B3, 147B3, 178B3, 195A4
Burgundian Kingdom 199B2
Burgundians 197E1
Burnum CRO *Ivoševci* 109H3, 131E3
Burrio UKG *Usk* 133C6
Busento fl. ITL 196D3
Butae IND *Buddas* 174D2
Buxentum ITL *Policastro Bussentino* 92E3
Büyüktepe-Bayburt TKY 3E1
Byblos LEB *Jebeil* 2D3, 74D2
Byllis ALB *Hekal* 152B4
Byzacena *(province)* TUN 188C4
Byzantium/Byzantion TKY *Istanbul* 19H1, 72B3, 159B1, 189F3

Cabirus fl. IND *Kāverī* 175F5
Cadder UKG 136B2
Çadır Höyük TKY 2C1
Cadousioi IRN 23E3
Caecina fl. ITL *Cecina* 81B3, 108D4
Caere ITL *Cerveteri* 81C5, 86A1, 109E5, 117A1
Caermote UKG 135A2
Caersws UKG 133C5
Caesaraugusta SPN *Zaragoza* 138D2
Caesarea ISR *Qesaria/Qaisariye* 131G5, 162A5, 168B3, 193G5
Caesarea TKY *Kayseri* 131G4, 159F3, 179G4, 189G4
Caesarea Germanice TKY *Tahtalı* 159B2
Caesarea Philippi SYR *Banias* 161H4, 168C1
Caesarobriga SPN *Talavera de la Reina* 138C2
Caesarodunum FRA *Tours* 147C3
Caesaromagus UKG *Chelmsford* 133E6
Caesena ITL *Cesena* 81C3, 109E3
Caiatia ITL *Caiazzo* 87B1, 89D3, 127C3
Caicus fl. TKY *Bakır Çay* 21E2, 31H3
Calabria ITL 111D1
Calacte ITL *Caronia* 113D3
Calagorris FRA *Saint-Martory* 99E1
Calagurris SPN *Calahorra* 138D2, 147B4
Calama ALG *Guelma* 144B1
Calatia ITL *S. Giacomo delle Galazze* 87B2, 89D3, 93B2
Cale POR *Vilanova da Gaia* 138A2
Caledonia UKG *Scotland* 132B3
Cales ITL *Calvi* 83D3, 93B2, 109G6, 127C3
Calingae IND 175G3
Callaeci/Callaecia SPN 99A1, 138A2, 195A4
Callatis ROM *Mangalia* 19F4, 68B1, 153E3
Calleva UKG *Silchester* 133D6
Callinicum SYR *Raqqa* 73G6, 162B4
Calor fl. ITL *Calore* 87C1
Calycadnus fl. TKY *Göksu* 2C2, 72D5, 159E4
Calydon GRE 14C2, 30B4, 33B5, 48B3
Camarina/Kamarina ITL *Camarina* 18B3, 43D4, 94C6, 113D4
Camarum Ins. YEM *Kamaran* 172D5
Cambodunum GER *Kempten* 149C4, 151D4
Camboglanna UKG *Castlesteads* 135B1
Camerinum ITL *Camerino* 89C1, 109F4
Cameroon, Mt. CMR 53B4
Campani ITL 85D3
Campania ITL **87**, 109G6, 188D3
Campi Catalauni FRA 196B1
Campi Phlegraei ITL *Campi Flegrei/Phlegraean Fields* 87B2
Campovalano ITL 83D2
Campus Vogladensis FRA *Vouillé* 199B2
Camulodunum UKG *Colchester* 133F6
Candidum Pr. TUN *Cap Blanc* 94A6
Cannae ITL *Canne* 95G3, **97**
Canon YEM *Qarnawu?* 172D5
Canopus EGY *Abukir* 74A4, 171B2
Cantabria SPN 138C1
Cantiaci UKG 104B1, 133E6
Cantium Pr. *see* Kantion Pr.
Canusium ITL *Canosa di Puglia* 83E3, 89F3, 109H6, 127D3
Capena ITL *Civitúcola* 86B1, 109E5, 117C1, 127A5
Capera SPN *Ventas de Cáparra* 138B2
Capestrano ITL 83D2
Capitulum ITL 89C2
Caporcotani ISR *Lejjun* 168B3, 179G5
Cappadocia TKY 2C2, 22B2, 68C2
Cappadocia *(province)* TKY 159E2, 189G4
Cappadox fl. TKY *Delice Irmak* 2C2, 159F2
Caprasia Ins. ITL *Capraia* 108C4
Capreae Ins. ITL *Capri* 87B3
Capsa TUN *Gafsa* 140D1, 144C3
Capua ITL *S. Maria Capua Vetere* 87B2, 93B2, 95G3, 109G6
Caracoticum FRA *Harfleur* 133E7, 147C2
Caralis ITL *Cagliari* 94A5, 113A2, 130D4, 178C4
Carcaso FRA *Carcassonne* 147D4

Carchemish SYR/TKY 2D2
Cardouchoi TKY 22D2
Caria TKY 2B2, 31H5, 68B2, 159A3
Caria *(province)* TKY 189F4
Cariati SAU *Qaryat al-Fau* 172D4
Carmania IRN 23F4, 61F3, 69F4, 173G2
Carmo SPN *Carmona* 99B3, 138B3
Carni ITL/SVN 85D1
Carnonacae *see* Karnonakai
Carnuntum AUS *Petronell* 131E2, 149E4, 152A1, 179E2
Carnutes FRA 147C2
Carpetana Iuga SPN 138C2
Carpetani/Carpetania SPN 94B3, 99B2, 138C2
Carpi TUN *Mraissa* 144D1
Carpi/Carpia MOL/ROM *NW Black Sea* 153E1, 180C1
Carpow UKG 132C3
Carrhae TKY *Altınbaşak* 73G5, 105G3, 162B3
Carricini ITL 85D3
Carriden UKG 136D1
Carsioli ITL 92D2, 117D1
Carsulae ITL *S. Damiano* 89C2, 109E5
Carteia SPN *El Rocadillo* 99B4, 138B4
Cartenna ALG *Ténès* 94C4, 138E4, 140C1
Carthaginiensis *(province)* SPN 188A4
Carthago TUN *Carthage* 95F4, 130D4, 141E1, 144D1
Carthago Nova SPN *Cartagena* 94C4, 99D3, 138D3, 188B4
Carvetii UKG *Cumbria* 132C4
Casilinum ITL *Capua* 87B2, 89D3, 93B2
Casinum ITL *Cassino* 89D3, 93A1
Caspiae Portae IRN *Sar Darreh pass* 53E2, 61E2
Caspiae Portae RUS *see* Kaspiai Portae
Caspioi? TKM 23F2
Caspium Mare *Caspian Sea* 23E1, 53D2, 69E2, 163G3
Castel di Decima ITL 81D5, 86B2
Castellina Chianti ITL 81B3
Castelluccio di Pienza ITL 81C4
Castellum Dimmidi ALG *Messad* 140C1
Castlecary UKG 136C1
Castlehill UKG 136B2
Castra Albana ITL *Albano* 178D3
Castra Exploratorum UKG *Netherby* 132C4, 135B1
Castra Hannibalis ITL 92F4
Castra Regina GER *Regensburg* 178D2
Castra Vetera GER *Xanten* 147E1, 149A2
Castrum Inui ITL 86B3
Castrum Novum ITL *Torre Chiaruccia* 92C2, 117A1
Castrum Novum ITL *Giulianova* 92D2, 109F5
Castrum Truentinum ITL *Martinsicuro* 89D2, 109F4
Castulo SPN *Cortijos de S. Eufemia y de Yangues* 94B4, 99C3, 138C3
Casuentus fl. ITL *Basento* 111C1
Catabathmus Maior EGY *Sollum* 141H2
Catada fl. TUN 94A6
Cataonia TKY 22C2
Catina ITL *Catania* 113E3
Catuvellauni UKG 104B1, 133D6
Cauca SPN *Coca* 99C2
Caucasiae Portae GEO 162D1
Caucasus M. *Caucasus* 3F1, 53D2, 68D1, 162C1
Caudini ITL 85E3

Caudium ITL 83D3, 89E3
Caulonia *see* Kaulonia
Caunus TKY *Dalyan* 2B2, 49H5, 72B5, 159B4
Cavares FRA 94D2
Çavuştepe TKY 3F2
Cayster fl. TKY *Küçük Menderes* 13E2, 16F2, 31H4, 155D2
Cebenna M. FRA *Cévennes/Massif Central* 147D4
Celadussae Inss. CRO *Kornati* 109G4
Celeia SVN *Celje* 109G1, 149E4
Celenderis TKY *Aydıncık* 2C3, 159E4
Celenza Val Fortore ITL 92E3
Celsa SPN *Velilla del Ebro* 138D2
Celtiberi/Celtiberia SPN 94B3, 99C2, 138D2
Celtici POR 99A3
Cemenelum FRA *Cimiez* 108A4, 147E4
Cenabum FRA *Orléans* 133F8, 147C2
Cenis, Mont FRA 95E2
Cenomani ITL 85B1, 95F2, 108C2
Centumcellae ITL *Civitavecchia* 117A1
Centuripae ITL *Centuripe* 48A6, 113E3
Cephallania (Ins.) GRE *Kephallenia* 30A4, 48A4, 56A3, 155A2
Cephaloedium ITL *Cefalù* 113D3
Cephissus fl. GRE 14D2
Cerbalus fl. ITL *Cervaro* 109H6
Cercina Ins. TUN *Grand Kerkenna* 95F5, 141E1, 144D2
Çesme Baglararasi TKY 7F8
Chaberis Emporion IND *Tranquebar* 175F5
Chaeronea GRE *Kapraina* 30C3, **57,** 60A2, 71C2
Chalandriani GRE 7E8
Chalandritsa GRE 6B4
Chalastra GRE *Anchialos?* 32D2
Chalcedon TKY *Kadıköy* 19H2, 49H1, 72B3, 159B2
Chalcidice GRE *Khalkidike* 16C1, 30D2, 48C2, 155B1
Chalcis *(on Euboea)* GRE *Khalkis* 16C2, 30D4, 71C2, 155C2
Chalcis ad Belum SYR *'Is, Qinnesrin* 74E1, 163H3
Chalcis sub Libano LEB *Husn esh-Shadur?* 74E3
Chalke Ins. GRE 49G5
Chalkis *(in Aetolia)* GRE *Kato Vasiliki* 14C2, 30B4, 48B4
Chalos fl. SYR *Qoueiq* 54D3
Chalybes TKY 54E2
Chamavi NET 147E1, 149A2
Chania GRE 9A2
Channunia TKY 74F1
Chaones/Chaonia ALB 30A2, 59A2
Chardaleon SAU 172C4
Charybdis ITL *Cariddi (whirlpool)* 43F2, 113F2
Chatriaioi IND *Khatri* 175E2
Chattenia SAU 173E3
Chatti GER 147F1, 149B3
Chauci GER 149B2
Cheimerion Pr. GRE *Akra Trophale* 30A3
Chelidonium Pr. TKY *Gelidonya Burnu* 159C4
Chelonatas Pr. GRE *Kyllinis* 33A6
Cherronesioi TKY 45D3
Cherronesitai TKY 45C1
Chersonasos GRE *Limin Khersonisos* 154C2
Chersonesos UKR 19G3, 153G2

Chersonesos Pr. GRE *Okhthonia* 33F5
Chersonesus TKY *Gallipoli peninsula* 21D1, 30A6, 59E2
Chersonesus Kimbrike DEN/GER *Jutland peninsula* 149B1
Cherusci GER 147F1, 149B2
Chianciano ITL 81C4
Chios (Ins.) GRE *Khios* 21D2, 31F4, 71E2, 155C2
Choba ALG *Ziama* 144A1
Chorasmia TKM/UZB 23F2
Chorienes' Rock UZB 61G2
Chrysas fl. ITL *Dittaino* 43D3
Chryse TKY *Şar* 73F4
Chrysopolis TKY *Üsküdar* 49H1, 54A1
Chrysoun M. FRA *Mt. Cinto* 108B5
Chulimath fl. ALG *Oued Chélif* 99E4, 138E4, 140B1
Chullu ALG *Collo* 95E4, 144B1
Chytroi CYP *Kythrea-Ag. Dimitrios* 156C2
Cibalae CRO *Vinkovci* 152B2
Cibyra TKY *Horzum* 72B5, 159C4
Ciciliano ITL 127B5
Cidamus LBY *Ghadamès* 140D2
Cilicia TKY 2C2, 22C2, 68B3
Cilicia *(province)* TKY 103E2, 163G1, 179G4, 189G4
Ciliciae Portae *see* Kilikiai Portae
Cilicius Aulon 156B1, 159E4
Cillium TUN *Kasserine* 144C2
Cilurnum UKG *Chesters* 135C1
Ciminius L. ITL *Lago di Vico* 81C5
Cimmerius Bosphorus UKR *Straits of Kerch'* **34**, 153H2
Çine Tepecik TKY 7G8
Cingulum ITL *Cingoli* 109F4
Circeii ITL *S. Felice Circeo* 92D3, 109F6
Circesium SYR *al-Busaira* 162C4
Cirta ALG *Constantine* 95E4, 140D1, 144B1, 188C4
Cissa Ins. CRO *Pag Is.* 109G3
Cissi ALG 138F4
Cissia IRN 23E3
Cissis *see* Kissa
Cithaeron M. GRE *Kithairon* 33D5
Civitas Camunnorum ITL *Cividate Camuno* 108C2
Civitas Namnetum FRA *Nantes* 147B3
Clanis fl. ITL *Chiani* 81C4
Clanius fl. ITL *Regi Lagni* 87B2
Clapier, Col du FRA/ITL 95E2
Clastidium ITL *Casteggio* 95E2
Claudia Ara Agrippinensium GER *Köln/Cologne* 147E1, 149A3, 151A1, 188C2
Claudianus M. EGY *Jabal Faṭīrah* 171C4
Claudiopolis TKY *Bolu* 159D2
Claudiopolis TKY *Mut* 159E4
Claudioseleucia TKY *Selef, Bayat* 159C3
Claustra Alpium Iuliarum CRO/SVN 109G2
Cleddans UKG 136A2
Clipea TUN *Kelibia* 94B6, 144D1
Clota fl. UKG *Clyde* 132C4, 136B2
Clunia SPN *Peñalba de Castro* 138C2
Clusium ITL *Chiusi* 81C4, 89B2, 92C2,109E4
Cluviae ITL *Piano Laroma* 89D2, 109G5
Clysma EGY *Kum el-Qolzum/Suez* 75B5, 172A1
Cnidus TKY *Burgaz?* 19F5, 31H5, 49G5
Cnidus TKY *Tekir* 71F3, 159A4, 161E2

Cocanges UKG *Chester-le-Street* 135D2
Codanus Sinus DEN/GER *Kattegat/Baltic Sea* 149B1
Coele Syria SYR 68C3
Colanica UKG *Camelon* 132B3, 136C1
Colapis fl. CRO/SVN *Kupa/Kolpa* 109G2
Colchians GEO 22D2
Colchis GEO 162C1
Coliacum Pr. IND *Callimere* 175F5
Collatia ITL *Lunghezza* 86C2
Colline Metallifere ITL 81B4
Colline Pass ITL 95F2
Collippo POR *S. Sebastião do Freixo* 138A3
Colophon TKY *Degirmendere* 16F2, 31G4, 49G4, 159A3
Colossae TKY 159C3, 161F2, 193F4
Columnae Herculis *Pillars of Hercules* 53A2, 138B4
Comama TKY *Serefönü, Ürkütlü* 159C4
Comana TKY *Şar* 73F4, 105G3, 162A3
Comana Pontica TKY *Kılıçlı* 73F3, 162A2
Combretovium UKG *Baylham House* 133F6
Çömlekçi Köy TKY 16F3
Commagene TKY 131H4, 162A3
Compsa ITL *Conza della Campania* 89E3, 95G3, 127D3
Comum ITL *Como* 83A1, 108B2, 127A1, 147F3
Conana TKY *Gönen* 159C3
Concordia ITL *Concordia Sagittaria* 92C1
Condate Redonum FRA *Rennes* 133D8, 147B2
Condatomagus FRA *La Graufesenque* 147D4
Condercum UKG *Benwell* 135D1
Congavata UKG *Drumburgh* 135A1
Conimbriga POR *Condeixa-a-Velha* 138A2
Consabura SPN *Consuegra* 138C3
Consentia ITL *Cosenza* 83E4, 92E4, 95G4, 111C2
Constantinopolis TKY *Istanbul* **187**, 189F3, 193F3, 197G3
Contestania SPN 138D3
Contrebia SPN *Cabezo de las Minas* 99D2, 138D2
Contributa SPN *Medina de las Torres* 138B3
Copais L. GRE *Kopais* 14D2, 30D4
Copia ITL *Sibari/Copia* 92E4
Coptos EGY *Qift* 2C6, 75C7, 171C4
Cora ITL *Cori* 86C2, 92B4, 117D3
Corcoras fl. SVN *Krka* 109H2
Corcyra (Ins.) GRE *Kerkyra/Corfu* 18D4, 30A2, 71A2, 155A1
Corcyra Nigra Ins. CRO *Korčula Is.* 152A3
Corduba SPN *Córdoba* 99C3, 130A4, 138C3, 178B4
Corfinium ITL *Corfinio* 83D2, 89D2, 104D2, 109F5
Coria UKG *Corbridge* 132D4, 135C1
Corieltauvi UKG 133D5
Corinium CRO *Karin* 109H3
Corinium UKG *see* Korinion
Corinthiacus Sinus GRE *Gulf of Corinth* 33C5
Corinthus GRE *Korinthos/Corinth* 30C4, 71C3, 131F4, 155B2
Coriosopitum UKG *Corbridge* 135C1
Cornovii UKG 133C6
Cornus ITL *S. Caterina di Pittinuri* 113A2
Coronaeus Sinus GRE *Gulf of Messene* 33C7
Coronea GRE *Pyrgos* 30D4
Corsi ITL 113A1

Corsica Ins. FRA *Corsica* 83A2, 95E3, **108,** 178C3
Cortona ITL *Cortona* 81C4, 89B1, 95F2, 109E4
Corycus TKY *Kızkalesi (Gorgos)* 73E5, 159F4
Cos Ins. GRE *Kos* 155D3, 161E2
Cosa ITL *Ansedonia* **90,** 92C2, 95F3, 108D5
Cossaei IRN 23E3, 60D2
Cossyra Ins. ITL *Pantelleria* 94B6, 113B4, 141E1
Costoboci 153E1
Cramond UKG 132C3
Crater fl. ITL *Crati* 111C2
Cremna TKY *Girme, Çamlık* 159C3
Cremona ITL *Cremona* 92B1, 95F2, 108C2, **121**
Creones *see* Kreones
Crepsa Ins. CRO *Cres* 109G3
Creta et Cyrene *(province)* GRE/LBY 103D2, 131E4, 179E4, 189F4
Creta Ins. GRE *Kriti/Crete* **9,** 16D4, 71D4, **154**
Creticum Mare *Kritiko Pelagos* 13C3, 31E6, 155C3
Crisia fl. HUN/ROM *Crişul Repede* 152B1
Crocus Field GRE 59C3
Croton ITL *Crotone* 18C2, 83F4, 92F4, 111C2
Croy Hill UKG 136C2
Crustumerium ITL *Marcigliana* 86B1
Ctesiphon IRQ *al-Ma'aridh* 162D5
Cubulteria ITL *S. Ferrante* 89D3
Cufis AFG *Kandahar* 69G3
Cuicul ALG *Djemila* 140D1, 144A1
Çukuriçi Höyük TKY 7G8
Cumae ITL *Cuma* 18A1, 87B2, 93B2, 109F6
Cunaxa IRQ 54E3
Cunei POR 99A3
Cuniculariae Inss. ITL 113B1
Cupra Maritima ITL *Cupra Marittima* 92D2, 109F4
Cupra Montana ITL *Cupramontana* 127C2
Cures ITL 83C2, 86C1, 117C1, 127A5
Curia SWI *Chur* 108C1, 147F3, 149B4
Curicta Ins. CRO *Krk* 109G2
Curubis TUN *Korba* 144D1
Cyclades Inss. GRE 7E8, 31E4, 155C2
Cydara fl. SRI *Arevi-ār* 175F6
Cydnus fl. TKY *Tarsos Çay* 2C2, 159F4
Cygnus GEO *Ochamchira* 162C1
Cyme TKY *Nemrut Limanı* 21D2, 31G3, 49F3, 71F2, 159A3
Cynoscephalae GRE 30C3
Cyparissius Sinus GRE *Gulf of Kyparissia* 33A6
Cyprus *(province)* CYP/CYX 131G4, 179G4, 189G5
Cyprus Ins. CYP/CYX **9,** 22B3, 74C2, **156**
Cyrenaica LBY 141G2
Cyrene LBY *Ain Shahat, Grennah* 18D6, 68A3, 141G2, **145**
Cyrene *(province)* LBY 131E5, 179E4
Cyreschata TAJ *Khojend* 23H2
Cyropolis TAJ *Kurkat?* 61G2
Cyrrus SYR *Nebi Ouri* 73F5, 131H4, 163H2
Cythera Ins. GRE *Kythera* 155B3
Cyzicus TKY *Belkız Kale* 19G2, 31H2, 72B3, 159B2

Dachinabades IND *Deccan* 175E3
Dacia *(kingdom)* ROM 105E2
Dacia *(province)* ROM 152D1, 179E2, 195D2
Dacia Mediterranea *(province)* BUL/SRB 189E3

Dacia Ripensis *(province)* BUL/SRB 189F3
Dades Pr. CYP *Cape Kiti* 156C3
Daha TKM 23F2
Dakhleh EGY 171A6
Daldis TKY *Nardi* 159B3
Dalmatia CRO 109H3, 131E3, 152A3, 178D3
Damascus SYR *Dimashq* 2D3, 74E3, 162A5, 172B1
Damnonii *see* Daunoni
Dan ISR *Tel Dan/Tell el Qadi* 2D3
Dandagula IND *Dantapura* 175G3
Dandarioi RUS 34C2
Danes DEN 199C1
Danuvius fl. *Danube* 53C2, 130D2, 151D3, 152A1
Daphnous GRE *Ag. Konstantinos* 32D4
Darabgird IRN 173F2
Darae ALG/MOR 140A3
Dardani/Dardania MKD/SRB 59B1, 152B3, 180C1, 189E3
Dardanos TKY 30A6, 49F2
Dareitai? IRN/TKM 23F2
Darioritum FRA *Vannes* 133C8, 147A2
Darnis LBY *Derna* 141G2, 189E5
Daskyleion TKY *Ergili* 2A1, 31H2, 49G2
Daulis GRE *Davleia/Kastro* 14D2, 33D5
Daunii ITL 85E3
Daunoni UKG 132B4
Dea Dia, T. ITL *Magliana* 117B2
Decantae *see* Dekantai
Deceangli UKG 133C5
Degirmentepe TKY 3E2, 7G7
Deire DJI *Ras Siyyan* 172D6
Dekantai UKG 132B2
Dekapolis 168C3
Dekeleia GRE 36C3, 48D4
Delion GRE *Dilesi* 33E5, 48D4
Delminium BOS *Lib u Borčanima* 152A3
Delos GRE *Delos* 16D3, 56D3, 71D3, **78–79**
Delos Ins. GRE *Delos* 13D3, 45C3, **79,** 155C2
Delphi GRE *Delphi* 16C2, 30C3, **39,** 71C2, 155B2
Delphinion GRE 49F3
Delta EGY *Nile delta* 171B2
Demetai UKG 133B6
Demetrias GRE *Volos* 71C2, 155B1
Demetrias GRE *Vasiliko* 71C3
Demirci Hüyük TKY 7I6
Dendera EGY 2C6
Deoua fl. UKG *Dee* 132D3
Der IRQ 3F3
Derbe TKY *Kerti Hüyük* 159E4, 161G2
Derris Pr. GRE *Ambelos* 32E3
Dertona ITL *Tortona* 92A1, 108B3, 147F3
Dertosa SPN *Tortosa* 94C3, 138E2
Derventio UKG *Papcastle* 132C4, 135A2
Derventio UKG *Malton* 133E5
Derventio fl. UKG *Derwent* 135C2
Desarene IND *Orissa* 175G2
Desarene *(region)* IND 175G3
Deultum BUL *Debelt* 153E3, 193F3
Deva UKG *Chester* 133C5, 178B1
Devade Inss. SAU *Farasan* 172C5
Dhaskalio-Kavos GRE 7E9
Dia Ins. GRE 154C1

Diakres GRE 45A2
Diakria GRE 36B3
Diakrioi GRE 45D4
Diana Veteranorum ALG *Zana* 144A2
Diana, T. ITL *near Nemi* 86C2, 117C2
Diana, T. ITL *S. Angelo in Formis* 87B1
Dianium SPN *Dénia* 138E3
Didyma TKY *Didim* 16F3, 31G5, 159A4
Didyme Ins. ITL *Salina* 43E1, 111A3
Dierna ROM *Orşova* 152C2
Digdida Selorum LBY *Wadi el-Harriga* 141F2
Dikaia GRE *Epanome?* 45A1
Dikaia GRE *E Abdera* 56D1
Dikte M. GRE *Mt. Modi* 154D2
Diktynnaion GRE 154A1
Dilkaya Höyük TKY 3E2
Dilmun BAH/KUW 3H5
Diluntum BOS *Stolac* 152A3
Dimini GRE 6C2
Dimitra GRE 6D1
Dinar see Kelainai 2B2
Diocaesarea ISR *Zippori/Saffuriye* 168C2
Diocaesarea TKY *Uzuncaburç* 159F4
Diomedeae Inss. CRO *Palagruža Iss.* 109H5
Dion GRE *Malathria* 30C2, 48D2, 71C1, 152C4
Dion *(on Euboea)* GRE *Likhas Kastri* 56C2
Dionysias EGY *Qasr Qarun* 171B3
Dionysopolis BUL *Balchik* 153E3
Dioscurias GEO *Sukhumi* 19H4, 73H2, 162C1
Dioskourides Ins. YEM *Socotra* 173F6
Diospolis ISR *Lud* 168B4
Diospolis TKY *Niksar* 73F3
Diospolis Magna EGY *Karnak/Luxor* 75C7, 171C4
Diospolis Mikra EGY *Hiw* 171C4
Diospontus TKY 189G3
Dispilio GRE 6B1
Divodurum FRA *Metz* 147E2, 149A3
Divona FRA *Cahors* 147C4
Diyala fl. IRN/IRQ 3F3
Djenné Djenno MLI 140A6
Dobunni UKG 133D6
Doclea MNE *Duklja* 152B3, 189E3
Dodekaschoinos EGY 171B5
Dodona GRE *Dodone* 13A2, 30B2, 71B2
Dokimeion TKY *İscehisar* 159D3
Doliana GRE 6A2
Doliche TKY *Dülük* 162B3
Dolopes? GRE 14C1
Dolopia GRE 27B2, 30C3, 59B3
Domavium BOS *Gradina* 152B2
Dora ISR *Burj et Tantura* 2C4, 74D3, 168B3
Dorion GRE *Malthi* 14C3
Doris GRE 30C3, 59B3
Doriskos GRE 22A2, 31F1, 59E2
Dorylaion TKY *Şarhüyük* 2B1, 72C4, 159C2
Doschoi RUS 34C2
Douekaledonios Oceanus *North Atlantic* 132B1
Doulichion? Ins. GRE *Koutsilaris* 14B2
Dounga Ins. IND *Salsette Is.* 175E3
Drangiane AFG/IRN 61F3, 69F3, 173H1
Drapsaka AFG *Qunduz* 69H3

Dravus fl. *Drau/Drava* 109G1, 149E4, 152A2
Dreinos fl. *Drina* 152B2
Drepanon CYP 156A3
Drepanon/Drepanum ITL *Trapani* 43A2, 94B5, 113C3
Dreros GRE *Neapolis/Ag. Antonios* 16E4, 21D4, 71E4, 154C2
Drilon fl. ALB/MKD *Drini/Drin* 30A1, 59B2, 152B3
Drobeta ROM *Turnu Severin* 152C2
Druentia fl. FRA *Durance* 94D2, 147E4
Dubis fl. FRA *Doubs* 147E3
Dumatha SAU 172C2
Dumna Ins. UKG *Harris and Lewis* 132A2
Dumnonii UKG 133B7
Duntocher UKG 136A2
Dura SYR 68C3, 73H6, 162C4, **166**
Duranius fl. FRA *Dordogne* 147C3
Duria Bautica fl. FRA/ITL *Doire Baltée/Dora Baltea* 108A2
Duria fl. FRA/ITL *Doire Ripaire/Dora Riparia* 108A2
Durius fl. POR/SPN *Duero/Douro* 94A3, 99A2, 104A2, 138A2
Durnovaria UKG *Dorchester* 133D7
Durobrivae UKG *Chesterton/Water Newton* 133E5
Durocortorum FRA *Reims* 130C2, 147D2, 178C2, 188C2
Duroliponte UKG *Cambridge* 133E6
Durostorum BUL *Silistra* 153E2, 179F3
Durotriges UKG 133C6
Durovernum UKG *Canterbury* 133F6
Dur-Sharrukin IRQ *Khorsabad* 3F2
Dyme GRE *Kato Achaia* 33B5, 71B3
Dyrrachium ALB *Durrës* 71A1, 95H3, 105E2, 152B4
Dystos GRE 33F5
Dytikos Oceanus 132A2

Ebora POR *Évora* 138A3
Eburacum UKG *York* 133D5, 178B1, 188B1
Eburodunum FRA *Embrun* 147E4, 188C3
Eburones GER 147E1, 149A3
Ebusus SPN *Eivisa/Ibiza* 94C4, 99E3, 138E3
Ecbatana IRN *Hamadan* 3G3, 23E3, 69E3, 163F4
Echinai Inss. GRE *Echinades* 14B2
Echinos GRE *Akhinos* 32D4
Echzell GER 151B1
Edeba SPN *Torrenueva* 138C3
Edessa GRE *Edessa* 30C1, 71B1
Edessa TKY *Şanlıurfa* 73G5, 162B3, 189H4, 193G4
Edeta SPN *Lliria* 138D3
Edetani/Edetania SPN 94C3, 99D2, 138D3
Edfu EGY 2C6
Edom ISR/JOR 2C4
Eetioneia GRE 36B4
Egesta ITL *Segesta* 43B2
Egra SAU *Meda'in Salih* 172C2
Egypt, Lower EGY **2B4**
Egypt, Upper EGY **2B6**
Eileithyiaspolis EGY *el-Kab* 171C5
Eion GRE 27C1, 32E2, 48D1
Eknomos M. ITL *Sole* 94C6
Elaea TKY *Kazıkbağları* 31G3, 71F2, 159A3
Elaia Pr. CYX *Cape Elaia* 156D2

Elaious TKY 19F2, 30A6, 49F2
Elaioussa TKY *Ayaş* 159F4
Elam IRN 3G4, 23E3
Elateia GRE *Drakhmani/Piperis* 6C3, 30C3, 71C2
Elatreia GRE *Paliorophon* 59B3
Elaver fl. FRA *Allier* 147D3
Elea ITL *Castellamare di Velia* 18B1, 111B1
Eleon GRE 6C3
Elephantine EGY *Geziret Aswan* 2C6, 22B5, 75C8, 171C5
Eleusiniakos Sinus GRE 36A4
Eleusis GRE *Eleusis* 6C4, 30D4, 36A4
Eleutherna GRE *Prines* 71D4, 154B2
Eleutheropolis ISR *Bet Jibrin* 168B5
Elimberrum FRA *Auch* 138E1, 147C4
Elimiotis GRE 59B2
Elis *(city)* GRE *Palaiopolis/ Kalyvia Elidos* 21B2, 30B4, 155B2
Elis *(region)* GRE *Elis* 14B3, 33B6, 48B4, 71B3
Elkab EGY 2C6
Elmali TKY 7I9
Elusa FRA *Eauze* 188B3
Elvira SPN *Granada* 192A4
Elymais IRN *Khuzistan* 69E3, 163F5, 173E1
Elymoi ITL 43B2
Elyros GRE *Rodovani* 154A2
Emathia GRE 13B1
Emerita Augusta SPN *Merida* 130A4, 138B3, 178A4, 188A4
Emerkingen GER 151C4
Emesa SYR *Homs* 74E2, 162A4, 189H5, 193G4
Emmaus ISR *Imwas* 168B4
Emona SVN *Ljubljana* 109G2, 149D4
Emporia TUN 95E5
Emporiae SPN *Empúries* 18A4, 94D3, 99F1, 138F2
Emporio GRE 7F8, 16E2
Engaddai ISR *'En Gedi* 168C5
Engyon ITL *Troina* 43E2, 113E3
Enienes GRE 14B1
Enkomi CYX 9C1
Enna ITL *Enna* 43D3, 94C6, 113D3
Enope GRE 14C4
Enosis Ins. ITL *Isola di San Pietro* 113A2
Entella ITL *Rocca d'Entella* 43B2, 113C3
Eordaia GRE 30B1, 59B2
Eordaikos fl. ALB *Devoli* 30A1, 152B4
Eous Oceanus 175G5
Epeioi GRE 14B2
Ephesus TKY *Selçuk* 7G8, 31H4, 71F3, 159A3
Ephyra GRE *Mesopotamon* 6A3, 14A2
Ephyra GRE *Kastro/Douraki* 71C2
Epiakon? UKG *Whitley Castle* 135C2
Epidamnos ALB *Durrës* 18D4, 48A1, 71A1
Epidauros GRE *Epidauros* 14D3, 30D4, 48C4, 71C3
Epidauros Limera GRE *Palaia Monemvasia* 30D5, 48C5
Epidaurum CRO *Cavtat* 152A3
Epidioi UKG 132A4
Epikteteis TKY 159C2
Epimaranitae UAE 173F3
Epiphaneia IRN *Hamadan* 69E3

Epiphaneia SYR *Hama* 74E2, 162A4
Epiphaneia TKY *Gözene/Gözeneler Harabesi* 163G2
Epirus ALB/GRE *Epeiros* 21A1, 30A2, 155A1, 179E4
Epirus Nova ALB/GRE 189E4
Epirus Vetus GRE 189E4
Episkopi GRE 6A2
Eporedia ITL *Ivrea* 92A1, 108A2
Erchia GRE 36C4
Erebuni ARM *Arinberd* 3F1
Eresos GRE *Skala* 31F3, 45C2, 49F3
Eretria GRE *Eretria* 16C2, 30D4, 45B2, 71C2
Eretum ITL 86C1, 89C2
Ericusa Ins. ITL *Alicudi* 111A3
Eridu IRQ *Abu Shahrein* 3F4
Erigon fl. MKD *Crna* 152C4
Erikodes Ins. ITL *Alicudi* 43D1
Erineos GRE 48C4
Erisane SPN 99B4
Erymandros fl. AFG/PAK *Helmand* 69G4, 173H1
Erymanthos M. GRE *Erymanthos* 14C3, 30B4
Erythraeum Mare *Red Sea* 22C4, 172B3
Erythraeum Mare *Indian Ocean* 53E3, 174B4
Erythraeum Mare *Persian Gulf* 173E2
Erythrai GRE *Darimari* 30D4, 33E5
Erythrai TKY *Ildır* 21D2, 31G4, 49F3, 71E2
Eryx ITL *Erice* 43A2, 94B5, 113C3
Erzerum TKY 54E2
Esbous JOR *Tell Hesban* 168D5
Esica UKG *Great Chesters* 135B1
Eskiyapar TKY 2C1
Etenna TKY *Sırt* 159D4
Eteocretans GRE 13D4
Etruria/Etrusci ITL **81,** 85B2, 108D4
Euboea Ins. GRE *Euboia* 13C2, 30D3, 59C3, 155C2
Euboean Hollows GRE 27D2
Euboicus Sinus GRE 30D3
Eudaimon Arabia YEM *Aden* 172D6
Euesperides LBY *Benghazi* 18D6, 141G2
Eukarpia TKY *Emirhisar* 159C3
Eulaeus fl. IRN 3G3, 163E5, 173E1
Eumeneia TKY *Işıklı* 72C4, 159C3, 193C4
Euonymon GRE *Trachones* 36B4
Euonymos Ins. ITL *Panarea* 43E1, 111B3
Eupalion GRE *Kastro Soule* 48C3
Eupatoria TKY 73F3
Euphrates fl. *Euphrates* 3F3, 22C3, 68D3, 162B2
Euripos GRE 33E5
Euromos TKY *Ayaklı* 31H5
Europa *(province)* TKY 189F4
Europos IRN *Ravy* 69E3
Europos SYR/TKY *Jerablous/Cerablus (Carchemish)* 73G5
Europus (Dura) SYR 68C3, 73H6, 162C4, **166**
Eurotas fl. GRE *Evrotas* 16C3, 21B3, 30C5
Eurydikeia TKY *Izmir* 71F2
Eurymedon fl. TKY *Köprü Çay* 2B2, 159D3
Eurymenai GRE *Kastritsa* 32A3
Eusebeia TKY *Kayseri* 73E4
Eutaia GRE *Lianou* 33C6
Eutresis GRE *Arkopodi* 6C3, 14D2
Exusta Inss. YEM *Jabal Tayr* 172D5

Fabrateria Nova ITL *Falvaterra* 93A1
Fabrateria Vetus ITL *Ceccano* 89C3
Faesulae ITL *Fiesole* 81B3, 89B1, 108D4, 196D2
Fagifulae ITL *S. Maria di Faìfoli* 89E3
Falerii ITL *Civita Castellana* 81D5, 83C2, 89C2
Falerii ITL *S. Maria di Falleri* 127A5
Falerio ITL *Falerone* 92D2, 109F4
Falisci ITL 85C2
Falkirk UKG 136C1
Fanococidi UKG *Bewcastle* 135B1
Fanum Fortunae ITL *Fano* 83D2, 92D2, 95F2, 109F4
Faventia ITL *Faenza* 81C2
Favoni Portus FRA 108C5
Fayum EGY 2B5, 75A5
Felsina (Bononia) ITL *Bologna* 81B2, 83C1
Ferentinum ITL *Ferentino* 86D2, 89C3, 127C3
Ferentium ITL *Ferento* 81C4, 109E5
Ferresanus Portus SAU 172D5
Fertur fl. ITL *Fortore* 109G6
Ficana ITL 86B2
Ficulea ITL *Marco Simone Vecchio* 127A5
Fidenae ITL *Borgata Fidene* 81D5, 86B1, 92C2, 117B2
Fikirtepe TKY 7H6
Finns 199D1
Firmum Picenum ITL *Fermo* 92D2, 109F4
Flaminia et Picenum ITL 188D3
Flanona CRO *Plomin* 109G2
Flavia Solva AUS *Wagna* 109H1, 149E4
Flavias TKY *Kadirli* 163G1
Flaviobriga SPN *Castro Urdiales* 138C1
Flevum L. NET *IJssel* 147E1, 149A2
Florentia ITL *Firenze/Florence* 92B3, 108D4, 127B2
Flusor fl. ITL *Potenza* 109F4
Forentum ITL *Lavello* 89F3
Formiae ITL *Formia* 89D3, 109F6, 127C3
Fortunatae Inss. SPN *Canary Is.* 53A2
Forum Appii ITL *Faiti* 160A1
Forum Clodii ITL *S. Liberato* 117B1, 127A5
Forum Cornelii ITL *Imola* 108D3
Forum Gallorum ITL 104C2, 108D3
Forum Hadriani NET *Voorburg* 147D1
Forum Iulii FRA *Fréjus* 147E4
Forum Iulii ITL *Cividale* 109F2
Forum Limicorum SPN *Monte do Viso* 138A2
Forum Novum ITL *Fornovo Taro* 108C3
Forum Popillii ITL 87B1
Forum Segusiavorum FRA *Feurs* 147D3
Forum Traiani ITL *Fordongianus* 113A2
Fossatum Africae ALG *Seguia Bent el Krass* 144A2
Frankish Kingdom 199B1
Franks 196C1
Fregellae ITL 89D3, 93A1, 109F6
Fregenae ITL 92C3
Frentani ITL 85D2
Fretum Oceani *Strait of Dover* 133F7, 147C1
Frigidus fl. SVN *Vipava* 109F2
Friniates ITL 85B1
Frisii/*Frisians* GER/NET 149A2, 199B1
Frusino ITL *Frosinone* 89D3
Fucinus L. ITL *Lago Fucino* 109F5
Fulginiae ITL *Foligno* 89C2

Fulvia TKY *Işıklı* 72C4
Fundi ITL *Fondi* 89D3, 127C3
Furculae Caudinae ITL *Forchia* 87C2, 89E3

Gaba ISR *Jaba'* 168B2
Gabellus fl. ITL *Secchia* 108C3
Gabii ITL *Castiglione* 86C2, 117C2
Gabrantouikes UKG 132D4
Gabreta Silva GER *Böhmerwald* 149D3
Gabrosentum UKG *Moresby* 135A2
Gadara JOR *Umm Qeis* 74D3, 168C2
Gadara JOR *Tell Jadur* 168C4
Gades SPN *Cadiz* 53A2, 99B4, 138B4, 182A2
Gaditanum Fretum *Strait of Gibraltar* 99B4, 138B4, 196A4
Gaetuli ALG/LBY 140D2
Gaetuli (Darae) ALG/MOR 140A3
Gagai TKY *Yenice* 159C4
Galata Ins. TUN *Ile de la Galite* 144C1
Galatas GRE 9C2
Galatia TKY 68B2
Galatia *(province)* TKY 131G4, 159E2, 179G4
Galepsos GRE 32E2, 48D1
Galilaea ISR *Galilee* 168B2
Galillenses ITL 113B2
Gallaecia POR/SPN 188A3, 196A3
Gallia *Gaul* 53B2, 104B1, **147**, 196C2
Gallia Cisalpina ITL 103C1
Gallia Transalpina 103B2
Galliae *(diocese)* 188B2
Galliai 195B3
Gallicum Fretum FRA/ITL *Straits of Bonifacio* 108B6
Gamala SYR *es Salam* 168C2
Gandara AFG/PAK 23H3
Gangaridae BAN/IND 175H2
Ganges fl. IND *Ganges* 53F3, 175F1
Ganges fl. SRI *Mahaweli Ganga* 175F6
Gangeticus Sinus *Bay of Bengal* 175G4
Gangra TKY *Çankırı* 72D3, 159E2, 189G4, 193G3
Ganos TKY 59E2
Ganzak IRN *Leilan* 163E3
Garama LBY 141E3
Garamantes LBY 141E3
Garganus M. ITL *Gargano* 109H6
Garizein M. PSE *Jebel et Tur* 168C4
Garumna fl. FRA *Garonne* 104B2, 147B4
Gaugamela IRQ 60D2, **64**
Gaulanitis SYR 168C2
Gaulos Ins. MLT *Gozo* 94C6, 113D4
Gaza PSE *el Ghazzel/Gaza* 2C4, 74D4, 168A5, 193G5
Gazara ISR *Tell Jezer* 168B4
Gebel el-Silsila EGY 2C6
Gedrosia IRN/PAK 23G4, 61F4, 69F4, 173H2
Gela ITL *Gela* 18B3, 43D3, 48A6
Gelas fl. ITL *Gela* 43D3
Gelidonya (shipwreck) TKY 7I9
Gemellae ALG *Mlili* 140C1, 144A2
Genava SWI *Genève/Geneva* 147E3, 149A4
Genèvre, Mont FRA 95E2
Genoni ITL 95E3
Genua ITL *Genova/Genoa* 83A1, 95E2, 108B3, 147F4
Georgiko GRE 6B2

Gepids 199D2
Geraistos GRE *Porto Kastri* 33F6
Geraistos Pr. GRE *Mandelo* 13C2
Geraneia M. GRE 30D4
Gerasa JOR *Jerash* 74E4, 162A5, 168D3
Gereonium ITL *Gerione* 95G3
Gergovia FRA *Gergovie* 104B2, 147D3
Germa TKY 159D2
Germania *Germany* 53B1, 147F1, **149**, 180B1
Germania I *(province)* 188C2
Germania II *(province)* 188C2
Germania Inferior *(province)* 130B2, 147D1, 149A3, 178C2
Germania Superior *(province)* 130C2, 147E2, 151A2, 178C2
Germanicopolis TKY *Ermenek* 159E4
Germanicum Mare *North Sea* 53B1, 132E3, 149A1, 196B1
Geronthrai GRE *Geraki* 33D7
Gerra SAU 173E2
Gerros fl. RUS *Sulak* 163E1
Gerros fl. UKR *Molochnaya* 153H1
Gesoriacum FRA *Boulogne* 133F7, 147C1
Getae 59E1, 153E2
Gezer ISR *Tell Jezer* 2C4
Ghassanids 199F4
Gheriat el-Garbia LBY 141E2
Gholaia LBY *Bu Njem* 141F2
Giali Ins. GRE 7G9
Gigthis TUN *Bou Grara* 141E2, 144D3
Gindaros SYR *Jenderes* 74E1, 105G3
Girba TUN *Houmt-Souk* 141E2, 144D3
Giricano TKY 3E2
Girnavaz TKY 3E2
Gischala ISR *Jish* 168C2
Gitana GRE *Gkoumani* 30A2
Giza EGY 2B4
Gla GRE 6C3
Glanum FRA 147D4
Glasgow Bridge UKG 136B2
Glevum UKG *Gloucester* 133D6
Glykys Limen GRE 30A3
Gnathia ITL *Egnazia* 83F3
Godin Tepe IRN 3G3
Golgoi CYP *Athienou-Ag. Fotios* 156C2
Göllüdağ TKY 2C2
Gomphoi GRE *Mouzaki* 30B3, 71B2
Gonnoi GRE *Dereli* 16C1, 30C2
Gophna PSE *Jifna* 168C4
Gordion TKY *Yassıhöyük* 2B2, 60B2, 72D4, 159D2
Gordyene TKY 162C3
Gorgippia RUS *Anapa* 34C3, 153H2
Gorsium HUN *Tác* 149F4, 152A1
Gortyna GRE *Ag. Deka* 13C4, 71D4, 131F4, 154C2
Gothi/Gothia 149F2, 180C1
Gothiscandza POL 149F1
Goths 197F2, 199F2
Gouola fl. FRA *Golo* 108B5
Gournia GRE 9D2
Goutsoura GRE 6A2
Grabaei MNE 59A1

Gracurris SPN *Eras de San Martín* 99D1, 138D2, 147B4
Granicus fl. TKY *Biga Çayı* 31G2, 60B2, **63**, 159A2
Graviscae ITL *Porto Clementino* 81C5, 83C2, 92C2, 108D5
Great St. Bernard pass SWI 95E2
Grosskrotzenburg GER 151C2
Grotta GRE 7E9, 16D3
Grumentum ITL *Grumento Nova* 89F4, 92E3, 95G3, 111B1
Gudme DEN 149C1
Gulf Islands IRN 23F4
Guntia GER *Günzburg* 151D3
Gunugu ALG *Sidi-Brahim* 138E4
Gurgan IRN 163H3
Guzana SYR 3E2
Gyaros Ins. GRE *Gyalos* 31E4
Gygaia L. TKY *Marmara Gölü* 13E2
Gymnesiae Inss. SPN *Mallorca, Menorca* 138E2
Gymnias TKY *Pasinler* 54D2
Gynaikon Limen PAK *Karachi* 174C2
Gyrtone GRE *Mourlari* 14D1, 48C2
Gytheion GRE *Gythion* 30C5, 48C5, 71C3

Habitancum UKG *Risingham* 135C1
Habur fl. SYR/TKY 3E3
Hacibektaş TKY 2C2
Hacilar TKY 7I8
Hacimusalar Höyük TKY 7I9
Hadria ITL *Atri* 92D2
Hadrianeia TKY *Dursunbey* 159B2
Hadrianoi TKY *Orhaneli* 159B2
Hadrianopolis TKY *Siledik, Yağmurlu* 159B3
Hadrianopolis TKY *Deliktaş* 159C4
Hadrianoupolis TKY *Edirne/Adrianople* 152D4, 189F3, 197F3
Hadrianoutherai TKY *Balıkesir* 159B2
Hadrian's Wall UKG **135**
Hadrumetum TUN *Sousse* 94A6, 141E1, 144D2, 188D4
Haemimontus *(province)* BUL/TKY 189F3
Haemus M. BUL 59D1, 152D3
Hagnous GRE 36C5
Hala Sultan Tekke CYP 9C2
Halaesa ITL *Alesa* 113D3
Halai GRE *Klimatariai* 33D5
Halai Aixonides GRE *Palaichori* 36B5
Halai Araphenides GRE *Loutsa* 36D4
Haliakmon fl. GRE *Haliakmon* 27B1, 30C2, 59B2, 152C4
Haliartos GRE *Kastri Maziou* 14D2, 33D5
Halicarnassus TKY *Bodrum* 16F3, 31H5, **41**, 72A5, 159B4
Halicyae ITL *Salemi* 43B2
Halieis GRE *Porto Cheli* 33D6, 48C4
Halimous GRE 36B4
Halonnesos Ins. GRE *Ag. Eustratios/Strati* 31E2, 59D3
Halos GRE *Alos* 27C2, 32D4, 59C3
Haltwhistle Burn UKG 135C1
Haluntium ITL *San Marco d'Alunzio* 113E3
Halykos fl. ITL *Platani* 43C3, 113C3
Halys fl. TKY *Kızıl Irmak* 2C1, 22C2, 73E4, 159F2
Hamaxitos TKY *Beşiktepe, Gülpınar* 49F2

Harborz M. IRN 3H2, 163G4
Harmozeia IRN 173G2
Harpagion TKY 49G2
Harpasos fl. TKY *Çoruh* 3E1, 54D2, 162C2
Harran TKY 3E2
Hasanlu IRN 3F2
Hasta ITL *Asti* 108A3
Hasta SPN *Mesas de Asta* 99B4
Hasta SPN *Cortijo el Rosario, Mesas de Asta* 138B4
Hatra IRQ *Hadhr* 162D4
Hatria ITL *Adria* 81C2, 83C1, 109E3
Hatria *(in Picenum)* ITL *Atri* 109F5
Hatti TKY 2C1
Haueris EGY *Hawwaret el-Maqta* 171B3
Hazor ISR 2D4
Heba ITL 92C2, 108D5
Hebron PSE *el Khalil* 168B5
Hebros fl. *Evros/Martisa/Meriç* 19F1, 31G1, 49F1, 152D3
Hebudes Inss. UKG *Inner Hebrides* 132A3
Hecatompylos IRN *Shahr-i Qumis* 61E2, 69F3, 163H4
Heddesdorf GER 151A1
Heirkte M./Oros ITL *Monte Pellegrino* 43C2, 95G4, 113C2
Hekale? GRE *Koukounarti* 36C3
Helike GRE 6B4, 33C5
Heliopolis EGY *Matariya* 2B4, 75B5, 171B2
Heliopolis LEB *Ba'albek* 74E2, 162A5
Hellas? GRE 14D2
Hellespontus TKY *Dardanelles/Çanakkale Boğazı* 13D1, 27E1, **30**, 159A2
Hellespontus *(province)* TKY 189F4
Heloros fl. ITL *Eloro* 43E4
Heloros/Helorus ITL *Eloro* 18B3, 43F4, 95G4, 113E4
Helos GRE *Ag. Stephanos* 14D4, 33D7
Helvetii SWI 104C1, 147E3
Hemeroskopeion SPN *Dénia* 94C4
Hemodos M. *Himalayas* 175G1
Heniochi M. TKY 162C2
Hephaistia GRE *Kastro Bouni* 31F2, 45C1
Heptanomia EGY 171B3
Heraclea/Herakleia TKY *Ereğli* 19F4, 54B1, 72C3, 159D1, 189F3
Heraclea ITL *S Metapontum* 83E3, 95G3, 111C1
Heraclea ad Latmum TKY *Kapıkırı* 31H4, 71F3, 159B3
Heraclea Minoa ITL *Eraclea Minoa* 94B6, 113C3
Heraclea (Perinthus) TKY *Ereğli* 159B2
Heraea M. ITL *Monte Altesina* 113D3
Heraia GRE *Ag. Ioannes* 33B6, 71B3
Heraion *(NW Argos)* GRE 16C3
Heraion *(on Samos)* GRE 7F8, 16E3
Heraion Teichos TKY *Aytepe* 59F2
Herakleia MKD *near Bitola* 30B1, 59B2, 152B4
Herakleia (Trachis) GRE 30C3, 71C2
Herakleia Minoa ITL *Eraclea Minoa* 43C3
Herakleia Salbakes TKY *Vakıf* 159B3
Herakleion GRE *Platamon* 30C2
Herakleion GRE *Irakleion* 154C2
Herakleopolis EGY *Ihnasya el-Medina* 2B5, 75A5, 171B3
Herbessos ITL *Montagna di Marzo* 43D3, 95G4

Herbita ITL 43D2
Herculaneum ITL *Ercolano* 87B2, **124**
Herculis Inss. ITL 113A1
Herdoniae ITL *Ordona* 89F3, 95G3, 109H6
Hermaia Pr. TUN *Cap Bon* 94B6
Hermandica SPN *Salamanca* 99B2
Herminius M. POR *Serra da Estrella* 99A2, 138A2
Hermione GRE *Ermione* 14D3, 33D6, 48D4, 59C4
Hermonassa RUS 34B3, 153H2
Hermonthis EGY *Armant* 75B7, 171C5
Hermopolis Magna EGY *Ashmunein* 2B5, 75A6, 171B3, 193F5
Hermunduri GER 149B3
Hermus fl. TKY *Gediz Çay* 2A2, 31G3, 72B4, 159A3
Hernici ITL 85C3
Herodeion JOR *Tell el-Hammam?* 168C4
Herodeion PSE *el Fureidis* 168C5
Heroonpolis EGY *Abu Suwayr, Tell el Maskhuta* 171C2
Heroopoliticus Sinus EGY *Gulf of Suez* 171C3
Heruli DEN/SWE 149C1
Hibera SPN *Tortosa* 99E2
Hibernia IRE/UKG *Ireland* 130A1, 133A5, 178A1, 188A1
Hibis EGY *el-Khargeh* 171B5, 172A3
Hiera (Hephaistou) Ins. ITL *Vulcano* 43E1, 111A3
Hiera Ins. ITL *Marettimo* 43A2
Hierakonpolis EGY *Kom el-Ahmar* 2C6
Hierakonpolis *(SE Alexandria)* EGY 74A4
Hierapolis SYR *Membidj* 73G5, 162B4, 189H4
Hierapolis *(in Phrygia)* TKY *Pamukkale* 72B5, 159C3, 193F4
Hierapolis *(in Cappadocia)* TKY *Şar* 73F4
Hierapolis *(in Cilicia)* TKY *Bodrum Kalesi* 73F5, 163G1
Hierapytna GRE *Ierapetra* 71E4, 154D2
Hierasos fl. ROM/UKR *Siret* 152D1, 153E2
Hierasykaminos EGY *el-Maharraqa* 171C6
Hierichous PSE *Jericho* 2D4, 74D4, 168C4
Hieron M. TKY *Ganos Dağı* 59E2
Hieros fl. ITL *Pabillionis* 113A2
Hieros fl. TKY *Girmir Çay* 2C1, 159E2
Hierosolyma ISR *Jerusalem* 105G4, **167**, 168C5, 193G5
Himera ITL *Imera* 18A2, 43C2
Himeras fl. ITL *Grande* 43D2
Himeras fl. ITL *Salso* 43D3, 113D3
Hippalon Mare 173F6
Hippana ITL *Monte dei Cavalli* 43C2
Hippo Diarrhytus (Akra) TUN *Bizerte* 94A6, 144C1
Hippo Regius ALG *Annaba* 95E4, 140D1, 144B1, 196C4
Hippokoura IND *Brahmapuri* 175E4
Hipponion ITL *Vibo Valentia* 18C2, 83E4
Hippos ISR *Horvat Susita/Qal'at el Husn* 74D3
Hirpini ITL 85E3
Hispalis SPN *Sevilla/Seville* 104A3, 138B3
Hispania POR/SPN **138**, 180A1, 196A3
Hispania Citerior *(province)* SPN 94B3, 103A2
Hispania Ulterior *(province)* SPN 94B4, 103A2
Hispaniae *(diocese)* 188A4
Hispellum ITL *Spello* 92C2, 109E4
Histiaia GRE *Kastro/Oreoi* 13B2, 30D3, 45A2, 71C2
Histonium ITL *Vasto* 109G5

Histri CRO 85D1
Histria ROM *Istria* 19F3, 68B1, 153E2
Histria *(region)* CRO *Istra* 109F2
Hit IRQ 3E3
Homonadeis TKY 159D4
Horreum Margi SRB *Ćuprija* 152B3
Horta ITL *Orte* 109E5
Hostilia ITL *Ostiglia* 108D2
Hunno UKG *Halton Chesters* 135C1
Huns 197H2
Hyampolis GRE *Exarkhos* 14D2
Hybla Gereatis ITL *Paternò* 43E3, 48A6, 113E3
Hybla Heraia ITL *Ragusa Ibla* 43E4, 113E4
Hydaspes fl. IND/PAK *Jhelum* 61H3, **65**
Hyde? (Sardis) TKY *Sart* 13E2
Hydissos TKY *Karacahisar* 45D3
Hydraotes fl. IND/PAK *Ravi* 61H3
Hydrea Ins. GRE *Hydra* 33E6
Hydruntum ITL *Otranto* 111D2
Hykkara ITL *Carini* 43B2
Hyllos fl.? TKY *Kum Çay* 13E2
Hymettos M. GRE *Ymittos* 36C4
Hypanis fl. RUS *Kuban Bug* 34D3
Hypanis fl. UKR *Bug Kuban* 19F3, 153F1
Hypata GRE *Hypati* 32C4
Hyperboreios Oceanus *North Atlantic* 132B1
Hyperesia GRE 14C2
Hyphasis fl. IND/PAK *Beas* 61H3
Hypsas fl. ITL *Belice* 43B2, 113C3
Hyrcania IRN/TKM 23F3, 61E2, 69F2, 163H3
Hyrcanium Mare *Caspian Sea* 23E1, 69E2
Hyria GRE *Tseloneri* 14E2
Hyrkania PSE *Khirbet Mird* 168C5
Hyrkanis TKY 71F2
Hyrtakina GRE *Temenia: Kastri* 154A2
Hysiai GRE *Akhladokampos* 21B3
Hytenneis TKY 22B3

Iabakchous fl. JOR *Wadi Zerqa* 168C4
Iacca SPN *Jaca* 99D1
Iader CRO *Zadar* 95G2, 109G3
Iaitas ITL *Monte Iato* 43B2
Ialysos GRE *Ialysos* 13E3, 31H6, 49G5
Iamneia ISR *Yibna* 168B4
Iamneia Paralios ISR *Minet Rubin* 168B4
Iamo SPN *Ciudadela?* 138F2
Iapudes CRO 104D2, 109G3
Iapyges ITL 85F3
Iasos TKY *Asınkalesi* 2A2, 31H5, 71F3, 159B4
Iathrippa SAU *Medina* 172C3
Iatros fl. BUL *Iskur* 152D3
Iaxartes fl. *Syr Darya* 23G1, 53E2, 69H2
Iazyges HUN 152B1
Iazyges UKR 153F1
Iberia GEO 162D1
Ibericum Mare 94B4, 99D4, 138E3
Iberus fl. SPN *Ebro* 94C3, 99C1, 138C1, 147A4
Icarus Ins. KUW *Failaka* 163F6, 173E2
Iceni UKG 133F5
Ichnae SYR *Tell al-Sadde?* 73G6
Ichthyophagi EGY 171D4
Ichthyophagoi IRN/PAK 173H3
Ichthys Pr. GRE *Katakolon* 33B6
Iconium/Ikonion TKY *Konya* 2C2, 54B2, 72D5, 159E3
Icosium ALG *Algiers* 94D4, 138F4, 140C1
Ida M. GRE *Idi/Pseiloritis* 154B2
Ida M. TKY *Kaz Dağ* 13D1, 31G2, 159A2
Idaion Antron GRE *Idaean cave* 9B2, 16D4, 154B2
Idalion CYP *Dali* 2C3
Idomene GRE *Palaiokoula* 48B3
Idoubeda M. SPN 99C1, 138C2
Idri LBY 141E3
Idumaea ISR 168B6
Idyma TKY *Kozlukuyu* 45E3
Ierusalem ISR *Jerusalem* 2C4, 73H6, **167**, 168C5
Ietas ITL *Monte Iato* 113C3
Igilgili ALG *Jijel* 140D1, 144A1
Igilium Ins. ITL *Isola del Giglio* 81B5, 108D5
Iguvium ITL *Gubbio* 83C2, 89C1, 109E4
Ikarion GRE *Dionyso* 36C3
Ikarion Mare 13D2
Ikaros Ins. GRE *Ikaria* 27E3, 31F4, 49F4, 155D2
Iklaina GRE 6B5
Ikos GRE *Kokkinokastro* 30D3, 56C2
Ilercaones SPN 99D2
Ilerda SPN *Lérida* 104B2, 138E2
Ilergetes SPN 94C3, 99E1
Iliberri SPN *Granada* 138C4, 192A4
Ilici SPN *Alcudia de Elche* 94C4, 138D3
Ilienses ITL *Mulgaria* 113A1
Ilipa (Magna) SPN *Alcalá del Río* 94A4, 99B3, 138B3
Ilipinar TKY 7H6
Iliturgi SPN *Cerro Máquiz* 94B4, 99C3, 138C3
Ilium TKY *Hisarlık/Troy* 30A6, 49F2, 71E1, 159A2
Illerup Ådal DEN 149C1
Illiberris FRA *Elne* 94D3
Illyricum 103C2, 152B4, 195C3
Ilorci SPN *Lorquí?* 94C4, 99D3
Ilva Ins. ITL *Elba* 81A4, 83B2, 108C4, 182D1
İmamoğlu Höyük TKY 2D2
Imaus M. *Himalayas* 175G1
Imbros (Ins.) TKY *Gökçeada* 13D1, 31F2, 59D2, 155C1
Imgur-Enlil IRQ *Balawat* 3F3
Inatos GRE *Tsoutsouros* 154C2
India 23H4, 53F3, **175**
India *S beyond Egypt?* 180D3
Indibilis SPN *Benicarló* 94C3
Indicum Mare *Indian Ocean* 23E6, 53E3, 173G5, 174B4
Indus fl. TKY *Dalaman Çay* 2B2, 159B4
Indus fl. *Indus* 23H4, 61G3, 69H4, 174D1
Industria ITL *Montheu da Po* 108A2, 127A1
Inferum Mare *Lower/Tyrrhenian Sea* 108B4
Ingauni ITL 85A1
Insani M. ITL *Marghine Mts.* 113B2
Insubres ITL 85A1, 95E2, 108B2
Insulae *(province)* GRE/TKY 189F4
Interamna Lirenas ITL 93A1
Interamna Nahars ITL *Terni* 83C2, 89C2, 109E5
Interamnia Praetuttiorum ITL *Teramo* 89D2, 92D2, 109F5
Intercatia SPN *Aguilar de Campos?* 138B2

Intercisa HUN *Dunaújváros* 152B1
Internum Mare *Mediterranean Sea* 53B2, 74A3, 130D4, 161E3, **182–83**
Inveravon UKG 136D1
Inveresk UKG 132C3
Iol Caesarea ALG *Cherchel* 130B4, 138E4, 140C1, 178C4
Iolkos GRE *Volos Kastro* 6C2, 14D1, 30D3
Iomanes fl. IND *Jumna* 175F1
Iomnium ALG *Tigzirt* 138F4, 140C1
Ionia TKY 2A2, 22B2, 31G4, 159A3
Ionium Mare/Ionion Pelagos *Ionian Sea* 13A2, 30B2, 71A3, 155A2
Ioppe ISR *Jaffa* 162A5, 168B4
Iordanes fl. ISR *Jordan* 2D4, 74D4, 162A5, 168C3
Ios (Ins.) GRE 31F5, 45C3, 56D4
Iotapata ISR *Khirbet Shifat* 168C2
Iouernikos Okeanos *Irish Sea* 133A5
Ioulis GRE *Khora* 31E4, 56C3
Ipnoi Pr. GRE *Pelion* 32D3
Ipsos TKY *Çayırbağ* 72C4
Iria Flavia SPN *Padrón* 138A1
Iris fl. TKY *Yeşil Irmak* 54C1, 73F3, 162A2
Irni SPN *Cerro del Castillejo* 138B4
Isara fl. FRA *Isère* 94D2, 147D3
Isara fl. FRA *Oise* 147D2
Isaura Nova TKY *Zengibar Kalesi* 159E4
Isauria *(province)* TKY 159D4, 189G4, 197G4
Isca (Silurum) UKG *Caerleon* 133C6, 178B2
Isca UKG *Exeter* 133C7
Isca fl. UKG *Usk* 133C6
Iscina LBY *Medina Sultan, Sort* 141F2
Isinda TKY *Alaettin Mahalle, Korkuteli* 159C4
Ismaros? (Maroneia) GRE *Ag. Kharalabos* 13D1
Israel ISR 2D4
Issa Ins. CRO *Vis* 109H4
Issicus Sinus TKY *Gulf of İskenderun* 163G2
Issus TKY *Yeşil Hüyük* 60C2, **63**, 73F5, 163G2
Istone M. GRE *Pantokrator* 30A2, 48A2
Isurium UKG *Aldborough* 133D5
Italia ITL *Italy* **83, 85, 108–109, 111,** 178D3
Italia *(diocese)* ITL *Italy* 188D3
Italica SPN *Santiponce* 94A4, 99B3, 138B3
Italiotes ITL 85E4
Itanos GRE *Erimoupolis* 71E4, 154D2
Ithaca (Ins.) GRE *Ithake* 13A2, 30A4, 33A5, 155B2
Ithome M. GRE *Ithome* 21B3, 30B5
Itouna fl. UKG *Eden* 135B2
Iudaea ISR/PSE *Judaea* 105G4, 131G5, **168**
Iulia Concordia ITL *Concordia Sagittaria* 109E2
Iulia Equestris SWI *Nyon* 147E3, 149A4
Iulia Gordos TKY *Eski Gördes* 159B3
Iulias ISR *et Tell/el 'Araj* 168C2
Iuliobona FRA *Lillebonne* 133F7, 147C2
Iuliobriga SPN *Retortillo* 138C1, 147A4
Iuliomagus FRA *Angers* 147B2
Iuliopolis TKY *Sarılar* 159D2
Iulium Carnicum ITL *Zuglio* 109F1, 149D4
Iuppiter Latiaris, T. ITL *Monte Cavo* 86C2
Iura M. FRA/SWI *Jura* 147E3, 149A4
Iuthungi GER 149C3

Iuvanum ITL *S. Maria di Palazzo* 109G5
Iuvavum AUS *Salzburg* 149D4, 151F4

Judah ISR/PSE 2C4

Kabalioi TKY 22B3
Kabeira TKY *Niksar* 73F3
Kabyle BUL *Yambol* 59E1, 152D3
Kadikalesi TKY 7G8
Kadiston M. GRE *Mt. Kadiston* 154C2
Kadoi TKY *Eski Gediz* 72B4, 159C3
Kaghyzman TKY 54E2
Kaidros fl. ITL *Cedrino* 113B1
Kainai IRQ 54E3
Kaine EGY *Qena* 171C4
Kakoulima, Mt. GIN 53A4
Kakovatos GRE 6B4
Kakyparis fl. ITL *Cassibile* 43E3, 48B6
Kalaiou Inss. OMN *Ad Daymaniyat* 173G3
Kalapodi (Abai?) GRE 6C3
Kalaureia (Ins.) GRE *Poros* 16C3, 33E6
Kalavasos CYP 9B2
Kale Akte ITL *Marina di Caronia?* 43D2
Kalhu IRQ *Nimrud* 3F3
Kaliour IND *Uraiyar?* 175F5
Kalliena IND *Kalyan* 175E3
Kalliga IND *Mukhalingam* 175G3
Kallinousa Pr. CYX *Petra tou Limniti* 156A2
Kalogeros GRE 6A4
Kaloi Limenes GRE *Liminones* 154B3, 161E3
Kalon M. OMN *Jebel Akhdar* 173G3
Kalos Limen UKR *Chernomorskoye* 153G2
Kalpes Limen TKY 54B1
Kalydnai/Kalydnioi Inss. GRE *Kalydaioi* 13E3, 45D3
Kalymna Ins. GRE 31G5
Kalynda TKY *Kozpınar* 45E3, 72B5
Kaman Kalehöyük TKY 2C2
Kamarina ITL *Kamarina* 43D4
Kambadene IRN 163E4
Kamigara PAK *Aror* 174D1
Kamir Blur ARM 3F1
Kamiros GRE 13E3, 31H6, 49G5, 71F4
Kana ISR *Kafr Kanna* 168C2
Kanastraion Pr. GRE *Kanastrio* 32E3
Kane YEM *Bir 'Ali* 173E5
Kanogiza IND *Kanauj?* 175F1
Kantanos GRE 154A2
Kantion Pr. UKG 53B1
Kapharnaoum ISR *Tell Hum/Capernaum* 168C2
Kaphereus Pr. GRE *Kavo Doro* 33F5
Kaphyai GRE *Chotoussa* 33C6, 71C3
Karambis Pr. TKY *Kerembe burnu* 159E1
Karanis EGY *Kom Awshim* 75A5, 171B3
Karaoğlan Mevkii TKY 7I7
Karatepe TKY 02D2
Kardamyle GRE *Kardamyle* 14C4
Kardamyle GRE *Marmaron* 31F3, 49F3
Kardia TKY *Baklaburnu* 19G2, 30B6, 49F2, 59E2
Kardouchoi TKY 54E2
Karkinitis Sinus UKR *Gulf of Karkinit* 153F2
Karmana IRN 69F4, 173G2

Karna YEM *Ma'in* 172D5
Karnak EGY 2C6
Karnonakai UKG 132B3
Karoura IND *Tirukkarur* 175F5
Karpasia CYX *Rizokarpaso-Ag. Filon* 156D1
Karpates M. *Carpathian Mts.* 149F3, 152D2
Karpathion Mare 31G6
Karpathos/Krapathos Ins. GRE *Karpathos* 13E3, 31G6, 155D3
Karphi GRE 9C2, 16E4
Kar-Shalmaneser SYR *Tell Ahmar* 2D2
Karthaia GRE *Poles* 56C3
Karun fl. IRN/IRQ 3G4
Karyai GRE *Analipsis* 48C4
Karyanda TKY *Salih Adası* 31H5
Karystos GRE 13C2, 31E4, 45B2, 56C3
Kāśī IND 175G2
Kasmenai ITL 18B3, 43E3
Kasos Ins. GRE *Kasos* 13D4
Kaspiai Portae RUS 163F1
Kassandreia GRE *Nea Potidaia* 68A2
Kassiope GRE *Kassiopi* 30A2
Kassope GRE *Kamarina* 30A3, 59B3, 71A2
Kastabala TKY *Bodrum Kalesi* 74E1
Kastanas GRE 6C1
Kastri GRE 7E8
Katakekaumene Inss. YEM *Jabal Tayr* 172C5
Katane ITL *Catania* 18B3, 43E3, 48B6
Kato Syme GRE 9C2
Kato Zakros GRE 9D2
Kaudos Ins. GRE *Gavdos* 154A3, 160D3
Kaulonia ITL *Monasterace Marina* 18C2, 83E4, 95G4
Kauśāmbī IND *Kosam Inam* 175G2
Kavousi GRE *Kastro* 16E4
Kawar NER 141E6
Kayalıdere TKY 3E2
Kayapınar TKY 2D1
Kaymakçi TKY 7G7
Kaystroupedion TKY 54B2
Kebren TKY *Fuğla Tepe, Çal Dağ* 45C1, 159A2
Keçiçayiri TKY 7J7
Keioi GRE 45B3
Kekryphaleia Ins. GRE *Kyra, Spalathronisi* 33D6
Kelainai TKY *Dinar* 2B2, 54B2, 68B2, 72C5
Keletron GRE *Kastoria* 32B2
Kellis EGY *Ismant el-Kharab* 171A5
Kemerhisar TKY 2C2
Kenan Tepe TKY 3E2
Kenchreai GRE *Kechriai* 33D6, 160D2
Kentoripa ITL *Centuripe* 43E3
Kentrites fl. TKY *Bohtan Su* 54E2
Keos Ins. GRE 27D3, 31E4, 56C3
Kephalari Magoula GRE 6B4
Kephale GRE 36D5
Kephaloidion ITL *Cefalù* 43D2
Kephisia GRE *Kephisia* 36C3
Kephisos fl. GRE 33E5
Kepoi RUS *Artyukhov/Sennaya* 34C2
Kerameis GRE 36B4
Keramon Agora TKY 54B2
Keramos TKY *Ören* 31H5, 45D3

Kerasous TKY *Giresun* 19H4, 54D1, 73G3
Kerinthos GRE *Kria Vrisi, Ag. Ilias* 13C2, 32E4
Kerkenes Dağ TKY 2C2
Kerkeosiris EGY *Kom el-Khamsin* 171B3
Kerkinitis UKR *Eupatoria* 19G3, 153G2
Kerkinitis L. GRE *Kerkines* 30D1
Kerobothros IND 175E5
Kerouinoi FRA 108B5
Keryneia CYX *Kyrenia* 156B2
Khargeh EGY 171B6
Khirokitia CYP 9B2
Khorsabad IRQ 3F2
Kidrama TKY *Yorga* 159C4
Kierion GRE *Pyrgos Kieriou* 32C4
Kieros TKY *Konuralp* 72C3
Kikones GRE 13D1
Kilikes TKY 13E2
Kilikiai Portae TKY *Karanlıkkapı* 159F4, 163H2
Kilise Tepe TKY 2C2
Kimmerikon UKR *Opuk* 34B3
Kimolos Ins. GRE 31E5, 59D4, 155C3
Kinaidokolpitai SAU 172C4
Kindye TKY *Sırtmaç* 45D3
Kinet Höyük TKY 2D2
Kinnamomophoros Chora SOM 173E6
Kinneil UKG 136D1
Kios TKY *Gemlik* 72B3
Kiperi GRE 6A3
Kirkbride UKG 135A1
Kirkidios fl. FRA *Porto* 108B5
Kirkintilloch UKG 136B2
Kirra GRE *Magoula Xeropigadas* 6B3, 21B2, 33C5
Kisamos GRE *Kastelli Kisamou* 154A1
Kish IRQ *Tell Uhaimir and Ingharra* 3F4
Kissa SPN 94C3
Kissi BFA 140B6
Kissonerga CYP 9A2
Kissos M. GRE *Khortiatis* 30D1
Kition CYP *Larnaka* 2C3, 9C2, 74C2, 156C3
Kizzuwatna TKY 2C2
Klarios fl. CYP *Potamos tou Kampou* 156A2
Klazomenai TKY *near Limantepe* 16E2, 19E5, 21D2
Klazomenai TKY *Klazümen* 31G4, 49F3, 71E2, 159A3
Kleides Inss. CYX 156D1
Kleitor GRE 33C6
Kleonai GRE *Ag. Vasileios* 14D3, 33D6, 48C4
Kleonai GRE *Daphne?* 45B1
Knossos GRE *Knossos* 9C2, 10, 21D4, 71D4, 154C2
Kokkonatou Inss. YEM *Sabuniyah, Samhah, Darsah* 173F6
Kolchikos Sinus IND/SRI *Gulf of Mannar* 175F6
Kolonai TKY 30B6
Kolonos GRE *Kolonos* 36B4
Kolossai TKY 54A2
Kom el-Hisn EGY 2B4
Kom Ombo EGY 2C6
Komar Pr. IND *Cape Comorin* 175E6
Komisene IRN 163H4
Kommos GRE 9B2
Kömür Adası TKY 7G8
Kopai GRE *Topolia* 14D2

Kophen fl. AFG *Kabul* 61G2
Koprates fl. IRN/IRQ *Ab-i Diz* 163F5, 173E1
Korakesion TKY *Alanya* 159D4
Koresia GRE *Livadi* 45B3, 56C3
Korinion UKG *Cirencester* 133D6, 188B2
Korkyra Melaina CRO 18C4
Korodamon Pr. OMN *Ra's al-Hadd* 173H3
Korone GRE *Petalidhi* 33B7
Koroneia GRE *Pyrgos* 14D2
Korsote IRQ 54E3
Koru Pedion TKY *Kasaba ovası* 72B4
Korydallos M. GRE *Korydallos* 36B4
Korykos M. TKY *Kıran/Koraka Dağ* 31G4, 49F4
Koryphasion Pr. GRE *Koryphasiou* 33B7
Kos (Ins.) GRE *Kos* 21E3, 31G5, 71F3, 159A4
Kossoura Ins. ITL *Pantelleria* 43A4
Kotiaeion TKY *Kütahya* 159C2
Kotyora TKY *Ordu* 19H4, 54D1, 73G3
Koukonisi GRE 7E6
Koumasenoi FRA 108B5
Kouphovouno GRE 6B5
Kourias Pr. CYP *Akrotiri Pr.* 156B3
Kourion CYP 2C3, 156B3
Kourion Bamboula CYP 9B2
Koutroulou Magoula GRE 6B3
Kranae Ins. GRE 14D4
Krane GRE *Argostolion* 30A4, 56A3
Krannon GRE *Kastro/ Douraki* 21B2, 32C4, 48C3, 71C2
Kreones UKG 132B3
Krestonia GRE 48C1
Kreusis GRE *Livadostro* 33D5
Krimisos fl. ITL *Freddo* 43B2
Kriou Metopon Pr. GRE *Cape Krios* 154A2
Krisa GRE *Ag. Varvara* 6B3, 14D2
Krithote TKY 30B6, 56E2
Krithote Pr. GRE *Tourkovigla* 33A5
Krokodilopolis EGY *Medinet el-Fayum* 75A5, 171B3
Krommyon GRE *Ag. Theodori* 33D6, 48C4
Krommyon Pr. CYX *Cape Kormakitis* 156B2
Kronion Oros ITL *Monte S. Calogero* 43B3
Krya GRE 6A2
Kryptos Limen OMN 173G3
Küllüoba TKY 7J7
Kültepe TKY 2C2
Kululu TKY 2D2
Kummuh TKY 2D2
Kumtepe TKY 7F6
Kunulua TKY *Tell Tayinat* 2D3
Kutha IRQ *Tell Ibrahim (al-Khalil)* 3F4
Kutrigur Huns 199F2
Kyamosoros fl. ITL *Salso* 43D2
Kyaneai TKY *Yavı* 159C4
Kydones GRE 13C4
Kydonia GRE *Khania* 21C4, 71D4, 154A1
Kyllandos TKY *Elmalı?* 45E3
Kyllene GRE *Kyllini* 30B4, 48B4
Kyllene M. GRE *Kyllene* 14C3, 30C4
Kynaitha GRE *Kalavryta* 71B3
Kynopolis EGY *el-Qeis* 171B3
Kynos GRE *Pyrgos/Livanates* 6C3, 14D2, 33D5
Kynossema Pr. TKY *Kilitbahir* 30A6, 49F2

Kynouria GRE 30C5
Kyparissia GRE 33B6
Kypros PSE *Tel el 'Aqabeh* 168C4
Kypsela TKY *İpsala?* 31G1, 152D4
Kyros fl. AZE/GEO *Mtkvari/Kura* 162D1
Kysis EGY *Douch* 171B5
Kythera (Ins.) GRE *Kythera* 13B3, 30D6, 48C5, 155B3
Kythnos (Ins.) GRE *Kythnos* 27D3, 31E5, 45B3, 56C3
Kytinion GRE *Paliokhori/Ag. Georgios* 33C5, 48C3

La Rustica ITL 86C2
Labicum ITL *Colonna* 92B3
Labraunda TKY 2A2
Lacedaemon GRE *Lakonia* 14C3, 30C5
Lachish ISR *el Qubeibe* 2C4
Laconia GRE *Lakonia* 48C5
Laconicus Sinus GRE *Gulf of Lakonia* 33C7
Lagina TKY *Turgut* 71F3
Lakhmids 199F3
Lakiadai GRE 36B4
Lamasba ALG *Henchir Merouana* 144A2
Lambaesis ALG *Lambèse* 140D1, 144A2, 178C4, 188C4
Lamia GRE *Lamia* 27B2, 30C3
Laminium SPN *Alhambra?* 138C3
Lamnaios fl. IND *Narmadā* 175E3
Lampsacus/Lampsakos TKY *Lapseki* 19G2, 30B6, 54A2, 71E1
Lamptrai GRE *Kitsi* 36C5
Lancia SPN *El Castro* 138B2
Langobardi GER 149C2
Lanuvium ITL *Lanuvio* 86C2, 89C3, 109E6, 117C3
Laodicea SYR *Lattaquié* 74E2, 162A4, 193G4
Laodicea ad Libanum SYR *Tell Nebi Mend* 74E2, 162A4, 193G4
Laodicea ad Lycum TKY *Eski Hisar* 72B5, 159C3, 189F4, 193F4
Laodikeia (Katakekaumene) TKY *Ladik* 72D4, 159E3
Laodikeia en te Phoinike LEB *Beirut* 74D3
Laos ITL *Marcellina* 18B1, 83E4
Laos fl. ITL *Lao* 111B2
Lapethos CYX 2C3, 9B1, 156B2
Lappa GRE *Argyroupolis* 154B2
Lapurdum FRA *Bayonne* 138D1, 147B4
Laranda TKY *Karaman* 159E4, 193G4
Larinum ITL *Larino* 83E3, 89E3, 109G5
Larisa TKY *Limantepe* 7F7, 13D2
Larisa Kremaste GRE *Pelasgia* 32D4
Larissa GRE *Larisa* 21B2, 30C2, 71C2, 155B1
Larissa IRQ *Nimrud* 54E3
Larissa SYR *Shaizar* 73F6
Larius L. ITL *L. Como* 108B2
Larsa IRQ *Tell Sinkara* 3F4
Las GRE *Passavas* 14D4, 48C5
Lasaia GRE 154C2, 161E3
Latium/Latini ITL 85C3, **86**, 109E6, **117**
Latmos TKY 45D3
Latmos M. TKY *Beşparmak Dağı* 31H5
Lato pros Kamara GRE *Ag. Nikolaos* 154D2
Latopolis EGY *Esna/Isna* 75B8, 171C5
Laureion GRE *Lavrio* 36D6
Laurentes ITL 86B2

Lauriacum AUS *Lorch* 149D4, 178D2
Laus Pompeia ITL *Lodi Vecchio* 108C2
Lautulae ITL 89C3
Lavatris UKG *Bowes* 132D4, 135C2
Lavinium ITL *Pratica di Mare* 86B2, 89B3, 117B3
Lebadeia GRE *Levadeia* 33D5, 59C3
Lebedos TKY *Kisik* 31G4, 49F4, 71F3
Lechaion GRE 33D6
Ledroi CYP *Lefkosia* 156B2
Lefkandi GRE 6C3, 16C2
Legio ISR *Lejjun* 168B3, 171D1
Legio VII Gemina SPN *León* 138B2, 178A3
Leipsydrion GRE *Gaitana?* 36B3
Lekton Pr. TKY *Bababurnu* 159A2
Lelantion Pedion GRE *Lelantine plain* 21C2
Lemannus L. SWI *Lac Léman* 147E3, 149A4
Lemba CYP 9A2
Lemnioi GRE 45B1
Lemnos Ins. GRE *Lemnos* 13D1, 31F2, 49E2, 155C1
Lemovices FRA 147C3
Leontini/Leontinoi ITL *Lentini* 18B3, 43E3, 95G4, 111E3
Leontion GRE *Kastritsi* 33B5
Leontopolis EGY *Tell el-Yahoudiyeh* 74B4, 171B2
Leontopolis EGY *Kom el-Muqdam* 75B5
Lepcis Magna LBY *Lebda* 95G5, 141E2, **143**, 188D5
Lepinus M. ITL *Monti Lepini* 86C2
Lepreon GRE 27B3, 33B6, 48B4
Lepti Minus TUN *Lamta* 94B6, 104C3, 144D2
Lerna GRE 30C4
Leros (Ins.) GRE *Leros* 31G5, 49F5, 56E3
Lesbos Ins. GRE *Lesbos* 13D2, 31F3, 49F3, 155C1
Lethaios fl. GRE *Geropotamos* 154B2
Letopolis EGY *Ausim* 75B5, 171B2
Leucas (Ins.) GRE *Lefkada* 21A2, 30A3, 59B3, 155A2
Leuci FRA 147E2, 149A4
Leuctra GRE *Parapoungia* 33D5, **55**
Leuka M. GRE *Lefka Mts.* 154A2
Leukaspis EGY *Marina el-Alamein, el-Bahrein* 171A2
Leuke Kome SAU *'Aynuna* 172B2
Leukimma Pr. GRE *Akra Lefkimis* 48A3
Leukolla CYP *Paralimni-Armyropigano* 156C2
Leukonion GRE 49F4
Leukonoion? GRE *Peristeri?* 36B4
Lianokladi GRE 6B3
Liatovouni GRE 6A2
Libanus M. LEB *Jebel Lubnan* 162A5
Libarna ITL *Serravalle Scrivia* 108B3
Libisosa SPN *Lezuza* 138D3
Liburnia CRO 109G3
Libya 22A4, 60A3, 141H2, 171A2
Libya Inferior *(province)* EGY/LBY 189F5
Libya Superior *(province)* LBY 189E5
Libycum Mare/Libykon Pelagos 43C4, 141G2, 171A1
Lidar Höyük TKY 2D2, 30C3
Liger fl. FRA *Loire* 104B1, 147B3
Ligures/Liguria ITL 85A1, 108B3
Ligures Baebiani ITL *Macchia di Circello* 127C3
Lilaia GRE *Kato Agoriani/Pyrgos* 30C3, 71C2
Lilybaeum/Lilybaion ITL *Marsala* 43A2, 94B6, 104D3, 113C3

Limantepe (near Klazomenai) TKY 7F8
Limenia CYX 156A2
Limnai TKY 19F2, 30A6
Limonum FRA *Poitiers* 147C3
Limyra TKY 2B3, 159C4
Limyrike IND *Malabar coast* 175E5
Lindos GRE *Lindos* 13E3, 31H6, 49G5, 71F4
Lindum UKG *Lincoln* 130B1, 133E5, 188B2
Lingones ITL 85C1, 147D2, 149A4
Lipara (Ins.) ITL *Lipari* 18B2, 43E1, 94C5, 113E2
Liparaeae Inss. ITL *Aeolian Is./Isole Eolie* 94C5
Liris fl. ITL *Garigliano* 87A1, 93A1, 109F5
Lisht EGY 2B5
Lisia Ins. UKG *Guernsey* 133C7, 147A2
Lissa Ins. CRO *Ugljan* 109G3
Lissos GRE *Ag. Kyrkos* 154A2
Lissus ALB *Lezha* 95H3, 105E2, 152B4
Liternum ITL 87B2, 93B2
Lithares GRE 6C3
Little St. Bernard pass FRA/ITL 95E2
Livias JOR *Tell er-Rama* 168C5
Lixus MOR *Tchemmisch* 94A5, 138B4
Lixus fl. MOR *Oued Loukos* 138B4
Locris Epiknemidia *(East)* GRE 21B2
Locris Opuntia *(East)* GRE 30C3, 59C3
Locris Ozolia *(West)* GRE 21B2, 30C4, 59B3
Logia fl. IRE *Lagan* 132A4
Lokra fl. FRA *Prunelli* 108B5
Lokroi Epizephyrioi ITL *Locri* 18C2, 83E4, 111C3, 127D4
Lombards 199D2
Londinium UKG *London* 130B2, 133E6, 178B2, 188B2
Longanos fl. ITL *Patri/Fantina* 43E2
Longovicium UKG *Lanchester* 135D2
Lopadusa Ins. ITL *Lampedusa* 141E1
Lopodunum GER *Ladenburg* 151B2
Lorium ITL *Castel di Guido* 117B2
Loryma TKY *Bozuk* 31H5, 49G5
Loudias L. GRE 30C1
Lourinon FRA *Castellu de Luri* 108C4
Lousoi GRE *Lousiko/Chamakou* 16B3
Lousones SPN 99D2
Luca ITL *Lucca* 92B2, 108C4
Lucani/Lucania ITL 85E3, 111B1
Lucania et Bruttii ITL 188D4
Lucentum SPN 99D3, 138D3
Luceria ITL *Lucera* 83E3, 92E3, 95G3, 109H6
Lucus Augusti SPN *Lugo* 138A1
Lucus Ferentinae ITL 86C2
Lucus Feroniae ITL 81D5, 86B1, 117C1, 127A5
Lugdunensis *(province)* FRA 130B2, 147C2, 178B2
Lugdunensis I *(province)* FRA 188C2
Lugdunensis II *(province)* FRA 188B2
Lugdunum FRA *Lyon* 130C3, 147D3, 178C3, 188C3
Lugdunum Convenarum FRA *St-Bertrand-de-Comminges* 138E1, 147C4
Lugii POL 149F2
Luguidunec ITL *Nostra Signora di Castro* 113A1
Luguvalium UKG *Carlisle* 132C4, 135B1
Lukka TKY 2B2
Luna ITL *Luni* 92B1, 108C3, 147F4

Luni sul Mignone ITL 81C5
Lupia fl. GER *Lippe* 147F1, 149B2
Lupiae ITL *Lecce* 83F3, 111D1
Lusitania *(province)* POR/SPN 130A4, 138A2, 178A3, 196A4
Lutetia FRA *Paris* **145**, 147C2
Lycaonia TKY 22B2, 159E3, 161G2, 180D2
Lychnidos MKD *Ohrid* 30B1, 71B1, 152B4
Lychnidus L. ALB/MKD *Ohrid* 30A1, 59B2
Lychnitis L. ARM *Sevan* 163E2
Lycia TKY 2B2, 22B3, 68B3, 159C4
Lycia et Pamphylia *(province)* TKY 131G4, 189G4
Lycium Mare 159B4
Lydda ISR *Lud* 168B4
Lydia TKY 2B2, 31H3, 68B2, 159B3
Lydia *(province)* TKY 189F4
Lykastos? GRE *Rokka* 13D4
Lykioi TKY 45E3
Lykopolis EGY *Asyut* 75B7, 171B4
Lykos fl. CYP *Kouris* 156B3
Lykos fl. TKY *Kelkit Çay* 2D1, 162B2
Lykos fl. TKY *Gördük Çay* 31H3
Lykosura GRE 33C6
Lyktos GRE *Xidas* 13D4, 21D4, 71E5, 154C2
Lyncestis MKD 48B1, 59B2
Lyrnessos? (Antandros) TKY *Devren/Avcılar* 13E2
Lysias SYR *Bourzey* 74E2
Lysimachea TKY *Hatıplar* 71E2
Lysimacheia GRE *Mourstianou* 71B2
Lysimacheia TKY *Baklaburnu* 68A2, 71E1
Lystra TKY *Hatunsaray* 159E3, 161G2

Maa Palaeokastro CYP 9A2
Macae LBY 141E2
Macae OMN/UAE 173G3
Macedonia 16B1, 30C1, **59**, 60A1
Macedonia *(province)* 103D2, 131E3, 152B4, 179E3
Macedonicum Mare 31E2
Macella ITL 94B6
Machairous JOR *Mekawer* 168C5
Macomades LBY *Sirte, Marsa Zaafran* 141F2
Macoraba SAU *Mecca* 172C4
Macra fl. ITL *Magra* 108C3
Macrones/Makrones TKY 22C2, 54D2
Mactaris TUN *Mactar* 144C2
Madaba JOR *Madaba* 162A6, 168D5
Madauros ALG *Mdaourouch* 144B1
Madiane SAU 172B2
Madnasa TKY *Göl?* 45D3
Madytos TKY *Eçeabat* 30A6, 49F2, 71E1
Maeander fl. TKY *Büyük Menderes* 2A2, 31H4, 72B5, 159B3
Maedi MKD 59C1
Maeonians TKY 13E2
Maeotis *Sea of Azov* 34B2, 153H2
Magis UKG *Burrow Walls* 135A2
Maglone UKG *Old Carlisle* 135A2
Magnesia *(region)* GRE *Magnesia* 27C2, 30C2, 59C2
Magnesia ad Maeandrum TKY *Tekke* 21E2, 31H4, 71F3, 159B3
Magnesia ad Sipylum TKY *Manisa* 31H3, 71F2, 159A3

Magnetes TKY 22B2
Magnetes? GRE 14D1
Magnis UKG *Carvoran* 135B1
Magnopolis TKY 73F3
Magnum CRO *Balina glavica* 109H4
Mago SPN *Mahón* 94D3, 138F3
Maia UKG *Bowness-on-Solway* 135A1
Maiandros fl. TKY *Menderes* 54A2
Maidum EGY 2B5
Maior Ins. SPN *Mallorca* 138E3
Maiotai RUS 34C2
Maipha YEM *Naqab al-Hajar* 173E5
Mais fl. IND *Mahī* 175E2
Maisolos fl. IND *Kṛṣṇa* 175F4
Maka 23F4, 173G2
Makriyalos GRE 6C2
Malabar Coast IND 53F3
Malaca SPN *Málaga* 94B4, 99C4, 138C4
Malaia M. SRI 175F6
Malaios Ins. UKG *Mull* 132A3
Malame GRE 9A1
Malanga IND *Kanchipuram* 175F5
Malao SOM *Berbera* 172D6
Mālavas IND 175E2
Malazgirt TKY 54E2
Malea Pr. GRE *Maleas* 13B3, 30D6
Maleventum ITL *Benevento* 83D3, 89E3
Malia GRE 9C2
Malichou Inss. YEM *Zubayr* 172C5
Malis GRE 27C2, 30C3, 59C3
Malloi IND 61H3
Mallos TKY 73E5, 159F4, 163G2
Malthi GRE 6B4
Malva ROM *Reşca* 152D2
Malvesa BOS *Skelani* 152B3
Mamaeum Litus SAU 172D5
Mamucio UKG *Manchester* 133D5
Manavia Ins. UKG *Isle of Man* 132B4
Mandalo GRE 6B1
Mandas fl. IND *Godāvarī* 175G4
Manduria ITL 83F3, 111D1
Manika GRE 6C3
Mannea IRN 3G2
Mantineia GRE *Mantineia* 14D3, 30C4, 48C4, 71C3
Mantua ITL *Mantova* 81B1, 83B1, 108D2
Mantua SPN *el Coto la Cepilla* 138C2
Marakanda UZB *Samarkand* 61G2, 69G2
Marandet NER 140D6
Marathon GRE *Marathon* 16C2, **25**, 27D2, 36D3
Marathos SYR *'Amrit* 74E2
Marcianopolis BUL *Reka Devniya* 153E3, 189F3
Marcina ITL *Vietri sul Mare* 87C3
Marcomanni CZE/GER 149D3
Mardioi? IRN 23E4
Mardoi IRN 23E3, 61E2
Mareia EGY *Kom el-Idris* 74A4
Mareotis L. EGY *Lake Mariout* 171B2
Margiana TKM 23G3, 61F2, 69G3
Margum SRB *Orašje* 152B2
Margus fl. *Morava* 152B3
Mariana FRA *La Canonica* 108C5, 147F4

Mariandyni TKY 22B2
Marianus M. SPN *Sierra Morena* 99C3, 138C3
Mariba YEM *Marib* 172D5
Marisa ISR *Tel Sandahanna* 74D4, 168B5
Marisos fl. HUN/ROM *Marosch/Mureş* 152B2
Marki Alonia CYP 9B1
Markiani GRE 7E9
Marmaridai LBY 141G2
Maroneia GRE *Ag. Kharalabos* 19F2, 31F1, 71E1, 152D4
Maroneia GRE *in Attica* 36D6
Maroneus M. ITL *Pizzo Carbonara* 113D3
Maroni CYP 9B2
Marrucini ITL 85D2
Marsi ITL 85D3
Marsiliana d'Albegna ITL 81B4
Marzabotto ITL 81B2, 83C1
Masada ISR *Es Sebbe* 168C6, **169**
Maşat Höyük TKY 2D1
Massa Marittima ITL 81B4
Massagetai UZB 23H2
Massalia/Massilia FRA *Marseille* 18A4, 53B2, 104C2, 147E4
Massicus M. ITL *Monte Massico* 87A1
Matiane L. IRN *Urmia* 163E3
Matiene IRN 22D3
Mauretania ALG/MOR 104A3, 180A2, 195A4
Mauretania Caesariensis *(province)* ALG 130B4, 140B1, 178B4, 188B4
Mauretania Sitifensis *(province)* ALG 188C4
Mauretania Tingitana *(province)* MOR 130A4, 140A1, 178A4, 188A5
Mauri MOR 199A3
Maurusii MOR 138C4
Maydos Kilisetepe TKY 7F6
Mazaka TKY *Kayseri* 73E4
Mazara ITL *Mazara del Vallo* 113C3
Mazara fl. ITL *Mazaro* 43B2
Medeon GRE *Ag. Theodoroi* 6C3, 16C2
Media IRN/IRQ 3G3, 23E3, 69E3, 163E4
Media Atropatene IRN 105H3, 163E3
Medinet el-Fayum EGY 2B5
Medinet el-Ghurob EGY 2B5
Mediolanum ITL *Milano/Milan* 83A1, 108B2, 147F3, 188C3
Mediolanum (Santonum) FRA *Saintes* 147B3
Mediomatrici FRA/GER 147E2, 149A3
Medion GRE *Katuna* 48B3
Medma ITL *Rosarno* 18B2, 111B3
Mefineis M. ITL *Monte Roccamonfina* 87A1
Mega Pedion ISR *Jezreel valley* 168B3
Megalopolis GRE *Megalopolis* 30C5, 59B4, 71B3
Megara GRE *Megara* 19E5, 30D4, 71C3, 155C2
Megara Hyblaia ITL *Megara Hyblaea* 18B3, 43F3, 48B6, 113E3
Megiddo ISR *Tel Megiddo* 2C4
Meir EGY 2B5
Mekestos fl. TKY *Simav Çayı* 2A2, 31H2, 159B2
Mekyberna GRE *Molivopirgos* 45A1, 48D2
Melan M. YEM 173E6
Melas fl. TKY *Manavgat Çay* 2B2, 159D4

Melas fl. TKY *Karasu* 162B3
Melas Sinus TKY *Saros Körfezi* 30B5, 31G1
Meliboia GRE 14D1
Melie TKY *Kale Tepe* 16F3
Melita (Ins.) MLT *Malta* 94C6, 113D4, 141F1, 160A3
Meliteia GRE *Avaritsa* 32C4
Melitene TKY *Eski Malatya* 162B3, 179H4
Melos (Ins.) GRE *Melos* 21C3, 31E5, 48D5, 155C3
Memphis EGY *Mit Rahina* 2B4, 22B4, 68B4, 171B2
Menai ITL *Mineo* 43E3, 113E3
Menapii BGM/NET 147D1
Mende GRE *Kalandra* 18D2, 30D2, 45A1
Mendes EGY *Tell el-Ruba* 2C3, 74B4, 171C2
Mendesion Stoma EGY 171C2
Meninge TUN *Bordj el-Kantara* 144D3
Meninx Ins. TUN *Gerba* 95F5, 144D3
Mercurii Pr. TUN *Cap Bon* 113A3, 144D1
Meroe SUD *Bagrawiya* 68C6, 172B5
Mersa Gawasis EGY 2C5
Merv TKM *Erk Kala/Gyaur Kala* 61F2, 69G2
Meschistha GEO *Mtskheta* 162D1
Mesembria BUL *Nessebar* 19F4, 153E3
Mesene IRN/IRQ 163E6, 173E1
Mesogis M. TKY *Aydın Dağları* 159B3
Mesopotamia 3E3, 22D3, 68C3
Mesopotamia *(province)* 162B3, 179H4, 189H4
Mesopotamium ITL 113D4
Mespila IRQ 54E3
Messana ITL *Messina* 18B2, 43F2, 94C5, 113E2
Messapii ITL 85F3
Messene GRE *Mavromati* 14C3, 30C5, 71B3, 155B2
Messenia GRE *Messenia* 16B3, 30B5, 48B4
Metagonium Pr. ALG *Cap Bougaroun* 94B5
Metalla ITL *Antas* 113A2
Metallum Vipascense POR *Aljustrel* 138A3, **139**
Metapontum ITL *Pantanello* 18C1, 83F3, 95G3, 111C1
Metaris Aestuarium UKG *Wash* 133E5
Metaurum ITL *Gioia Tauro* 18B2
Metaurus fl. ITL *Metauro* 95F2, 109E4
Metellinum SPN *Medellín* 138B3
Methana GRE 33E6, 48D4, 71C3
Methone GRE *N Pydna* 19E4, 32C2, 48C2, 59C2
Methone GRE *Methoni* 30B5, 48B5
Methone GRE *Nevestiki* 32D4
Methora IND *Mathura* 175F1
Methydrion GRE *Nemnitsa* 48C4
Methymna GRE *Methymna* 21D2, 31F3, 49F3, 56E2
Metropolis TKY *Yeniköy* 2A2
Metropolis *(SE Eumeneia)* TKY *Tatarlı* 159C3
Metropolis TKY *Oyneş* 159C3
Metulum CRO *Viničica* 104D2, 109G2
Mevania ITL *Bevagna* 89C2, 109E4
Mevaniola ITL 109E3
Meydancıkkale TKY 2C3
Midaion TKY *Karahüyük* 159D2
Midas City TKY *Yazılıkaya* 2B2
Mikro Vouni GRE 7E6
Milatos? GRE 13D4
Miletopolis TKY *Melde* 159B2
Miletus TKY *Balat* 2A2, 16F3, 31G4, 40, 71F3, 159A3
Milev ALG *Mila* 144A1, 192C4

Miltenberg GER 151C2
Milyai TKY 22B2
Milyas TKY 159C4
Mimas M. TKY *Boz Dağ* 13D2, 31G3, 49F3
Minaei YEM 173E5
Mincius fl. ITL *Mincio* 108C2
Minervium ITL *Roccelletta* 92E4
Minius fl. POR/SPN *Minho/Miño* 99A1, 138A1
Minnagar PAK *Bahmanabad?* 69H4, 174D2
Minnagara IND *Baroda* 175E2
Minor Ins. SPN *Menorca* 138F3
Minturnae ITL 87A1, 89D3, 93A2, 109F6
Mirobriga POR *Santiago do Cacém* 138A3
Mirobriga SPN *Ciudad Rodrigo* 138B2
Mirobriga SPN *Cerro del Cabezo* 138B3
Misenum ITL *Miseno* 87B3, 104D2, 111A1
Mishrifeh see Qatna
Mistea TKY *Beyşehir* 159D3
Mitrou GRE 6C3
Mittani TKY 3E2
Moab JOR 2D4, 168C6
Mochlos GRE 9D2
Modiin PSE *el Midiye* 168B4
Modoura IND *Madurai* 175F6
Modoutou Emporion SRI *Mullaitivu?* 175F6
Moenus fl. GER *Main* 147F2, 149C3, 151C2
Moeris L. EGY *Birket Qarun* 171B3
Moesia *(province)* 131E3
Moesia Inferior *(province)* BUL/ROM 152D3, 179F3, 189F3
Moesia Superior *(province)* MKD/SRB 152B3, 179E3, 189E3
Moesiae *(diocese)* 189E3
Mogentiana HUN *Tüskevár* 149F4, 152A1
Mogontiacum GER *Mainz* 130C2, 149B3, 151B2, 178C2
Molaria ITL *Mulgaria* 113A1
Molibodes Ins. ITL *Isola di Sant'Antioco* 113A3
Molossis GRE 30A2, 56A2
Mona Ins. UKG *Anglesey* 133B5
Monastiraki GRE 9B2
Montana BUL *Mihajlovgrad* 152C3
Monte Giove ITL 92D2
Monte Sirai ITL 94A5
Monteriggioni ITL 81B3
Mopsouestia TKY *Yakapınar* 73E5, 163G2
Morgantina ITL *Serra Orlando* 43D3, 95G4, 113E3
Moridunum UKG *Carmarthen* 133B6
Morikambe Aestuarium UKG *Morecambe Bay* 133C5
Morini FRA 147C1
Mortuum Mare *Dead Sea* 74D4, 168C5, 171D1
Mosa fl. *Meuse/Maas* 104C1, 147E1, 149A2
Mosarna PAK *Pasni* 174C2
Moschi 22D2
Mosella fl. FRA/GER *Moselle/Mosel* 104C1, 147E2, 149A3, 151A2
Mossynoeci TKY 22C2, 54D2
Mosylon Emporion SOM *Bandar Cassim or Candala* 173E6
Mothis EGY *Mut* 171A5
Motya ITL *Mozia* 43A2
Moundou SOM *Heis?* 173E6

Mounichia GRE *Tourkolimani* 36B4
Mouza Emporion YEM *Wahija* 172D6
Mulucha fl. ALG *Oued Moulouia* 138C4, 140A2
Mumrills UKG 136D1
Munda SPN *Cerro de las Camorras?* 104A3
Municipium Iasorum CRO *Daruvar* 152A2
Munigua SPN *Dehesa de Mulva* 138B3
Murgi SPN 138C4
Murlo ITL 81B4, 83C2
Mursa CRO *Osijek* 152A2
Muş TKY 54E2
Musasir IRQ *Mergasur* 3F2
Müsgebi TKY 7G9
Musti TUN *Henchir-Mest* 144C1
Musulamii ALG/TUN 144C2
Muthul fl. ALG/TUN *Oued Mellègue* 140D1, 144B2
Mutina ITL *Modena* 81B2, 92B1, 104C2, 108D3
Muziris IND *Cranganūr* 175E5
Mycale M. TKY *Samsun Dağ* 13E2, 27F3, 31G4
Mycenae GRE *Mykenes* **11,** 13B2, 33D6
Mygdonia GRE 27C1, 48C1
Mykalessos GRE *Rhitsona* 48D3
Mykonos (Ins.) GRE *Mykonos* 27D3, 31F5, 45C3, 71D3
Mylae ITL *Milazzo* 18B2, 43F2, 94C5, 113E2
Mylasa TKY *Milas* 2A2, 31H5, 71F3, 159B4
Myndos TKY *Gümüslük* 31G5
Myonnesos (Ins.) TKY *Çıfıt Kale* 31G4, 71E3
Myos Hormos EGY *Quseir el-Qadim* 53D3, 75D7, 172B2
Myous TKY *Afşar* 31H4, 45D3, 49G4
Myra TKY *Demre* 131G4, 159C4, 179F4, 189G4
Myriandros TKY *Ada Tepe* 54C3, 163G2
Myrina GRE *Kastro/Myrina* 31E2, 45B1
Myrina mouth of Koca Çay 45D2, 71F2
Myrkinos GRE 48D1
Myrleia TKY *Mudanya* 72B3
Myrmekion UKR *Karantinnaya* 34B2
Myrrinous GRE *Merenda* 36D5
Myrtoion Mare GRE 30D5
Myrtos GRE 9C2
Myrtou Pighades CYX 9B1
Mysia TKY 2A2, 22B2, 31H2, 159B2
Mysians TKY 13E1
Mytilene GRE *Mitilini* 2A2, 31G3, 71E2, 155D2

Nabataea/Nabataei JOR 105G4, 131G5, 171C2, 172B1
Naissus SRB *Niš* 152C3
Nakoleia TKY *Seyitgazi* 159D2
Nakrason TKY *Maltepe?* 71F2
Namades fl. IND *Narmadā* 175E3
Namnetes FRA 147B2
Nanagounas fl. IND *Tapti* 175E3
Napata SUD *Barkal* 172A4
Napoca ROM *Cluj-Napoca* 152C1
Nar fl. ITL *Nera* 109E5
Naraggara ALG *Sakiet Sidi Youssef* 95E4
Narbo Martius FRA *Narbonne* 104B2, 138F1, 147D4, 178C3
Narbonensis *(province)* FRA 130B3, 178B3
Narbonensis I *(province)* FRA 188B3
Narbonensis II *(province)* FRA 188C3

Narce ITL 81D5
Narmouthis EGY *Kom Medinet Madi* 171B3
Narnia ITL *Narni* 92C2, 109E5
Naro fl. BOS/CRO *Neretva* 152A3
Narona CRO *Vid* 152A3
Narthakion GRE *Limogardi* 32C4
Nasamones LBY 141G3
Natiso fl. ITL *Natisone* 109F2
Naucratis EGY *Kom Gajef* 2B4, 19F6, 74A4, 171B2
Naulochos ITL 104D3, 113E2
Naupactus GRE *Navpaktos* 21B2, 30C4, 48B3
Nauplia GRE *Nauplion* 33D6
Nauportus fl. SVN *Ljubljanica* 109G2
Nautaka UZB *Shahr-i-Sabz?* 61G2
Navan UKG 132A4
Naxos (Ins.) GRE *Naxos* 31F5, 45C3, 71E3, 155C2
Naxos ITL *Giardini-Naxos* 18B2, 43F2, 48B5, 113E3
Nazareth ISR *Nazareth* 168C2
Nea Nikomedeia GRE 6B1
Nea Paphos CYP *Kato Paphos* 2B3, 156A3
Nea Pleuron GRE *Kato Retsina* 48B3
Neaethus fl. ITL *Neto* 111C2
Neaiton ITL *Noto* 43E4
Neapolis CYP *Lemesos* 156B3
Neapolis GRE *Kavalla* 19E2, 32F2, 59D2, 161E1
Neapolis ITL *Napoli/Naples* 18B1, 83D3, 87B2, 127C3
Neapolis *(Sardinia)* ITL *S. Maria de Nabui* 113A2
Neapolis PSE *Shechem/Nablus* 162A5, 168C3
Neapolis *(on Propontis)* TKY *Erikli* 45D1
Neapolis *(in Pisidia)* TKY *Kiyakdede* 159D3
Neapolis TUN *Nabeul* 94B6, 113A4, 144D1
Nebrodes M. ITL *Monti Nebrodi* 113E3
Neckarburken GER 151C2
Neiloupolis EGY *Dalas* 193F5
Nelkynda IND *Nirkunnam* 175F6
Nemausus FRA *Nîmes* 147D4, 188C3
Nemea GRE *Herakleion* 16C3, 30C4, 48C4
Neocaesarea TKY *Niksar* 162B2, 189H4, 193G3
Nepet ITL *Nepi* 81C5, 92C2, 127A5
Neptunia ITL *Taranto* 92F3
Nertobriga SPN *Cabezo Chinchón* 99D2
Nertobriga SPN *Valeria la Vieja* 138B3
Nervii BGM/FRA 147D1
Nestos fl. GRE *Nestos/Mesta* 27D1, 31E1, 59C1, 152D4
Nether Denton UKG 135B1
Netum ITL *Noto* 113E3
Neviodunum SVN *Drnovo pri Krškem* 109H2, 149E4
Newbrough UKG 135C1
Nicaea FRA *Nice* 18B4
Nicaea TKY *İznik* 72B3, 159C2, 193F4
Nicer fl. GER *Neckar* 147F2, 149B3, 151C2
Nichoria GRE 6B5, 16B3
Nicomedia TKY *İzmit* 72C3, 131G4, 159C2, 189G4
Nicopolis EGY 179F5
Nicopolis GRE *Palaio-Preveza* 155B2, 160C2, 179E4, 189E4
Nicopolis ISR *Imwas* 168B4
Nicopolis TKY *Yeşilyayla* 105G2, 162B2
Nicopolis ad Istrum BUL *Nikiup* 152D3
Nicopolis ad Nestum BUL *Gârmen* 152C4
Nida GER *Heddernheim* 151B1

Niederbieber GER 151A1
Niger fl. 53B3, 140B6
Niger M. LBY *Gebel Soda* 141F3
Nikaia GRE *Ag. Triada/Palaiokastro* 32C4, 59C3
Nikaia PAK 61H3
Nikonion UKR *Roksolanskoye* 153F2
Nikopolis EGY *Alexandria suburb* 131G5
Nikopolis TKY *Yeşil Hüyük* 73F5
Nilus fl. *Nile* 2C6, 53C3, 75B5, 171B3
Nimrud IRQ 3F3
Nineveh IRQ *Kuyunjik* 3F3, 162D4
Ninica TKY *Mut* 159E4
Nippur IRQ *Nuffar* 3F4
Nisa TKM 69F2
Nisaia GRE 33E6
Nisibis SYR/TKY *Nusaybin* 73H5, 162C3
Nissia CYP 9D1
Nisyros (Ins.) GRE *Nisyros* 13E3, 45D3, 56E4
Noiodounon FRA *Sées* 133E8
Noiodounon Diablintum FRA *Jublains* 133E8, 147B2
Nola ITL *Nola* 87C2, 89E3, 93C2, 109G6
Nomentum ITL 89C2, 117C1, 127A5
Noouantai UKG 132B4
Noouios fl. UKG *Nith* 132B4
Nora ITL *Pula* 83A4, 94A5, 113A3
Norba ITL 86C3, 92C4
Norba SPN *Cáceres* 138B3
Norchia ITL 81C5
Noricum *(province)* 109F1, 130D2, 149D4, 178D2
Noricum Mediterraneum *(province)* 188D3
Noricum Ripense *(province)* AUS 188D2
Norşuntepe TKY 3E2
Notion TKY 31G4, 49G4
Novae BOS *Runović* 152A3
Novae BUL *Svishtov* 131F3, 152D3, 179F3
Novaesium GER *Neuss* 130C2, 147E1, 149A3
Novantae see Noouantai
Novaria ITL *Novara* 108B2
Novem Populi FRA 188B3
Novilara ITL 83C2
Noviodunum FRA *Neung-sur-Beuvron* 147C2
Noviodunum ROM *Isaccea* 153E2
Noviomagus FRA *Noyon* 149A2
Noviomagus GER *Speyer* 147F2, 151B2
Noviomagus GER *Neumagen* 149B3
Noviomagus NET *Nijmegen* 147E1, 149A2
Noviomagus UKG *Chichester* 133E7
Noviomagus Lexoviorum FRA *Lisieux* 133E8
Nubia/Nubaei EGY/SUD 2C6, 68B5, 172A5
Nuceria *(in Umbria)* ITL *Nocera* 109E4
Nuceria Alfaterna ITL *Nocera* 87C3, 89E3, 92D3, 95G3
Nufar IRQ *Nuffar* 163E5
Numana ITL *Numana* 83D2
Numantia SPN *Numancia* 94B3, 99D1, **100**, 138D2
Numerus Syrorum ALG *Lalla Maghnia/Marnia* 138D4, 140B1
Numidia ALG 95E5, 104B3, 130C4
Numidia *(province)* ALG 140D1, **144**, 178C4
Numidia Cirtensis *(province)* ALG 188C4
Numidia Militiana *(province)* ALG 188C5

Nursia ITL *Norcia* 89C2, 109F5
Nymphaion UKR *Geroyevka* 34B3
Nymphaion Pr. GRE *Nymphaion* 32F3
Nysa ISR *Beisan Beth Shean* 74D3, 171D1
Nysa TKY *Sultanhisar* 72B5, 159B3

Oai GRE *Papangelaki* 36C4
Oarakta Ins. IRN *Qeshm Is.?* 173G2
Oasis Magna EGY 171B4
Oasis Parva EGY 171A3
Oberstimm GER 151E3
Oblivio fl. POR/SPN *Lima/Limia* 99A1
Obulco SPN *Porcuna* 99C3, 138C3
Ocelum Duri SPN *Zamora?* 138B2
Ocriculum ITL *Otricoli* 89C2
Octodurus SWI *Martigny* 108A1
Odessus BUL *Varna* 19F4, 72B2, 153E3
Odrysae BUL 153E3
Oe? GRE 36B3
Oea LBY *Tripoli* 95G5, 141E2
Oeneus fl. BOS *Una* 109H3
Oenoanda TKY *İncealiler* 72B5, 159C4
Oenotri ITL 85E3
Oescus BUL *Gigen* 131F3, 152D3, 179F3
Oglasa Ins. ITL *Isola di Montecristo* 108C5
Oglyos Ins. GRE *Antikythera* 33D8
Oichalia GRE *Kastri/Ano Potamia* 33F5
Oineon GRE *Klima Evpaliou/Magoula* 48C3
Oiniadai GRE *Trikardo* 33A5, 48B3
Oinoe GRE *Viokastro* 33D5
Oinoe GRE *Ninoi* 36A3
Oinoe GRE *Myopolis* 36C3
Oinoe *(on Ikaros)* GRE 31F4, 45C3, 56E3
Oinophyta GRE *Staniates* 33E5
Oinoussai Inss. GRE *Sapientza, Schiza* 33B7
Oisyme GRE *Vrasidas* 19E2, 32F2, 48D1
Oitylos GRE *Oitylos* 14D4, 33C7
Okelis YEM *Khor Ghurayrah (Shaykh Sa'id)?* 172D6
Okilis SPN *Medinaceli* 99D2
Olba TKY *Ura* 74C1
Olbasa TKY *Belenli* 159C4
Olbia FRA *L'Almanarre* 18A4
Olbia *(Sardinia)* ITL *Olbia* 83B3, 95F3, 113B1
Olbia UKR *Parutino* 19F3, 68B1, 153F1
Old Church UKG 135B1
Old Durham UKG 135D2
Old Kilpatrick UKG 136A2
Old Smyrna TKY 16F2
Olgassys M. TKY *Ilgaz Dağları* 159E1
Oliaros Ins. GRE *Antiparos* 31E5
Olgassys M. TKY *Ilgaz Dağları* 159E1
Olisipo POR *Lisboa/Lisbon* 99A3, 138A3, 182A2
Olizon GRE *Ag. Andreas/Palaiokastro* 14D1, 32D4
Ollius fl. ITL *Oglio* 108C2
Olooson GRE *Elassona/Panayia* 14C1, 32C3
Olophyxos GRE *Akte?* 45B1
Olous GRE *Elounta* 16E4, 154D2
Olpai GRE *Agrilovouni* 32A4, 48B3
Olympia GRE *Olympia* 6B4, 30B4, 35, 71B3, 155B2
Olympos M. CYX *Kinanero Vouno* 156D1
Olympos M. TKY *Nif Dağ* 31G4
Olympus TKY *Deliktaş* 159C4

Olympus M. GRE *Olympos* 13B1, 30C2, 155B1
Olympus M. TKY *Ulu Dağ* 159C2
Olynthos GRE *Nea Olynthos* 27C1, 30D2, 48D2, 59C2
Omana UAE *ed-Dur* 173G3
Omboi EGY *Kom Ombo* 75C8, 171C5
Onchestos GRE *Kazarma* 14D2
Onoba SPN *Huelva* 138B3
Opis IRQ *Tell Mujeili'* 3F3, 54F3, 60D3
Oplontis ITL *Torre Annunziata* 87C3
Opoeis GRE 14D2
Opone SOM 173F6
Opous GRE *Atalandi* 21B2, 27C2, 33D5
Oppidum Novum ALG *Ain Defla* 138E4, 140C1
Orbetello ITL 81B5
Orcades Inss. UKG *Orkney* 132C1
Orchomenos GRE *Kalpaki* 14C3, 30C4, 48C4, 71C3
Orchomenus GRE *Skripou* 6C3, 13B2, 30D3, 48C3
Ordovices UKG 133C5
Oreine Ins. ERT *Dissei* 172C5
Oreos GRE *Pyrgos* 30D3, 59C3
Orestis GRE 30B2, 59B2
Oretani/Oretania SPN 94B3, 99C3, 138C3
Orgus fl. FRA/ITL *Orco* 108A2
Oriens *(diocese)* 189F5
Orientale Mare *Bay of Bengal* 175G4
Orikon ALB *Orikumi* 71A1, 95H3, 105E2
Oriza SYR *Tayibe* 162B4
Orkas Pr. UKG 53A1
Orneae GRE 14D3, 48C4
Oroatis fl. IRN *Zoreh* 163G6, 173F1
Orongis SPN *Jaén* 99C3
Orontes fl. SYR/TKY *Nahr el-Asi* 2D3, 19G5, 74E1, 162A4
Oropia GRE *Oropia* 36B2
Oropos GRE 30D4, 36C2, 48D4, 71C2
Orospeda M. SPN 99C3, 138C3
Orthoura IND *Uraiyar?* 175F5
Ortona ITL *Ortona* 109G5
Ortopla CRO *Stinica* 109G3
Orvieto ITL 81C4
Osca SPN *Huesca* 94C3, 138D2, 147B4
Osci ITL 85D3
Osismii FRA 133B8
Osrhoene SYR/TKY 105G3
Osrhoene *(province)* SYR/TKY 162B4, 179H4, 180D2, 189H4
Ossa M. GRE 14D1, 30C2
Ossonoba POR *Faro* 138A4
Osterburken GER 151C2
Osteria dell'Osa ITL 86C2
Ostia ITL *Ostia Antica* 86B2, 109E6, 117B2, **119**
Ostrakine EGY *el Felusiyat* 171C2
Ostrogothic Kingdom 199C2
Ostrogoths 197E2
Otadinoi UKG 132D4
Othoca ITL *S. Giusta* 113A2
Othrys M. GRE 30C3
Otrous TKY *Yanık Ören* 193F4
Otzaki GRE 6B2
Oualentia ITL *Nuragus* 113A2
Ouasada TKY *Bostandere* 159D3

Ouedra fl. UKG *Wear* 135D1
Ouenikones UKG 132C3
Ouergionios Okeanos *Celtic Sea* 133A6
Ouiadoua fl. *Oder* 149E2
Ouindinon FRA *Le Mans* 133E8, 147C2
Ouindion M. IND *Vindhya range* 175E2
Ouindogara Sinus UKG *Irvine Bay* 132B4
Oulatha ISR *Hule plain* 168C1
Oulippada SRI 175F6
Ourania CYX 156D1
Oustika Ins. ITL *Ustica* 43B1
Outioi? IRN 23F4
Ouxenton M. IND 175G2
Ouxioi IRN 23E4, 61E3
Ovilava AUS *Wels* 149D4, 188D2
Oxus fl. *Amu Darya* 23G2, 53E2, 61F2, 69G2
Oxyrhynchus EGY *el-Bahnasa* 75A6, 171B3
Oylum Höyük SYR 2D2
Ozene IND *Ujjain* 175E2

Pachynos Akra/Pachynum Pr. ITL *Capo Passero* 43F4, 94C6, 113E4
Pactolus fl. TKY *Sart Çay* 31H4
Padus fl. ITL *Po* 18B3, 83B1, 108B2, 147F3
Paeligni ITL 85D2
Paeonians GRE 13B1
Paestum ITL *Paestum* 83E3, 89E4, 92E3, 111A1
Pagai GRE *Alepochori* 33D5, 48C4
Pagasaeus Sinus GRE *Pegasetic Gulf* 32D4
Pagasai GRE 30D3, 59C3
Paiania GRE *Liopesi* 36C4
Paiones/Paionia MKD 59B1, 152C4
Paionidai GRE 36B3
Paisos TKY 30B6
Paithana IND *Paithan* 175E3
Paktye TKY 30B6
Palaeogoni SRI 175F6
Palaesimundum SRI *Anurādhapura* 175F6
Palaestina ISR/PSE *Palestine* 22C3, 60C3
Palaestina *(province)* ISR/PSE 180D3, 189G5, 195F5
Palaikastro GRE 9D2
Palaipaphos CYP *Kouklia* 2B3, 9A2, 156A3
Palaiperkote TKY 30B6
Palaisimoundou Ins. SRI *Sri Lanka* 175G6
Palantia SPN *Palencia* 138C2
Pale GRE *Lixouri* 27A2, 56A3
Palibothra IND *Patna* 175G2
Palinurus Pr. ITL *Cape Palinuro* 111A2
Palla FRA *Bonifacio* 108B6
Pallakotas Canal IRQ 54A4
Pallantia SPN *Palenzuela* 99C1
Pallantion GRE *Berbati* 33C6
Pallene GRE *Kassandra* 27C1, 30D2
Pallene GRE *Stavros* 36C4
Pallia fl. ITL *Paglia* 109E5
Palma SPN *Palma de Mallorca* 138F3
Palmyra SYR *Tudmur* 2D3, 162B4
Paloura IND *Dantapura* 175G3
Pamisos fl. GRE 30C5
Pamphylia TKY 2B2, 22B3, 68B2, 159D4
Pamphylium Mare *Antalya Körfezi* 159D4

Panaztepe TKY 7F7
Pandion IND *Pāṇḍya* 175F6
Pandosia GRE *Trikastro* 30A3, 59B3
Paneas SYR *Banias* 168C1
Paneas *(region)* SYR 168C1
Paneion M. GRE *Paneion* 36C5
Panermos GRE 7E9
Pangaion M. GRE 31E1
Panionion TKY 21E2
Pannonia *(province)* 131E3, 180B1, 195C3, 197E2
Pannonia Inferior *(province)* 149F4, 152A2, 179E3, 189E3
Pannonia Superior *(province)* 109G2, 152A1, 178D3, 189E3
Pannoniae *(diocese)* 188D3
Panopeos GRE *Ag. Vlasios* 14D2
Panopolis EGY *Akhmim* 75B7, 171C4
Panormos GRE *Tekes* 48B4
Panormos ITL *Palermo* 43C2, 94B5, 113C3
Pantikapaion UKR *Kerch'* 19G3, 34B2, 73F1, 153H2
Pantimathoi? IRN 23F2
Panzano ITL 81B3
Paphlagonia TKY 2C1, 22B2, 159E1, 189G3
Paphos CYP *Kato Paphos* 74B2, 131G4, 161G3, 179G4
Pappa TKY *Yunisler* 159D3
Paraetacene IRN *Luristan* 61E3, 163F5, 173E1
Paraetonium EGY *Marsa Matruh* 141H2, 171A2
Parapamisos AFG 23H3
Parauaea ALB 59B2
Parentium CRO *Poreč* 92D1, 109F2
Parihedri M. ARM 162D2
Parikanioi? IRN 23E3
Parikanioi? PAK 23G4
Parisii FRA 147C2
Parisoi UKG 133E5
Parium TKY *Kemer* 19G2, 31G2, 71F1, 159A2
Parlais TKY *Barla* 159D3
Parma ITL *Parma* 81A2, 92B1, 108C3
Parnassus M. GRE 14D2, 30C3
Parnes M. GRE 30D4, 36B3
Parnon M. GRE 30C5
Paropamisos M. *Hindukush* 61F2
Paros (Ins.) GRE *Paros* 19E5, 21D3, 31F5, 155C2
Parrasia? GRE 14C3
Parsa IRN 69E4
Parthenios fl. TKY *Bartın Su* 54B2
Parthia *(empire)* 131H4, 179H4
Parthia *(region)* IRN/TKM 23F3
Parthini ALB 105E2
Parthyene IRN/TKM 61F2, 69F2
Pasargadae IRN 3H4, 23E4, 61E3, 163H6
Pasitigris fl. IRN/IRQ *Karun* 163F6, 173E1
Passaron GRE 32A3
Patala PAK *Bahmanabad?* 61G4, 69H4, 174D2
Patara TKY *Gelemiş* 2B3, 72B6, 159C4, 161F3
Patavium ITL *Padova/Padua* 83C1, 109E2
Pathissus fl. *Tisza* 152B2
Pathyris EGY *Gebelen* 171C5
Patinga SUD *Kawa* 172A4
Patmos (Ins.) GRE *Patmos* 31G5, 49F4, 56E3, 161E2
Patnos TKY 3F2

Patous RUS *Novorossiysk* 34C3
Patrae GRE *Patras* 6B3, 30B4, 71B2, 155B2
Patrasys RUS *Garkushi* 34B2
Patulcenses Campani ITL *Parteoli* 113B2
Pausikani? TKM 23F2
Pautalia BUL *Kjustendil* 152C3
Pax Iulia POR *Beja* 138A3
Paxos Ins. GRE 30A3
Pazarlı TKY 2D1
Pedalion Pr. CYP *Cape Gkreko* 156D2
Pedalion Pr. TKY *Kurdoğlu Burnu* 159B4
Pedasos? (Assos) TKY *Beyramkale* 13D2
Pedum ITL 89C2
Pefkakia GRE 6C2
Peiraieus GRE 30D4, 36B4
Peiraieus TKY *Samsun* 73F3
Peiraion GRE *Perachora* 33D5
Pelagonia MKD 59B2
Pelendones SPN 99C1
Pelikata GRE 6A3
Pelinna GRE *Palaiogardiki* 32C3
Pelion M. GRE 14D1, 30D3
Pella GRE *Pella* 30C1, 59C2, 71C1, 152C4
Pella JOR *Tabaqat Fahl* 74D3, 168C3
Pella SYR *Qalaat el-Moudiq* 74E2
Pellene GRE *Zugra* 14D2, 33C5, 48C4, 71C3
Peloponnesus GRE *Peloponnese* 27B3, 30B4, 47B3, 155B2
Peloris Akron/Pelorus Pr. ITL *Capo Peloro* 43F2, 95G4, 113F2
Pelousiakon Stoma EGY 171C2
Pelso L. HUN *Balaton* 149F4
Peltai TKY 54B2
Peltuinum ITL *Civita Ansidonia* 89D2, 109F5, 127C2
Pelusium EGY *Tell el-Farama* 2C4, 74C4, 171C2, 195F6
Pelva BOS *Lištani* 152A3
Peneios fl. GRE *Peneios* 13B2, 30C2, 59B2, 155B1
Peneios fl. *(in Peloponnese)* GRE *Peneios* 30B4, 33B6
Penna Sant'Andrea ITL 83D2
Pentapoleis LYB 195D6
Pentapolis GRE 6C1
Pentelikon M. GRE *Pentelikon* 36C3
Pentri ITL 85D3
Peparethos GRE *Skopelos* 30D3, 45B2, 56C2
Perachora GRE 16C2
Peraea JOR 168C3
Peraiboi GRE 14B1
Perati GRE 16D3
Pergamum TKY *Bergama* 31G3, 71F2, **77**, 131F4, 159A3
Perge TKY *Aksu* 72C5, 159D4, 161F2
Pergus L. ITL *Lago di Pergusa* 43D3
Perinthos/Perinthus TKY *Ereğli* 19G2, 72B3, 131F3, 153E4
Peristeria GRE 6B4
Perkote TKY 30B6
Peroz-Shapur IRQ 162D5
Perraibia GRE 27B1, 30C2, 59B2
Persepolis IRN 3H4, 23E4, 25, 69E4, 173F2
Persia *(empire)* **22–23**

Persicus Sinus *Persian Gulf* 23E4, 53D2, 69E4, 173F2
Persides Pylae IRN 61E3
Persis IRN 3H4, 23E4, 69E4, 173F1
Pertalis IND *Tribeni?* 175H2
Perusia ITL *Perugia* 81D4, 89C1, 104D2, 109E4
Pessinous TKY *Ballıhisar* 68B2, 72C4, 159D2, 180D2
Petelia ITL *Strongoli* 83F4, 95H4, 111C2
Petra JOR *Wadi Musa* 68C4, 75D5, 162A6, 172B1
Petras GRE 9D2
Petrocori FRA 147B3
Petuaria UKG *Brough-on-Humber* 133E5
Peucetii ITL 85E3
Peukelaotis IND *Charsada* 61H2
Phaino JOR *Feinan* 162A6, 171D2
Phaistos GRE *Ag. Ioannis* 9B2, 16D4, 71D4, 154B2
Phaleron GRE 30D4, 36B4
Phanagoreia RUS *Sennaya* 19G3, 34C2, 153H2
Pharai GRE 33B5, 71B3
Pharbaithos EGY *Horbeit* 171C2
Pharkadon GRE *Klokoto* 32C3
Pharnakeia TKY *Giresun* 73G3
Pharsalus GRE *Pharsala* 21B2, 30C3, 71C2, 105E3
Pharus Ins. CRO *Hvar Is.* 95G2, 109H4
Phasaelis PSE *Khirbet Fasayil* 168C4
Phaselis TKY *Tekirova* 45F3, 60B2, 159C4
Phasis GEO 19H4, 73H2, 162C1
Phasis fl. GEO *Rioni* 162D1
'Phasis' fl. *Araks* 54F2
Phatnitikon Stoma EGY 171C1
Phazania LBY 140D2
Pheia GRE *Ag. Andreas/Pontikokastro* 48B4
Phellos TKY *Çukurbağ* 159C4
Pheneos GRE *Kalyvia* 14C3, 33C6
Pherai GRE *Kalamata* 14C3
Pherai GRE *Velestino* 6C2, 14D1, 30C3, 59C3
Phigaleia GRE *Phigaleia* 33B6, 71B3
Philadelpheia EGY *Gharabet el-Gerza* 75B5
Philadelpheia EGY *Kom el-Kharaba el-Kebir* 171B3
Philadelpheia JOR *Amman* 74E4, 162A5, 168D4, 172B1
Philadelpheia TKY *Alaşehir* 72B4, 159B3, 161F2, 193F4
Philae Ins. EGY *Bilaq* 75C8, 171C5
Philaidai GRE *Brauron* 36D4
Philetaireia TKY 71E2
Philia CYX 9B1
Philippeia JOR *Tabaqat Fahl* 74D3
Philippi GRE *Krenides* 31E1, 59D2, 105E2, 152D4
Philippopolis BUL *Plovdiv* 59D1, 152D, 189F3
Philippoupolis GRE 59C2
Philistia 2C4
Philomelion TKY *Akşehir* 72C4, 159D3, 193F4
Philosophiana ITL *Sofiana* 113D3
Philoteria ISR *Beth Yerah/Khirbet el Kerak* 74D3
Phintias ITL *Licata* 43D3, 113D3
Phlamoudhi CYX 9C1
Phleious GRE *Nemea* 30C4, 48C4, 71C3
Phlya GRE *Chalandri* 36C4
Phocaea TKY *Foça* 19E5, 31G3, 49F3, 159A3
Phocis GRE 21B2, 30C3, 59C3
Phoebiana GER 151D3
Phoenice *(province)* 189G5, 195F6

Phoenicia 2D3, 22C3, 161H3
Phoenicium Mare 156C3, 162A4
Phoenicusa/Phoinicousa Ins. 111A3*Filicudi* 43E1, 111A3
Phoimios fl. ALG *Oued Sahel* 140C1
Phoinike ALB *Finiq* 30A2, 71A1, 95H3
Phoinix GRE *Loutro* 154A2, 160D3
Pholegandros Ins. GRE 31E5
Phraaspa IRN *Zohak Qal'eh* 105H3, 163E3
Phrada AFG 61F3
Phrearrioi GRE 36D5
Phrygia TKY 2C2, 22B2, 68B2, 159C3
Phrygia *(Hellespontine)* TKY 22A2, 60A2, 68A2
Phrygia I *(province)* TKY 189G4
Phrygia II *(province)* TKY 189G4
Phthia? GRE 14D2
Phthiotis GRE 27B2
Phygela TKY *Kuşadası* 49G4
Phyle GRE 36B3
Physkos TKY *Marmaris* 159B4
Physkos fl. IRQ 54B3
Piazza Armerina ITL 113D3
Picentes/Picenum ITL 85D2, 109F4
Pictones FRA 147B3
Picts UKG 199A1
Pidasa TKY *Cert Osman Kale* 45D3
Piercebridge UKG 135D2
Pieria GRE 13B1
Pieria M. TKY *Kızıl Dağ* 163G2
Pietrabbondante ITL 83D3, 89D3
Pikrai Limnai EGY *Lake Timsah* 02C4, 171C2
Pillars of Hercules see Columnae Herculis
Pinara TKY *Minare* 159C4
Pindasos M. TKY *Madra Dağ* 159A2
Pindus M. GRE 30B3, 47B2, 155B1
Pinna ITL *Penne* 89D2
Piramesse EGY *Qantir* 2C4
Pisa GRE 33B6
Pisae ITL *Pisa* 81A3, 92B2, 95F2, 108C4
Pisatis GRE 21A2
Pisaurum ITL *Pésaro* 92D2, 109E4, 127C1
Pisida LBY *Bu Chemmasc* 141E2, 144D3
Pisidia *(region)* TKY 22B2, 159D4, 161F2
Pisidia *(province)* TKY 189G4
Pistoriae ITL *Pistoia* 95F2, 108D3
Pitane TKY *Çandarlı* 21D2
Pithekoussai ITL 18A1, 83D3, 87A3
Pitinum Mergens ITL *near Acqualagna* 109E4, 127B2
Pitinum Pisaurense ITL *Macerata Feltria* 109E4
Pitoura IND *Dharanikota* 175F4
Pityeia TKY *Lapseki* 13D1
Pityous GEO *Bichvinta/Pitsunda* 162C1
Pityoussa Ins. GRE *Spetsai* 33D7
Pityussae Inss. SPN *Ibiza and Formentera* 94C4
Placentia ITL *Piacenza* 81A2, 92B1, 95F2, 108C2
Planasia Ins. ITL *Pianosa* 108C5
Plataea GRE *Kokkla* 14E2, **29**, 30D4, 48D4
Platamodes Pr. GRE 33B7
Platia Magoula Zarkou GRE 6B2
Plavis fl. ITL *Piave* 109E2
Pleistarcheia TKY *Kapıkırı* 71F3

Plemmyrion Akron ITL *Punta della Maddalena* 43F4
Plestia ITL *Colfiorito* 89C2
Pleuron GRE *Gyphtokastro/Petrovouni* 14B2, 33B5
Plotinoupolis GRE *Didymoteikhon* 152D4
Podouke IND *Arikamedu, Virampatnam* 175F5
Poetovio SVN *Ptuj* 109H1, 131E3, 149E4
Poggio Buco ITL 81C4
Poiessa GRE *Poiesses* 56C3
Pola CRO *Pula* 92D1, 109F3
Polemonion TKY 162B2
Poliochni GRE 7E6
Polla ITL 92E3
Pollentia ITL *Pollenzo* 108A3
Pollentia SPN *Alcudia de Polensa* 138F3
Polyrrenia GRE *Epano Palaiokastro* 71C4, 154A1
Pompei Tropaea SPN *Panissars* 138F2, 147D4
Pompeia JOR *Umm Qeis* 74D3
Pompeii ITL *Pompei* 87C3, 92D3, **123**
Pompeiopolis TKY *Viranşehir* 73E5, 159F4
Pompeiopolis TKY *Taşköprü* 159F1
Pompelo SPN *Pamplona* 138D1, 147B4
Pomptinae Paludes ITL *Pianura Pontina* 86C3
Pons Aeli UKG *Newcastle upon Tyne* 135D1
Pons Aeni GER *Pfaffenhofen am Inn* 149C4, 151E4
Pontecagnano ITL 83E3
Pontia Ins. ITL *Ponza* 92D3
Pontica *(diocese)* TKY 189G4
Pontus TKY 2D1, 68C2, 131H4, 162A2
Pontus Euxinus *Black Sea* 19F4, 68B1, 153F3, 162A1
Pontus Polemoniacus TKY 189H3
Populonium ITL *Populonia* 81B4, 83B2, 89A2, 108C4
Porolissum ROM *Moigrad-Jac* 152C1
Porphyrites M. EGY *Gebel Abu Dukhan* 171C4
Porsuk TKY 2C2
Porthmia UKR 34B2
Portunata Ins. CRO *Dugi otok* 109G3
Portus ITL 109E6, 117B2, **120**, 182D1
Portus Blendium SPN *Suances* 138C1, 147A4
Portus Dubris UKG *Dover* 133F6
Portus Lemanis UKG *Lympne* 133F6
Portus Luguidonis ITL 113B1
Portus Macedonum PAK 174C2
Poseidonia ITL *Paestum* 18B1, 83E3, 87D3
Poseidonion Pr. GRE *Kassandras* 32E3
Posideion SYR *Ras el-Bassit* 19G5, 74E1
Potaissa ROM *Turda* 152C1, 179E3
Poteidaia GRE *Nea Potidaia* 18D2, 30D2, 48D2, 59C2
Potentia ITL *Potenza* 89F4, 111B1
Potentia *(in Picenum)* ITL *Porto Recanati* 92D2, 109F4
Praeneste ITL *Palestrina* 83C3, 92B3, 109E5, 117D2
Praesidium FRA 108B5
Praetorium Agrippinae NET *Valkenburg* 147D1
Praetuttii ITL 85D2
Praevalitana *(province)* ALB/MNE 189E3
Praisos GRE *Vaveloi* 21D4, 154D2
Prasiai GRE *Paralio Leonidi* 33D7, 48C5
Prasias L. GRE 32E2
Prasii IND *Magadhas* 175G1
Premis EGY *Kasr Ibrim* 171C6
Priansos GRE *Kastellos* 154C2
Priapus TKY *Karabiğa* 49G2

Priene TKY *Güllübahçe* 31G4, **41,** 71F3, 159A3
Prinias GRE 16D4
Privernum ITL *Madonna di Mezzagosto* 83D3, 89C3, 92C4
Probalinthos GRE 36D3
Prochyta Ins. ITL *Procida* 87A3
Proconnesus TKY *Marmara* 31H1, 49G2, 56E1, 159B2
Proerna GRE *Gynaikokastro* 32C4
Promona CRO *Tepljuh* 104D2
Pronnoi GRE *Poros* 56A3
Prophthasia AFG 61F3, 69F4
Propontis TKY *Sea of Marmara* 13E1, 31H1, 59F2, 159B2
Prosymna GRE 16C3
Prusa TKY *Bursa* 72B3, 159C2
Prusias ad Hypium TKY *Konuralp* 72C3, 159D2
Prusias ad Mare TKY *Gemlik* 72B3, 159C2
Prymnessos TKY *Sülün (Süğlün)* 159C3
Psaros fl. TKY *Seyhan Nehri* 54C2
Pseira GRE 9D2
Pselchis EGY *El-Dakka* 68B5, 171C6
Psessoi RUS 34D1
Psophis GRE *Psophis/Tripotamoi* 33B6
Psychro cave GRE 9C2
Psyra Ins. GRE *Psara* 13D2, 31F3
Pteleon GRE *Gritsa* 14D1, 32D4
Ptolemais EGY *El-Mansha* 189G6
Ptolemais ISR *Tell Acco* 74D3, 161H4, 168B2, 171D1
Ptolemais LBY *Tolmeta/Tulmeitia* 141G2, 189E5
Ptolemais TKY *Kisik* 71F3
Ptolemais TKY *near Fığla Burnu* 72D5
Ptolemais Euergetis EGY *Medinet el-Fayum* 75A5, 171B3
Ptolemais Hermiou EGY *Menshyah* 68B4, 75B7, 171C4
Ptolemais Hormou EGY *el-Lahun* 171B3
Ptolemais Theron SUD 172C4
Pulchri Pr. TUN *Ras Sidi-Ali-el-Mekki* 94A6
Puṇḍranagara BAN *Mahasthan(garh)* 175H2
Pupput TUN *Souk-el-Abiod* 144D1
Pura PAK 23G4
Puteoli ITL *Pozzuoli* 87B2, 93B2, 109G6, 160A1
Pydna GRE 30C2, 59C2, 71C1
Pygela TKY *Kuşadası* 45D3
Pyla Kokkinokremos CYP 9C1
Pylai IRQ 54E3
Pylos GRE 6B5, 30B5, 48B5, 51
Pyramos fl. TKY *Ceyhan Nehri* 54C2, 73F5, 163H1
Pyrasos GRE *Nea Ankhialos* 14D1, 32D4
Pyrenaei M. FRA/SPN *Pyrenees* 94C2, 138D1, 147B4, 196B3
Pyretos fl. UKR 153E1
Pyrgi ITL *Santa Severa* 81C5, 86A1, 109E5, 117A1
Pyrra GRE *Megale Limne* 31G2, 49F3, 56E2
Pythion GRE 32C3
Pytho GRE *Delphi* 14D2

Qadesh SYR 2D3
Qarqar SYR 2D3
Qasr ash-Sharraba LBY 141E3
Qatna SYR 2D3
Qaw el-Kebir EGY 2B5

Quadi CZE/SVK 149E4
Quintana GER *Künzing* 149D3, 151F3
Quinto ITL 81B3
Quiza Cenitana ALG *el Bénian* 138E4, 140B1
Qumran PSE 168C5

Raeti ITL 85C1
Raetia *(province)* 108C1, 149C4, 151E3, 178D2
Rājagṛha IND *Rajgir* 175H2
Raphaneai SYR *Rafniye* 131G5, 162A4, 179G4
Raphia ISR *Tell es Sheikh Suleiman* 68C3, 74D4, 168A6, 171D2
Ratae UKG *Leicester* 133D5
Ratiaria BUL *Archer* 152C3, 189F3
Ravenna ITL *Ravenna* 81C2, 83C1, 109E3, 196D2
Reate ITL *Rieti* 83C2, 89C2, 95F3, 109E5
Red Sea see Rubrum Mare
Regae ITL *Le Murelle* 81C5
Regiae ALG *Arbal* 138D4
Reginoi UKG 133E6
Reginum GER *Regensburg* 149C3, 151E3
Regium ITL *Reggio di Calabria* 83E4, 92E4, 94C5, 111B3
Regium Lepidum ITL *Reggio nell'Emilia* 108D3
Regulbium UKG *Reculver* 133F6
Remesiana SRB *Bela Palanka* 152C3
Remi FRA 147D2
Resaina SYR *Tell Fakhariya* 162C3, 179H4
Resculum ROM *Bologa* 152C1
Rha fl. RUS *Volga* 23E1, 53D2, 69E1
Rhagai IRN *Ravy* 61E2, 69E3, 163G4
Rhaidestos TKY *Tekirdağ* 72A3, 153E4
Rhaikelos GRE 21B1
Rhambakia PAK *Khandewari?* 61G4
Rhamnous GRE *Rhamnous* 33F5, 36D2
Rhapta TAN *Dar es-Salaam* 53D4
Rhegion ITL *Reggio di Calabria* 18B2, 43F2, 48B5
Rheneia Ins. GRE 31E5, 79
Rhenus fl. ITL *Reno* 81B2, 108D3
Rhenus fl. *Rhein/Rhine* 104C1, 130C2, 147E1, 151A2
Rhinocolura EGY *El-Arish* 74C4, 171D2
Rhion Pr. GRE *Rion* 33B5
Rhithymna GRE *Rethymnon* 154B2
Rhizon MNE *Montenegro* 95H3
Rhoda SPN *Ciutadella de Roses* 99F1
Rhodanus fl. FRA/SWI *Rhône* 94D1, 108A1, 147D4, 149A4
Rhodios fl. TKY *Kocaçay* 30B6
Rhodope *(province)* BUL/GRE 189F3
Rhodope M. BUL/GRE *Rhodope* 22A2, 31E1, 152C3
Rhodopolis GEO *Vardtsikhe* 162D1
Rhodos (Ins.) GRE *Rhodos/Rhodes* 21E3, 31H6, 71F4, 155D3
Rhoiteion TKY *Baba Kale* 30A6, 49F2
Rhosos TKY *Uluçınar* 74E1, 163G2
Rhotanos fl. FRA *Tavignano* 108B5
Rhyndakos fl. TKY *Orhaneli/Koca Dere* 2B1, 72B4, 159B2
Rhytion? GRE *Rotasi* 13D4
Rider CRO *Danilo* 109H4
Riotinto SPN 138B3

Risinium MNE *Risan* 152A3
Risstissen GER 151C3
Rocca San Felice ITL 92E3
Roda SPN *Ciutadella de Roses* 94D3
Roma ITL *Roma/Rome* 86B2, **91, 101, 116,** 117B2, **128, 184**
Romula ROM *Reşca* 152D2
Rossano di Vaglio ITL 83E3
Rotomagus FRA *Rouen* 133F7, 147C2, 188B2
Rouession FRA *St-Paulien* 147D3
Rough Castle UKG 136C1
Roxolani ROM 152D2, 153E1
Rubi ITL *Ruvo di Puglia* 83E3
Rubico fl. ITL *Pisciatello/Rubicon* 104C2, 109E3
Rubrum Mare *Indian Ocean* 173G5
Rubrum Mare *Red Sea* 22C5, 53D3, 172C4, 179G6
Rudiae ITL *Rugge* 83F3
Rufrae ITL *Presenzano* 89D3
Rusaddir SPN *Melilla* 94B5, 138C4, 140B1
Rusazus ALG *Azeffoun* 138F4, 140C1
Ruscino FRA *Château Roussillon* 138F1, 147D4
Rusellae ITL *Roselle* 81B4, 89B2, 92C2, 108D4
Rusguniae ALG *Tementfoust* 138F4
Rusicade ALG *Ras Skikda* 95E4, 140D1, 144B1
Rusippisir ALG *Taksebt* 138F4
Ruspina TUN *Henchir-Tenir* 104C3
Rusuccuru ALG *Dellys* 94D4, 138F4, 140C1
Rutupiae UKG *Richborough* 133F6

S. Giovenale ITL 81C5
Saalburg GER 151B1
Saba YEM 172D5
Sabatha YEM *Shabwa* 173E5
Sabatinus L. ITL *Lago di Bracciano* 81C5, 86A1, 117B1
Sabha LBY 141F3
Sabini ITL 85C2
Sabinum ITL 117C1
Sabirian Huns 199F1
Sabis fl. FRA *Sambre* 147D1
Sabratha LBY *Sabrata, Zuaga* 95F5, 141E2
Sabrina fl. UKG *Severn* 133C5
Sachalitis OMN 173F5
Sacrum Pr. FRA *Finocchiarola* 108B4
Sacrum Pr. POR *Cabo de S. Vicente* 99A4, 138A4
Sadenoi IND *Śātavāhanas* 175E3
Saena ITL *Siena* 108D4
Saepinum ITL *Altilia* 89E3, 93C1, 109G6, 127C3
Saetabis SPN *Xátiva* 138D3
Sagalassos TKY 159C3
Sagrus fl. ITL *Sangro* 109G5
Saguntum SPN *Sagunto* 94C3, 99D2, 138D3
Sahara Desert 53B3
Saipros fl. ITL *Flumendosa* 113B2
Sais EGY *Sa el-Hagar* 2B4, 74A4, 171B2
Saittai TKY *Sidas Kale* 159B3
Saka UZB 23G1
Sakai IND/PAK *Śakas* 174D2
Sakasene AZE 22D2
Sakçagözü TKY 2D2
Sala HUN *Zalalövő* 149E4, 152A1

Sala MOR *Chellah/Rabat* 140A1
Sala Consilina ITL 83E3, 92E3
Salacia POR *Alcácer do Sal* 138A3
Salamis CYX 2C3, 74C2, 156C2, 161G3
Salamis (Ins.) GRE *Salamis* 14E3, **29,** 30D4, 36A5, 48D4
Salapia ITL *Lupara* 83E3
Salassi ITL 95E2, 108A2
Salbake M. TKY *Bozdağ* 159B4
Saldae ALG *Béjaïa* 94D4, 140C1, 144A1
Salernum ITL *Salerno* 87D3, 92E3, 111A1
Saliagos GRE 7E9
Salike Ins. SRI *Sri Lanka* 175G6
Salinae ITL 86B2
Sallentinum Pr. ITL *Capo Santa Maria di Leuca* 111D2
Salluvii FRA 147E4
Salmantica SPN *Salamanca* 138B2
Salmydessos TKY *Midye* 54A1
Salo fl. SPN *Jalón* 99D2, 138D2
Salona CRO *Solin* 109H4, 131E3, 152A3, 183E1
Salpensa SPN *Cortijo de la Coria* 138B4
Salpia ITL *Salpi* 95G3
Salvium BOS *Vrba* 152A3
Sam'al TKY *Zincirli* 2D2
Samaria PSE *Sebastiya* 2C4, 74D3, 168B3
Samaria *(region)* ISR/PSE 168B3
Samarobriva Ambianorum FRA *Amiens* 147C2
Same *(settlement)* GRE *Same* 30A4, 56A3
Samnites/Samnium ITL 85D3, 109G5
Samonion Pr. GRE *Cape Sideros* 154D2, 161E3
Samos (Ins.) GRE *Samos* 19E5, 31G4, 71F3, 155D2
Samos Ins. *(= Cephallania)* GRE 13A2, 14B2
Samosata TKY *Samsat* 2D2, 73G5, 162B3, 179H4
Samothrace (Ins.) GRE *Samothrake* 13D1, 31F1, 45C2, 155C1
Samsat see Samosata
Samum ROM *Cășei* 152C1
Samus fl. HUN/ROM *Someș* 152C1
Sane GRE *Tripiti?* 45B1, 48D2
Sangarius fl. TKY *Sakarya* 2B1, 60B2, 72C3, 159C2
Sant' Angelo ITL 93B2
Santicum AUS *Villach* 109F1
Santones FRA 147B3
Saphar YEM *Zafar* 172D5
Saqqara EGY 2B4
Sarangia AFG 23F3
Sarapis Ins. OMN *Masirah Is.* 173G4
Sarcapos ITL *Muravera* 113B2
Sardinia Ins. ITL *Sardinia* 88A3, 95E3, **113,** 178C4
Sardis TKY *Sart* 2A2, 22B2, 71F2, 159B3
Sardonyx M. IND *Satpura range* 175E3
Sardoum Mare 113A1
Sardus Pater, T. ITL *Temple of Antas* 113A2
Sarepta LEB *Sarafend* 161H3
Şarhöyük TKY O2B1
Sarmatia/Sarmatae 153E1, 180C1, 195D2
Sarmaticus Oceanus 149D1
Sarmizegetusa ROM *Grădiştea Muncelului* 179E3
Sarnus fl. ITL *Sarno* 87C2
Saronicus Sinus GRE *Saronic Gulf* 36A5

Saros fl. TKY *Seyhan Nehri* 2C2, 73E5, 162A4
Sarpedon Pr. TKY 31F1
Sarsina ITL *Sarsina* 89B1, 109E4
Sarteano ITL 81C4
Saspeires IRN 23E2
Satala TKY *Sadak* 162B2, 179H3
Saticula ITL *S. Agata dei Goti* 93C2
Satnioeis fl. TKY *Yermidere Çay* 13D2
Satrachos fl. CYP *Dhiarrizos* 156A3
Satricum ITL *Borgo Le Ferriere* 81D6, 86C3, 92B4, 117C3
Sattagydia AFG 23H3
Saturnia ITL *Saturnia* 81C4, 92C2, 108D5, 127A6
Sava fl. ALG *Oued bou Sellam/Oued Summam* 144A1
Savaria HUN *Szombathely* 149E4, 152A1, 189E2
Save YEM *as-Sawa* 172D6
Savia *(province)* BOS/CRO 188D3
Savo ITL *Savona* 95E2
Savus fl. *Sava* 104D2, 109G1, 152A2
Saxa Rubra ITL *Grottarossa* 117B1
Saxons 196B1
Scadinavia NOR/SWE 149D1
Scaldis fl. BGM/NET *Escaut/Schelde* 147D1
Scallabis POR *Santarém* 138A3
Scamander fl. TKY *Menderes Çay* 13D1, 31G2
Scarbantia HUN *Sopron-Scarbantia* 149E4, 152A1
Scardona CRO *Skradin* 109H4
Sciathus Ins. GRE 27C2
Scitis Ins. UKG *Skye* 132A3
Scodra ALB *Shkodra* 95H3, 105E2, 152B3
Scolacium (Minervium) ITL *Roccelletta* 92E4
Scordisci CRO 152A2
Scultenna fl. ITL *Panaro* 108D3
Scupi MKD *Skopje* 152B3, 189E3
Scylletium/Scolacium ITL *Roccelletta* 92E4, 111C3
Scyrus Ins. GRE *Skyros* 13C2, 49E3, 59D3, 155C2
Scythia 34B1, 53D1, 60C1, 153E1
Scythia (Minor) *(province)* ROM *Dobrogea* 153E2, 189F3, 197G2
Scythopolis ISR *Beisan Beth Shean* 74D3, 162A5, 168C3, 171D1
Seabegs UKG 136C1
Sebaste PSE *Sebastiya* 74D3, 168B3
Sebaste *(in Phrygia)* TKY *Selçikler* 159C3
Sebaste *(in Cilicia)* TKY *Ayaş* 159F4
Sebasteia TKY *Sivas* 162B2, 189H4
Sebastopolis GEO *Sukhumi* 162C1
Sebastopolis *(in Caria)* TKY *Kızılca* 159C3
Sebastopolis *(in Pontus)* TKY *Sulusaray* 162A2
Sebennytikon Stoma EGY 171B1
Sebennytos EGY *Sammanud* 2B4, 74B4, 171B2
Sebethus fl. ITL 87C2
Sebinnus L. ITL *L. Iseo* 108C2
Sedetani SPN 99D2
Segeda SPN *Poyode Mara/Durón* 99D2, 138D2
Segedunum UKG *Wallsend* 135D1
Segesta ITL *Segesta* 94B5, 113C3
Segobriga SPN *Cerro de Cabeza del Griego* 99C2, 138C3
Segodunum FRA *Rodez* 147D4
Segontia SPN *Sigüenza* 94B3, 99C2

Segovia SPN 138C2
Segusio ITL *Susa* 147E3, 188C3
Seleucia IRN *Ja Nishin* 69E4
Seleucia IRQ *Tell Omar* 68D3, 105H4, 162D5
Seleucia TKY *Selef, Bayat* 72C5
Seleucia ad Calycadnum TKY *Silifke* 74C1, 159F4, 189G4
Seleucia ad Eulaeum IRN *Shush* 69E3
Seleucia ad Maeandrum TKY *Aydın* 71F3
Seleucia Tracheia TKY *Silifke* 74C1
Seleucis SYR 68C3
Seleukeia JOR *Tell Abil* 74E3
Seleukeia *(W Side)* TKY 72C5
Seleukeia Pieria TKY *Kapısuyu/Kaboussié* 73F6, 163G2, 183G2
Seleukeia pros to Pyramo TKY *Yakapınar* 73E5
Selge TKY *Zerk* 72C5, 159D4
Selgoouai UKG 132C4
Selinous TKY *Kale Tepe, Gazipaşa* 159D4
Selinous/Selinus ITL *Selinunte* 18A3, 43B3, 94B6
Sellasia GRE *Palaiogoulas* 33C7, 71C3
Selymbria TKY *Silivri* 19H1, 49G1, 59F2, 153E4
Semnus fl. ITL *Sinni* 111B1
Sena Gallica ITL *Senigallia* 92D2, 95G2, 109F4
Sena Iulia ITL *Siena* 92B3
Senia CRO *Senj* 104D2, 109G3
Senones FRA 147C2
Senones ITL 85C2
Sentinum ITL 89C1, 109E4
Sepias Pr. GRE *Ag. Georgios* 32D3
Sepphoris ISR *Zippori/Saffuriye* 168C2
Septem Maria ITL 109E3
Sequana fl. FRA *Seine* 104B1, 133F8, 147C2
Sequani FRA 147E3
Sequania *(province)* FRA 188C3
Serabit el-Chadim EGY 2C5
Seraglio GRE 7G9, 16F3
Serapeum EGY 75B5
Serdica BUL *Sofia* 152C3, 189E3, 193E3
Sermylia GRE *Ormylia?* 32E2, 45A1, 48D2
Servia GRE 6B2
Sesklo GRE 6C2
Sestinum ITL *Sestino* 127B2
Sestos TKY *Yalikabat?* 13D1, 30A6, 71E1, 152D4
Setaea GRE *Siteia* 154D2
Setantioi UKG 133C5
Setia ITL *Sezze* 92C4, 117D3
Sevan L. ARM 3F1
Sexi SPN *Almuñécar* 94B4, 99C4, 138C4
Seyitömer TKY 7I7
Shechem PSE 2D4
Sicca Veneria TUN *el Kef* 94A6, 144C1
Sicignano ITL 92E3
Sicilia *(province)* ITL *Sicily* 130D4, 178D4, 188D4
Sicilia Ins. ITL *Sicily* **43, 48, 113,** 182D2
Sicoris fl. AND/SPN *Segre* 104B2
Siculum Fretum ITL *Strait of Messina* 113E3
Sicyon GRE *Vasiliko* 14D3, 30C4, 48C4, 71C3
Side TKY *Selimiye* 60B2, 72C5, 159D4
Side *(in Pontus)* TKY 183H2
Sideris fl. IRN/TKM *Atrek* 163H3

Sidicini ITL 85D3
Sidon LEB *Saida* 2C3, 74D3, 161H3, 162A5
Sidyma TKY *Dodurga* 159C4
Sierra Leone SLE 53A4
Siga ALG *Takembrit* 94C5, 99D4, 138D4, 140B1
Sigeion TKY *Yenişehir* 19F2, 30A6, 49F2
Signia ITL *Segni* 92C4, 117D2
Sigon SYR *Sahyoun* 73F6
Sikanoi ITL 43C3
Sikelikos Porthmos ITL *Strait of Messina* 43F2
Sikeloi ITL 43D3
Sikinos (Ins.) GRE *Sikinos* 31E5, 56D4
Sila M. ITL *Sila* 111C2
Silandos TKY *Kara Selendi* 159B3
Sile EGY *Tell el-Ahmar* 2C4
Silia Ins. UKG *Guernsey* 133G7, 147A2
Silina Inss. UKG *Scilly Is.* 133A7
Sillyon TKY *Asar Köy* 159D4
Silures UKG 133C6
Simitthu TUN *Chemtou* 140D1, 144C1
Simoeis fl. TKY *Dümruk Su* 13D1
Sinai EGY 2C4, 171C2, 197G5
Sinda CYX 9C1
Sindike RUS 34C3
Sindikos Limen RUS *Anapa* 34C3
Sindimana PAK 61G4
Singara IRQ *Balad Sinjar* 162C4, 179H4
Singidunum SRB *Beograd/Belgrade* 152B2, 179E3
Singitikos Sinus GRE *Kolpos Agiou Orous/Singitic Gulf* 32F3
Singos GRE 32E3, 45B1, 48D2
Sinope TKY *Sinop* 19G4, 73C2, 162A1, 183H1
Sinthos fl. *Indus* 174D1
Sinuessa ITL *Torre S. Limato* 87A1, 93A2
Siphai GRE *Aliki* 48C4
Siphnos (Ins.) GRE *Siphnos* 21C3, 31E5, 45B3, 56D3
Sipontum ITL *Siponto* 83E3, 92E3, 109H6, 127D3
Sippar IRQ *Tell Abu Habba* 3F4, 54A4
Sipylos M. TKY *Manisa Dağı* 13E2, 31H3
Sirenae T. ITL 87B3
Siris ITL 18C1
Sirmium SRB *Sremska Mitrovica* 152B2, 189E3, 197E2
Siscia CRO *Sisak* 104D2, 109H2, 152A2, 189E3
Sissi GRE 9C2
Sithonia GRE 30D2
Sitifis ALG *Sétif* 140C1, 144A2, 188C4
Sittacene IRQ 22D3
Sittake IRQ 54F3
Sızma Höyük TKY 2C2
Skardon M. MKD *Šar planina* 152B4
Skarkos GRE 7E9
Skepsis TKY *Kurşunlu Tepe* 31G2, 45C1, 71E1
Skiathos (Ins.) GRE *Skiathos* 30D3, 56C2
Skillous GRE *Makrisia* 33B6
Skione GRE 18D2, 30D2, 45A1, 48D2
Skiritis GRE 30C5
Sklavokambos GRE 9C2
Skotoussa GRE *Ag. Triada/Souphli* 32C4
Skudra BUL/GRE 22A2
Skylakion M. ITL 111B3

Skyllaion Pr. GRE *Spathi* 33E6
Skyros (Ins.) GRE *Skyros* 31E3, 45B2, 56D2
Slavs 199E1
Smyrna TKY *Izmir* 21E2, 31G4, 71F2, 159A3
Smyrnophoros Chora DJI/SOM 172D6
Sogdian Rock UZB 61G2
Sogdiana UZB 23G2, 61G2, 69G2
Sohar OMN 173G3
Soknopaiou Nesos EGY *Dima* 75A5, 171B2
Sollentia Ins. CRO *Šolta* 109H4
Sollion GRE 48B3
Soloeis ITL *Solanto di Santa Flavia* 43C2
Soloi CYX 74C2, 156B2
Soloi TKY *Viranşehir* 60B2, 73E5, 159F4
Soloke IRN *Ja Nishin* 69E4
Solorius M. SPN *Sierra Nevada* 99C4, 138C4
Solous ITL *Solanto di Santa Flavia* 94B5
Soluntum ITL *Solunto* 113D3
Solygeia GRE *Galataki* 48C4
Solyma M. TKY *Furuncuk* 13F3
Sonus fl. IND *Son* 175G2
Sophene TKY *Dersim* 162B3
Sopianae HUN *Pécs* 149F4, 152A2, 189E3
Sora ITL *Sora* 93A1
Sorabile ITL *Fonni* 113B1
Soracte M. ITL *Monte Soratte* 86B1
Sorai IND 175F5
Sorviodurum GER *Straubing* 149D3, 151F3
Sos Höyük TKY *Yiğittaşı* 3E1
Sotira CYP 9B2
Soudeta M. GER *Erzgebirge?* 149C3
Sounion GRE 36D6, 48D4
Sounion Pr. GRE 14E3, 31E4
Soura SYR *Sourriya* 162B4
Sousia IRN *Tus* 61F2
Spalatum CRO *Split* 109H4, **186**
Spania POR/SPN *Iberian peninsula* 195A4
Sparta GRE *Sparti* 13B3, 30C5, **40**, 71C3, 155B2
Spartolos GRE 32D2, 45A1, 48C2
Spasinou Charax IRQ *Jebel Khayabir* 69E4, 163E6, 173E1
Spathes GRE 6B2
Spercheios fl. GRE *Spercheios* 13B2, 30C3
Sphakteria Ins. GRE 30B5, **51**
Sphettos GRE 33E6, 36C4
Spina ITL *Valpega* 18C3, 81C2, 83C1, 109E3
Splonum BOS *Gor. Vrtače* 152A2
Spoletium ITL *Spoleto* 83C2, 92C2, 95F3, 109E5
Sporades Inss. GRE 31G4
Śrāvastī IND *Set Mahet* 175G1
Stabiae ITL *Varano* 87C3
Stageira GRE 18D2, 32E2, 48D2, 59C2
Stektorion TKY 159C3
Steno GRE 6A3
Stobi MKD *Pustogradsko* 152C4
Stolos GRE 45A1, 48D2
Stracathro UKG 132C3
Stratonicaea TKY *Siledik, Yağmurlu* 72B4, 159B3
Stratonikeia TKY *Eskihisar* 7G8, 71F3, 159B4
Stratonos Pyrgos ISR *Qesaria/Qaisariye* 168B3
Stratos GRE *Sourovigli* 33B5, 48B3, 71B2

Strepsa GRE *Basilika?* 45A1
Strongyle Ins. ITL *Stromboli* 43F1, 111B3
Strophades Inss. GRE 30B5
Strymon fl. BUL/GRE *Struma* 18D1, 30D1, 59C1, 152C3
Stuberra MKD *Čepigovo* 152B4
Stymphaia GRE 30C2
Stymphalos GRE *Stymphalia* 14D3, 33C6
Styra GRE *Nea Styra* 13C2, 33F5, 45B2
Styx fl. GRE *Mavronero* 14C2
Suana ITL *Sovana* 81C4
Suarattaratae IND 174D2
Sublaqueum ITL *Subiaco* 117D2
Sububus fl. MOR *Oued Sebou* 140A1
Sucro SPN *Algemesi?* 99D3
Sucro fl. SPN *Júcar (Xúquer)* 94C3
Suebi GER 149C2, 196D2
Suebicum Mare *Baltic Sea* 149D1
Suel SPN *Sohail* 138C4
Suessa Aurunca ITL *Sessa Arunca* 83D3, 87A1, 89D3, 93A2
Suessa Pometia? ITL 86C3
Suessetani SPN 99D1
Suessula ITL 83D3, 87C2, 93B2, 127C3
Suevic Kingdom 199A2
Sufasar ALG *Amoura* 138F4
Sufes TUN *(Henchir) Sbiba* 144C2
Sufetula TUN *Sbeitla* 140D1, 144C2
Sulcis ITL *S. Antioco* 83A4, 95E4, 113A2
Sulcis fl. ITL *Cixerri* 113A2
Sulmo ITL *Sulmona* 83D2, 109F5
Sumelocenna GER *Rottenburg am Neckar* 151B3
Summerston UKG 136B2
Superaequum ITL 109F5
Surrentum ITL *Sorrento* 87B3
Susa IRN *Shush* 3G4, 23E3, 69E3, 163F5
Susiana IRN *Khuzistan* 60D3, 69E3
Sutrium ITL *Sutri* 81C5, 92C2, 109E5
Syagros Pr. YEM *Ras Fartak* 173F5
Syangela TKY *Kaplan Dağ* 45D3
Sybaris ITL *Sibari/Copia* 18C1, 83E4
Sybota Inss. GRE *Sivota* 30A3, 48A3
Sybrita GRE *Thronos* 154B2
Syedra TKY 159D4
Syene EGY *Aswan* 68B5, 75C8, 171C5, 195F8
Syia GRE *Sougia* 154A2
Symaethus/Symaithos fl. ITL *Simeto* 43E3, 113D3
Syme (Ins.) GRE *Syme* 13E3, 31H5, 49G5
Syna M. EGY *Jabal Mūsā* 171D3
Synaos TKY *Simav* 159B3
Synnada TKY *Şuhut* 72C4, 159C3, 189G4, 193F4
Syracusae/Syrakousai ITL *Siracusa/Syracuse* 18B3, 43F3, **51**, 113E3, 130D4
Syrakousanos Limen FRA *Golfe de Porto Vecchio?* 108B6
Syrastrene IND *Saurāṣṭra* 174D3
Syria 2D3, 22C3, 161H3, 195F5
Syria *(province)* 105G3, 131H4
Syria Coele *(province)* SYR/TKY 162B4, 179G4, 189H4
Syria Palaestina *(province)* 162B6, 179G5
Syria Phoenice *(province)* 162A5, 179G4, 180D2

Syros (Ins.) GRE *Syros* 31E5, 56D3
Syrtica LBY 141F2
Syrtis Maior LBY *Gulf of Sidra* 95H6, 141F2
Syrtis Minor TUN *Gulf of Gabès* 95F5, 144D3

Tabai TKY *Tavas Kale* 159B3
Tabala TKY *Burgaz* 159B3
Taboca QAT *Qatar* 173F3
Tacape TUN *Gabès* 141E2, 144D3
Tader fl. SPN *Segura* 94B4
Tadinae ITL *Gualdo Tadino* 89C1, 109E4
Tadmor SYR *Tudmur* 2D3
Taexali *see* Taixaloi
Tafilalt MOR 140A2
Tagara IND *Ter* 175E3
Tagili SPN *Tijola* 138C3
Tagus fl. POR/SPN *Tejo/Tajo* 94B3, 99A2, 138E3
Taima SAU *Tayma'* 2D5
Tainaron GRE 33C8
Tainaron Pr. GRE *Tainaron* 30C6
Taixaloi UKG 132C3
Takyris EGY *Dahshur* 2B5
Tamalites IND *Tamluk* 175H2
Tamaros fl. UKG *Tamar* 133B7
Tamassos CYP 156B2
Tameia UKG *Cardean* 132C3
Tamesis fl. UKG *Thames* 133D6
Tamynai GRE 33F5
Tanager fl. ITL *Tanagro* 111B1
Tanagra GRE 30D4, 36A2, 48D4
Tanais fl. RUS *Don* 34D1
Tanarus fl. ITL *Tanaro* 108A3
Tanis EGY *San el-Hagar* 2C4, 74B4, 171C2
Tanitikon Stoma EGY 171C2
Tannetum ITL *Taneto* 108C3
Taochoi TKY 54E2
Taouion TKY *Büyük Nefes* 159F2
Taphros Fretum FRA/ITL *Straits of Bonifacio* 108B6
Taposiris Megale EGY *Abu Sir* 171B2
Taprobane Ins. SRI *Sri Lanka* 53F4, 175G6
Tapurioi IRN 23E3
Tara IRE 133A5
Taras ITL *Taranto* 18C1
Tarbelli FRA 147B4
Tarentum ITL *Taranto* 83F3, 92F3, 95H3, 111C1
Taricheai ISR *Mejdel* 168C2
Tarne? (Atarneus) TKY *Kale Tepe* 13E2
Tarnis fl. FRA *Tarn* 147C4
Tarquinii ITL *Tarquinia* 81C5, 83C2, 89B2
Tarracina ITL *Terracina* 83D3, 89C3, 109F6, 127C3
Tarraco SPN *Tarragona* 94C3, 99E2, 130B3, 138E2
Tarraconensis *(province)* SPN 130A3, 138C2, 178A3, 188B3
Tarsatica CRO *Trsat* 109G2
Tarsos/Tarsus TKY *Tarsos* 2C2, 54C2, 74C2, 159F4
Tartarus fl. ITL *Tartaro* 108D2
Tarus fl. ITL *Taro* 108C3
Tatta L. TKY *Tuz Göl* 159E3
Taucheira LBY *Tocra* 18D6, 141G2
Taulantioi ALB 59A2
Taurasia ITL 95E2

Taurike Chersonesos UKR *Crimea* 153G2
Taurini ITL 95E2
Taurisci CRO/SVN 109F1
Tauroi UKR 153G2
Tauromenion/Tauromenium ITL *Taormina* 43F2, 94C6, 113E3
Taurus M. TKY *Toros Dağları* 2D2, 159E4, 162B3, 197G4
Tavium *see* Taouion
Tavsan Adasi TKY 7G8
Taxila IND *Taxila* 61H3, 69H3
Taygetos M. GRE *Taygetos* 14C4, 30C5
Teanum Apulum ITL 83E3, 89E3
Teanum Sidicinum ITL *Teano* 83D3, 87B1, 89D3, 95G3
Teate ITL *Chieti* 89D2, 109G5
Tebtynis EGY *Tell Umm el-Buregat* 75A5, 171B3
Tectosages TKY 159E2
Tectoverdi UKG 132D4
Tegea GRE *Piali/Episkopi* 14D3, 33C6, 48C4, 71C3
Tegyra GRE *Pyrgos* 33D5
Teichioussa TKY 49G4
Teichos Dymaion GRE *Araxos* 6B4
Telamon ITL *Talamonaccio* 81B4, 89B2
Telandria Ins. TKY *Tersane Ada* 45E3
Teleboas fl. TKY *Kara Su* 54D2
Telesia ITL *S. Salvatore Telesino* 89E3, 93C2
Tell Balamun EGY 2B4
Tell el-Maskhuta EGY 2C4
Tell Halaf see Guzana
Tell Sukas SYR 19G5
Tell Tayinat see Kunulua
Telmessos TKY *Fethiye* 45E3, 72B5, 159C4
Telos GRE *Telos* 56E4
Tembris fl. TKY *Porsuk Çayı* 2B1, 159D2
Temenouthyrai TKY *Uşak* 159C3
Temnon M. TKY 159B2
Temnos M. TKY *Demirci/Simav Dağ* 159B3
Temos fl. ITL *Temo* 113A1
Tempe GRE 27B1
Tempsa ITL *Nocera Tirinese/Piano della Tirena* 92E4, 111B2
Tenedos (Ins.) TKY *Bozcaada* 31F2, 45C1, 49F2, 56D2
Tenos (Ins.) GRE *Tenos* 31F4, 45B3, 71D3, 155C2
Tentyra EGY *Dendera* 75C7, 171C4
Teos TKY *Sığacık* 19E5, 31G4, 71E2, 159A3
Tepe Nush-i Jan IRN 3G3
Tepebağları TKY 2C2
Terabdon Sinus PAK *Sonmiani Bay* 174C2
Terenouthis EGY *Kom Abou-Billou* 171B2
Tergeste ITL *Trieste* 92D1, 104D2, 109F2
Terias fl. ITL *S. Leonardo di Lentini* 43E3
Terina ITL *S. Eufemia Vetere* 18C2
Termera TKY *Asarlık* 45D3
Termes SPN *Montejo de Tiermes* 99C2
Termessos TKY *Güllük Dağ* 72C5, 159C4
Termessos Mikra TKY *İncealiler* 72B5
Terventum ITL *Trivento* 109G6
Tetios fl. CYP *Tremithios* 156B2
Tetrapolis GRE 36D3
Teurnia AUS *Sankt Peter in Holz* 109F1, 149D4

Teutloussa Ins. GRE *Seskli* 49G5
Teutoburgiensis Saltus GER *Teutoburger Wald* 147F1, 149B2
Thabor M. ISR *Tabor* 168C2
Thabraca TUN *Tabarca* 94A6, 144C1
Thabudeos ALG *Tehouda* 144A2
Thaenae TUN *Henchir-Thina* 141E1, 144D2
Thagaste ALG *Souk Ahras* 144B1
Thaima SAU *Tayma'* 2D5
Thamanaioi? IRN 23E3
Thamna PSE *Khirbet Tibne* 168B4
Thamugadi ALG *Timgad* **139**, 144A2
Thapsacus/Thapsakos SYR 54D3, 60C2
Thapsos Akron/Thapsus Pr. ITL *Penisola Magnisi* 43F3, 48B6
Thapsus TUN *Ras-Dimas* 94B6, 104C3, 144D2
Tharros ITL *S. Giovanni di Sinis* 83A4, 95E3, 113A2
Thasos (Ins.) GRE *Thasos* 21C1, 31E1, 49E1, 155C1
Thaumakoi GRE *Domokos Kastri* 32C4
Theadelpheia EGY *Kharabet Ihrit* 75A5, 171B3
Theangela TKY *Etrim* 72A5
Thebae GRE *Thivai/Thebes* 13C2, 30D4, 71C2, 155C2
Thebai EGY *Karnak/Luxor* 2C6, 75C7, 171C4
Thebai Phthiotides GRE *Akitsi/Mikrothivai* 32D4
Thebais EGY 171B4
Thebais *(province)* EGY 189G6
Thebe? TKY 13E1
Thekoa PSE *Khirbet et Tuqu* 168C5
Thelepte TUN *Medinet-el-Kedima* 144C2
Thenteos LBY *Edref? Zintan?* 141E2
Theodosia UKR *Feodosiya* 19G3, 34A3, 153H2
Theopetra cave GRE 6B2
Thera (Ins.) GRE *Santorini* 7E9, 19E5, 31F6, 155C3
Therma GRE 56E3
Thermae Himeraeae/Thermai Himeraiai ITL *Termini Imerese* 43C2, 94B5, 113D3
Thermae Selinuntinae ITL *Sciacca* 113C3
Thermaicus Sinus GRE *Thermaic Gulf* 30C2, 155B1
Therme GRE 27C1
Thermi GRE 7F7
Thermodon fl. TKY *Terme Çay* 54D1
Thermon GRE 16B2, 33B5, 71B2, 155B1
Thermopylae GRE 27C2, **28**, 30C3
Thespeia/Thespiai GRE *Erimokastro* 14D2, 33D5, 48C4, 71C2
Thesprotia/Thesprotoi GRE 13A2, 30A2, 59A2
Thessalia GRE *Thessaly* 16B2, 59B3, 105E3, 155B1
Thessalia *(province)* GRE 189E4
Thessaliotis GRE 30B3
Thessalonica GRE *Thessalonike/Salonica* 30D1, 71C1, 131F3, 155B1
Theveste ALG *Tébessa* 95E5, 130C4, 140D1, 144B2
Thibilis ALG *Announa* 144B1
Thiges TUN *Henchir-Ragoubet* 144C3
Thisbe GRE *Kakosi* 14D2, 33D5
Thmouis EGY *Tell Timai el-Amdid* 171B2, 193F5
Thorikos GRE *Thorikos* 16D3, 33F6, 36D6, 48D4
Thospitis L. TKY *Lake Van* 162D3
Thouria GRE *Aithaia/Hellenika* 33C7
Thracia *Thraki* 21D1, 31F1, 68A2
Thracia *(province)* 131F3, 189F3

Thraciae *(diocese)* 189F3
Thracium Mare 31E2
Thria GRE 36A3
Thronion GRE *Palaiokastro eis ta marmara* 14D2, 32D4, 48C3
Thronoi CYP *Tornos* 156C2
Thryoessa? GRE 14C3
Thubactis LBY *Gasr Ahmed, Misurata Marina?* 141F2
Thubunae ALG *Tobna* 144A2
Thuburbo Maius TUN *Henchir-Kasbat* 141E1, 144C1
Thubursicum Numidarum ALG *Khamissa* 144B1
Thugga TUN *Dougga* 140D1, 144C1
Thule? NOR 53B1
Thule? Ins. ISL 53A1
Thule? Ins. UKG *Shetland* 53B1, 132E1
Thurii ITL *Sibari/Copia* 83E4, 92E4, 95G3, 111C2
Thuringians 199C1
Thyateira TKY *Akhisar* 72B4, 159B3, 161F2
Thymbrion TKY 54B2
Thyrea GRE *Kynouria* 21B3, 33C6, 48C4
Thyrides Pr. GRE *Pounta* 33C8
Thyron GRE 14C3
Thyrreion GRE *Thyrion* 32A4, 71B2
Thyrsos fl. ITL *Tirso* 113A1
Thysdrus TUN *el-Djem* 144D2
Thyssos GRE *Skala Zographou* 45B1, 48D2
Tibareni TKY 22C2, 54D2
Tiberiadis Mare *Sea of Galilee* 168C2
Tiberias ISR *Tiberias* 168C2
Tiberiopolis TKY *Yunisler* 159D3
Tiberis fl. ITL *Tevere/Tiber* 81C3, 86B2, 92C2, 109E4
Tibiscum ROM *Jupa* 152C2
Tibiskos fl. ROM/SRB *Timis* 152B2
Tibula ITL *S. Teresa di Gallura* 113B1
Tibur ITL *Tivoli* 86C2, 89C2, 109E5, 117C2
Ticinum ITL *Pavia* 108B2
Ticinus fl. ITL/SWI *Ticino* 95E2, 108B1
Tieion TKY *Hisarönü* 72D3, 159D1
Tifata M. ITL *Monti di Maddaloni* 87B2, 95G3
Tifernum Mataurense ITL *S. Angelo in Vado* 109E4, 127B2
Tifernum Tiberinum ITL *Città di Castello* 109E4
Tifernus fl. ITL *Biferno* 109G6
Tigani GRE 7F8
Tigava ALG *Bel-Abbès/Ouled-Abbès* 138E4
Tigisis ALG *Ain el Bordj* 192C4
Tigranocerta TKY 68D2, 73H5, 162C3
Tigris fl. *Tigris* 3G4, 23E3, 54E3, 162C3
Tijirhi LBY 141F4
Tikarios fl. FRA *Taravo* 108B5
Til Barsip SYR *Tell Ahmar* 2D2
Tiliaventum fl. ITL *Tagliamento* 109F2
Tille TKY 2D2
Tillibari TUN *Remada* 141E2
Tilmen Höyük TKY 2D2
Timbuktu MLI 53A3
Timgad ALG **139**
Timna ISR 2C4
Tin Hinan ALG 140C4
Tinea fl. UKG *Tyne* 135C1
Tingi MOR *Tangier* 94A5, 130A4, 138B4, 140A1

Tinna fl. ITL *Tenna* 109F4
Tios TKY *Hisarönü* 19F4, 72D3
Tipasa *(E Iol Caesarea)* ALG *Tipasa* 94D4, 138E4, 140C1
Tipasa *(S Hippo Regius)* ALG *Tifech* 140D1, 144B1
Tiryns GRE *Tirynthos* 14D3, 27C3, 33D6
Titius fl. CRO *Krka* 109H4
Tittoi SPN 99D2
Tlos TKY *Düver* 159C4
Tmolus M. TKY *Boz Dağ* 13E2, 31H4, 159B3
Toletum SPN *Toledo* 99C2, 138C3
Tolfa ITL 81C5
Toliatis Ins. UKG *Thanet* 133F6
Tolistobogioi TKY 159D2
Tolosa FRA *Toulouse* 138E1, 147C4, 196B2
Tombouze MLI *Timbuktu* 140B6
Tomis ROM *Constanţa* 19F3, 153E2, 183F1, 189F3
Tonzos fl. BUL/TKY 152D3
Topaklı TKY 2C2
Toprakkale TKY 3F2
Torboletai SPN 99D2
Toretai RUS 34C3
Torikos RUS *Gelendzhik* 34C3
Toronaikos Sinus GRE *Gulf of Kassandra* 32E3
Torone GRE *Torone* 6D2, 18D2, 32E3, 48D2
Tosale IND *Dhauli?* 175H3
Toubios fl. UKG *Tywi* 133B6
Toumba GRE *Thessaloniki suburb* 6C1
Toumba tou Skourou CYX 9B1
Trachis GRE 14D2, 30C3, 71C2
Traianoupolis GRE *Loutra Traianopolis?* 152D4, 189F4
Traiectum NET *Utrecht* 149A2
Tralles TKY *Aydın* 31H4, 72B5, 159B3, 193F4
Transpadana ITL 108A2
Trapezous/Trapezus TKY *Trabzon* 19H4, 54D1, 73G3, 162C2
Trasumennus L. ITL *Lago Trasimeno* 81C4, 95F2, 109E4
Traversette, Col de la FRA/ITL 95E2
Trea ITL 109F4
Treba ITL *Trevi* 89C2
Trebia fl. ITL *Trebbia* 95E2, 108B3
Trebula Mutuesca ITL *Monteleone Sabino* 89C2
Trebula Suffenas ITL 89C2
Tremithous CYP 156C2
Tres Tabernae ITL 117C3, 160A1
Treveri GER/LUX 147E2, 149A3
Triakontaschoinos EGY/SUD 172A3
Trianda GRE 7G9
Tricasses FRA 147D2
Trichonis L. GRE *Gavalou* 33B5
Tricorii FRA 94D2
Tridentum ITL *Trento* 108D1
Trifanum ITL 89D3
Trikka/Trikke GRE *Trikkala/Ag. Nikolaos* 14C1, 32B3
Trikorynthos GRE 36D3
Trimithis EGY *Amheida* 171A4
Trinius fl. ITL *Trigno* 109G5
Trinobantes UKG 104B1, 133E6
Triokala? ITL *Caltabellotta* 113C3

Triopion TKY *Kumyer* 31H5, 49G5
Triphylia GRE 30B4
Tripolis LEB *Tarabulus/Tripoli* 74E2, 162A4
Tripolis ad Maeandrum TKY *Buldun* 159B3
Tripolitana LBY/TUN 141E2, 188D5
Tripuri IND *Tewar* 175F2
Tris Langades GRE 6A3
Trisantona fl. UKG *Trent* 133D5
Tritaia GRE *Ag. Marina* 33B6
Triton fl. GRE *Platyperama/Giophyros* 154C2
Tritonis L. LBY *Mugtaa el-Chebrit* 141G2
Tritonis Palus TUN *Chott el Jérid* 144B3
Trivicum ITL 127D3
Troesmis ROM *Igliţa* 153E2
Trogodos M. CYP *Olympos/Troodos* 156A2
Trogodytae EGY 171D6
Trogodytice ERT/SUD 172C5
Troia TKY *Hisarlık/Troy* **4–5**, 13D1, 30A6, 71E1, 159A2
Troizen GRE *Damala* 14E3, 30D4, 48D4, 71C3
Trokmoi TKY 159F2
Tropaeum Augusti FRA *La Turbie* 108A4, 147E4
Tropaeum Traiani ROM *Adamclisi* 153E3
Troulli CYX 9C1
Truentus fl. ITL *Tronto* 109F5
Trypiti GRE 9C3
Tsangli GRE 6C2
Tsikalario GRE 16E3
Tsoungiza GRE 6B4
Tubusuctu ALG *Tiklat* 138F4
Tucca ALG *Merdja* 144A1
Tucci SPN *Martos* 99C3, 138C3
Tuder ITL *Todi* 83C2, 89C2, 92C2, 109E5
Tulliassi ITL 108C1
Tullum FRA *Toul* 147E2, 149A3
Tungri BGM 147D1
Tunip SYR *Asharne* 2D3
Tunis TUN 94A6
Turdetania/Turdetani SPN 94A4, 99B3, 138C3
Turduli SPN 99B3
Turris Libisonis ITL *Porto Torres* 108B6, 113A1
Turris Tamalleni TUN *Telmine* 144C3
Tuscana ITL 81C5
Tuscia et Umbria ITL 188D3
Tusculum ITL *Tuscolo* 86C2, 89C3, 109E6, 117C2
Tushpa TKY *Van* 3F2
Tuwat ALG 140B3
Tyana TKY *Kemerhisar* 2C2, 54C2, 73E5, 159F3
Tylissos GRE 9C2
Tylos Ins. BAH *Bahrain* 173F2
Tymphaia GRE 59B2
Tyndaris ITL *Tindari* 43E2, 94C5, 113E2
Tyndis IND *Ponnāni* 175E5
Tyndis fl. IND *Mahanadi* 175G3
Tynnas fl. IND *Pennar* 175F4
Tyrambe RUS *Stanitsa Peresyp* 34C2
Tyras UKR *Belgorod-Dnestrovskiy* 19F3, 153F2
Tyras fl. MOL/UKR *Dniester* 153F1
Tyriaion TKY *Teke Kozağacı* 54C2, 159D3
Tyritake UKR *Arshintsevo* 34B2
Tyrrhenoi ITL 85C2

Tyrrhenum Mare *Tyrrhenian Sea* 83C3, 95F3, 108B4
Tyrus LEB *es-Sur/Tyre* 2C3, 60C3, **64**, 74D3, 168B1

Ubii GER 147E1, 149A3
Ubus fl. ALG *Oued Seybouse* 144B1
Üçtepe TKY 3E2
Ulpia Traiana GER *Xanten* 147E1, 149A2
Ulpia Traiana Sarmizegetusa ROM *Sarmizegetusa* 152C2
Ulpiana SRB *Gračanica* 152B3
Ulubrae ITL 92B4
Uluburun (shipwreck) TKY 7I9
Ulucak TKY 7G8
Umbri/Umbria ITL 85C2, 109E4
Umbro fl. ITL *Ombrone* 81B4, 108D4
Ur IRQ *Tell Muqayyar* 3F4
Urartu 3F2
Urbana ITL 93B2
Urbanus fl. BOS *Vrbas* 152A2
Urbs Salvia ITL *Urbisaglia* 89D1
Urgo Ins. ITL *Isola di Gorgona* 108C4
Urmia L. IRN 3F2
Urso SPN *Osuna* 94B4, 99B3, 138B3
Uruk IRQ *Warka* 3F4, 68D3, 163E6
Urvinum Mataurense ITL *Urbino* 127B2
Uselis ITL *Usellus* 113A2
Usha ISR *Khirbet Hushe* 168B2
Ustica Ins. ITL 113C2
Utica TUN *Henchir-bou-Chateur* 94A6, 104C3, 144D1
Uticensis Sinus TUN *Gulf of Tunis* 113A3
Utigur Huns 199F2
Uxellodunum FRA *Capdenac* 147C4
Uxelodunum UKG *Stanwix* 135B1
Uzentum ITL *Ugento* 83F4

Vaccaei SPN 94A3, 99B1
Vada Sabatia ITL *Vado Ligure* 108B3
Vada Volaterrana ITL *Vada* 81A4, 108C4
Vadimonis L. ITL *Laghetto di Bassano* 89C2
Vaga TUN *Beja* 144C1
Vaiśālī IND 175G1
Valentia FRA *Valence* 147D3
Valentia ITL *see* Oualentia
Valentia SPN *Valencia* 99D3, 138D3
Valeria SPN *Valeria de Arriba* 138D3
Valeria *(province)* HUN 189E3
Valtos GRE 6C2
Van Kalesi TKY 3F2
Van L. TKY 3E2
Vanacini FRA 108B4
Vandal Kingdom 199B3
Vandals 197E1
Varus fl. FRA/ITL *Var* 108A3, 147E4
Vascones SPN 99D1
Vasilika GRE 6C1
Vasiliki GRE 9D2
Vectis Ins. UKG *Isle of Wight* 133D7
Vedra fl. *see* Ouedra fl.
Vegium CRO *Karlobag* 109G3
Veh Ardashir IRN *Abu Khshaim* 173G1
Veii ITL *Veio* 81D5, 83C2, 86B1, 117B1

Veldidena AUS *Wilten* 149C4, 151E4
Veleia ITL *Velleia* 92B1, 108C3, 127A1
Veleia SPN *Iruña* 138C1
Velestino (Pherai) GRE 6C2
Velia ITL *Castellamare di Velia* 83E3, 89E4, 95G3
Veliocasses FRA 133E7
Velitrae ITL *Velletri* 86C2, 89C3, 92B4, 117C3
Venafrum ITL *Venafro* 93B1
Veneti FRA 133C8, 147A2
Veneti/Venetia ITL 85C1, 109E2
Venetia et Histria 188D3
Venicones *see* Ouenikones
Venonis UKG *High Cross* 133D6
Venta (Belgarum) UKG *Winchester* 133D6
Venta (Icenorum) UKG *Caistor-by-Norwich* 133F5
Venta (Silurum) UKG *Caerwent* 133C6
Venusia ITL *Venosa* 89F3, 92E3, 111B1
Verbanus L. ITL *L. Maggiore* 108B2
Vercellae ITL *Vercelli* 83A1, 108B2, 147F3
Vercovicium UKG *Housesteads* 135C1
Verona ITL *Verona* 83B1, 108D2
Verteris UKG *Brough-under-Stainmore* 135C2
Verucchio ITL 81D3
Verulae ITL *Veroli* 89D3
Verulamium UKG *St. Albans* 133E6
Vesontio FRA *Besançon* 147E3, 149A4, 188C2
Vestini ITL 85D2
Vesunna FRA *Périgueux* 147C3
Vesuvius M. ITL *Monte Vesuvio* 87C2
Vetera GER *Xanten* 130C2, 178C2
Vettones/Vettonia SPN 99B2, 138B2
Vetulonia ITL *Vetulonia* 81B4, 83B2, 89A2, 108D4
Via Aemilia ITL 108C2
Via Annia ITL 109E2
Via Appia ITL 86C3, 87A1, 111C1, 117D3
Via Aurelia FRA/ITL 108C3, 117A1, 147E4
Via Caecilia ITL 109F5
Via Campana ITL 87B2
Via Cassia ITL 109E4, 117B1
Via Claudia Augusta 108D1, 149C4, 151D4
Via Clodia ITL 117A1
Via Domitia FRA 147D4
Via Domitiana ITL 87A2
Via Egnatia 105F2, 152B4, 155B1
Via Flaminia ITL 109E4, 117B1
Via Hadriana EGY 171B3
Via Iulia Augusta ITL 108A4, 147F4
Via Latina ITL 86D2, 87A1, 109F6, 117C2
Via Nomentana ITL 117C2
Via Nova Traiana 162A6, 168C6, 171D2
Via Popilia ITL 87C2, 109E2
Via Postumia ITL 108D2
Via Praenestina ITL 117C2
Via Salaria ITL 109F5, 117C1
Via Sebaste TKY 159C3
Via Severiana ITL 117C3
Via Tiburtina ITL 117C2
Via Traiana ITL 109H6
Via Valeria ITL 109F5, 117C1
Viadua fl. *see* Ouiadoua fl.
Vibo Valentia ITL *Vibo Valentia* 92E4, 111B3, 127D4

Vicetia ITL *Vicenza* 83C1, 108D2
Victoria UKG *Inchtuthil* 132C3
Vicus Alexandri ITL *Forte Ostiense* 117B2
Vicus Augustanus Laurentium ITL *Tor Paterno* 117B2
Vicus Aurelianus GER *Öhringen* 151C3
Vidiśā IND *Besnagar* 175F2
Viducasses FRA 133D8
Vienna FRA *Vienne* 147D3, 188C3, 192C3
Viennensis *(diocese)* FRA 188B3
Vignacourt FRA 195B3
Villa Domitiani ITL *Castel Gandolfo* 117C2
Villa Hadriani ITL *Villa Adriana* 117C2
Villa Magna ITL 117D2
Villa Neronis ITL 117D2
Villa Traiani ITL 117D2
Villanova ITL 81C2
Viminacium SRB *Kostolac* 131E3, 152B2, 180C1, 189E3
Vindhya M. IND *see* Ouindion
Vindinum FRA *see* Ouindinon
Vindobona AUS *Vienna* 149E4, 152A1, 178D2
Vindogara Sinus *see* Ouindogara Sinus
Vindolanda UKG *Chesterholm* 135C1
Vindomora UKG *Ebchester* 135D1
Vindonissa SWI *Windisch* 130C2, 147F2, 151B4
Vindovala UKG *Rudchester* 135D1
Vinovia UKG *Binchester* 135D2
Vipasca *see* Metallum Vipascense
Virāta IND *Bairat* 175E1
Viroconium UKG *Wroxeter* 130B2, 133C5
Viromandui FRA 147D2
Virunum AUS *Zollfeld* 109G1, 130D2, 149D4, 188D3
Visentium ITL *Monte Bisenzio* 81C4, 109E5
Visigothic Kingdom 199A2
Visigoths 196B2
Vistula fl. POL *Wisla/San* 149F2
Visurgis fl. GER *Weser* 147F1, 149B2
Vitellia ITL 92B4
Vivara Ins. ITL 87B3
Vivisci FRA 147B3
Vocontii FRA 147E4
Voghiera ITL 81C2
Voidokilia GRE 6B5
Volaterrae ITL *Volterra* 81B3, 89A1, 108D4
Volcae FRA 94D2
Volcae Arecomici FRA 147D4
Volcae Tectosages FRA 147C4
Volos see Iolkos
Volsci ITL 85C3
Volsiniensis L. ITL *Lago di Bolsena* 81C4, 109E5
Volsinii ITL *Bolsena* 81C4, 83C2, 89B2, 109E5
Volturnum ITL 87A2, 93A2
Volturnus fl. ITL *Volturno* 87B1, 93B2, 109G6
Volubilis MOR *Ksar Pharaoun* 140A1
Voreda UKG *Old Penrith* 135B2
Vorgium FRA *Carhaix* 133C8, 147A2
Vosegus M. FRA *Vogesen /Vosges* 147E2, 151A3
Votadini *see* Otadinoi
Vounous CYX 9B1
Vrokastro GRE 16E4
Vrysi CYX 9B1
Vulci ITL 81C5, 83C2, 89B2, 108D5

Waddan LBY 141F3
Wadi Draa MOR 140A2
Wadi Sirhan SAU 172C1
Wargla ALG 140D2
Watling Lodge UKG 136C1
Westerwood UKG 136C1
Wilderness Plantation UKG 136B2

Xanthos TKY *Kınık* 2B3, 60B2, 72B6, 159C4
Xanthos fl. TKY *Esen Çay* 13F3
Xynias L. GRE 30C3
Xypete GRE 36B4

Yassıhöyük see Gordion
Yenibademli Höyük TKY 7E6
Yumuktepe-Mersin TKY 2C2

Zabas Megas fl. IRQ/TKY *Greater Zab* 3F2, 54E3, 162D3
Zabas Mikros fl. IRQ *Lesser Zab* 3F3, 54E3, 162D4
Zabi ALG *Bechilga* 138F4, 140C1, 144A2
Zacynthus (Ins.) GRE *Zakynthos* 13A2, 30B4, 48B4, 155A2
Zadrakarta IRN 53E2, 61E2, 69E3
Zagora GRE 16D3
Zagrus M. *Zagros* 3F3, 68D2, 163E4
Zama Regia TUN *Jama* 94A6, **97**, 144C1
Zancle/Zankle ITL *Messina* 18B2, 43F2, 83E4
Zapatas fl. IRQ/TKY *Greater Zab* 54E3
Zarai ALG *Zraia* 140D1, 144A2
Zarangiane AFG/IRN *Helmand basin* 173H1
Zarax GRE *Ierakas* 33D7
Zariaspa AFG *Balkh* 61G2, 69G2
Zas cave GRE 7E9
Zegrenses MOR 138B4
Zela TKY *Zile* 73E3, 105G2, 162A2
Zeleia TKY *Sarıköy* 13E1, 31H2, 72A3
Zenobiou Inss. OMN *Kuria Muria* 173G5
Zephyrion Pr. CYP *Cape Zephyros* 156A3
Zerelia GRE 6C3
Zeugma TKY *Kavunlu* 68C2, 73F5, 162B3
Zeytinlibahçe Höyük TKY 2D2
Zilil MOR *Dchar Jedid* 138B4, 140A1
Zincirli TKY 02D2
Zitha TUN *Zian* 144D3
Ziyaret Tepe TKY 3E2
Zominthos GRE 9B2
Zoster Pr. GRE *Kavouri* 33E6
Zucchabar ALG *Miliana* 138E4
Zugmantel GER 151B1
Zuwila LBY 141F3